S0-AFM-794

"Thank you for the copy of *Better Off Without 'Em*, but I'm afraid it's New York and San Francisco that I think should secede."
—P. J. O'Rourke

Praise for Chuck Thompson's *Better Off Without 'Em*

"[*Better Off Without 'Em*] is a book that will prompt guffaws in some, an urge to shoot it through the spine in others, and everyone to agree that it will only stoke the election-year bonfire."
—*Vanity Fair*

"A fun, engaging read—let's call it speculative nonfiction—and would make for a fine night of beer-fueled argument."
—Wonkette.com

"Underneath all the macho bombast, there are some serious ideas at play. . . . Thompson writes passionately and persuasively about the disastrous long-term effects that de facto segregation and systematic underfunding of public schools will have on the U.S. economy."
—*The Boston Globe*

"Funny in the mode of P. J. O'Rourke and Joe Queenan."
—*Arkansas Democrat-Gazette*

"An entertaining and worthwhile read. . . . [Thompson] amasses data, and somewhere in between the fire and the brimstone, plans of serious argument are laid down."
—DailyKos.com

"[Thompson] is awesomely talented and wickedly funny."
—*Philadelphia Inquirer*

"[Thompson] presents an intriguing and plausible plan, with a touch of humor, that just may be the only way out of the political poison that has spread across this country and endangers the future for all of us. Plus it's a darn good history lesson."
—*Boulder Daily Camera*

MAR – – 2014

"Hilariously over-the-top. . . . Thompson's mix of vitriol, bewilderment, humor, and research holds the seemingly disparate elements together and makes for an entertaining, if absurdly hyperbolic, read. . . . Thought-provoking."

—*Publishers Weekly*

"Often thoughtful, always irreverent. . . . a raucous road trip through the South with a funny, informed, sardonic and opinionated Yankee."

—*Kirkus Reviews*

"A surprisingly worthwhile read. . . . A confrontational, extreme—and occasionally convincing—argument for cutting the South loose, peppered with hilarious anecdotes."

—ShelfAwareness.com

"Fry yourself some grits, unfurl that Confederate flag, and read this gem of a book. Chuck Thompson doesn't have a politically correct bone in his Yankee body. He skewers the South mercilessly, and hilariously—and backs up his barbs with facts. *Lots* of facts. *Better Off Without 'Em* is sure to set hearts racing, on both sides of the Mason-Dixon Line."

—Eric Weiner, *New York Times* bestselling author of *The Geography of Bliss*

WITHDRAWN

ALSO BY CHUCK THOMPSON

To Hellholes and Back

Smile When You're Lying

The 25 Essential World War II Sites: European Theater

The 25 Best World War II Sites: Pacific Theater

CHUCK THOMPSON

BETTER OFF WITHOUT 'EM

A NORTHERN MANIFESTO FOR SOUTHERN SECESSION

SIMON & SCHUSTER PAPERBACKS

NEW YORK   LONDON   TORONTO   SYDNEY   NEW DELHI

Mount Laurel Library
100 Walt Whitman Avenue
Mount Laurel, NJ 08054-9539
856-234-7319
www.mtlaurel.lib.nj.us

Certain names and identifying characteristics have been changed.

Simon & Schuster Paperbacks
A Division of Simon & Schuster, Inc.
1230 Avenue of the Americas
New York, NY 10020

Copyright © 2012 by Chuck Thompson

All rights reserved, including the right to reproduce this book or
portions thereof in any form whatsoever. For information address
Simon & Schuster Paperbacks Subsidiary Rights Department,
1230 Avenue of the Americas, New York, NY 10020

First Simon & Schuster trade paperback edition July 2013

SIMON & SCHUSTER PAPERBACKS and colophon are registered trademarks
of Simon & Schuster, Inc.

For information about special discounts for bulk purchases,
please contact Simon & Schuster Special Sales at
1-866-506-1949 or business@simonandschuster.com.

The Simon & Schuster Speakers Bureau can bring authors
to your live event. For more information or to book an event,
contact the Simon & Schuster Speakers Bureau at
1-866-248-3049 or visit our website at www.simonspeakers.com.

Designed by Akasha Archer

Manufactured in the United States of America

10 9 8 7 6 5 4 3 2 1

The Library of Congress has cataloged the hardcover edition as follows:

Thompson, Chuck.
    Better off without 'em : a Northern manifesto for Southern secession / Chuck Thompson.
        p. cm.
    Includes bibliographical references and index.
        1. Southern States—Politics and government—1951- 2. Southern States—Description
    and travel. 3. Political culture—Southern States. 4. Secession—Southern States.
    I. Title. II. Title: Better off without 'em.
    F216.2.T46 2012
    306.20975—dc23
                                    2011052521

ISBN 978-1-4516-1665-1
ISBN 978-1-4516-1666-8 (pbk)
ISBN 978-1-4516-1667-5 (ebook)

CONTENTS

INTRODUCTION   ix
Divided We Stand (Sort Of)

CHAPTER 1   1
Religion: Georgia, Kentucky, End Times,
and the Rise of KKKristian Zombies

CHAPTER 2   41
Politics: South Carolina and the Seven Deadly Sins of Southern Gub'mit

CHAPTER 3   85
Race: Alabama, Bigotry, Wildman, and the White Spike Lee

CHAPTER 4   125
Football: Louisiana State, ESPN, BCS,
and the Gridiron Delusion of the SEC

CONTENTS

CHAPTER 5   153

Education: Arkansas, Mississippi, and the Three Rs of Southern
Schools—Revenue, Resentment, Resegregation

CHAPTER 6   195

Economics: Florida, Texas, the U.S. Military,
and the Fiscal Future of Secession

EPILOGUE   231

The South's Gonna Do It Again . . . and Again . . . and Again

ACKNOWLEDGMENTS   259

NOTES   269

INDEX   295

INTRODUCTION

Divided We Stand (Sort Of)

Hang out in my living room on any national election night and at some point in the evening, usually around 7 p.m. Pacific time, you're almost certain to hear me scream something like: "Why in the hell does the United States—and by extension the entire free world, capitalist dominion, and all of Christendom—allow its government to be held hostage by a coalition of bought-and-paid-for political swamp scum from the most uneducated, morbidly obese, racist, morally indigent, xenophobic, socially stunted, and generally ass-backwards part of the country?"

Catch me after some earnest academic with Cambridge and Ivy credentials has to appear on NPR to defend evolution against the latest onslaught on public education from Book of Dipshits creationists, and you'll likely bear witness to a Thompson rage-gasm along the lines of: "What in Christ's name happened to that confederation of Mason-Dixon mouth breathers that got them so intimidated by science and facts and book larnin' that they can't even walk past a library or look through a microscope without quoting Habakkuk and Deuteronomy to each other until the threat of intellectual enlightenment goes away?"

Crack a beer in my TV room on any autumn Sunday when the BCS college football rankings come out or, God help you, kick back on my sofa the week the annual bowl game matchups are announced and the Southeastern Conference is once again gifted a national championship opportunity based on some rigged illusion of the down-home gridiron greatness of a conference that wouldn't know its latest recruiting violation from a kicking tee if it ever left home after September to play in the snow, sleet, or any genuine football temperatures, and you'll definitely need to stop me from slashing my wrists before hearing me wail in agonized sports martyrdom: "Vanderbilt? Kentucky? Mississippi State? You call that strength of schedule? You're honestly standing there and telling me with a straight face that nonconference wins against Troy State, Charleston Southern, and Florida International, *at fucking home*, are legitimate?"

Stop by when a brain-dead zealot is yammering her way through a hypocrisy-laden justification for simultaneously being pro-life and pro-death penalty while some mewling cipher of a FOX "News" "reporter" bobs his head in vacant acquiescence and . . . well, you already know how the rest of this Stars and Bars tangent goes.

And you already know how it goes because (a) You've said or felt pretty much the same things yourself about the slave states at some point or (b) you're from the South, have people there, or otherwise possess a degree of affection for the region such that you're sick and tired of its honor being traduced and its culture blamed for every American malady by hillbilly-bashing, know-it-all knob polishers such as myself (however impressively informed and well intentioned we might be).

You already know most of the other backwoods-bumpkin insults that I could layer into this opening salvo because if there's one thought that at one time or another has connected American minds from Seattle to Savannah it is this: It's too bad we didn't just let the South secede when we had the chance.

A short time ago, I began scribbling down notes for a book with the working title "The Divided States of America." I'd gotten the idea from a brilliant website of regional/tribal drumbeating that lays out the case for something called the Republic of Cascadia. The site is the brainchild of a guy named Lyle Zapato, a mystery man who refuses to be interviewed by anyone other than Daljit Dhaliwal, the semi-hot, bob-haired London-born Punjabi Sikh former host of PBS's *Worldfocus*.

Zapato's Republic of Cascadia is an imaginary place that combines the "former" American states of Oregon and Washington and the "former" Canadian province of British Columbia into a sovereign nation consisting of 330,411 square miles and fifteen million inhabitants generating an annual GDP of $515 billion.[1]

Rather than being tied to the vagaries of a federal government with an agenda that, beyond national defense, rarely lines up with local needs, the more or less like-minded residents of Cascadia live in a paradise of mist-shrouded mountains and mossy forests; a utopia of organic composting and innovative light-rail transportation where all the cows are grass-fed, all the chickens roam free, many of the herbs are smokable, plastic bags are outlawed, citizens mail their post-consumer-waste commitment-ceremony announcements with Cascadian Postal Authority stamps honoring such cultural touchstones as proper kayaking protocol, and nonobese children salute a flag emblazoned with a pinecone resting on a field of tolerant rainbow colors.

The philosophical underpinning of Cascadia is simple: shared values, cultural norms, and manageable geography—not the chance tentacles of history and insatiable federal bureaucracy—are what unite, or at least what should unite, a given population.

Cascadia works in the imagination because to a large degree it already exists in real life. That imaginary beer you were drinking during my BCS football meltdown? An "uncompromised, unfiltered" golden wheat Widmer Hefeweizen brewed, bottled, and sucked down like teat milk every day by the masses in Portland, Oregon.

Better still, the concept is eminently transferable. With Cascadia as inspiration, I began imagining the U.S. map carved into similarly cohesive cultural blocs.

Heartlandia, for example, would stretch from the area east of the Rockies in Montana, Wyoming, and Colorado across the breadbasket to the foothills of the Appalachian Mountains.

Mormonia would claim all of Utah and adjacent parts of Idaho and Nevada.

Biblestan would cut a massive swath across the lower half of the existing United States, but also include noncontiguous pockets of Heartlandia, claiming dominion over chunks of Missouri, Kansas, and the rural South-west (which, if you don't know, is a lot more Bible-thumpy than all the adobe and golf courses lead you to imagine).

The Northeast would be rechristened Greater Soxany.

Like Singapore and the Vatican, New York and Los Angeles would be conferred city-state status.

Mexifornia would stay Mexifornia.

Tracing new national boundaries out of obsolete American states got me excited about writing a bestselling travel book from the point of view of a first-time visitor to each of these culturally united lands. As I shifted my attention from the map and started compiling imaginary atlas statistics, however, the broader limitations of my redistricting project quickly became apparent.

With its national seal bearing the image of a man in overalls pointing toward an endless horizon of corn syrup and thank-you notes for "nice vis-its" with aging relatives, Heartlandia possessed an undeniable appeal. But was life there really all that different from the day-to-day grind in Biblestan or Mormonia?

Sure, the people of Greater Soxany and the Federated Boroughs of New York had their differences, but one loudmouth is pretty much like any other, and hipsters get just as uppity about recycling in Burlington as they do in Brooklyn.

And when you got into the nitty-gritty details of pinecone politics, Cascadia felt an awful lot like old Maine, New Hampshire, and Vermont, right down to the organic spunk of damp wool, flax brownies, and $1,200 Restoration Hardware couches covered in dog hair at the well-attended neighborhood association meetings.

Anyone wanting to blow holes in my gerrymandering could see as plain as prairie that half a century of Interstate travel, mass media, and nacho cheese flavoring had done its grim work. Every region of the country has its own natural splendors and personality ticks, but aside from a few wacky religious differences and all that goddamn salad dressing they insist on drowning their iceberg lettuce with in the Midwest, I realized that life in These Homogenized States wasn't all that dissimilar from sea to warming sea.

With one exception: The South. The Confederacy. The Rebel states. The land of pickled pig knuckles, prison farms, coon-hunting conservatives, NASCAR tailgaters, prayer warriors, and guys who build million-dollar careers out of bass fishing.

The more I looked at my map and considered each "new" republic, the more the South stood out as the only truly exotic region left in America, the only nation within a nation, the only place separated from the rest by its own impenetrable morality, worldview, politics, religion, personality, and even language.

Grits, Gravy, and Gumbo: An Unauthorized Definition

After abandoning the idea of redrawing the social and political boundaries of the entire United States in favor of a more thoroughgoing examination of the South, the first issue I had to address was defining my subject. This turned out to be unexpectedly tricky.

When forming a mental picture of "the South," the first impulse is to recall the original Confederate States of America, that farsighted group that voted to secede from the Union in 1861, thereby touching off the Civil War. Using history as a guide, today's South would logically seem to follow the imprimatur of the proudly seditious and eternally defeated states of the C.S.A.

Alas, history is almost never as neat as we'd like it to be. It turns out that a total of eleven states officially made up the Confederacy. Seven states were original signatories to the C.S.A.; four joined shortly afterward.

Amazingly, for Civil War novices anyway, Kentucky and West Virginia, two states that even the least worldly Yankee sixth grader of today would identify as part of the Skynyrd universe, were not members of that regionally hallowed organization. Even more startling, given its reputation for naked racism and attachment to cranky public figures such as ex-Klansman senator Robert Byrd, West Virginia was created specifically as a non-Confederate state, a Unionist part of Virginia.

Now consider that Texas was among the original seven states that declared secession even before Abraham Lincoln took office on March 4, 1861, and you can see that defining the South isn't anything near an open-and-shut case. An all-around pain in the ass insofar as categorization goes, and never much of a team player, anyway, Texas had its own motives for dropping its long johns in the direction of Washington, D.C. And even back then its reputation was far more cowboy than cow tipper.

Filled with Jews, Cubans, and meth labs, today's Florida is, like Texas, impossible to characterize in prototypically southern terms. Nevertheless, Florida demands Confederate consideration for being yet another of the original seven rebel states, as well as the geographic anchor of the region, and an easy target of ongoing jokes about its penis-like shape. (Which I'll do my best to refrain from as we move along, but no promises.)

Even more troublesome to the fledgling ethnographer, during the Civil War parts of at least five other states and territories were claimed by the Confederacy without formal secession or control ever being established. These included areas of Oklahoma and Missouri—benighted burgs according to certain contemporary prejudices, perhaps, but not places one immediately associates with Rachel Maddow effigies or guys named Skeeter and Possum.

With membership in the Confederacy not guaranteeing a punched ticket into the modern southern fraternity, I turned for help to the famed Mason-Dixon line. From a purely metes-and-bounds point of view, however, this turned out to be an even more complicated and confusing line of inquiry.

Presumed by many to exist as a physical line of division between northern and southern states, the original Mason-Dixon line was actually laid out in the 1760s merely to establish the legal boundary between soon-to-be abolitionist Pennsylvania, slave-friendly (in a manner of speaking) Maryland, and the territory that would come to be known as Delaware. Doing the laying out were a pair of British astronomers named Charles Mason and Jeremiah Dixon. According to *American National Biography* writer Edwin Danson, the latter was such an "ethically weak" soul that he'd once been kicked out of a Quaker meetinghouse for excessive drinking, thus making him a perfect candidate to be dispatched to America to help settle a ferocious land dispute.

That dispute had raged for nearly eighty years between three generations of landowning Penn (as in Pennsylvania) and Calvert (as in Maryland's Calvert city, county, and peninsula) family dynasties. At the core of the fight was the jurisdiction of Philadelphia, and whether the future American capital was to be located within the legal boundaries of Pennsylvania or Maryland.

The Penns and Calverts were so intractable regarding property lines that their territorial pissing match eventually led to a series of armed skirmishes between colonial militias, events known as Cresap's War, named for Thomas Cresap, aka the "Maryland Monster," whose fierce loyalty to the cause of Maryland expansion provoked numerous outbursts of mob violence on his person. That as an adolescent my Calvert County nephew Erik used to refer to a certain feature of his anatomy as the "Maryland Monster" is mere unhappy coincidence and immaterial to the larger historical discussion at hand.

Almost a century after Mason and Dixon had undertaken their peacemaking survey, which resulted in an accepted border between Pennsylvania and Maryland, more and bigger land disputes were coming to a boil across the United States. By the time abolitionist Abe ascended from his murky Illinois backwater to the national stage, the term "Mason-Dixon line" had morphed in popular usage from a recognized boundary delineating Pennsylvania free territory from Maryland slave territory, into a symbolic line separating all free and slave states and, eventually, states that seceded from the Union.

Yet even that imaginary border was maddeningly fluid. Some of that era's authorities referred to the then undecided states of Missouri, Maryland, and Kentucky as being "above" the Mason-Dixon line, i.e., free states. Others spoke of those same states as being situated below it, i.e., slave states.[2]

Authorities today are even more abstract on the subject of what constitutes "the South."

"It's an interesting question and I don't have any expectation your answer to it will meet with anyone's satisfaction," one of those authorities, Dr.

Charles Joyner, told me after I'd asked him for a definitive description of southern geography.

In addition to being the Burroughs Distinguished Professor of Southern History and Culture at Coastal Carolina University, as well as extraordinarily patient in the face of insistent cold callers from the West Coast, Joyner is the author of several acclaimed books on southern society, including *Shared Traditions: Southern History and Folk Culture*. If anyone could define "the South" for me, Joyner seemed like the guy.

In the sufficiently intimidating tones of the southern gentleman scholar, however, the first thing Joyner said when I asked him where the South began and where it ended was, "I'm not authorized to give out that information."

"Not authorized?"

"That is correct. And nobody else is authorized to do so, either."

Joyner went on to explain that a universally accepted definition of the South has never existed. He pointed out that the great southern diaspora had made places like Bakersfield, California, Flint, Michigan, and Harlem in some ways feel more southern than modern-day Atlanta.

"A lot of what was part of the old Confederacy doesn't seem much like the South anymore," Joyner said. "And there's a part of southern Ohio known as Little Dixie."

The greatest label-busting southerner of all time, Joyner told me, was Stand Watie, a slave-owning Cherokee Indian from Oklahoma who rose to the rank of brigadier general in the Confederate Army. If a Native American from Oklahoma could be a rabid southerner thirsty for Yankee blood, so went the implication, who couldn't?[3]

Joyner, who somewhat troublingly defied my condescending grits 'n' gravy stereotype, even flashed a bit of enigmatic southern humor when I asked him to clear up one of the most perplexing issues of my early research.

"The Confederacy officially comprised eleven states," I said. "So how come the Confederate flag has thirteen stars?"

"Apparently they were numerically challenged," Joyner replied. "Otherwise they wouldn't have started a war with the United States."

Defining "the South" for purposes of this book was obviously going to require a combination of historic empathy, a contemporary feel for the culturally distinct, and a hide thick enough to deflect the protests of hometown experts resentful of a stubborn prick in a Seattle Mariners cap interpreting their culture for them.

With Texas standing as the most debatable omission, the Appalachian anomaly of West Virginia as the most contentious inclusion, and Florida the most difficult case of all, I eventually settled on a South encompassing twelve contiguous states: Alabama, Arkansas, Florida, Georgia, Kentucky, Louisiana, Mississippi, North Carolina, South Carolina, Tennessee, Virginia, West Virginia. Though if border Missourians in Dunklin, Pemiscot, and Ozark counties feel unhappy about being left out, they have my blessing to crash the party.

Bluff Called: Gentlemen, Ladies, You Are Free to Leave

Anticipating a white-hooded Dixie backlash after signing the Civil Rights Act into law in 1964, President Lyndon Johnson famously told an aide, "We have lost the South for a generation."[4]

For the Democratic Party he was right. Unfortunately, the rest of us are still stuck with the South. And, save for some superficial concessions to modern conformity, the South is in many ways still stuck in 1964.

There's a reason the "We want our country *back*" Teabaggers held their first national convention in Nashville in 2010. With China and India cranking out thousands of newly minted computer engineers every week, any *forward*-thinking part of the country would have laughed Sarah Palin and her $100,000 populist pose off the stage for suggesting that electronic technology is a mere prop for out-of-touch liberals and that instead of using a fancy-pants TelePrompTer she should just keep her notes written on her hands—just like every eighth grader who was ever too lazy to study for the test or too stupid to remember the dick-simple material from the remedial textbook.

Incidentally, in terms of politics my issue in this book isn't with Republicans, as much as it is with southern obstructionists and fanatics who want to conflate biblical law with U.S. law. When they're doing their fiscally responsible, missionary-hump-values routine, the Republicans are fine.

Ignorant, rude, and fractious though they are, the Teabagging Repubs and their southern power base have raised the notion of cultural separation to lofty heights, inspiring all sides of a politically energized generation to ponder the increasingly attractive question: What would happen if we simply jettisoned the 566,466 square miles and 78,385,623 million people responsible for generating so much of the willful ignorance and Jim Crow–style hatred that keeps the rest of the country from moving ahead?[5]

Everyone has joked about a modern-day secession. Politicians, like Texas governor and presidential hopeful Rick Perry, have even threatened it. But what would the measurable impact be if it actually happened? Would one or the other or both sides come out economically, politically, or culturally improved? Other than having to redesign the flag, what would happen to the United States if we just went ahead and let the South secede?[6]

In the short term, the United States would lose a few assets—Bourbon Street, South Beach, Augusta National, a lot of great musicians, a few good writers. With the Kennedy Space Center, Pensacola Naval Air Station, and other important military installations, Florida would require delicate handling. The Gulf Coast is by far the U.S. leader in petroleum refinery capacity, so a rock-solid energy treaty or two would have to be inked.

Economic pacts guaranteeing unfettered access to genetically modified hogs and NFL-caliber wide receivers would need to be negotiated. Losing the Everglades would be a bummer, but after that it's just a lot of third-tier national parks down there, half of which are more or less just stone monuments dedicated to Rebel soldiers.[7]

For romantic souls already growing melancholy at the thought of losing all that quality bourbon and Spanish moss, it's worth noting that splitting up the Union doesn't have to mean losing *access* to most of the good stuff from the South. In fact, for both sides, an exciting by-product of separation would be an explosion of southern tourism.

Think about it. Freed from its standing as a hind tit, guilt-by-association international embarrassment to the rest of the country, the politically repressive religious monarchy of the born-again Confederacy would be transformed overnight into a travel destination swarming with trendsetting elites.

Just like they do with Myanmar, Venezuela, and more conservative parts of the Middle East, instead of loathing redneck Amerikkka and all it stands for, *Lonely Planet* types from around the world would immediately embrace the South as a bastion of traditional culture nobly holding out against the "so-called progressive" agenda of modernity; an indigenous society teeming with underappreciated folk wisdom, ancient values, and fascinating dialects deserving of fierce protection and a slew of new expat-financed eco-lodges. With time, Americans would start thinking of the South as another Mexico, only with an even more corrupt government.

The Civil War didn't come out of nowhere. Long before Confederate seditionists fired on Americans at Fort Sumter in 1861 to launch the bloodiest war in the nation's history, plenty of southerners were dissatisfied with the very idea of a United States of America. Many had fought bitterly against joining it.

Along with brother Edward, John Rutledge attempted to derail the Declaration of Independence at the Continental Congress of 1776, with Edward writing that there was "no wisdom in a Declaration of Independence, nor any other purpose to be answered by it."

The Rutledges' position was largely informed by the fact that John was at the time a near-monarchial head of what residents then considered the independent republic of South Carolina. It wouldn't be until 1778 that Rutledge would abdicate his position as South Carolina's "president." (The southern gentry has always felt more comfortable with British elitism, rule of law, and all-around wankiness, which is why to this day the League of the South secessionist organization insists on using British spelling in all of its documents and correspondence, defending Oxford standard usage against what it calls the "bastardisation" of "Webster's so-called 'American' English.")[8]

Throwing a massive hissy fit over a newly enacted tariff in 1828, vice president and South Carolinian John C. Calhoun articulated his doctrine of nullification, an argument that essentially said that if a state didn't like a particular federal law it could simply ignore it—no matter that it had already pledged its allegiance to upholding the federal compact. In effect, and in true self-absorbed southern manner, Calhoun wanted the South to continuing enjoying all of the benefits that come with being part of the country without having to make any of the necessary sacrifices or compromises.[9]

His screed is widely acknowledged as having galvanized South against North and laying the foaming and frothing groundwork for the Civil War. Today, Calhoun's plantation home is a lovingly restored attraction on the campus of Clemson University in South Carolina.

In light of the South's long-standing cantankerousness about being part of the United States, it could be and often has been argued that North and South essentially proceeded out of the gate as separate countries, political and social entities at fundamental odds with one another.

By the 1790s, American writers were already identifying the South as a threat to national development and ideals, with the North emerging as the essence of the nation and the South as its antithesis, "a negative reference point" to the rest of the country, according to University of Georgia historian James C. Cobb in *Away Down South: A History of Southern Identity.*[10]

The same conditions led famed literary critic Edmund Wilson to write in his masterful *Patriotic Gore* that in the 1800s North and South had "become so distinct from one another that they were virtually two different nations; they were as much two contending units—each of which was trying to expand at the other's expense—as any two European countries."[11]

Look at the way current southern politicians repeatedly sabotage national debate or, for just one economic example, examine the way the South has operated like a competing nation in cannibalizing and degrading Michigan and the American auto industry—points to be taken up in greater detail in Chapters 2 and 6—and it becomes clear that little has changed.

Add on wildly opposing approaches to such civic building blocks as religion, politics, race relations, education, and catfish consumption, and you start to see something beyond a mere alliance of uneasy and often combative economic frenemies—what this union has primarily always been. You see two distinct societies fated to an eternal struggle that prevents both sides from fulfilling their destinies. Or at least moving in a direction most of their respective citizens and leaders see fit.

One way or another, the social, political, and economic gridlock that's paralyzing this country has got to be broken. There are a lot of people running for office who claim they know how to do it, but none is bold enough to acknowledge the Rebel elephant in the room. None is willing to consider the possibility that breaking up the country through peaceful secession might be the most sane and effective way of saving it.

I am.

Growing up in Juneau, Alaska, barely a decade after statehood and with the rhetoric of the Alaska Independence Party in full flower, I understood even then the attraction of flipping a middle finger at the rest of the country.

Physically distant though it may have been, Alaska had much in common with the South. Less than two decades removed from statehood (1959) and the massive land and resource grab that commenced with the discovery of oil in Prudhoe Bay in 1968, there was at the time plenty of casual talk in certain beery quarters about the travesty of compromise that came with statehood and economic surrender to a government thousands of miles and cultural light-years away.

The Alaska Independence Party was a fringe but nevertheless tolerated part of the political landscape. At eighteen, I briefly toyed with an impulse to check AIP on my voter registration form before ticking the box next to "Independent."

There's nobility in sticking to your guns, in not selling out, in remaining a rebel forever. By eighteen, however, I was already coming to the realization that there's also a great measure of stupidity—and, more dangerous, a toxic mixture of self-pity and self-destruction—in clinging to willful obstinacy for obstinacy's sake.

Even so, few of us ever sell out completely, and I'm no more immune than any one to anguished cries for "Freeeeeeedom!" Ridiculous and predictable as they are, I can't help empathizing a little bit with guys like Georgia Republican U.S. representative Paul Broun, who, in the midst of a crucial national debate, seriously advanced the idea that, "If Obamacare passes, that free insurance card that's in people's pockets is gonna be as worthless as a Confederate dollar after . . . the Great War of Yankee Aggression!"

Hysterical jackasses like Broun, and plenty like him I met on my travels through the South, really just want the same thing that I do: a country liberated from the tyranny of morons and seditionists, and the freedom to say about the other side, in all honesty and with complete accuracy, that we just might be better off without 'em.

CHAPTER 1

Religion: Georgia, Kentucky, End Times, and the Rise of KKKristian Zombies

Nothing separates North and South like religion. Not politics, not racism, not Paula Deen's butter popsicles.

That's not just my opinion. It's a gospel view vouchsafed by southerners occupying every point of the social spectrum, from tin shack crazies and riding mower moderates, to the trailer park gentry and ascot-and-snifter set hobnobbing in university clubs.

"Of all the things that divide the South from the rest of the country, the first one has got to be fervent Christianity," says Dr. Michael Hill, president of the League of the South, the secessionist group he founded in 1994. "The South historically has been a very Christian society. That has defined its worldview. We realize men have evil hearts and can't be trusted."

Although he's polite and engaging when I get him on the phone, the swaggering godsmack from a fringe guy like Hill comes as no surprise. After all, this is a man who encourages people to "personally secede from the corrupt and corrupting influence of post-Christian culture in America" and who used to show up on Glenn Beck's show as a serious guest. In fact, Hill's "radical" view of the South as a place fundamentally segregated from the rest of America by intransigent religious dogma merely reflects mainstream southern opinion.[1]

Virtually any respected academic or social organization will say the same thing.

As explained by no less an authority than the *Encyclopedia of Southern Culture* (a mammoth academic achievement from the Center for the Study of Southern Culture at the University of Mississippi and published by the University of North Carolina Press): "The South is the only society in Christendom where the evangelical family of Christians is dominant . . . making the South the 'religious region' that it is and marking off the South from patterns, practices and perspectives prevalent in other parts of America."[2]

As important as the sheer number of believers is the intellectual cell in which the general population of the South is held captive by religion—which most of the time means evangelical Baptist or Methodist.

"Though some [southerners] resist such a worldview, they cannot give up religion or get away from it," continues the *Encyclopedia.* "They are so deeply indoctrinated in the orthodox faith that they cannot articulate alternative formulations to it, much as they wish they could."[3]

All of this leads to a point that, in anticipation of the predictable southern response to outside criticism, I'm going to return to in some form or another several times over the course of this book: Yes, extreme evangelical religiosity exists in every state in the Union. But establishing a moral or cultural equivalency between South and North by pointing out this obvious fact is misleading. You can find barbecue joints, Walmart fatties, and crooked elementary school football teams in the North, too, but that doesn't make the North the South.

To respond to a critique of southern religious lunacy by shouting, "You should see how batshit crazy they are in Arizona!" is to employ the classic schoolyard rhetorical misdirection, "Oh, yeah, I'm stupid? Well, guess what, you're ugly." This counterblast of moral reprobation from the South is the same one that followed the 1852 publication of *Uncle Tom's Cabin,* when no fewer than fourteen pro-slavery novels were published in three years in an effort to debunk the unflattering portrait of slavery presented by Harriet Beecher Stowe.[4]

No shit, there are religious kooks everywhere, but the South is to radical Christianity what Afghanistan and Pakistan are to radical Islam.

According to a seven-hundred-plus-page 2011 Barna Group study titled *Diversity of Faith in Various U.S. Cities,* the cities with the highest proportion of residents who describe themselves as Christian are all in the South. These include Shreveport (98 percent), Birmingham (96 percent), Charlotte (96 percent), Greenville (94 percent), and a lot of other cities loaded with motel rooms whose carpets you wouldn't want to walk across barefoot.

The cities with the lowest percentage of self-described Christians include all the expected sinner dens: New York, Boston, Los Angeles, San Francisco, Seattle, and Portland, Oregon, the latter of which Bush I staffers used to call "Little Beirut," an epithet local liberals still regard as a badge of honor.[5]

David Kinnaman, who led the Barma study, said that the research "confirmed many spiritual assumptions about various regions of the country. The South hosts many of the nation's Christians, while the West and Northeast play to more secular stereotypes."[6]

Unlike most statisticians summarizing reports, Barma project director Doug Colby, who compiled the study's three years of data, was unequivocal. He told me flat-out, "You're absolutely correct in saying the faith of folks in the South is more dominant and prominent than in most of the U.S. The data we have supports this."

It's not just the overwhelming percentage of believers in the South, it's the attitudes they bring to—or from—their religiosity. In 2009, a Pew Forum "Importance of Religion" study measured a number of variables (frequency of prayer, absolute belief in God, and so forth) to determine the degree of religious fervor in all fifty states.

Led by Mississippi, Alabama, and Arkansas, nine of the top ten most religious states were southern. Oklahoma ruined Dixie's perfect record by sneaking in at number seven. Of all southern states, only D.C.-infected Virginia and Semitic Florida finished just outside the top fifteen, edged out by such powerful fanatics as the Mormons of Utah and the pious enigmas of Kansas. The bottom half of the list presented a representative cross section of the rest of the country: Michigan, New Mexico, Iowa, Illinois,

Wisconsin, Montana, New York, California, Maine, and, cordially sharing most hellbound honors, New Hampshire and Vermont.[7]

Not only is the South the place where 50 percent of American evangelicals live, it's also the region from which the national movement draws its ideas and through which most of its fame and profit are harvested. Rabid believers are disproportionately southern—with around a third of the national population (counting Texas), the South accounts for 55 percent of the "electronic church" audience.

Nearly every important evangelical figure of the past century has come from the South (Californian Rick Warren being an exception). A recent Trinity Broadcast Network program touting the national influence of southern Christianity proclaimed that Virginia was the most important state for "birthing national leaders on the religious front."[8]

In the nineteenth century, the South's religious platform was articulated by men such as Baptist minister and slaveholder Iveson Lewis Brookes, who proclaimed that "every intelligent man of the South making a philosophical investigation into the institution of Negro slavery with the Bible in his hand . . . must come to the conclusion with me that it is God's institution." The slightly more contemporary outlook is articulated by men such as the Austin Lounge Lizards, whose cheerful ditty "Jesus Loves Me (But He Can't Stand You)" offers similar insight, but which is much easier to dance to. Assuming your Baptist minister isn't peeking around the corner.[9]

Mark Potok, an editor at the nonprofit civil rights organization Southern Poverty Law Center, with whom I spent an afternoon in Montgomery, Alabama, tells the story of a casual encounter with the region's church-based Us vs. Assholes philosophy.

"We were walking through a park in Montgomery and came across this little local fair, games for kids, hot dogs, that sort of thing," Potok says. "We stopped to check it out and pretty quickly figured out we'd walked into a church event."

"What tipped you off?" I ask.

"A couple minutes after we got there a guy walks over to us holding three sets of stickers—green, yellow, and red. Very politely he asks for our religious affiliation. I tell him and he takes a red sticker out of his hand and presses it on my shirt. I ask him, 'What's that for?' He says, 'The green stickers are for Baptists, the yellow stickers are for non-Baptist Christians, and the red stickers are for the people who are going to hell."

I laugh and tell Potok I don't believe a word of his story, but he swears it's true. Over the next few months I repeat this tall tale to at least ten southerners and not one blinks.

"Totally believable," says a friend who's spent most of his life in the Florida Panhandle. "In fact, I'd be less likely to believe the story if it *didn't* happen that way."

Along with abortion clinic bombings and accidental exposure to Christian rock, Potok's is the kind of anecdote that calcifies the hearts of northern devil worshippers against the nauseating smugness of southern scripture donkeys. What's insidious about this reaction, however, is that the secularists' instinctive aversion to hypocritical judgment is actually *embraced by evangelicals*, who use it as the mortar to add more bricks to the wall separating themselves from the rest of the country.*

Subject yourself to evening Bible studies or Christian radio and you'll eventually get an earful of Luke 6:22, the venerated Bible verse through which evangelical alchemists convert hatred to strength: "Blessed are ye, when men shall hate you, and when they shall separate you from their company, and shall reproach you, and cast out your name as evil, for the Son of man's sake," writes Luke, sanctifying odium and ecclesiastic bile for all infinity.

Scripture whappers who tire of Luke can joyfully fall back on Mark 13:13, which makes a similar point: "And you shall be hated by all men for my name's sake."

In the contentious aftermath of both of Bush II's fake electoral victories, Luke 6:22 and Mark 13:13 echoed from Christian pulpits across the

---

* The "rest of the country," by the way, will heretofore be referred to as "the North." Though it's possible to scare up a minor debate on the matter, "North" still suffices down South as an all-purpose handle to describe all heathen American land outside of Dixie. An exchange I had with a five-ten, seventeen-year-old member of the Georgia Pistols AAU girls basketball team who hit me up for a donation in a Walmart parking lot in Atlanta illustrates the point.

Five-ten superstar: We say 'up North' for everywhere outside the South.
Me: Even to reference Minnesota or Montana or California?
Five-ten superstar: Yes.
Me: Even for Hawaii?
Five-ten superstar: Yes!!!
Me: Okay, here's your five dollars. Thank you for talking to me.

country. "Praise God that they hate you! Praise God that your name has become of evil!" shouted Eleanor Lancaster on the Living Waters Program on November 4, 2004, in a Family Values Radio broadcast, a typical voice among millions exalting that day.[10]

Few of the devout could have been surprised. Rather than a devotion to the family of man, the southern evangelical church's long-standing mission has been to maintain the deep divisions that beget such troublesome cultural touchstones as *The Help* and *Blue Collar Comedy Tours.*

The Black Side of the Ledger: Eddie Long, Jesus Politics, and the Prosperity Gospel in the African American Church

If you imagine all of this would make the northern novitiate's first trip to a southern church a holy-rolling buzz kill, you'd be as wrong as a menorah at midnight Mass. In the flesh, southern religion is awesome!

Well, at least for the first twenty minutes of the 8 a.m. Sunday service I attend at New Birth Missionary Baptist Church in Lithonia, Georgia, it is.

Am I actually in church? It's hard to tell. From the outside, the New Birth complex rises from a leafy Atlanta suburb like a college basketball arena, all green roofline, soaring angles, contoured white walls, and parking lot. Inside, it's part tent revival, Kanye concert, and Best Buy showroom.

"Make some noise! Who wants to bounce a little bit? Give praise this morning!"

At the stroke of eight, a handsome, young male tenor charges onto New Birth's wide, circular stage and immediately gets in the crowd's business.

"Get up, people! Stand up! Let's make some noise!"

Across 6.8 acres of church—that's 296,634 square feet of SRO lower bowl and half-filled upper deck—about six thousand black people and, from what I can see, four scattered whities, rise to their feet. Their facial expressions are like those I once saw in a British pub when a sweaty rugby team swarmed to the bar in spellbound expectation of the first drink of the day.

A swirling organ and rat-a-tat snare drum announce the opening of a rhythmically irresistible number whose refrain—"Lo-ooord, you are awesome!"—explodes like cannon fire from a fifty-member choir that pivots, dips, and raises its hands in unison at stage left. The solo tenor at the lip of the stage riffs over the ebullient "Awesome" refrain—"If it wasn't for Your love, I don't know where I'd be! C'mon, church, sing the words!"

A cigarette-thin drummer rides his crash cymbal like Dave Grohl, circa 1991, while the heartbeat whomp of bass and kick drum throbs at 82 beats per minute. Polished white speaker towers hang on wires throughout the auditorium. There's not a nightclub in New York or Miami that wouldn't trade up today for New Birth's sound system.

New Birth Church starts to dance. Even me, sort of. Notoriously inhibited, especially when explicitly pressured to dance in that wedding reception, "Everybody here tonight must boogie" kind of way, even I can't help feeling the rhythm of the spirit. With so little Thompson family honor to protect in Lithonia, Georgia, it's easy to give in to the vibe—and no matter how lame my moves are, they're no worse than the clunky hip rumble of the sixty-year-old lady next to me who smells of bacon grease and methane.

"Awesome" and a follow-up number called "Our God Is Greater" showcase New Birth's Grammy-worthy production values. Singing, dancing, lighting, sound . . . what you get at New Birth is hitting-your-mark stagecraft at its pinnacle.

Video cameras on giant booms float over the crowd like mechanical predators. Massive screens surrounding the stage alternate between sweatbead close-ups of the performers onstage and roving fan-cam shots of the audience. Some of the flock appear in various stages of early-morning rapture, others mug for the lens like kids on a stadium JumboTron.

The "worship arts," as they're actually called here, turn service into show. It's fun. Upbeat. Personal. Way more inspirational than *Rent* or *Jersey Boys*. Compared with the constipated Catholic Sundays I grew up with, it's the difference between watching an elderly couple holding hands on the Hallmark Channel and actually fucking a pair of thousand-dollar Paris prostitutes in La Villa Saint-Germain with the room service tab at five large and running.

If you asked me to name one not-to-be-missed tourist attraction in the

South, a Sunday service at New Birth Missionary Baptist Church would be it. Ask about a recommendation for spiritual guidance, however, and I'd be a little less sanguine about the place.

For me, the New Birth experience begins to unravel almost as soon as the music stops and the solicitation—aka "preaching"—begins.

Before the main sermon, several burly deacons pass the microphone to take care of some church business. A natty guy in a shiny coat and tie emphasizes the importance of civic duty by leading the first call-and-response segment of the day. When he says, "I said vote!" the crowd responds, "Vote!" When he says, "I said, I WANT YOU TO VOTE!" the crowd shouts, "VOTE!"

To me, politics and church go together about as well as politics and children—both combinations are unseemly, as Sarah Palin proves on both counts—but at first I think, no big deal, they're not advocating any particular position, just dispensing the mindless every-vote-counts claptrap that anyone with a rudimentary understanding of statistical probability and Ohio 2004 knows is total bullshit.

Then the deacon asks two men in the audience to stand. He introduces each as a local politician facing a stiff challenge in next week's election. The crowd is implored to give praise in honor of the candidates' decisions to worship at New Birth this morning. To call this an implication of whom you're supposed to vote for is to call a Budweiser Super Bowl commercial a polite suggestion for what beer you might consider purchasing next time you're at the grocery.

Tacitly recognizing while never officially endorsing candidates is, of course, the shady business of churches all over the country. In this wink-wink-nudge-nudge way Bible thumpers piss on secular law, protect their tax-exempt 501(c)(3) status as charitable organizations, and involve themselves as deeply in the muck of politics as Pontius Pilate and Judas Iscariot.

For those wondering exactly how much wiggle room nonprofits have to engage in the political process, the answer is: not much. IRS language is uncharacteristically clear regarding tax-exempt entities:

All section 501(c)(3) organizations are absolutely prohibited from directly or indirectly participating in, or intervening in, any political campaign on behalf of (or in opposition to) any candidate for elective public office. . . . Voter education or registration activities with evidence of bias that (a) would favor one candidate over another; (b) oppose a candidate in some manner; or (c) have the effect of favoring a candidate or group of candidates, will constitute prohibited participation or intervention.[11]

If anyone from the government is in church today, the case of New Birth Missionary Baptist Church vs. the IRS would be open-and-shut before anyone has time to set out the free coffee and donuts in the foyer. As an individual who helps keep the IRS in business, I find this is highly discouraging. Tax-exempt laws for churches have become a lot like "bedtime" and "behave yourself" in this country. The regulations may be on the books, but almost nobody has the balls to enforce them.

This isn't just a few stray shekels the country is being cheated out of. In a 2010 interview with CNN, Hartford Seminary professor of sociology and religion Scott Thumma estimated the average megachurch in the United States hauls in about $6.5 million a year.

"If you put together all the megachurches in the United States, that's easily several billion dollars," Thumma said.

For comparison, Major League Baseball's annual gross revenues are about $7 billion a year. The American cotton industry takes in $4.376 billion. Big Church may not quite be Big Oil or Big Bank or Big Insurance, but it's not for lack of emulating their strategies of fiscal evasion.[12]

Or marketing.

After the smile, the first thing they give you when you walk in the double doors of New Birth Church is a coupon good for 10 percent off at the gift shop. The coupon is validated when you write your name and email address on the back. Just what I need—a bunch of endless God spam competing with entreaties from Nigerian princes and solicitations to make my dick huger than it already is.

Hanging near the entry at New Birth, a large banner reads: "CORPORATELY GOING AFTER THE GLORY. ISAIAH 40:5." In the gift shop I pick up a copy of the New King James Bible—New Birth's sanctioned version—and flip to Isaiah 40:5. It reads: "The glory of the LORD shall be revealed, And all flesh shall see it together; For the mouth of the LORD has spoken." The corporate tie-in between New Birth and Isaiah isn't precisely clear.

Resisting the lure of church-logo pens, church-logo attaché cases, church-logo water bottles, church-logo toys, church-logo tote bags, church-logo backpacks, and church-logo sweatshirts, I settle for a non-church-logo apple, piece of pound cake, and bottle of water: $3.25. Turns out I was wrong about the free coffee and donuts.

Big business masquerading as religion is nothing new—the Papal States and Vatican haven't survived twelve hundred years because the Catholic Church isn't a shrewd real estate investor—but black churches in the South are particularly ruthless about high-pressure tithing.

Describing the small African American church she attended in Dallas, a friend told me that collections there were counted as soon as they were taken, with amounts donated by each parishioner immediately announced in front of the congregation.

"The emphasis on money was intense," Tracie told me. "If the first collection was not enough, they would literally get up and say 'C'mon, now, the reverend needs his chicken dinner tonight.' And they'd take a second collection."

In Selma, Alabama, tall and burly B. J. Ryan, a retired Marine who served as part of the Marine Barracks as White House guard under three presidents in four years—"Nixon, Ford, and Carter, that's the answer to a great trivia question"—tells me he's got stories about black churches "that'd blow your hair back."

I tell him to blow away.

"They talk about 10 percent as your tithe, right?" Ryan says. "The pastor of the church I attend says that any person that does not give that 10 percent is cursed. With an actual curse! They actually have people giving what they call 'sacrificial donations,' which is people getting their phones and lights turned off because they are trying to make the sacrifice that the pastor asked for, but can't really afford it. And the church don't give them a quarter to get their lights turned back on. I know this for a fact, I have actually seen that happen.

"About three or four years ago—now remember what I told you about sacrificial donations—our pastor called me asking me to find him the prices of a new BMW. Because I'm good with the Internet and I know how to find a good price with AutoFinder and other sites. I gave him some prices. So he goes to a car lot and gets himself a brand-new 740i BMW.

"He drove to church and told the congregation, 'You go outside and see what the Lord has blessed the pastor with!' He told them all he was gonna get a Cadillac, but in a vision the Lord told him he deserved the best car he could get and he went back and got a BMW. That is a true story."

"To me, that's as much the parishioners' fault as the pastor's," I say. "Why do people put up with that?"

"People are not well educated here," Ryan says. "A lot of people get their degree, but very few in the South get an education."

Actually, U.S. Census Bureau figures don't even support the "get an education" part of Ryan's argument. According to the bureau's state-by-state ranking of adults with high school degrees, eight of the bottom ten states are in the South (counting Texas), with residents of Mississippi and Texas "leading" the least-educated pack.[13]

Because of generally poor education, Ryan tells me, pastors in southern churches have enormous power and influence over the people in their churches.

"They command huge respect," he says. "It's not so easy to say 'no' as you think."

"I came to work today!" Bishop Terrell Murphy shouts, repeating the running theme that began with him standing at a lectern reading methodically from an Apple PowerBook.

Filling in today in the absence of New Birth founder Bishop Eddie Long, Murphy is the dynamic young pastor of New Birth's Charlotte chapter. A former youth minister at the Lithonia church, he's an Eddie Long protégé, and a loyal one. Murphy often strays from the main points of his sermon for stream-of-consciousness homilies praising the exalted demagogue of New Birth.

"You think he puts his pants on one leg at a time just like you, but the difference is his are more anointed," Bishop Murphy says of the New Birth leader. He really kisses Eddie's ass, but, then, so does everyone here.

Well, almost everyone. After the bit about the anointed pants legs, Murphy surveys the half-seated arena and twists his head in anger.

"You should *never* sit when I honor our bishop!" Murphy shouts.

Slowly, shamed, like disobedient children, the rest of the assembly stands for more Bishop Eddie touting.

Like the Boss playing the Meadowlands, Murphy came out promising a show and, after a near-comatose start, he's finally living up to his word. He prowls the stage like a panther in estrus as he ratchets up the tempo of his message of martyrdom, slander, and holy retribution.

The sermon is hard to follow. Murphy veers from references to the Jewish high priest Caiaphas, who supposedly led the plot to crucify Jesus, to a smattering of the Book of Zechariah, to more acid renunciations of those who oppose Bishop Long.

"God is angry with our enemies," Murphy warns. "His warring angels are mounting up and ready to do the work that needs to be done!"

Murphy proclaims the enemies of Eddie Long are slavering at the prospect of discrediting him and the church, but assures the audience that God's avenging angels will smite all Eddie-opposing infidels. There's palpable paranoia in his tone, but it is true that Bishop Long has a number of detractors.

One is Julian Bond, the civil rights legend and former Georgia legislator. Bond openly boycotted the 2006 funeral of Coretta Scott King, held at New Birth and presided over by Bishop Long with President George W. Bush at his side. Explaining the boycott, Bond told an Atlanta TV station, "[Long] said that homosexuality is worthy of death. He is a raving homophobe."

Long's legendary gay-bashing, "homosexual cure" programs, and public opposition to same-sex marriage inspired the Southern Poverty Law Center to call him "one of the most virulently homophobic black leaders in the religiously based anti-gay movement." No small achievement in the African American community.

Bishop Murphy's paranoia about the fragility of Eddie Long's reputation turns out to be prescient. Several weeks after my visit to New Birth, four young men from the church accuse Long of coercing them into sex when they were seventeen- and eighteen-year-olds. After drawn-out and nasty negotiations, Long eventually strikes an undisclosed, out-of-court settlement with his accusers while denying any wrongdoing.[14]

The local media goes berserk and for a while I think about turning the scandal into a surprise kicker for this entire chapter. Then I abandon the idea when it occurs to me how unshocking it is anymore when your friendly neighborhood gay-bashing religious-conservative community leader turns out to be your friendly neighborhood gay-bashing religious-conservative community leader with benefits.

"Hey, We Hate Gays, Too!" How Shared Values Bring Blacks and Whites Together on the Most Segregated Day of the Week

Even the most committed defenders of southern racial harmony will admit that if there's one thing blacks and whites in the South don't do together it's worship. Sunday remains the most segregated day of the week in America. Homophobia, however, is the one thing that unifies black and white Christians.

Because its influence has spread across the country, it's possible to interact with southern church gay bashing pretty much anywhere from Lithonia, Georgia, to, let's say, a Southwest Airlines flight from Phoenix to Columbus, Ohio, that I happen to board one bright spring afternoon. Even before we've lifted off the blazing Arizona tarmac, the older guy next to me—he by the window, me in the accursed middle seat—leans over, breathes into my *Wall Street Journal*, and offers an unsolicited comment on the article I'm reading. John Candy couldn't have pried open the conversational door any better in *Planes, Trains and Automobiles*.

Sixty years old and looking every week of it—overweight, gray hair, thick fingers, watery blue eyes, hearing aid, Activia breath—Bill is on his way home to Beckley, West Virginia. Undeterred by my steadfast effort to pretend to read, he lays another plank on the "Won't you be my neighbor?" bridge.

"I'm an ordained Baptist minister," Bill says. "Southern Baptist. I'm not American Baptist."

"Other than the accent, what's the difference?" I ask.

"Doctrinally, there is no difference. But American Baptists are more prone to succumbing to societal pressures. They allow homosekshewalls in their church."

I put the paper on my lap. For the next five minutes Bill talks nonstop about the nightmare of sharing a pew with homosekshewalls.

"Tell me something," I say, when he stops to suck in some air. "What is it with the whole gay thing for Southern Baptists? Why is it such a big deal? I never cared about this issue before it became part of your national platform and I still don't understand why I'm supposed to care about it."

This is where the conversation gets interesting. Not just for me, but for rows 12, 13, and 14, all of whose occupants are in range of Big Bill's unrepentant oratorical sphere.

"Let me show it to you like this," Bill says.

Placing the tip of his pen in the margin of his Sudoku booklet, Bill draws a large "G." Directly beneath this he draws a large "BR." Beneath this a capital "L."

"We don't admit practicing gays in the church to worship with us, just the same as we don't admit bank robbers or liars in the church to worship with us," Bill explains, stabbing at the G for "gays," the BR for "bank robbers," and the L for "liars."

Instead of blurting out the words in my mind—"Wait, what the fuck? How did bank robbers enter into this?"—I merely smile in the way of the tolerant international traveler I've become, a curious social discoverer who respects even the most illogical foreign perversions with open-minded courtesy. Anyone who's ever spent time teaching English to Japanese businessmen or explaining "Peace Corps" to tribal warlords in Uzbekistan knows what I'm talking about.

Emboldened by this liberal-hearted kindness, the emphatically "Southern" Baptist Bill adds to his diagram an "A" for adulterers and an "E" for embezzlers, two more proscribed Baptist personality types. Again, I choke back comment. Like so many I will meet on my travels, Bill brings to life the concept of the South as its own country, making the idea feel less like an absurd thought experiment and more like a reality that already exists.

Stay with Me Here: The Rise of KKKristianity in the Southern Church

How in God's name could organizations supposedly founded upon principles of love and fellowship be transformed into avatars of distrust and separation? Why does the pattern of southern black, homophobic, politically corrupt churches exist side by side with the pattern of southern white, homophobic, politically corrupt churches? You don't have to be Shelby Foote to guess at the sad predictability of the answers.

If you believe that every white sheet and southern segregationist were expunged with the passing of civil rights legislation and ensuing march toward the United States of Half-Asian Children, kindly allow a brief digression into the background of the white church in the South, which the *Encyclopedia of Southern Culture* says "was the ideological linchpin of racism and segregation" and which nowadays "has mainly been a conservative, reinforcing agent for traditional values of white southern society." This is the same church that "formed the institutional base for evading public school desegregation by founding private 'Christian academies' and promoting reactionary policies through the electronic church and the New Christian Right in the 1970s and 1980s."[15]

Extreme church-based intolerance of outsiders began after the Civil War as a means of preserving what was feared to be the endangered remnants of the region's biscuits-and-boneheads culture—a reactionary emotion born of the great postwar "Lost Cause" period of southern self-pitying.

An even more intoxicating church-abetted belief in the South as Raped National Martyr flowered after the white South's second great military defeat; this one at the hands of the national guardsmen, activist throngs, and courageous African Americans who after decades of battle finally succeeded in forcing desegregation and civil rights on the obdurate region. This cataclysm of southern humiliation and public shaming led to what I would personally and perhaps rashly deem the darkest and most rarely acknowledged chapter in twentieth-century American religion—the subsumption of modern southern evangelical churches by elements of the Ku Klux Klan.

Church as Klan? Crazy, I know, but follow me for a minute. The road from Iveson Lewis Brookes to Pat Robertson isn't as twisted as you might imagine.

In 1973—the year of Watergate, official defeat in Vietnam, and what then appeared to be the final spasm of the God-fearing right's sleeper hold on American society—a small group of defeated but still defiant Jim Crow radicals saw an opportunity to regroup undetected within southern churches while simultaneously using them as vehicles for tilting society back in the direction of evil-is-the-heart-of-man extremism. Having mostly stayed on the sidelines during the civil rights struggles of the 1960s, southern white churches had already shown themselves to be at least open to the hyper-conservative ideas of Klan and Klan-types, who were often already members anyway.

Nineteen seventy-three was also the year Presbyterian minister R. J. Rushdoony (a transplanted New Yorker in California) published the highly influential *Institutes of Biblical Law*. Latched on to by these same aggrieved conservatives, the book helped form the basis of a southern-based religious movement that, in an ironic reference to the bitter post–Civil War years, was called "Christian Reconstructionism." Then as now the movement's aim was to establish an American theocracy through the electoral takeover of local, state, and federal governments by church-approved candidates.[16]

Pursuing the widespread influence they'd lost during the civil rights struggles, Christian Reconstructionists adopted segregationist philosophies and bullying tactics that unnervingly paralleled those employed by the KKK. With one fundamental difference. Having been thoroughly trounced on the issues of race music and separate drinking fountains, *racial segregation* hereafter would be publicly replaced by *religious segregation*. If it helps to imagine this shift in terms of historic precedent, think of the way Jim Crow replaced slavery.

Revamped "Christian" promises of empowerment were particularly welcomed in poor, less-educated rural areas. These were burgs filled with newly disenfranchised populations whose segregationist beliefs had become anathema to a mainstream America suddenly controlled by Jews, Catholics, atheists, coloreds, drug pushers, gays, university professors, miscegenationists, people who named their babies Che, Fidel, and Shaquille, and pretty much anyone who went to college or considered themselves "smart."

Concurrently, the Christian Identity movement—a fundamentalist philosophy that grafts "Christianity" to white supremacy, sexism, and antigay beliefs; the "glue of the racist right," according to political science professor Michael Barkun of Syracuse University—was finding purchase in some southern churches.[17]

Anxious to follow this thread with an expert, I call legendary Mississippi investigative reporter Jerry Mitchell at Jackson's *Clarion-Ledger* daily newspaper. Most famous for work that helped put Byron De La Beckwith behind bars for the 1963 assassination of NAACP leader Medgar Evers, Mitchell has received more than thirty national awards and was a Pulitzer Prize finalist in 2006 for "masterly stories on the successful prosecution of a man accused of orchestrating the killing of three Civil Rights workers in 1964," aka the *Mississippi Burning* murders.[18]

"They [Klansmen] obviously did go into the churches," Mitchell tells me. "Here's another part of it; they already were in the churches. Most of these fundamentalist guys were already church members."

The church's first post-Klan hero was Jerry Falwell, who cofounded the Moral Majority in 1979 in Lynchburg, Virginia. As the Christian right's leading blowhard and pastor of Lynchburg's Thomas Road Baptist Church, Falwell was dogged by Klan-sympathizer accusations his entire life. In 1964, a group from the Congress of Racial Equality noisily protested discrimination at Falwell's Thomas Road Baptist Church. The "Christian academy" Falwell opened in 1967 was criticized as a segregationist pillar, one of those controversial new private schools built for the kids of white parents stubbornly resisting integration at public schools across the South. (More on this in Chapter 5.) A 2002 episode of the Showtime cartoon *Queer Duck* featured an unhooded Falwell rejecting a place in heaven after finding out that gays are allowed in.[19]

As converts were recruited through churches, associated political organizations were fitted with crude but effective doublespeak labels designed to shroud the movement's separationist beliefs behind a benign veil of "Christianity." Traditional Values Coalition. Concerned Women for America. Family Research Council. Council of Conservative Citizens. Through this assumed connection with mainstream attitudes, and with dispiriting support from greedy and conveniently homophobic black ministries, the Invisible Empire reasserted itself through white southern churches by means of an insidious duplicity that in my more beer-injected moments I insist on calling KKKristianity.

Putting together the sort of evidence you need to build an airtight Klan-to-Osteen case isn't easy—they don't call the empire "invisible" for nothing—and the lack of smoking guns to support the preceding words of circumstantial rant makes the argument at best a three-legged mule. Even so, in the same way you'll never know the full story behind the cobra tattoo on her inner thigh your daughter brought home from college, you can recognize a bad influence when you see it.

Despite the lack of visible white sheets in southern pews, I can't help feeling that I'm on to something. I put the question of Klan influence in contemporary southern churches to dozens of people.

"You understand the Council of Conservative Citizens is the Klan in suits and ties, not robes, don't you?" says renowned civil rights activist Rims Barber in Jackson, Mississippi, now in his sixth decade of battling for equal rights in the South. "The CCC has clearly gone into the Baptist churches. And maybe the Klan is in some of the Pentecostals. I don't know enough about that to tell for certain, but people have certainly gone underground in that sense. I don't know that it was a planned maneuver, it just sort of culturally happened."

Like every black person I put the question to, church bass player B. J. Ryan in Selma laughs at yesterday's news.

"You are being a little generous in suggesting that they needed to go underground," he tells me. "That part of your theory is never needed down here. They didn't go underground. They wear a cross now instead of a sheet. They changed it over to a religious deal where it's all done in the name of Jesus Christ."

Rarely is it a good idea to have the cell number of an actual Klansman programmed into your iPhone, but, several months after our first encounter, I call and put the question of KKK infiltration into southern churches to self-professed Grand Dragon John Howard. (I'll explain more about our unlikely acquaintance in Chapter 3.) Among other things, the sixty-seven-year-old Howard runs the Redneck Shop in Laurens, South Carolina, where you can walk in the door, plonk down $125, and walk out with an authentic Klan outfit, all ready for cross burnings and midnight horseback rides.

Given Howard's self-preservationist habit of obfuscation, it's not surprising that I get a response from him that is equal parts confirmation and contradiction.

"The number one thing I can tell you about southern people going to church in the 1920s and '30s and '40s is they had different denominations and different beliefs, but they had a common cause: America for Americans," Howard says, instantly firing away in his informed redneck, Machine Gun Kelly style. "There were from five to nine million men, women, and children in the Klan and this is something you need to ask yourself. What happened to these people I do not know, but they were judges, lawyers, senators, city officials, businessmen, just plain, common people. Who do you think these people are, atheists? William Joseph Simmons [founder of the second Ku Klux Klan in 1915] was an ordained evangelical Methodist minister."

"So disappearing within the church in the '60s and '70s seems like a natural move," I say.

"You need to open your eyes! There hasn't been a Klan since 1948 [when it went bankrupt following a federal lawsuit for tax delinquency]. The Klan ended there. All those people died out."[20]

"But their ideas and attitudes weren't killed by a court case."

"They did! If you're looking for racist groups of white people today, you won't find them."

"The child of yesterday is the man of today," I say, delivering my zinger.

"The only way to get a group of white people together nowadays is for a nigger ball game!"

"Or a Toby Keith concert."

"Well, that, too, I suppose."

Perhaps the saddest response to my inquiry comes from an Alabama Baptist pastor named Charles Gibbs, who politely dismisses the suggestion that the Klan or ex-Klan has a significant presence in southern churches. Yet almost immediately, as if suddenly remembering something that might help me out, he tells me the story of quitting his first job as minister of a church in Biloxi, Mississippi, after the church's council of deacons came to him insisting that no blacks be allowed as members. In 1981.

Good-natured with messy gray hair, a doughy face, and friendly smile, Pastor Gibbs is an Air Force veteran who speaks slowly and simply, deploying the kind of hayfoot facade that has fooled outsiders for years. Beneath the rustic demeanor lurks what my mom would call "a sharp cookie."

Over an hour of conversation, Gibbs displays an easy, broad knowledge of world history, military affairs, and modern politics. While never precisely giving in to my more incendiary accusations, he offers a number of sympathetic sighs and vaguely supportive anecdotes.

"Just within the last year, an older black man came to our church," Gibbs tells me. "After I greeted him he asked, 'Do y'all let black folk come to this church?'"

Gibbs's hangdog expression seeps into the floor.

"That broke my heart, it really did," he says. "I thought to myself, 'Do people still have to ask that question after all this time?'"

Six New Mosques! The Muslim Menace Comes to Mobile

The answer to Pastor Gibbs's question is: Where have you been? This I learn at Gibbs's own West Mobile Baptist Church, where I drop in unannounced on a Wednesday evening for an advertised concert and ice cream fellowship.

Though its logo and branding make it look like a high-powered HMO or credit union—the official motto is the businesslike "Partnering With God To Change Lives"—West Mobile Baptist Church is in many respects the antithesis of the modern southern megachurch. On ugly, flat Airport Boulevard, almost ten miles from downtown Mobile, West Mobile Baptist is one of tens of thousands of nondescript little churches you pass every three blocks in the South.[21]

Absolutely nothing distinguishes the concrete and wood building where four hundred to five hundred, nearly all white, active members crowd weekly into a dingy main hall with stained acoustic ceiling tiles, fluorescent office lights, and worn curtains. If Eddie Long walked into this place he'd personally rip out the 1980s carpet, open his speed dial, and get one of his interior designers on the line. If Long's New Birth Church is the Yankee Stadium of southern religion, West Mobile Baptist is an unmowed high school field hosting the Greensboro Grasshoppers in a Tuesday matinee against a semipro team from Hattiesburg.

The Wednesday gathering at West Mobile features what a promotional poster calls one of the "hidden jewels of Mobile," a guest singer-preacher named Alicia Williamson Garcia. I arrive ten minutes late—as a veteran traveler I really should know that at any time of day the traffic on a street named Airport Boulevard is going be rage-worthy—to find Garcia already onstage belting out a contemporary religious number.

A weighty, attractive black woman in her early forties, Garcia's powerful gospel voice recalls the late-era Gladys Knight. There's no choir or band, just her and a recorded music bed playing through a reasonably good sound system. As she sings, lyrics appear on two pull-down projector screens behind her. The music is not quite white, not quite black. Call it whitewashed Negro spiritual karaoke.

Garcia knows how to work a crowd. Delivered in spoken riffs between songs, her primary message to the entirely white assemblage in attendance for tonight's service is that Christian women need to be more understanding of their husbands' and sons' shortcomings.

She tells a story about her own exasperating, video-game-obsessed husband that draws a round of sympathetic church chuckles. She encourages the ladies in the house to take the first difficult, pride-swallowing steps toward reconciliation after arguments.

She speaks to the crowd like she's voicing a puppet show for second graders. This type of singsong condescension drives me absolutely bonkers, but the congregation eats it up.

In the middle of the set, Garcia takes a break so that three church members can get onstage to talk about a recent missionary trip to Guatemala. Each speaks enthusiastically of distributing food, medicine, and soul-redeeming Bibles. The trip's most inspirational episode came when the group climbed to the top of a hill of garbage with impoverished local children for an impromptu prayer service. It's impossible to miss the little-brown-brother tone.

The most fascinating part of the Guatemala recap is the testimony of a guy named Scott. A fit, forty-something Everyman, Scott makes the astonishing and very specific claim that Satan attempted to derail his trip to Guatemala by making a valve in the water heater in his house go on the fritz just days before he was set to fly out of Atlanta.

"How was I supposed to leave the country and leave my wife and family with no hot water?" Scott implores the crowd. "That was Satan trying to keep me from doing the Lord's work."

A troubled murmur spreads through the church. Scott says it again. Literally, the Prince of Darkness monkeyed with the valve in his water heater in a wicked yet ultimately unsuccessful attempt to upset his journey to the landfills of Central America.

Where do they come up with this stuff? Cutting off some dude in my rush to make this service on time, I'd nearly been T-boned by a Chevy half-ton in a busy intersection and it never once occurred to me that the Great Diabolus himself might be trying to prevent me from attending a midweek Baptist service.

Back onstage, Garcia belts out another tune before turning the congregation's attention to more worldly demons.

"Do you understand the times we're living in?" she challenges the two hundred churchgoers in attendance. "What God has done in lifting the cover off of our country? Since 9/11 the United States has supported the division of Israel and now God's judgment is upon us."

After chiding America for betraying Israel—and promising dire consequences—Garcia starts harping on the dangers of Islam. Then she drops a bomb that rattles the church even more than Scott's story about the devil futzing with his water heater.

"Islam is upon us . . . They are planning to build six mosques in Mobile!" Garcia tells the dumbfounded crowd. "Do you know what it means when they build a mosque? It means, 'We have conquered!'"

Six mosques? Right here in Mobile? You can literally see the story spreading from pew to pew like a collection plate. You just know that by tomorrow morning on some religious radio call-in show it's going to be ten mosques and a Muslim recruitment center located on the foredeck of the USS *Alabama* right in the middle of Battleship Park on Mobile Bay.

Dying to ask Alicia for details on the Muslim takeover of Mobile, I try to chase her down after the service. But she disappears after signing copies of her CD. It's called *We Win!* and sells for $15 at a table set up near the doors of the main hall.

Hoping to spot her later mingling behind the church at the ice cream fellowship, I sidle up to Pastor Gibbs near the ladies dishing out Blue Bell ice cream.

"Are six mosques really going to be built in Mobile?" I ask him.

"I don't exactly know," he says offhandedly. Like everyone else, he's trying to finish his Butter Crunch before it melts in the 90-degree heat. "I hadn't heard about that."

A man and woman nearby admit that tonight is also the first they've heard the news—so now it's news—but they tell me there's a large Muslim population in Mobile.

"Large enough to support six new mosques?" I ask.

"It just might."

Moments later I fall into a classic southern conversation with a balding, middle-aged, fact-spewing birther named Marvin, who for thirty minutes stands next to a wife he doesn't bother to acknowledge or introduce. When I tell him what I'm up to, Marvin rearranges his glasses and starts vomiting out the FOX "News"–approved righty line—Barack Obama is a liar, a socialist, a hater of Israel, an enemy of freedom, a foreigner, the tip of the Muslim advance into America. The supposedly elegant Michelle has cankles and could stand to drop twenty pounds.

"To get in the Indonesian mosque school as a kid, Obama had to become an Indonesian citizen," Marvin says, reeking of conspiracy-style authority. "Because Indonesia doesn't allow dual citizenship, he had to revoke his American citizenship. And now he wants to come back here and be president?"

"Well, actually, he doesn't *want* to be president, he is president," I say.

Ignoring the fact that renouncing American citizenship contradicts the basis of the argument Marvin had made ninety seconds earlier about Obama not being an American citizen in the first place—since as everyone who's paying attention knows Obama wasn't even born in this country—I attempt to establish a point of conciliatory commonality.

"Okay, let's say it's true that Obama renounced his citizenship to get into a mosque as a kid." I take a deep breath. "Are we really supposed to hold a lapse in judgment made by a nine-year-old against him for the rest of his life? George Bush was an alcoholic well into adulthood and nobody seemed to begrudge him that."

"Obama is a socialist."

"So are fire departments and libraries and cotton-industry subsidies and roads and the military. Want to get rid of all of those?"

The only thing that would make Marvin's prideful ignorance more of a stereotype is if his name were Jasper or Bocephus. The height of his spittle-and-bile performance is a non sequitur attack on John Kerry. You'd think old Kerry would be out of the crosshairs by now, but Marvin actually lays the blame for America losing the Vietnam War directly at Kerry's feet.

"We know now through the release of records that the North Vietnamese were ready to surrender," Marvin extemporizes. "They were finished. They knew it. When they saw Kerry protesting the war in Washington, D.C., and agitating all the protesters, the Vietcong suddenly knew they could win, so they decided not to ask for surrender."

You hear a lot about southerners wanting to refight the Civil War. What you don't hear is that far more of them want to refight the 1960s. During the give-and-take banter part of her concert-sermon, Garcia had walked to the side of the church, pointed to a Bieberesque teen with bangs in his eyes and hair on his shoulders and said, "With that long hair you've got, I can't tell if you're a boy or a girl!" The insult drew an appreciative laugh from the crowd, the sort of jeer not heard in most parts of the country since 1975. "Where does all the antipathy and venom come from?" I ask Marvin. "Why are southern religious conservatives so hateful toward the left?"

At this, silent wifey nearly tips over.

"All the hatred comes from the liberals!" she snarls, revealing a cob of small, gray teeth. "The hatred starts in them."

"It's not just a southern thing; there are evangelical Christians in every state in the country," Marvin says, his cheeks purpling. "There are more Southern Baptists in Oklahoma than in most southern states."

There it is again, the North-is-South argument. I tell Marvin that mine is not an inquest into northern issues. It's about the South, which, in the case of religion, is clearly the head, heart, and tail of the fundamentalist Christian snake. From the southern headquarters of church power, the KKKristian agenda is extended all the way to hamlets like Wasilla, Alaska (forty-fifth most religious state, according to that aforementioned Pew Forum study), as I'm reminded when Marvin brings up the patron saint of Winn-Dixie whiners.

"Sarah Palin is not from the South," Marvin reminds me.

"So what?" I say. "Hitler wasn't from Germany, either. Palin wouldn't exist if not for the South."

This shuts Marvin up for about half a second; my only undisputed debate tally of the night. And, please, spare me the phony "He compared Palin to Hitler! He compared Palin to Hitler!" histrionics. If everyone could make a deal to stop pretending to have emotional breakdowns every time someone dots their point with a rhetorical flourish the culture war conversations would be a lot more fun.

It's called hyperbole, it's not against the fucking law. No one's saying Palin wants to launch a Holocaust against the liberals. Just that she'd look pretty good in a swastika. And might be open to an invasion of Russia.

I might not sound as though I have a lot of empathy, but the truth is I understand the difficult position in which devoted evangelicals find themselves. Born again allegiance to God simply isn't compatible with allegiance to a mortal (i.e., evil-hearted) entity. These are mutually exclusive concepts that cause tremendous internal dissonance among more intelligent believers, whose entire social life is built around the church. If you're really living according to the religious principles that dominate southern society, you almost *have* to agitate for a government that puts God above country, biblical law against reason.

"The difference between the southern religious conservative and others is that we truly fear God and believe he sits in judgment of our country and that he doesn't like what he sees right now," Pastor Gibbs explains. "For conservatives not to stand against the Democrats is to betray the Lord. . . . We will never stop fighting. That's not gonna happen."

I believe him. Just like I believe America's social and political gridlock won't end until one side gains an overwhelming numerical majority (an obvious motivation behind the breakneck evangelical effort to recruit like-minded voters outside the saturated home region) or, like two scorpions in a bottle, the two antagonists are separated. Or one kills the other.

"What about secession?" I suggest as the ice cream fellowship crowd starts heading for their trucks. "Imagine a country in which you wouldn't have to waste time and resources battling abortion. You could just make it illegal and be done with it. You could outlaw mosques. Force gays out of your military. Make the Ten Commandments the basis of your legal system and get on with life. So could the rest of the country."

"With secession, both sides might want the same thing," Marvin allows philosophically.

"Exactly!" I say. "Each might say, 'You know what, we're better off without 'em,' and have a reasonable case. Maybe it's a win-win."

This is precisely the kind of intellectual exercise I've been imagining having with southerners during my first few months of travel, but any hopes I have of a productive give-and-take on how a peaceful separation might be hammered out are smote when Marvin quickly downshifts into another round of Coulterized lefty bashing, harping on Democrats for destroying America with their love of socialism and Mexicans.

Sensing my impatience, or maybe just wanting me the hell out of his ice cream social, Pastor Gibbs hands me a pamphlet titled *How to Get to*

Heaven from Mobile, Alabama. I act interested, but I'll be tossing it in the garbage as soon as Gibbs is out of sight. The fastest route from Mobile to a better world is called I-10 West and I already know the way to the on-ramp.

The coda to my Mobile visit comes the following morning when, driving out of the city, I place a call to the *Mobile Press-Register* newsroom and ask for the paper's religion editor. A third-generation southerner, Roy Hoffman has been at the *Press-Register* for a decade. You can tell great reporters within a minute of getting them on the phone by the way they pay attention to your opening spiel and double-check your name. Hoffman proves to be an authority on just about anything you'd want to know about faith in the South.

I tell him about the service at West Mobile Baptist Church and Sister Garcia's story about the construction of six mosques in Mobile.

"I've heard nothing about that," Hoffman says. "The Muslim presence in Mobile is small. There's a small Turkish community and a small Indian Muslim community. It's the least represented non-Christian religious group that's here.

"There is a Southeast Asian influx throughout the South and there are some Buddhist temples around," he adds, trying to be helpful.

"Where does a story like that come from?" I ask. "Shouting 'Mosque!' in a crowded Baptist church is like shouting 'Fire!' in a crowded theater. Why would she make such a confident assertion if it wasn't based in fact?"

"My best guess would be some sort of paranoid fantasy she picked up, maybe off of an extreme website or paranoia site. She sounds like a nut."

"Is it at all possible that six mosques could be built here?"

"Six would be unprecedented," Hoffman says. "I can't think of any faith here that could support six new churches. Usually the challenge is to get enough Muslims together. I've been scratching around myself trying to find some contacts to do a story on Ramadan and not having much luck."

"I spent an hour online last night looking for anything about new mosques in Mobile and found nothing."

"You probably won't."

Befriending Giant, Imaginary Squirrels, Deriding Descartes, and Other Creationist Pastimes

To be a modern evangelist is to submit to the nullity of reason. Sometimes, as with Sister Garcia, this means resorting to untruths. Sometimes, as with ice-cream-social Marvin, it means accepting the compulsory sacrifice of open-mindedness. Sometimes it simply requires identifying with an over-bearing suspicion of higher education. This is because, as every southern churchgoer can tell you, people lose their faith by degrees: first bachelors, then masters, then doctorate.

"There are a lot of really smart, good people involved in the churches and universities, but they are so committed to certain ways of interpreting biblical text that they have to apply a kind of mental gymnastics to reach the conclusions they want," says Kristin Swenson.

Swenson is a fortyish professor of religious studies at Virginia Commonwealth University and author of the assiduously unbiased *Bible Babel: Making Sense of the Most Talked About Book of All Time*. "Wishful thinking" is how she describes the efforts of Bible thumpers who twist scripture and common sense to support "a morally questionable purpose."[22]

I meet Swenson on a Sunday night in the open-beamed, colonial-style bar at the C&O restaurant in Charlottesville, Virginia. Even if she hadn't told me, I might have guessed at her Minnesota Lutheran roots—straight blond hair, blue eyes, agreeable smile, loose green shirt, jeans. No Marge Gunderson, but a few stray "Oh yaaaaaas?" pepper her conversation.

"There is a real suspicion in places of education itself—it's not like you and I share the assumption that education is good," Swenson tells me. "Too often there's an inability to think critically, to bring intellectual capacity to bear.

"Then you get somebody like Ken Ham, who is a pretty smooth talker and who dissuades you from learning more about the Bible. He comes quickly to this position of, 'If you don't believe what I'm saying, you are calling God a liar.' He's become very influential in Christian homeschool circles."

One of the most successful Bible entrepreneurs of the young century, Ken Ham is the visionary behind the seventy-thousand-square-foot Creation

Museum in Petersburg, Kentucky. In significant ways, the South might be said to start in the museum's parking lot, just across the Ohio River from Cincinnati. Passing between the pair of large stegosauruses that flank the entry gate, one gets a palpable sense of crossing the threshold from mere redneck America into the pathology of modern Dixie.

Dinosaurs are the primary fixation of the museum. This is because, even more than the story of Noah's ark, the Bible-literalist explanation of dinosaurs as creatures who hung out with Adam and Eve establishes in believers a radically different relationship with science than the rest of mainstream America—including much of the North—which at least to some degree grasps the limitations of relying on a book with so many built-in contradictions as the basis of historical and scientific knowledge.

The Creation Museum has a number of displays that refute "Human Reason" by pitting science against "God's Word," which usually amounts to some vaguely applicable Bible verse. One example is the signage that accompanies a lifelike model of a twelve-foot-long dinosaur with talons like meat hooks and forty-eight angry teeth ready to rip apart flesh, bone, and gristle:

Human Reason: The Utahraptor lived in the early Cretaceous world about 125 million years ago and evolved through millions of years of change.

God's Word: The Utahraptor lived in the pre-Flood world about 4,300 years ago. *God made the beasts of the earth (Genesis 1:25).*

The idea here is to set up an academic equivalency between religion and science (and imply that Utahraptors are mentioned in the Bible), so as to more effectively crush academia as one moves through the exhibits. The museum is filled with cartoon cutouts of kids with big speech bubbles above their heads saying things like, "I never heard this before in school," suggesting some sort of grand government conspiracy against facts and truth. This theme is expanded upon with displays of alleged scientific knowledge underscored with Bible passages such as, "Let God be true but every man a liar. Rom 3:4."

Refuting scientific consensus of earth as billions of years old, evangelicals often bolster their Bible-based cosmic timeline by complaining that

egghead explanations of seemingly incomprehensible ideas traffic in an elit-
ist mumbo jumbo that all but demands pious ridicule. Yet in places such as
Great Basin National Park in Nevada, 4,600-year-old bristlecone pine trees
grow on glacial moraine, and dead ones can be found as old as ten thousand years. That's at least four thousand years older than earth, according to
evangelical belief.[23]

And by what convoluted theoretical scientific guesswork can the rest of
us determine that a tree is ten thousand years old? By matching the rings of
living trees with identical rings of older trees from overlapping generations
and counting the number of rings! It's that fucking simple.

I'll admit, once into the millions and billions of years, some of the more
complicated explanations of natural history require leaps of faith for the
layman. Potassium-argon dating sounds a lot like one of those GEO 101
terms I managed to forget even before the midterm I barely passed more
than twenty years ago.

But at least there's a body of scholarship behind the idea of using radio-
active decay to determine the age of minerals. If I'm going to take a leap of
faith I prefer to do it with the people whose impenetrable magic has given us
airplanes, spaceflight, sonograms, cell phones, GPS, Trader Joe's microwav-
able tikka masala, and *A Very Harold & Kumar 3D Christmas,* not the family
values bozos whose singular, ancient text provides justification for slavery,
prohibitions on menstruating women in public, and instructions on goat
sacrifice.

A big part of the problem is a stubborn resistance to the rigors of education. In front of that fearsome dinosaur with all the teeth, an inquisitive
five-year-old girl demands that her mother tell her what sort of dinosaur
she's looking at. Mom shambles over—easy to imagine her being carted
though the concourse to gate C-37 at DFW airport—struggles silently
with the signage, but soon gives up on "Utahraptor" and walks away without a word, leaving her daughter to stare in silent, imbecilic awe at the
mysterious creature.

My visit to the Creation Museum is propitious. Some might say providen-
tial. Founder Ken Ham happens to be on the premises.

The intercom announcement of his appearance in the main hall at 4 p.m. raises a cheer throughout the museum. I get in line at 3:45 and snake through rope barriers for half an hour while people ahead of me pose for pictures and have Ham autograph homeschool textbooks claiming that dinosaurs roamed the earth 4,300 years ago.

You may never have heard of Ham, but to many Americans he's a folk hero. At one point during the wait, a middle-aged woman in front of me titters, "This is so exciting! I can't wait to get home and tell everyone who I got to meet on vacation!"

Ham is a thin, robust Australian, about five-ten with Friar Tuck bangs high on his forehead and gray beard trimmed in the fashion of a dour country parson. He wears a blue shirt and blue tie and surrenders a flinty smile here and there, but mostly his is a veneer of gravity and determination.

He's not uncomfortable, but you can sense the obligation. Watching Ham interact with the Creation Museum crowd is not unlike watching a CEO interact with shareholders at an annual board meeting. The only difference is Ham does his meet-and-greet in front of a life-size model of a mischievous cavegirl feeding a carrot to a giant gray squirrel while baby dinosaurs cavort in the foreground.

When I get to Ham, I ask why he decided to locate his museum in Kentucky. As if my smirking liberal ass doesn't know. Turns out, I don't.

"This spot is within a one-day drive of two-thirds of the American population," Ham says. "Chicago, New York, Ohio, Florida. You can get to here from there in a day."

If nothing else, you've got to admire the man's business savvy. Hand over the national economy to guys like Ham and Eddie Long and Joel Osteen, and we might have the budget balanced and trade deficits straightened out in time to avoid the real apocalypse that's on the way.

"What's with the fixation on dinosaurs?" I ask. "I expected more intelligent design and fewer T. Rexes."

"Dinosaurs are one of the main examples used to teach that the earth is millions of years old, and they are a source of fascination for just about everyone," he says, conspicuously not refuting the idea that the earth is millions (actually billions) of years old, even when I ask a follow-up designed to lead him into that tar pit. Ham isn't up for an argument today. He's here to press palms and sell books, not debate another cookie-cutter "progressive" know-it-all.

I tell him the museum is impressive and, since I don't feel like buying one of his books or CDs, get him to sign my ticket stub. This seems an appropriately Barnumesque souvenir to have from a man whose full-of-bullshit museum attracted 1.2 million visitors in its first three years of operation and got me to cough up the $24.95 adult entry fee.

And who in 2010 convinced the state of Kentucky to blur the lines between church, state, and private enterprise by extending him generous tax breaks to build a $150 million Noah's ark replica and museum, to be located near the Creation Museum. This, apparently, is the kind of socialism Kentuckians can believe in.[24]

To my rational northern brethren, the Creation Museum scene might sound harmless and quaint and perhaps a little hilarious—just some nutty Christians wanking off to themselves in the backwoods of Kentucky. But here's the problem with lumping this crowd in with snake handlers, moonshiners, and other picaresque characters of the South—they're infecting public schools all over the country with this same pigheaded stupidity.

The most troubling evidence of this appears to me in the form of Zachary, an offensive-lineman-size youth pastor, Bible counselor, and, as luck would have it, history teacher at a public high school in Cleveland, Ohio. In the museum's main hall, I shamelessly eavesdrop on a one-sided bloviating session Zachary is forcing on a pair of teenage boys in baggy shorts and Carolina Panthers T-shirts.

Behind a dark, flexing mane and full, throbbing beard, Zachary provides a sweeping review and summary dismissal of a millennium or so of Western philosophy. In that congenial and weirdly convincing hit-and-run rhetorical style perfected by the overheated ecumenical set, Zachary introduces the cornered boys to the lives, ideas, and principal shortcomings of Kant, Pascal, Kierkegaard, Nietzsche, Sartre, and other titans of Western thought.

"Descartes sought truth and original knowledge within himself," Zachary tells the boys. "Big problem!" Zachary has that uncanny knack for speaking in exclamation points, even when he's not shouting.

With the cavalier trashing of Descartes, I'm unable to hold my trembling intellect at bay any longer. This is the moment in *Annie Hall* when Woody Allen produces Marshall McLuhan to destroy a braying know-it-all in front of his date in line for a movie. I barge in beside the boys and tell Zachary that I find it strange that, him being a teacher and all, he'd discourage students from individual thought.

Zachary responds by tossing off a little Proverbs 3:5: "Trust in the Lord with all your heart; and don't lean on your own understanding."

"The Bible is infallible, every word is true, I believe every word," Zachary continues, stroking his beard as though enhancing its intimidating natural sheen.

Zachary tells me he attended the Southern Baptist Theological Seminary in Louisville, so I already sort of know how the rest of this conversation is going to go. As Mario Livio noted of Galileo's troubles with the church in *Is God a Mathematician?*: "As the dark clouds were gathering on the horizon, Galileo continued to believe that reason would prevail—a huge mistake when it comes to challenging faith." [25]

Nevertheless, I didn't come all the way to Kentucky to avoid stupid arguments.

"So, do you teach the biblical version of world history to your high school students?" I ask.

"Of course," Zachary says.

"Is that approved curriculum in Cleveland public schools? Is there any blowback from that sort of thing?"

"Who cares? It's the truth."

Zachary is positively jaunty about using his public school pulpit to push utterly unprovable theories. Dangerous are men with high opinions of their own opinions.

"What if it's not the truth?" I ask.

"It is."

"Are Cleveland students receptive to the biblical message?"

"Kids today are looking for guidance. Anyway, schools are supposed to be teaching creationism."

"What schools? Ohio schools?"

"All schools."

"What do you mean 'supposed' to teach creationism? By whose order?"

"The verdict of the Scopes trial was just to add evolution to curriculum, not to stop teaching creationism."

Actually, that's completely false. After only nine minutes of jury deliberation, the 1925 verdict in the Scopes Monkey Trial went against teacher John Thomas Scopes, the ACLU, and the pro-evolution crowd. The court actually upheld the existing Tennessee law prohibiting the teaching of evolution in schools, a decision that emboldened other southern states to enact their own laws banning the teaching of evolution.

W. J. Cash had the inexhaustible supply of willfully delusional Bible literalists nailed when he wrote in 1941's *The Mind of the South*, "A great Southern characteristic which deserves to be examined more thoroughly [is that] his world-construction is bound to be mainly a product of fantasy, and that his credulity is limited only by his capacity for conjuring up the unbelievable."[26]

As southern-educated history teacher Zachary might say, "Don't lean on your own understanding." Or, apparently, on the history books.

With Apologies to the Drive-by Truckers, Satan Is a Southerner—and He Votes

From museums to schoolrooms to courthouses to legislatures, the South's obsession with Bible literalism remains as fixed a part of regional identity today as it was in Cash's time. So is the evangelical resolve to transform the United States government into a theocracy modeled after its own beliefs. For non-KKKristians this is the real threat posed by southern religion, the endgame from which we must finally separate ourselves in order, perhaps, to save ourselves.

Churches in the South have always doubled as political forums. Preachers were expected to keep up Confederate morale during the Civil War. Black churches were central to the success of the civil rights movement. The Moral Majority's anti-everything political platform—abortion, gay rights, evolution, immigration—seeded national political debates over red herring issues we're wasting time on to this day. Just as Zachary is the heir to the Monkey Trial zealots, so are modern southern politicians pawns to an unbroken assembly line of church power brokers.

Conflating scripture with secular knowledge and legislative process isn't only the provenance of Ken Ham and Kentucky lawmakers. Southern legislators cite biblical teachings all the time, quoting the Bible as though it were official law of the land. For just one extraordinary example, while fulminating against government funding of Planned Parenthood in 2010, Virginia Republican state delegate Bob Marshall flipped to Exodus 13:12 to make the watertight point that children born with defects are God's way of punishing women who have aborted earlier pregnancies.

Virginia, of course, is the state with the governor who earned a master's degree in public policy from Pat Robertson's Regent University ("Christian Leadership to Change the World"), though at the time Governor Bob Mc-Donnell attended it was still known as CBN University, named for Robertson's Christian Broadcasting Network. So, a pretty rigorous academic institution.

McDonnell opened his 2010 term as governor by signing an executive order stripping homosexuals of protection under Virginia's antidiscrimination laws, an extension of policies he outlined in his 1989 CBNU master's thesis, "The Republican Party's Vision for the Family: The Compelling Issue of the Decade," asserting that, as reported by the *Washington Post*, "government policy should favor married couples over cohabitators, homosexuals, or fornicators." [27]

These sorts of asinine proclamations receive aggressive electoral support on Sunday mornings in places like the Freedom Baptist Church in Hiddenite, North Carolina, whose website notes, "We believe in the total depravity of man kind [sic]." In case you never get to a Sunday service there, the one I caught on the radio ended with a defiant reminder to parishioners that "The government doesn't call the shots. My Father calls the shots." [28]

Though leaning on fractional Bible wisdom for legislative justification is commonplace among southern pols, the viral outlook grips fundamentalists across the country. The northerner most infamously pulled into the Bible "logic" trap is Republican representative John Shimkus. From an area of southern Illinois settled almost entirely by farmers from Kentucky,

Shimkus earned notoriety in 2009 by informing a House subcommittee on energy and the environment that there was no need to worry about global warming, since God had promised Noah he would never again destroy the world by flood.

Citing the Book of Matthew as evidence, Shimkus declared, "The earth will end only when God declares its time to be over. Man will not destroy this earth. . . . I do believe God's word is infallible, unchanging, perfect." And, yes, this is the same Shimkus who, in 2004, led the glorious charge to defeat EPA rules controlling mercury emissions from coal-fired generators.[29]

By the way, is it me or does God's whole no-more-floods promise to Noah sound suspiciously open-ended? We can rest easy about a planet-engulfing deluge, great, but it feels to me like the Almighty left Himself an ark-load of wiggle room for all-consuming fires, meteor showers, alien attacks, or even a "permanent conservative majority" in Washington, D.C.

The argument here isn't that the southern evangelical power base is wrong. Or necessarily evil. Simply that a union based on such diametrically opposed approaches to societal organization—uncompromising Bible literalism versus protean secular law—is like a bad marriage that needs to end in order to save the children from turning into the same dysfunctional assholes as the parents.

It doesn't matter which side you see as "good" or "bad." Compromise is impossible when on one side you have people who literally believe that God is punishing America for not shipping more fighter jets to Israel, that anyone who supports legal abortion is a murderer, and that Satan spends his free time dicking around with their household appliances; and on the other side, a group comfortable with a president whose middle name is Hussein, defend the right to abortion, and don't see the Lord of Darkness behind every malfunctioning toaster or lightbulb.

"In God's reality there is no separation of church and state." A popular sentiment in the land of Bible zombies, I pick up this quote from a Christian radio show called *Awakening Young Voters*, which is produced by a group called Issues in Education that broadcasts in nine southern states and around the country. Because to most Americans, hand-washing the skid marks out of Bill O'Reilly's underwear is preferable to pulling a ten-minute shift listening to one-sided Bible study arguments for a Bush III regime, there's a tendency to underestimate the Christocracy imperative nurtured in evangelical churches—and to lose sight of the fact that, as the *Encyclopedia of Southern Culture* notes, "What is mainstream in the South, is peripheral elsewhere."[30]

League of the South founder Michael Hill makes a pair of chilling points to me:

"The South still reveres the tenets of our historic Christian faith. Our primary allegiance is to the Lord Jesus Christ and His Holy Church."

"Southerners are the second most populous stateless nation included in the encyclopedia, after the Tamils of southern India. The thirteen-state South remains twelfth in population of all the nation-states of the earth."

If Hill makes it sound as if the South is already its own God-based country that enjoys feeding a Tamil terrorist-style martyrdom, that's because in some fundamental ways it is.

Worse, it's a country that wants to take over mine. Then drown it in the same unshakable delusion that forms the basis of its religion and broadly defined regional character.

A big problem—maybe the biggest problem—with Born Agains and evangelicals is not only that they believe the world is destined to end in their lifetimes, but that it'd be a privilege to see that prophecy fulfilled. Understandable, perhaps, among a population faced with such modern indignities as the alleged songcraft of Taylor Swift, overseas customer support centers, and black presidents, but a severe handicap when addressing such concerns as resource depletion, angry Arabs, and Tim Tebow's fantasy draft valuation.

There was something buried in Sister Garcia's testimony that night in West Mobile that, had it not been for the blindsiding weirdness of her "six mosques" tocsin, would have stuck out like a pig in a python, to respectfully borrow from the regional vernacular.

"Do you understand the times we're living in?" Garcia had asked by way of guiding the flock toward the waters of apocalypse.

Attend a few Bible studies or ice cream fellowships and pretty quickly you'll hear some iteration of this portentous phrase. "The times we're living in." KKKristian code for "End Times." The triumphal or nightmarish—depending on how often you fantasize about your children being reduced to ashes in a world-swallowing inferno—return of the sweet and bleeding Jesus, guaranteed by such stalwarts of reason as the Creation Museum and New Life Family Worship Center Pentecostal Church in suburban Dallas, the latter of which, when I was there, was offering regular classes in End Times instruction.

"End Times" psychosis—the *Left Behind* Rapture book series has reportedly sold 65 million copies—is great for KKKristian business and those with upside-down mortgages; not great for anyone who's been feeding a SEP IRA for the past fifteen years. If you really believe the world is coming to a near and fateful end, of course, there's no need to worry about credit deficits or ensuring that public schools are properly funded. No need to place value in science, business, banks, governments, or other institutions that allow societies to guarantee a decent standard of living for future generations. Who's got time to worry about environmental degradation and the fact that we're tethered like a junkie to a needle to Middle East oil when it's all going to be swept away in a year or two or five, anyway?[31]

Famine. Pestilence. Earthquakes. Plague of frogs. San Francisco liberals. It's a fine, dramatic vision and I'm happy to leave it to the Lost Cause quitters who wallow in it. That's because the millions of southerners who not only believe the world is going to end on their watch, but *can't wait for it to end on their watch*, are a threat to those of us still interested in keeping alive the quivering flame of American optimism.

I'm so tired of the nonstop talk of fear and judgment from these people. It's pathetic the way briar patch prophets and their followers give up so easily. Then again, what's to be expected from a nation within a nation whose primary spiritual fonts have been converted into corporate vessels whose main obstacle to fiscal salvation is human enlightenment, who cite an "increase in knowledge" as a sign of the apocalypse (Daniel 12:4), and whose disciples believe all their problems will be solved by some mysterious entity and then behave like children when someone suggests a solution based in fact rather than Rush Limbaugh's latest meltdown.

To understand why the *Encyclopedia of Southern Culture* says "the South is the only society in Christendom where the evangelical family of Christians is dominant" (according to the Pew Forum on Religion & Public Life, in states such as Alabama, Arkansas, Kentucky, and Tennessee, evangelicals make up about half or more of the population), one need look no further than the Civil War and subsequent decades of woe-be-unto-us spin fashioned by the self-righteous, willfully delusional, and suicidal losers who started it.[32]

All these gloom and doomers giving up on the United States, quoting scripture, imagining God's rage, and whining about a world on the brink of extinction are descendants of the Lost Cause defeatism fostered and fetishized in post–Civil War southern churches—the same churches that have been hanging the blade of extermination over their people with the grim determination of a Dark Ages executioner ever since the final Union looter walked out the door with the last of the family silver. They haven't gotten over their issues in 150 years, so it's unrealistic to expect them to do so anytime soon.

CHAPTER 2

Politics: South Carolina and the Seven Deadly Sins of Southern Gub'mit

It's not easy to look into the twinkling eyes of a seventy-seven-year-old grandmother—a short woman in a pink T-shirt and floppy, white beach hat, the maker of someone's favorite sweet potato pie, a woman who says "God bless you with an extra dose of sugar"—and tell her that a life spent in the dim-bulb, backwater dumbfuckery of the smallest town in Alabama has so warped her political perspective that she and the rest of the citizens of Winston County deserve nothing less than a fast and merciless banishment to the same tar pits of American political history occupied by Stephen Douglas, George Wallace, Uncle Remus, and Herman Cain.

It's not easy to speak truth to a kindly old woman amid the tall grass of rural Alabama, but I think I might just be the guy to do it.

I've already been in Natural Bridge, Alabama (population twenty-seven), a couple hours longer than I'd planned. Now, listening to Emma Fields rant about Barack Obama's communist/Muslim/land-stealing ambitions, my courteous patience for southern political foaming and frothing has reached untested frontiers.

The encounter with Emma had begun in an ordinary way. Wanting only a $2.50 admission ticket, I'd wandered into the shop where she and her seventy-nine-year-old husband, Will, guard the entry to the town's only attraction.

The namesake natural land bridge is a 148-foot-long, 60-foot-high stone arch that spans a pretty patch of forest in a corner of northwest Alabama otherwise notable for its flea markets and outdoor junk sales. In the gift shop you buy your ticket, pass through a gate, and walk a short path to the natural bridge.

After some howdee-do chitchat and "yer darn tootin's" about the awful humidity and the couple's ten children—two military veterans, a minister, a nurse, and eight college grads among them—Emma announces for no apparent reason that all politicians are crooked. When I ask which ones in particular have gotten under her skin she practically spits the name Lyndon Johnson, whom she personally blames for the entire welfare state and subsequent slackening of American morals.

"They are all corrupt, going back to Lincoln," Emma pronounces, placing her hands on her hips like a gymnast sticking a perfect landing.

Stirred by the name of the loathsome commander in chief of the satanic blue marauders, Will comes to life with a story about a Reconstruction-era killing. He speaks as though the crime occurred last week.

"There was a Confederate veteran who lived here by the name of Kennedy who was killed by Union troops on a hill just fifty yards from here," Will says, pointing out the door. Will wears jeans, suspenders over his stretched-out white T-shirt, a camouflage-print baseball cap, and big, old-guy glasses. "His wife and children stayed with his body all night so that it would not be eaten by wild boars. Can you imagine that?"

Will is a member of the Sons of Confederate Veterans. He recounts for me various local crimes of Union rapists, carpetbaggers, and assorted scallywags. He actually uses the word "scallywag."

I ask if the Sons of Confederate Veterans are active in the area and Will tells me about several grave markers they've recently erected and the Confederate flag the organization maintains in front of City Hall.

"The blacks are allowed to preserve their heritage, but we are not, people don't like it," Emma adds.

I didn't come to Natural Bridge to talk politics. I actually just happen to be in a neighborhood almost no one ever just happens to be in. But southerners have a lot of opinions, especially about the South and being southern. I imagine this is burdensome for them, but it helps immensely in my research, because it turns virtually everyone I meet into an interview subject.

"Obama does not like going down to Arizona," Emma says when a news story about immigration comes on the radio behind the counter. "He won't go down there because he knows he probably won't come back."

"What do you mean by that? That he'll be shot?"

"That's right. That's right."

"Like JFK in Dallas?"

"That's exactly right!"

Emma straightens her beach hat and launches into a roiling stem-winder about socialists, the Illuminati, and federal corruption dating to 1776. The liberals are engaged in a massive land grab. The communist Obama intends to seize all private property in America.

"Where do you come by this news?" I ask.

"We saw an ad on TV. A black man in a suit was talking."

"Why would the federal government want to seize all private land? Think of all the property tax revenues that would vanish. Every local government in the country would collapse."

"I'm saying that the communists have been a part of everything from the start. They are involved in all of that."

Emma calls Russia a "sleeping giant," and tells me that China has a one-million-man army currently sitting on a Caribbean island "just waiting."

"Which island? Waiting for what? Have they got a navy sitting over there?" I act alarmed, which I sort of am. Not by the idea of a million Chinese clogging up the beaches in Barbados, but by this naked display of southern electoral ignorance.

Emma can't answer. She keeps spinning her yarn about the government seizure of land, somehow tying this nightmare scenario to the savings and loan scandal of the 1980s and her own mortgage account or retirement portfolio or something being transferred from a bank in Texas to one in New York to one in Chicago to one in Germany.

"I heard about that Chicago bank transfer and that made my ears perk up, let me tell you," Emma says, her sagacious nod tacitly turning Obama into an accessory to every shady activity that's gone down in Chicago since Al Capone got sent up the river for tax evasion.

Emma and Will aren't crazy. Or dumb. They're college-educated, experienced, sharp-minded, business- and family-oriented people who speak in punctilious, grammatical English. Despite pushing eighty, they remain completely lucid.

The point in recounting my conversation with them is not to demonstrate how extraordinary they are. Quite the opposite. Theirs is, in my experience, a near-perfect distillation of the prevailing southern political outlook, a group-thought vendetta against liberals and other foreigners that is so besotted with religion, race, militarism, ancient grudges, and hidebound demagogic exaggeration that productive discourse and open exchange of ideas with outsiders become a virtual impossibility.

But, really, shit, what did I expect from the smallest jerkwater shtetl in Alabama?

Conservative, Republican, Jackass, or Just Plain Southern?

When entering into a discussion of contemporary American politics, it's important to distinguish between Republican conservatism and southern sabotage. Though today the two have become almost inextricably intertwined, it's not a given that they must always be the same thing.

Hanging on a wall in the office where I work at home is a framed 14 x 8½-inch document. Inscribed in bold blue letters at the top of the document are the words "State of Alaska Certificate of Vote." Below is a paragraph of fancy script that reads:

> We, the undersigned, being the duly elected, qualified and acting presidential electors for the State of Alaska, do hereby certify that on the 17th day of December, 1984, A.D., at and within the City of Juneau, State of Alaska, duly and regularly met and convened and then and there, by the authority of law in us vested, voted for President of the

United States of America, with the following result: For President: Ronald Reagan.

At the bottom of the page, next to an embossed gold foil seal of the state of Alaska, are three signatures. The last one belongs to James L. Thompson. My father.

The document is an original legal certification of one of Alaska's three electoral votes in the 1984 U.S. presidential election, all of which went to Ronald Reagan. With the exception of his marriage license, the birth certificates of his children, and one or two other papers absolving him of all wordly debt, I don't think there was a document in this world to which my dad was ever more proud to affix his name.

Jim Thompson was active in the Alaska Republican Party for years—as a kid I waved to Fourth of July crowds from a campaign parade float supporting one of Wally Hickel's gubernatorial runs, the one that followed Hickel's term as Richard Nixon's secretary of the interior. Earning the honor to cast the vote for Reagan was both the ultimate reward for and high point of Dad's years of service to the conservative cause.

The political review that follows is not a renunciation of Republicans or the widely held notion of "conservatism" as understood in the modern American political sense. Though I did not and would not ever vote for Ronald Reagan, I grew up in a staunch GOP household and retain an abiding respect for people such as my father who pursue their political convictions with a strong, yet open-minded and honest intelligence. Though he never campaigned for one, my dad did occasionally vote for the opposition. The lone Democrat he ever supported for the presidency was John Kennedy.

"He was the better candidate," my dad would tell you, as if this should be the self-evident criterion for one's choice in any election.

Such intellectual honesty rarely dares show itself in today's southern-dominated Republican Party. And when it does, it gets beaten, flayed, and run out of the system faster than you can say Arlen Specter.

Conservatives and liberals in the United States have traditionally acted as ballast for the other's less admirable traits and more harmful tendencies, in the process creating a yin-yang codependency that's uniquely American. In the hands of its reactionary overlords, however, today's GOP isn't so much a group that leans right against the left as it is a group that pushes South against the North.

The Republican veneer may make southern politics appear no different than the brand of conservatism that prevails across the mountain states, Southwest, Midwest, and even large pockets of the presumably communist Pacific Northwest. Stripped of the bogus facade of party colors, however, the game of division practiced by Dixie reactionaries today is the same as the fathomlessly fraudulent politics that split the country in 1861 and in significant ways has kept it apart ever since.

Rejecting mainstream American values has been the leitmotif of southern politics from the moment the idea of "the South" was articulated. In order to affirm his own tribe, the southerner has always depended first on resisting the northern one and all that it stands for—resist freedom for blacks, resist collective rights for workers, resist gays, resist immigrants, resist public aid for the poor, resist liberals, resist nonbelievers, resist those with whom you disagree, and, most important, resist Washington, D.C. In his 1964 book, *Who Speaks for the South?*, South Carolina author James McBride Dabbs summarized the psychosis: "What a Southerner is, and what he is supposed to do besides resist, nobody knows."[1]

The question remains unanswered. With sesquicentennial celebrations of secession and the Civil War sweeping through the South in the first half of the present decade, the urge to resist the rest of the country grows more vigorous. And absurd. As economist Paul Krugman has noted of the party of the South: "If [Obama] came out for motherhood, the G.O.P. would declare motherhood un-American."

Michael Lind, Whitehead Senior Fellow at the New America Foundation, said it even better in a 2009 *Daily Beast* article: "The battle in Washington is not between liberals and conservatives; it is between the Union and the South. The rest of the country needs to understand . . . this [Republican Party] is the party [whose] spiritual ancestors are the old Southern conservative Democrats, like John C. Calhoun and Jefferson Davis and Strom Thurmond and Orval Faubus."[2]

Lind nails it. The unified southern resistance to every initiative from any "liberal" administration has deep historic roots.

The persistent defiance of every Democratic attempt to deal intelligently with national problems—be they recession, debt, or childhood diabetes—has nothing to do with political ideology, taxes, health care, or acceptable degrees of federal authority. It has everything to do with nullification, disruption, zealotry, and division. It's part of a time-sharpened effort to debilitate nearly every northern-led government by injecting it with the Seven Deadly Sins of Southern Politics: demagogic dishonesty, religious fanaticism, willful obstruction, disregard for own self-interest, corporate supplication, disproportionate influence, and military adventurism.

Here's how it breaks down itself, and everything it touches.

Sin #1: Demagogic Dishonesty

Match the hysteria below with the speaker and year to which each belongs:

1. "[The opposition] are atheists, socialists, communists, jacobins on the one side, and the friends of order and regulated freedom on the other. In one word, the world is a battleground—Christianity and atheism the combatants; the progress of humanity the stake."

2. "[The opposition's] secular socialist philosophy is profoundly in conflict with the heart of the American system and is a repudiation of the core lessons of American history. . . . With God's help, and with our willingness to humble ourselves, to always seek His guidance, and always do His bidding, we will overcome our radical secular opponents."

3. "[The opposition] are farmer murderers, poor-folk haters, shooters of widows, and orphans, international well-poisoners, charity hospital destroyers, spitters on our heroic veterans, rich enemies of our public schools, private bankers, European debt cancelers, unemployment makers, pacifists, communists . . . and skunks who steal Gideon Bibles!"

A. College of South Carolina president Dr. J. H. Thornwell, rebuking liberals during a pro-slavery speech in 1850

B. U.S. senator Theodore Bilbo of Mississippi, rebuking liberals during a campaign speech in 1934

C. Former U.S. House speaker and 2012 presidential candidate Newt Gingrich of Georgia, rebuking liberals during a book tour speech in 2010[3]

Before getting to the answers, sit back for a moment and behold the stunning consistency with which unhinged political raving has emanated from the South's most respected leaders across three centuries.

"Staying on message" is hardly an invention of the FOX "News" Republican sheeple era. Even as Abraham Lincoln was campaigning in the presidential election of 1860, the secessionist commissioners who traveled the South to stir up anti-American sedition without fail referred to the opposition solely as the "Black Republican" party. Repeating this scripted talking point with nauseating insistence made men such as South Carolina secession commissioner Andrew Pickens Calhoun and his Mississippi compatriot Fulton Anderson the Steve Doocy and Megyn Kelly of their day.[4]

The answers are:

1. a
2. c
3. b

But would it be any less believable if I told you that the answers were 1. c, 2. b, and 3. a? Or substituted the names Orval Faubus, Jabez Lamar Monroe Curry, and Spencer Bachus for Thornwell, Bilbo, and Gingrich? Or replaced any of those quotes with one from Georgia congressman Paul Broun, who reacted to a harmless 2010 Centers for Disease Control telephone survey meant to determine the eating habits of Americans by wailing in the press, "This is socialism of the highest order!"

The southern playbook hasn't changed. Thus can one reach to 1860 to find Alabama congressman Jabez Lamar Monroe Curry predicting "a saturnalia of blood" following Lincoln's electoral victory. Or achieve the same effect 150 years later by citing Alabama Republican national committeeman Paul Reynolds's gastric declaration that Democrats legally voting in the 2010 Alabama Republican gubernatorial primary amounted to "the biggest theft in American political history." Robert Bentley—the Republican front-runner in that primary, who predictably became governor of Alabama—practically wept on the front page of the *Montgomery Advertiser* that the election was "being hijacked by the liberal Democrat machine."

Some machine. Democrats have lost five of the last six gubernatorial races in Alabama. The state hasn't sent a Democrat to the U.S. Senate since 1997.[5]

No matter. Hyperventilation in the service of falsehood remains the go-to move of Dixie politicians, whose constituents have collectively agreed that hyperbole and lies are the same thing as wisdom and truth. Wonder where they might have come by that idea? Ah, yes, sin number two.

Sin #2: Religious Fanaticism

In June 2010, at the height of the ineffectual effort to cap the BP Deepwater Horizon oil gusher on the floor of the Gulf of Mexico, the Louisiana State Senate devised a novel solution. Specifically, on the sixty-sixth day of the environmental tragedy, the men and women duly elected to deal with Louisiana's many and varied problems declared a statewide Day of Prayer, beseeching God to bring a swift end to the undersea petro geyser.

The resolution passed unanimously, meaning that while one of the greatest man-made disasters in history spewed acres of gook and roving tar balls off of their coastline, not a single senator in all of Louisiana had the brains or balls to stand up and say, "Are you guys fucking kidding me with this shit?"

Governor Bobby Jindal made the Day of Prayer official by signing a decree that included twelve proclamations starting with the highfalutin conjunction "Whereas." Not one of these proclamations fell within the useful, self-searching domain of a well-placed:

"Whereas we resent that just eighteen days ago BP chief executive Tony Hayward told *Forbes* magazine that the BP Gulf spill would lead to record oil industry profits (Hooray!)"; or,

"Whereas we really need to start taking a closer look at the incompetent subcontractors working offshore in Louisiana, we hereby decree an immediate overhaul of our impotent state regulatory agencies be undertaken."

In defense of the resolution, flummoxed Republican senator Robert Adley said, "Thus far efforts made by mortals to try to solve the crisis have been to no avail. It is clearly time for a miracle for us."

The prayer did not work. BP's gusher wasn't stopped until July 15, three weeks after the Day of Prayer, and then only when a mortal-made, 150,000-pound cap was lowered onto the wellhead and cemented into place. Yet as the unanimous senate vote confirmed, the Day of Prayer was viewed as a perfectly reasonable response in a part of the country where Obama is a Muslim and alligator nuggets are a delicacy.[6]

Once in Washington, the effects of hidebound religious dogma hogtie progress. Those who hold that God's law is immutable arrive in the nation's capital armed not with the diplomat's skills of persuasion and compromise, but with the fanatic's conviction that negotiation with infidels equals sin. If it is God's law that abortion is an abomination, to cite the most potent example, then anyone who disagrees is a reprobate soul on the fast road to hell. To compromise with such a blackguard is to compromise, literally, with a murderer of babies.

Once this position is fixed in the religious "conservative" mind, it makes a moral imperative of opposing the heathen's political interests, no matter how logical or goodly, be they tax relief for the poor or calls to combat childhood obesity. Thus is put into play the unbending "no compromise" plot lines that have stymied debate and brought this country to its current state of political stalemate.

Because their cultures and political structures depend entirely upon paternalistic absolutes, religious fundamentalists deprive themselves of the typical human capacity for concession. As played out in the South, this pathology is, in essence, Islamic fundamentalism writ small. A devoted

Muslim is no more capable of compromising the Koran than a politicized Born Again is capable of compromising the crucibles of his faith.

Like the widespread certainty that Obama is a Muslim socialist born in Indonesia, in the South, Jesus-based public policy is no nutty aberration. It's the basis of mainstream political thought.

It's not that religious freaks won't compromise. It's that they can't. If they could they wouldn't be religious freaks in the first place. And wouldn't get elected to office. Not in the South, anyway.

Insofar as 1860s southerners were concerned, after all, Abraham Lincoln's most unforgivable sin had nothing to do with his abolitionist views. Plenty of southerners were sympathetic to the antislavery cause.

The South's real trouble with the Great Emancipator was that he wasn't a member of any church. Lincoln's major crimes included being a firm believer in evolution, and not accepting that the Bible was the divine revelation of God.[7]

Sin #3: Willful Obstruction

Two atomic bombs and the specter of the Red Army didn't hurt, but the reason the United States was able to turn totalitarian enemies into friendly allies with such ease in postwar Germany and Japan—in a way it was never able to do after vanquishing the South in the Civil War—is that the lack of powerful religious institutions in those countries enabled the rise of cooperative, logic-driven governments. The Americans, Germans, and Japanese of the post–World War II period were able to jointly build and maintain modern and profitable government apparatuses because the principal parties understood and embraced politics, which is to say, the art of compromise.

In other words, they were able to find common points of interest and behave as rational actors in mutually beneficial social and economic arrangements.

Hand in glove with evangelical radicalism has been a heroic refusal to engage in traditional horse-trading. With the southern caucus in Washington reaching for any branch it can to keep its mulish platform alive, that never-say-tie tenacity threatens the future of the country today more than at any time since 1860.

While China economically colonizes half of Africa, builds the world's greatest high-speed-rail network, and stockpiles U.S. banknotes, southerners force America to dither over Obama's allegedly hidden religiosity and contraception and gays getting married, while grudge-bearing state legislators such as Republican delegate Bob Marshall of the Virginia General Assembly call on his state to begin minting its own gold and silver coins, so that Virginia's economy might forever be divorced from that great failed currency known as the U.S. dollar.

In case you don't believe me, language in Marshall's 2011 Virginia House Joint Resolution No. 557 claimed, "many widely recognized experts predict the inevitable destruction of the Federal Reserve System's currency through hyperinflation in the foreseeable future." The discontented Yankee will search in vain for a more perfect representation of a kamikaze political statement that brings to bear the South's eternal grudge against America—and the End Times madness that imbues southern KKKristianity, and, by extension, all southern politics.[8]

In the introduction to *Patriotic Gore*, his 1962 survey of Civil War literature, Edmund Wilson wrote of his fellow southerners: "They have never entirely recognized the authority of the Washington government." Even now, the "Southerner first and American second" ethos remains a popular attitude that goes a long way to explaining the results of a 2010 survey in which 23 percent of Republicans queried said they believed their state should secede from the Union.[9]

Within the narrow-minded confines of the Us-against-the-North worldview of Lost Cause victimhood, recognizing the ultimate sovereignty of the U.S. government amounts to a verboten admission of weakness. As a result, the South no longer sends politicians to Washington. It sends blinkered warriors whose job is to represent the unbending naysayer impulse inscribed on the southern mind from cradle to church to football tailgater to grave.

Worse, no longer are southern pols even the seditious but gifted white-maned officer orators of the Senator Claghorn days. At least those guys had style. Today the South consigns to Washington mere foot soldiers whose Men's Wearhouse political dexterity renders most congressional debate as erudite and elegant as an employee smoke break in the parking lot behind the Waffle House.

You see the South's resistance obsession manifested all the time in pissy little Napoleons like South Carolina senator Jim DeMint, who openly plotted to make the major policy initiative of a sitting American president (health care, Obama) "his Waterloo." You see it when another South Carolina senator, Lindsey Graham, actually gets censured in 2009 and 2010 by Republicans in his home state for attempting to cooperate with Democrats—Scandal! Outrage!—on a bipartisan energy bill meant to fix the future security and prosperity of the country.

The first of those censures called out Graham for "tarnishing the ideals of freedom, rule of law, and fiscal conservatism"—all for sitting down at a table with that infamous liberal traitor John Kerry, the only military veteran the South ever met whose ability to reload an automatic weapon after emptying its magazine in the direction of foreigners didn't instantly confer upon him demigod status.[10]

There's no more reason now to expect the South will start cooperating with the rest of the country than there was in 1860 or 1960. The city of Vicksburg, Mississippi, after all, refused to celebrate the Fourth of July until 1941, when Congress first declared Independence Day a paid federal holiday. As a Confederate flag supporter in Georgia told the *Atlanta Journal-Constitution* in 2004 after his side lost a referendum to keep Confederate symbolism on the state's flag: "We will keep our anger alive. We shall be grim and unconvinced and wear bitterness like a medal."[11]

Sin #4: Disregard for Own Self-Interest

Year in and year out, an influential percentage of poor, uneducated, underserved, insurance-less white southerners continue to cast votes for candidates whose agendas clearly conflict with their own self-interest. Rank-and-file southern voters—who have lower average incomes than other Americans—resoundingly defeated Barack Obama in 2008; the eventual president carried just 10, 11, and 14 percent of the white vote in Alabama, Mississippi, and Louisiana, respectively.

Obama was trounced in the South despite the fact that his campaign platform included more tax breaks for those earning less than $100,000, more public education funding, and more public health care benefits for the populace than did the McCain-Palin ticket. That's not interpretation, that's fact.[12]

What accounts for the southern voter's apparent disassociation from his own interests? Why was it that, as southerners are quick to tell you, almost none of the poor bastards who got bayoneted for slavery in the Civil War actually owned any slaves or land themselves? Why in continually supplicating himself to political and commercial interests demonstrably hostile to his own, does the southern voter so fluently assume the role of the battered woman in an abusive relationship, a cringing figure who nevertheless keeps returning to her tormentor for more abuse because she is scared and believes herself to be powerless and without options?

To answer these questions, or at least get a close-in look at the social environment that produces them, I dropped one warm summer evening into the most redneck bar in the entire South. Prior to arriving in South Carolina I had not been aware of its status as the region's reigning meeting ground of gizzard shiners, closet Clampetts, and slave days nostalgics, but when I ventured one afternoon into Wallace Creations African American barbershop in Laurens, South Carolina, and asked where the passing Tocquevillian might avail himself of the shit-kickingest, domestic, light, and cold beer joint in the state, the response was immediate and unanimous: Little Louie's.

For the traveling writer, few encounters are actually worth the trouble it takes to have them. Like panning for gold, digging for fossils, or waiting for a decent *Saturday Night Live* skit, disappointment is the field researcher's closest companion. Occasionally, however, you get a Schweddy Balls or More Cowbell. This happens for me at Little Louie's Bar-N-Grill on State Highway 14 between Laurens and Barksdale, where I pull in at just past eight on a Friday night.

Slapped on the back of a rusty Ford F-150 in the muddy, potholed parking lot, a bumper sticker helps sets the tone: "I don't discriminate, I hate everybody." But it's the distorted blare of "The South's Gonna Do It Again" from a three-piece band of ZZ Top–looking dudes called the Nite Krawlers that ushers me into a world in which the name Copenhagen is more often associated with a refreshing dip than a European capital.

Breaching the Little Louie's threshold I overhear one guy tell another, "I'm gonna kick that motherfucker's ass!" This is articulated in that uniquely keg-party way in which it's impossible to tell if the speaker is drunk, sober, joking, serious, or all of the above.

I pay $1.50 for a Miller Lite at the bar and no sooner is the icy can shoved into my hand than the Nite Krawlers launch into, in order—and I am in no way making this up for dramatic effect—the Skynyrd version of "Call Me the Breeze," Charlie Daniels's "Long Haired Country Boy," and Hank Jr.'s "A Country Boy Can Survive" (which should, but of course still does not, include a verse about the southerner's native ability to survive by cashing government assistance checks).

Little Louie's is a biker bar with a concrete floor, cinder-block walls, a low ceiling, and bathrooms for "Pigs" and "Piglets." I walk in wearing a short-sleeved, dark blue T-shirt from Old Navy, beat-up black Levi's, and torn Nikes that look like they've been dragged through the grime of about twenty states, because they have.

This casual all-purpose look is appropriate in most of dive-bar America, but at Little Louie's I might as well be wearing a top hat and carrying a jewel-encrusted walking stick. Half the crowd wears absolutely filthy T-shirts, hole-y denims, and greasy baseball caps, uniforms that make them look like they just got done dropping a bored-out 454 into the '71 Chevelle Super Sport up on blocks in their stepsister's side yard. The other half sports Harley T-shirts with cut-off sleeves, thick-soled boots, wallet chains, and a history of neglectful dental care.

One hand resting on a pool table, a whale-gutted guy in his fifties is engaged in a chugging contest with a tall, muscular kid who must be playing Division I football somewhere. They guzzle beer from pint glasses. Shamu wins both times, but just barely. When he finishes, he yowls in agony/ecstasy and slams his glass on the table hard enough to startle the bar—even over the din of the Nite Krawlers, who, it must be said, aren't terrible—and glares at the football player without a trace of humor.

When the Nite Krawlers go on break, I make an innocuous comment about the band and the guy leaning against a section of wood-paneled wall next to me offers what I choose to interpret as a friendly grunt. Gus is the rough-and-tumble-sort, a fifty-nine-year-old owner of a scrap-metal yard.

Big, rough hands with deep grooves and divots in the fingers. I'd put the over-under on divorces at three.

When I ask how the scrap metal business is going he shakes his head.

"In 2006, I had nine or ten guys working for me," Gus says. "Now I've got four, and one of 'em's my kid."

Gus delivers a brief soliloquy, the usual lament of the struggling small business owner, but allows that he's guardedly optimistic about the future. BMW has a big manufacturing facility in nearby Spartanburg that's supposed to be ratcheting up production. Better still, a Korean company is about to open an electric car plant in Spartanburg County.

Gus is indeed up on the local news. In summer 2010—four months *before* the nation swept the Republicans back into power in the U.S. House of Representatives with orders to resurrect the economy—Seoul-based CT&T Ltd. announced plans to spend $21 million to begin assembling small electric vehicles in the nearby town of Duncan. The factory is expected to bring four hundred jobs to the area. State officials lauded the plant as "the unleashing of a green technology revolution" in the state. What's more, once operating at full speed, the assembly line will use all U.S.-sourced parts obtained from factories in South Carolina, Georgia, and elsewhere.[13]

"Sounds good," I say, deciding to chance a little liberal philosophy. "We gotta get off the Arab oil nipple sooner or later. Bankrupting ourselves to China to fight an oil war in the Middle East has never made much sense to me."

"The economy has gotten better in the last year or two," Gus says, ignoring the geopolitical bait. "Plants are getting built. Now we just need to get Obama out of office and we'll get back on track."

Wait. What?

"If the economy's picking up, why not stick with what's working?" I ask.

Gus shrugs, takes a swig. If the Nikes and Old Navy hadn't already red-flagged me, now I've really given myself away. Though he says nothing, I can feel the Miller Lite can in my hand actually getting colder!

"Green initiatives are a big part of Obama's agenda," I press on, as delicately as possible. "If electric cars are coming to the county, that's good. New cars means more scrap metal, more jobs, more money, right?"

"There's a lot goes into that," Gus says enigmatically.

"I'm sure. But auto factory deals don't get settled overnight. Bringing heavy manufacturing and green technology to South Carolina seems like a win-win for everyone. Why abandon an administration that's been spearheading that?"

Gus smiles and shakes his head, like I just don't get it. Like I'm missing some key piece of the puzzle that would explain why a man with a livelihood directly linked to the auto industry would complain about his business declining, yet be so anxious to get rid of a president who's been laying out money and pushing to bring long-term business deals with powerhouse Asian economies to the area in which he lives.

Truth is, Gus is right. I don't get it. I've heard the "Gotta get rid of the activist Dems at all costs" argument over and over in the South and it's never once made any sense to me, at least not in economic terms.

Or most others. All the ubiquitous Emma and Will–style bitching about power-mad Obama's "socialist" agenda is manifestly delusional. No matter how much the Tea Party bellyaches, no laws passed in the last four years have been as assholish or liberty-thieving as Prohibition and the 55 mph national speed limit, both pushed by Republicans.[14]

"You think there's a single Obama vote in this bar?" I ask, looking around at the forty or so Friday-night drinkers in Little Louie's.

Gus laughs. Not a cynical snort or rueful chuckle, a real laugh, the way you'd laugh at a stand-up comedian who'd just broke off a hilarious line.

"What do you think?" he asks me.

"I highly doubt it."

"I highly think you're right."

I come back from the bar with two more beers, but the conversation spins its wheels in an all-too-familiar way. Gus speaks with the quiet, deliberate authority of an intelligent, well-informed man. For reasons that go unarticulated, however, he insists that Obama is simply unacceptable. The Democrats are radicals hell-bent on destroying the country and nothing will be right until they're gone. No specifics are offered to support this point of view—it's all knee-jerk anger presented as gospel truth.

When the Nite Krawlers hoist themselves back onstage, I shake hands with Gus, drink-walk to the front of the room with three beers for the band, and request some Marshall Tucker. The lead singer consults the band and shakes his head.

"Don't know none," he says.

"'Heard It in a Love Song'? 'Can't You See'? 'Fire on the Mountain'? 'This Ol' Cowboy'? 'Silverado'?"

"Nope."

Three southern-fried rock pilgrims in the honky-tonk badonkiest bar in South Carolina can't summon a single tune from the pride of Spartanburg? Jesus Chrysler, am I the only real redneck in this joint? The disappointment feels like an omen.

Mindful that it's always better to leave a party thirty minutes too early than thirty minutes too late, I toss my empty into a lidless garbage can full of cans, bottles, peanut shells, and potato chip bags (Recycling? Ha ha ha ha!), make a pit stop in the little pigs' room, and head for the door.

In the parking lot I walk past a rusting Camry, inside of which a ratty blonde is giving a BJ to a guy in the front seat. I stare inside the windows just long enough to make sure of what I'm seeing, then head to my car. With the exception of me and possibly the guy in the Camry, no one in this whole place seems to be acting with regard to anything close to his own best interests.

Sin #5: Corporate Supplication

Gus, it turns out, is key to explaining the fifth great millstone of southern politics. It isn't so much Obama that he objects to (though I'm sure that in the South "Harvard-educated black lawyer" carries the equivalent weight that "David Duke apostle" might in the North) as it is the liberal reputation for defending the rights of workers vis-à-vis the radical Republican reputation for defending the rights of businesses to exploit workers.

Neither intellectual nor populist, the modern political South is more accurately described as a captive tool of corporate ideology. Regional politics reflect this reality with an unwavering drive to confirm the conviction that the industrialization of the South is not only sacred, but attainable only through cheap labor and laws that maintain a perpetually impoverished lower class from which to draw it.

When viewed through the prism of short-term need, the mystifying alliance of lower-income southerners and avaricious corporate vultures makes a little more sense. The South's large and beleaguered lower class tends to need food right now, they need to pay their overdue bills right now, they have little savings, business is down, debt is crawling up their asses. That's a near-perfect description of scrap metal Gus.

For different reasons, corporations are also addicted to short-term profit. "You need to eat today, we need to satisfy third-quarter projections—vote for us, we'll both win, and worry about tomorrow tomorrow, which as we all know is gonna suck, assuming that Armageddon doesn't come first, which it probably will if you all don't obey the rules." (Witness Sin #2.) This shortsighted attitude is also a reason so few southern states bother to adequately fund public education.

For cash-strapped southerners, it makes sense to side with strength, no matter how bad the deal looks in the short term. Need a job, even an underpaying one? How about a war? Why not? I was probably gonna end up in the family business, anyway.

The anti-workingman irony reeks badly in places like rural Winnfield, Louisiana (population 5,040 and dropping). Signage around town celebrates Winnfield as the home of three governors, including the great southern populist Huey P. Long, the man who served as governor, then U.S. senator in the 1920s and '30s, and later thespian muse of both Broderick Crawford and Sean Penn. The preternatural Willie Stark character in *All the King's Men* was based on the portrayal of Long in the novel of the same name by Robert Penn Warren.

I take pictures of the Long statue near his birthplace at the corner of Main and North Jones Streets and walk through his old neighborhood, a fairly well-maintained mix of lower- and middle-income homes. Most of the owners of these homes would no doubt consider stoning any candidate today who got up and spoke, as Long constantly did, of a great Share Our Wealth Society designed to redistribute public funds and corporate taxes. Long's "socialist" administration, of course, built all those Louisiana roads, bridges, schools, football stadiums, and hospitals southerners happily use today, as if they just appeared by magic and no one actually paid for them.[15]

In few sectors is the exaltation of corporations and exploitation of workers carried out with more coldhearted efficiency than in the auto industry. Like Mexico, the South has spent the past four decades systematically siphoning auto jobs from Michigan and the Midwest by keeping its workers' salaries low and inhibiting their right to organize by rendering their unions toothless.

The comparison with Mexico is not offered frivolously. Corporate America has a long-standing habit of treating the South like a Third World nation. Southern politicians love touting the South's "pro-business climate," a euphemism that lets multinational cartels operating in the South know that they won't be troubled by pesky unions or competitive labor costs. Just as it is south of the nation's border, the driving force behind America's new "Auto Alley" that ranges from Texas to South Carolina is cheap labor—the South's primary economic bargaining chip since the days of you know what.

For years now, Michael Lind has articulated the way in which the contemporary South engages the rest of the country more often as a rival than a partner. With both nerve and accuracy, Lind wrote in *The Daily Beast*, "Unable to compete on the basis of public investment and public education, the South of the 21st century, like a broken-down banana republic, now uses anti-union laws and low taxes to lure corporate investment [from the rest of the country]."[16]

For just one example, average wages for autoworkers in the South are 20 to 30 percent lower than in Michigan, the now pillaged hub of a once dominant American industry. (More on this in Chapter 6.)[17]

True, in any market economy supply and demand are king, and undercutting the competition with a cheaper product or service is part of the deal. Losers get crushed and sent home. But just because quasi-feudal southerners have been forced to swallow incessant public relations messaging that blames the wage-working underclass for the sins of executive mammon doesn't mean the rest of the country has to follow along selling out its own people so that multinationals can treat them like Amazon villagers.

The South is bad for the American economy in the same way that

China and Mexico are bad for the American economy. By keeping corporate taxes low, public schools underfunded, and workers' rights to organize negligible, it's southern politicians who make it so. By separating itself from this suppurating cancer in our midst, the rest of the country would at least be able to deal with the South as it would any other Third World entity, rather than as the in-house parasite that bleeds the country far more than it contributes to its collective health.

Sin #6: Disproportionate Influence

All of this leads back to a familiar question: So what? I'm not a religious nut or blind to my own self-interest or an unemployed autoworker or a southern voter. What do I care if the South has a self-destructive habit of devaluing its laborers? If some poor slackjaw in South Carolina wants to work his fingers to the nub for 30 percent less than a guy in Michigan and expose himself to industrial accidents and shitty health care and go to church on Sunday to pray that God forgives his state representative for fondling that eighteen-year-old male aide in the bathroom of the congressional lounge (allegedly), more diminished power to him.

The reason we all need to care, the reason for this entire dissection of southern politics, is that southern politics are not confined to the South. Thanks to its outsized influence in the federal government, Americans from Hilo to Huntsville are now hostage to the South's martyr-infused dysfunction.

The "Solid South" is a term that for most of post-Reconstruction history has been used to describe the single-party system under which all southern politics operated. Until the passage of civil rights legislation in the 1960s and subsequent "Christian" takeover of the southern Republican Party in the 1970s and 1980s, the South's single political entity of influence was the Democratic Party.

The Democrats' hold on the South was so ferocious that from 1919 to 1948, Democrats won 113 of 114 gubernatorial elections and 131 of 132 senatorial elections in the region. With the exception of 1928, the South gave every single one of its electoral votes to Democrats in the seventeen presidential elections between 1880 and 1944. That's not a political process. That's North Korea.[18]

Because the ripple of white voters who left the Democratic Party for the Dixiecrats in 1948, and then the Republican Party after *Brown v. Board of Education* in 1954, turned into a tsunami of complete political conversion unleashed by the destruction of Jim Crow and the empowerment of black voters in the 1960s, political observers today tend to refer to the "Solid South" as a thing of the past.

But it isn't.

The Solid South today is very much the same as it has been for most of the past century and a half. It's simply changed colors from blue to red. The intolerants that run today's Republican Solid South are every bit as in control of regional politics and committed to reactionary, anti-American radicalism as their fathers, grandfathers, and great-grandfathers were when they ran the region under the Democratic banner.

Old patterns remain fixed. No electoral presidential votes from the South went to Democrats in 2000. No electoral votes from the South went to Democrats in 2004. The Democratic ticket carried only three southern states in 2008 (Virginia, North Carolina, Florida). When the 112th Congress convened in January 2011, there were but sixteen white southern Democratic House members out of 105 seats in Alabama, Arkansas, the Carolinas, Florida, Georgia, Kentucky, Mississippi, Tennessee, and Virginia.[19]

It's true that in predominantly African American districts the Democratic Party exists and in some cases prevails. Insofar as the rest of the country is concerned, on national matters, there is but one party in the South and it is single-minded to its core.

One has to go back to 1976 to find a year in which a Democratic presidential candidate carried the South—that was southerner Jimmy Carter, who in addition to a Jawjuh drawl and Southern Baptist background benefited from a campaign run in the wake of Gerald Ford's ineffectual half-presidency. Not to mention the final sputterings of influence of the old-guard Democratic machine that fell apart with the dramatic shift in party allegiance that occurred following the federal legislative triumph of civil rights.

Excepting the singular anomaly of Barack Obama, whose ethnicity invigorated historically unreliable youth and African American voters, southerners refuse to recognize any Democratic presidential ticket unless a member of the southern tribe shares the ballot, thus dooming any mainstream northern Democrats' run for the U.S. presidency. This is yet another way in which the South's insular mind-set holds the rest of the country—and by extension the free world—hostage to its intransigent politics and petty truculence toward the North. "The greatest regional prize in modern presidential politics," as Earl and Merle Black, coauthors of *The Rise of Southern Republicans*, called the South, is jealously guarded by a comparatively small and radical sect of southern voters.[20]

"Right now in most of Dixie it is culturally unacceptable to be a Democrat," said Democratic campaign strategist Dave "Mudcat" Saunders, in an AP story titled "White Southern Democrats Nearly Extinct," which appeared shortly after the 2010 landslide Republican victory in national congressional elections.[21]

The Solid South's evangelical rigidity of thought not only confers upon the region an inordinate influence in presidential politics, it enables the South to assume a disproportionate control of Congress through the assumption of congressional committee chairmanships. The seniority system for chairmanships adopted by Congress in 1910 has allowed change-fearing southern voters—who tend more than others to return the same officials to Washington year in and out—to seize control of House and Senate leadership positions. Thus have the most reactionary and entrenched politicians in the country wrested control of the laws and policies of the entire nation.[22]

"The result of having a secure electoral base is that you stay around Washington a very long time," University of Georgia political science professor Charles Bullock told me. "That means you can to some degree ignore your constituents to spend time doing favors for your cohorts, building alliances with other Congress members."

So, now you know why so many GOP heads on TV speak with a southern accent.

As it has been for decades, today's Republican congressional delegation is disproportionately southern. In 2012, the Senate minority leader is Mitch McConnell of Kentucky. After House speaker John Boehner (the tanning-butter sensation is from Cincinnati, a city whose airport is actually

across the Ohio River in Kentucky, or as close to Petersburg, Kentucky's
Creation Museum as you can get without Michael rowing your boat
ashore), the two most powerful House posts belong to southerners: Majority Leader Eric Cantor of Virginia and House Financial Services Committee chair Spencer Bachus of Alabama.

Upon assuming his position in 2010, Bachus, whose committee's dominion includes the Federal Reserve, World Bank, and International Monetary Fund, unapologetically articulated the lickspittle southern approach
to corporate supplication.

"In Washington, the view is that the banks are to be regulated, and my
view is that Washington and the regulators are there to serve the banks,"
Bachus told the *Birmingham News*.

This is the sort of outlook that made the dramatic yet ultimately impotent Occupy Wall Street movement a necessity in the minds of many
frustrated northern liberals, and a joke on the several southern college cam-
puses I visited in 2011 during the storm.[23]

For most of the 1950s, with barely 20 percent of the nation's population, Dixie politicians controlled approximately 60 percent of the congressional committee chairs. What makes the South's control of Washington
even more frightening today is the region's torrid population growth. From
1960 to 2000, the population of the South nearly doubled, increasing at
more than twice the growth rate of the rest of the country.

Today, more than one-third of Americans live in the South (including
Texas). For the rest of us, that's a prospect more unpleasant than babies on
a plane. And snakes in the cockpit.[24]

The certainty of expanding national influence has southern politicians
giddy. Based on the most recent census figures, 2012 reapportionment
gives Florida two more seats in the House of Representatives, while Georgia and South Carolina will each gain one seat. Texas gains four new seats.

Silver-lining progressives who hope that the region's immigrant-driven
population boom portends a more liberal, pro-American electorate may be
sobered not only by the results of recent elections, but by the research of Tufts
University political science professor and acclaimed author James M. Glaser.

"While the South is now home to unprecedented numbers of migrants
and immigrants, the political culture of the region does not simply pass

from generation to generation, it permeates the environment, shaping the attitudes of those who live there, native and newcomer alike," writes Glaser in his 2005 book *The Hand of the Past in Contemporary Southern Politics.* "Migrants to the South often appear to adopt the racial-political attitudes of their neighbors. The southern political culture is thus self-sustaining, perpetuating itself in myriad ways."[25]

In other words, don't think that just because Bobby Jindal is an Indian American that he's going to break a centuries-old model of political addiction to Lost Causes, or be above counting on God to cap oil spills, help the LSU Tigers win the national football championship, and occasionally lend a hand in solving the state's lesser problems.

Sin #7: Military Adventurism

The ultimate cost of all of this northern kowtowing to the unreconstructed mix of southern political perversions has been America's unseemly history of military adventurism. The mania for soldierly joyrides, on which the South not only usually occupies the driver's seat but also insists on riding shotgun, has led to a series of martial escapades that conclude in national disgrace, disaster, or massive debt roughly once a generation.

The southerner's enthrallment with war and bloodshed, his veneration of defeat and disaster, his zeal for religious crusade, and easy compliance with the corporate profit motive, has repeatedly dragged the nation into unnecessary wars. Lately, these gunboat exploits have led to not only the diminution of America's influence abroad, but a paralyzing depletion of public treasuries.

"The long-standing determination of so many southerners to show their 'Americanness' through ostentatious professions of patriotism and an aggressive 'my country right or wrong' attitude [has] typically translated into historically high levels of military participation and enthusiasm for military action," writes University of Georgia history professor James Cobb of the "fundamentally military nature of the [southern] collective purpose."[26]

I can hear the southern chorus already. Placing the blame on the South for wars the entire country has fought—and often as not profited from—is preposterous. Whatever slim margin of credibility I might have been hold-ing on to this far into my Yankee fantasy of southern political liability has been irrevocably mixed in with last week's hog suet.

To those who would argue that it's unfair to blame the South for Amer-ica's never-ending love of cannon fire, assault rifles, and limbless foreign children—as well as the political and financial disasters that now reliably occur as a result of this pathology—I suggest an examination of the record.

The greatest calamity in the nation's history is a perfect place to begin. Because it has long passed into the etched-in-granite annals of national legend, Americans have completely lost sight of the single most important fact about the Civil War, which is that it absolutely, positively, in no way had to happen. Taking the long view of history, one might actually make a reasonable case that in its entire existence the United States has fought only two necessary wars (Revolutionary War and World War II, though I'll listen to arguments for action in Korea and Afghanistan). As modern wars go, however, the Civil War was as easy to talk yourself out of as your annual colonoscopy.

This becomes clear when you read the prewar history and discover that—as southerners love pointing out—far from being a saintly emanci-pator of slaves, Abe Lincoln was quite willing to allow southerners to keep their Negroes shackled till doomsday if it meant avoiding secession and war. Lincoln was above all things a politician, which means he was a nego-tiator, a role he continued to try to play even as the conflict dragged on to Rebel detriment.

The War That Did Not Have to Happen occurred for the sole reason that a great number of influential southerners wanted it to happen. These plantation battle hawks agitated for war in the press, in the halls of gov-ernment, and in public forums. Exactly like modern Gingrichian culture warriors who conjure dragons from the northern ether, the Civil War was provoked by military fanatics such as Stephen Fowler Hale, Alabama's in-fluential secession commissioner.

Tall, lanky, as pleasant as a bunion, and renowned for his bulbous and slightly deformed head, Hale was the son of a Baptist minister who traveled the South in 1860 warning anyone who would listen that Lincoln and his Black Republican Party were "arming their emissaries to cut the throats of southern men, women, and children." Lincoln and the Black Republicans, he fulminated in typical demagogic Baptist fashion, meant to subjugate southerners by unleashing a slave revolt upon them.

Lincoln, of course, had no more interest in subjugating southerners than he had in having yet another four-hour, middle-of-the-night "we need to talk" session with Mary Todd or moving back to the dismal Kentucky backwoods. But, then as now, evangelically driven southerners were incapable of negotiation, indulging instead in an impulse for self-destruction that led to the burning of Atlanta—though, even if you don't give a damn, also to an all-time classic Hollywood film much beloved by southerners. So, not a complete loss for Dixie.

Hale was a living, or rather, dying example. The fiery Alabama agitator with the big head was fatally wounded at the Battle of Gaines' Mill in 1862. In fairness, his death did help the South hang on to its capital of Richmond for a few more years. Though these days anyone taking a quick tour of the weary Virginia capital and its row of "second-place trophies" along Rebel-centric Monument Avenue might be moved to question the value of Hale's ultimate sacrifice.[27]

Even after not-always-honest Abe struck a conciliatory "We are not enemies, but friends" note in his March 1861 inaugural address—and explicitly supported a piece of black betrayal called the Corwin Amendment that would have allowed slavery to continue in the South, saying he "had no objection to [slavery] being made express and irrevocable"—it was flagitious southerners who fired the first shots that would lead to the deaths of more than 600,000 Americans. Not just the first shots, actually, but forty consecutive hours of heavy artillery bombardment upon Fort Sumter, South Carolina, in April 1861, just to make sure Lincoln, the North, and the fort's eighty-five Union defenders got the message that the South was not simply prepared for war, but had a purple hard-on for it.[28]

Eighteen sixty-one wasn't the first time the country had been led into an unnecessary war by southerners, nor would it be the last.

It was a particularly belligerent class of freshman legislators from the South and West that agitated in Congress for the War of 1812—remember that at the time, America's far "western" states were Ohio, Kentucky, Tennessee, and Georgia. The southern demand for war against Great Britain was so aggressive that the threat of northern secession cast a pall over the 1814–15 Hartford Convention, a gathering called to convey the New England Federalists' formal opposition to the ongoing war.[29]

Popular South Carolina writer of southern-centric novels and pro-slavery spokesman William Gilmore Simms was influential in rallying fellow gun toters in support of the morally baseless Mexican War. Simms provided a measure of posterity to the southern obsession for war with the godless Mexicans in an 1847 letter to South Carolina senator James H. Hammond.

"You must not dilate against military glory," Simms fairly ejaculated into his great fan-shaped beard. "War is the greatest element of modern civilization, and our destiny is conquest. . . . The Mexicans are in the condition of those whom God seeks to destroy having first made mad."

Mary Chesnut, the great Civil War diarist, echoed Simms's "God damned" southern justification for starting wars against foreigners. When asked why the Almighty might be presumed to be on their side, she passed along the cultured response given in parlors and ballrooms across the South: "Of course, He hates the Yankees. You'll think that well of Him."

The South has also provided the key political push for more recent military blunders. As C. Vann Woodward noted in *The Burden of Southern History*, "Not only had the strongest support for the Vietnam war come from the South, but so also had the President and the Secretary of State who led the crusade."

Given all of this, can anyone be surprised by a 2002 poll that showed about two-thirds of southerners supported an invasion of Iraq, as opposed to barely half of Americans in general? Or a late 2002 nationwide survey that showed that, even as the effort in Iraq grew into a legit quagmire and evidence of government dissembling became overwhelming, the South was the only region of the country in which a majority of residents still supported the Bush administration's chaotic pursuit of an ill-defined military strategy; a strategy that nevertheless with lethal efficiency padded the fortunes of Halliburton, Bechtel, General Dynamics, KBR, and the usual petro-imperialists, while selling out the country's financial future to Chinese government loan sharks?[30]

Just as the Civil War could easily have been avoided, so, too, might have the money and virtue pit of Iraq been sidestepped had not all the Armageddon bullshit and demagogic bluster about threats to "our freedom" yet again worked their sinister magic on the hoi polloi. As though any power in history has ever had the navy or air support to sail across the Atlantic or Pacific with the ten million or so heavily armed and supplied troops it'd require to conquer America.

Here's a secret intel bulletin for all y'all who've never left Yoknapatawpha County and imagine the United States is constantly on the precipice of enemy invasion—the only way this country is ever going to surrender its liberty to a foreign power is if it keeps electing corrupt officials who auction it away to multinational corporations and overseas government interests in exactly the fashion that southern star chambers have been doing to their own people throughout their entire dyspeptic history.

And, yes, just as finger-in-the-wind politicians voted to save their seats by going to war in 1861 against each other and in 1964 against the Vietcong, so were congressional members in this century bent into cowardice and passivity by the specter of disproportionate southern political might. Elected leaders from every state in the country approved Bush's fool's errand in Iraq.

Though let's be honest, Bush would never have been elected fucking dogcatcher without the South. How depressing that we already know that the next Republican warmonger to sweep into power will do so on the same tarnished epaulets of military fanaticism enabled by the outsized influence of the southern polity on electoral America. As one North Carolina Civil War enthusiast told Tony Horwitz in 1998's *Confederates in the Attic*: "Southerners are a military people. We were back then, still are today."[31]

The Secret to Coping with Southern Politics: Beer

Standing at the devil's crossroads of the South's seven political malevolencies—and my pick for most dysfunctional state in the Union—is South

Carolina. Long before Jon Stewart praised the state's reliable stream of bumbling political characters by labeling it "America's whoopee cushion," the "cradle of secession," and first state to up and quit its signatory obligation to the nation in 1860, South Carolina was renowned for producing politicians as slimy as the inside of a pumpkin.[32]

Upholding remarkable standards of cretinism set by their forebears, the twenty-first century's rogues' gallery of Palmetto State politicians is, nevertheless, impressive in its own right. Consider that since just 2008, South Carolina has given the nation: the weepy marital misdeeds of Governor Mark "Appalachian Trail" Sanford; Lieutenant Governor André Bauer likening kids receiving government-assisted school lunches to a pack of stray animals; Lieutenant Governor Ken Ard resigning in 2012 just fourteen months into his first term for multiple campaign funding and ethics violations; State Treasurer Thomas Ravenel being sent to federal prison on cocaine charges; former chair of the state election commission Rusty DePass comparing Michelle Obama's ancestors to an escaped gorilla from the Columbia Zoo; two state Republican chairmen publicly lauding Senator Jim DeMint for acting like a "Jew" while "watching our nation's pennies"; Congressman Joe Wilson shouting "You lie!" at President Obama during the 2009 State of the Union address; State Senator Jake Knotts referring to Indian American gubernatorial candidate Nikki Haley as a "raghead"; and the deeply twisted spectacle of a dazed, unemployed senatorial "candidate" and likely plant Alvin Greene running for office on the Democratic ticket minus only the dunce cap and hooting band of rednecks stringing a noose over a tree branch behind him on the campaign stump.[33]

It's no coincidence that the most convincing parodist of American right-wing political buffoonery, Stephen Colbert, comes from South Carolina. Nor that I would be drawn to the state capital of Columbia like a stray animal to a pile of rotting garbage.

Though few outside the capital have heard of them, two of the most interesting figures on the South Carolina political scene are Phil Bailey, director of the South Carolina Democratic Caucus, and Wesley Donehue, a highly regarded Republican political consultant whose clients include the infamous Joe "You Lie!" Wilson. Somehow remaining friends while occupying fiercely opposing positions, the two young political junkies decided in 2010 to bridge the cultural divide in South Carolina by cohosting a weekly webcast they named *Pub Politics*. From a revolving lineup of local bars, *Pub Politics* features the hosts and various guests casually bantering about state and national politics beneath the slogan: "Beer . . . bringing Democrats and Republicans together."

Followed by local government insiders, *Pub Politics* achieved a brief inferno of national prominence in 2010 when during a live webcast State Senator Jake Knotts referred to both Barack Obama and then gubernatorial candidate Nikki Haley as ragheads. Specifically, Knotts said, "We've already got a raghead in the White House, we don't need another raghead in the governor's mansion."

"The minute it happened I knew it was going to blow up," says Donehue, his smile indicating to me how little a Republican consultant in South Carolina has to worry about racist gaffes. "Peter Hamby of CNN was watching the show live and within fifteen minutes CNN was already tweeting about it."

"The next day, my fully charged cell phone had a dead battery on it by ten in the morning," adds Bailey.

We meet at a bar called the Publick House, not far from the capitol. It's a raucous, college-type pub, a sausage fest with reasonably cute waitresses and a very loud trivia contest under way as I walk in the door. "Which of the two following substances did Lindsay Lohan test positive for when stopped by police?" Etc. Even louder than the trivia, the music is American eclectic. Eddie Money followed by MGMT.

Though not quite caricatures, both Bailey and Donehue sort of live up to party stereotypes. Born and raised in Columbia and a 2003 graduate of the College of Charleston, Democrat Bailey is a burly, bearded, bighearted guy in a plaid shirt and jeans. He's friendly, easygoing, deceptively intelligent, and a little defensive about his Everyman credentials. Finishing an anecdote about dove shooting over the weekend he says, "Democrats here, we hunt."

A 2002 University of South Carolina grad from Goose Creek, South

Carolina, Republican Donehue is a clean-cut frat guy type, vaguely canine in a blue Oxford shirt and tan slacks. Angular, polished, and athletic, his borderline aggressive personality exudes confidence and intelligence. "My grandfather is a Civil War reenactor," he informs me.

Befitting the *Pub Politics* slogan, all three of us order beer. Donehue has a Modelo with lime. Bailey some local IPA thing. I start with a Coors Light, then switch to Modelo in a neurotic, chicklike effort to connect with Donehue. Two hours later, it'll still be impossible to know if the ploy worked.

"It's got to be hard being a Democrat in this state," I say to Bailey.

"You have to go for broke," Bailey replies. "The strategy often is to shame the Republicans to get what we want. We know we're not going to win the votes."

"But you have to remember that the vast majority of Democrats who vote here are conservatives," Donehue adds.

Bailey offers a resigned nod of assent.

Beyond the usual guilty fascination with train-wreck public figures, the real reason South Carolina is so monumentally important to my investigation is because it's so monumentally important to national politics. Even in overly influential Dixie, South Carolina casts an inordinately long and dark shadow upon the rest of the nation.

The state's outsized power is due to what is locally referred to as the "Triple P," or presidential preference primary. "Preference" is an understatement. South Carolina's Republican primary has become practically a mustwin hurdle for any serious GOP presidential candidate.

From 1980 to 2008, every winner of the state's bellwether Republican primary has gotten the GOP nomination. That's the reason that while other Republican hopefuls were deep-throating corn dogs at the Iowa Caucus in August 2011, Texas governor Rick Perry stole the show by shrewdly traveling to South Carolina to formally announce his candidacy for president. It is also where Newt Gingrich's campaign rose from the ashes with a huge victory over the then-inevitable Republican nominee, Mitt Romney, in 2012, prolonging the cannibalistic GOP primary process.

The state's political sleaze merchants—their specialty has been called "the dark arts of South Carolina politics"—have made the Triple P a killing field of promising presidential campaigns. Notable among these was John McCain's 2000 Straight Talk Express, which rolled into South Carolina on the heels of a tide-turning victory over George W. Bush in the New Hampshire primary.

Once in South Carolina, however, the old war hero's reputation was mauled and his campaign derailed by rumors allegedly spread by Bush's South Carolina operatives that McCain was mentally unstable, a homosexual, and that his adopted Bangladeshi-born daughter, Bridget, was actually an illegitimate half-black child conceived by McCain out of wedlock. McCain's campaign never recovered from the lies and the United States sailed more or less effortlessly—after a little southern-fried political chicanery in Florida—into nine years of an oil war started by an ex–oil man president whose cabinet was stocked with oil execs.[34]

For those who might take exception to these statements, okay, but at least please spare me the "conspiracy theory" accusation. The Bush-era oil cartel profiteering under the guise of government was more or less conducted in the open, which sort of takes the "conspiracy" part out of the equation. They named a state after Washington. They named cities and schools after Jefferson and Lincoln. They named a national park after Teddy Roosevelt. They named an aircraft carrier after FDR. They named a space center after Kennedy. They named a Chevron oil tanker after Condoleezza Rice. These are not coincidences.

Chastened but educated, McCain returned to South Carolina in 2008 a changed man. As described by John Heilemann and Mark Halperin in the 2008 presidential campaign summary, *Game Change*, McCain's campaign arrived ready to "harness the right-wing freak show to its advantage" in a state in which "everything always somehow boiled down to race." The gelded "maverick" won the 2008 South Carolina primary and became the Republicans' presidential nominee.[35]

"The Triple P is everything here," Donehue tells me. "If not for the Triple P, you wouldn't have so many political operatives and loud, colorful politicians in the capital. Residents in Georgia are not much different from South Carolina, but you don't have the same political influence because of the Triple P. We've got a ton of consultants here, we've got national attention on us because of it. I wouldn't be here doing this without it."

Fifty Years of the Code: A-T-W-A-T-E-R = A-S-S-H-O-L-E

South Carolina, Donehue and Bailey explain, is a "firewall" state in the Republican presidential primary process, the state in which unacceptably moderate candidates like McCain who might win northern primaries in Iowa and New Hampshire can be snuffed out of the race by the party's radical evangelical base.

"What is it with South Carolina voters?" I ask. "Politics are crooked everywhere, but the things that people here support, or at least tolerate, would never fly outside the South."

"Look at their levels of education," says Bailey. "This goes back to right after Reconstruction. It was a business decision to keep the population dumb. That went on for a couple of generations. There were generations of neglect of public education. We're still seeing the effects of that today. Level of education is a big factor in your politics in the South."

"Bigger than race?" I ask, intoning the name of the godfather of contemporary South Carolina politics, Lee Atwater.

The radical right political operative and dark prince of Republican politics, Lee Atwater was the man who originally maneuvered to push the South Carolina primary into the GOP spotlight. He's most prominently remembered, however, as the brains behind the Republican "southern strategy," a term coined to refer to Richard Nixon's post–civil rights plan to win the South's white, blue-collar vote by appealing to regional voters using coded racial language. A crafty manipulation of the region's native racism, the southern strategy is the campaign blueprint that helped sweep the radical KKKristian right into power in the South in the 1970s and helps maintain its hold on regional politics to this day.

The southern strategy reached the apex of its unmasked cynicism in 1980, when candidate Ronald Reagan inaugurated his presidential run by making the first stop of his campaign in the white supremacist stronghold of Philadelphia, Mississippi, site of the killing of three civil rights workers in 1964. Loosely depicted in the film *Mississippi Burning*, the murders were among the most infamous in American history.

Rather than recall or make any mention of the tragedy—at the time, the town's only claim to fame and still a festering racial wound—Reagan instead told the crowd, "I still believe in states' rights." This was an obvious appeal to locals who resented federal efforts to desegregate their schools, buses, drinking fountains, and high school proms.

"Everybody watching the 1980 campaign knew what Reagan was signaling," wrote Bob Herbert in the *New York Times*. "Whites and blacks, Democrats and Republicans—they all knew. The news media knew. The race haters and the people appalled by racial hatred knew. And Reagan knew. He was tapping out the code."[36]

In 1981, Atwater gave an interview to Case Western Reserve University professor Alexander Lamis in which he laid out the nefarious process behind the southern strategy and its code.

"You start out in 1954 by saying, 'Nigger, nigger, nigger,'" explained Atwater. "By 1968, you can't say 'nigger'—that hurts you. Backfires. So you say stuff like 'forced busing,' 'states' rights,' and all that stuff. You're getting so abstract now [that] you're talking about cutting taxes, and all these things you're talking about are totally economic things, and a by-product of them is [that] blacks get hurt worse than whites."[37]

"You still can't talk about politics in South Carolina period without talking about race," Bailey says with a shrug. "It's a huge factor. If someone tells you differently, they're bullshitting you."

"That's right," says Donehue.

"I don't think you can talk about South Carolina at all without talking about race," I say. "Isn't the reason southern politicians regularly make racist or other 'shocking' outbursts is because they're simply appealing to their like-minded constituencies? Wasn't Joe Wilson calling Obama a liar a premeditated act? Wasn't Rusty DePass comparing Michelle Obama to a gorilla calculated? Wasn't Jake Knotts calling Nikki Haley a 'raghead' a signal to his people that he was not backing off of their core beliefs?"

"I know Joe Wilson. That thing was not calculated, not planned," says Donehue. "The gorilla comment was dumb."

"On the raghead comment, I believe there was a level of calculation to that," says Bailey. "Jakey's a bubba. A lot of his district is middle- and lower-class whites, aka bubbas."

Donehue nods. "Everyone's explanation for it was, 'That's just Jakey being Jakey,'" he says.

Bailey and Donehue remind me of Sam Sheepdog and Ralph Wolf, the old Merrie Melodies antagonists who were sworn enemies by day, but who, once the five o'clock whistle blew, exchanged friendly good nights and remained on respectful terms until the next workday. Good-natured gamesmanship defines their relationship, which began when both were working on opposite sides of a 2005 state senate race in Aiken County.

"I beat him in that one," Donehue says.

"By a hundred votes." Bailey grimaces.

"But you have a decided advantage working for the GOP in South Carolina," I say to Donehue.

"Not in that county, I didn't!" Donehue replies with a sneaky smile.

The most striking thing about Bailey and Donehue is how young they are and yet how old they seem. These aren't hair-in-the-ear backroom party hacks, bitter products of civil rights era chaos. They text and tweet and drink fancy beer.

They're also set up to be power brokers for years to come. This is fine inasmuch as they both seem like decent, smart guys. But, in the most dysfunctional state in the nation, the one whose seal of approval very often determines half of the choices in every American presidential race, they're also long-term players fully vested in the damaging racial, religious, and ideological certitudes that comprise the twisted backbone of southern politics.

Talk to people like Bailey and Donehue and countless others I hung out with in the South and, if you share a little bit of my travel history, you might eventually come to the unexpected and somewhat counterintuitive conclusion that southerners are an awful lot like the Chinese. As individuals, they're great—kind, generous, friendly, funny, hospitable, obsessed with food, addicted to cheap labor, and prone to ancestor worship. Get them in a group, however, and these same good-natured folk somehow manage to rally around the most oppressive political philosophy this side of a mob book burning—though they're not above that sort of intemperance either, especially if the possibility of losing a little face is on the line.

Like most of those I've encountered in the Middle Kingdom, Bailey and Donehue are decent, intelligent people who nevertheless perpetuate poisonous political dogma—and afterward throw down just enough beer to allow them to sleep at night.

Columbia, South Carolina: Let Us Now Pause to Glorify Racism

"Symbols matter. They are profoundly important. By telling us where we came from, they tell us who we are and what causes ought to be defended."

So writes South Carolina restaurateur, businessman, and folk hero Maurice Bessinger in his autobiography, *Defending My Heritage: The Maurice Bessinger Story (Growing Up Southern)*. The passage comes from a chapter creatively titled "Symbols Are Profoundly Important and Must Be Defended."[38]

Bessinger is famed throughout South Carolina as the cantankerous owner of Maurice's BBQ Piggie Park restaurant chain. A more tightly packaged Colonel Sanders type, whose gleaming white suit jackets match his trimmed white mustache, the snazzy Korean War veteran bears the look of a man who enjoys his own farts. He's been a popular and active figure in state business and politics since 1966 when, after refusing to integrate his restaurants in accordance with the Civil Rights Act of 1964, he was sued by the NAACP.

Bessinger refused to comply with federal laws requiring equal rights for African Americans. His restaurants would remain open to whites only. After various appeals that dragged him through the state and federal court system, Bessinger's case eventually went before the U.S. Supreme Court. To no one's surprise, the Supreme Court ruled against him.

Though he lost his legal battle and grudgingly integrated his restaurants,

Bessinger had won the hearts of mainstream South Carolinians forever. Walk into the Piggie Park Columbia flagship restaurant today (South Carolina has been kind to Bessinger, there are now fourteen restaurants in his chain) and you'll find the walls plastered with Civil War memorabilia and framed testimonials from patrons, most written within the last decade, praising this "modern-day patriot" for his courageous defense of real American values.

Bessinger's gasbagging autobiography is one of the most weirdly entertaining summations of the delusional southern cultural mind-set ever printed. My favorite line about growing up southern: "White people are the best friends, historically, that blacks have ever had."[39]

I've read that whopper thirty or forty times and it's never once failed to make me laugh.

Splenetic race rants aside, I admit to sharing Bessinger's regard for symbols. Since I, too, believe in their cultural significance, and since after my night with the convivial Bailey and Donehue at the Publick House I'm anxious to fling myself with renewed cooperative vigor into the cultural chasm that divides North and South, I decide the following morning to walk from my hotel to the grounds of the South Carolina State House. This way I can see for myself what types of symbols the great state of South Carolina has seen fit to maintain by way of informing its citizens, "where we came from . . . who we are and what causes ought to be defended."

The capitol is a shock. True, tooth-and-nail battles over the placement of Confederate flags in public places have only been tenuously resolved in several southern states in the past decade. Nevertheless, I'm astonished to find that the grounds of the gorgeous classical revival–style South Carolina State House double as a shrine to slaveholders, racial oppressors, demagogues, and hominy-munching political obstinacy.

Walking counterclockwise from the north side of the domed capitol facing Gervais Street, I encounter a large bronze statue of Ben Tillman, South Carolina governor from 1890 to 1894 and U.S. senator for more than twenty years, from 1895 to 1918. The accompanying plaque notes that the monument was erected by the legislature, Democratic Party, and private citizens of South Carolina.

It does not mention that old "Pitchfork Ben" was one of the most vehement white supremacists this country has ever produced, a man who publicly advocated lynching all black people uppity enough to vote. Tillman once said of African Americans, "We have scratched our heads to find out how we could eliminate every last one of them. We stuffed ballot boxes. We shot them. We are not ashamed of it."[40]

Those with shorter memories or aversion to history books might find the next larger-than-life bronze statue, this one of longtime senator Strom Thurmond, a tribute to more palatable, modern southern ethos. The career of the "statesmen—soldier—educator," however, might just as effectively be represented by bookend depictions of his 1948 Dixiecrat pro-segregationist run for the U.S. presidency, and the revelation shortly after his death in 2003 that as a twenty-two-year-old he'd fathered a baby after banging his family's sixteen-year-old black housekeeper, an act that in many places would fall under the classification of statutory rape. For the sake of preserving his political career, the statesman, soldier, and educator ignored his own daughter for most of her life. (I love, by the way, how Barack Obama is always "black," but when it comes to the miscegenistic lustspawn of guys like Thurmond, it's "Well, she's half-black.")[41]

That's a snapshot of Thurmond the man. The most revealing insight into Thurmond the politician's commitment to public service can be prized from the names of his most important constituents, which, as on the Ben Tillman monument, are inscribed on the base of his statue: Wachovia Bank, Bank of America, Alcoa, Blue Cross Blue Shield, and Bell South among them.

Next, I stand beneath a larger-than-life Wade Hampton on horseback upon a high pedestal. Hampton was the undeniably talented Civil War commander who in 1860 also happened to be one of the largest slave owners in the world. Following the war and Reconstruction, Hampton led the charge to deny blacks equal rights under the law and reestablish white rule in South Carolina, first as governor in 1876, then as a U.S. senator. Even as statuary, this is a man who looks like anything he says can and will be used against him.[42]

Hampton departed the Senate in 1891, leaving South Carolina's interests in the capable hands of men such as the aforementioned "Pitchfork Ben" Tillman and Coleman Blease, who as governor reportedly took the severed finger of a lynched black man and buried it in the gubernatorial garden. As a U.S. senator, Blease's single service to his constituents, as one writer of the day noted, "was to keep before the startled gaze of the nation the vision of their eternal assault on the black man."[43]

In more subtle forms, that assault continues just fifty yards from Hampton. Here I spend ten minutes in front of the capitol's African American History Monument. Erected in 2001, it's a handsome piece of work with curved granite walls depicting scenes from the African American experience. Panels representing different eras in South Carolina history loom over the skeletal imprint of a slave ship packed with horizontal bodies.

Though no doubt conceived with noble intentions, it's significant to note that, per orders of the African American Monument Commission set up by the state legislature to oversee its design, the monument was not allowed to "represent any actual human being who actually lived," according to Kenneth Davis, a member of the commission. Figures such as slave revolt leader Denmark Vesey were censored out of the original design. Unlike every other monument on the State House grounds, few words nor any interpretive signage are offered to explain the meaning or record the achievements of those depicted on the African American monument.

The man who chaired the African American Monument Commission in 2001 was not black. That honor was bequeathed to state senator Glenn McConnell, a prominent politician who also happens to be a member of the Sons of Confederate Veterans and who was a vociferous supporter of keeping the Confederate flag on display on the State House grounds, even after legislators had voted to remove it from the capitol dome in 2000.

Today, McConnell is South Carolina's lieutenant governor (prior to assuming the position in 2012 he was the longtime president pro tempore of the state senate) and, according to both Bailey and Donehue, the most powerful man in the state. Online, you can find pictures of McConnell all dressed up pretending to be a Confederate officer. And not on Halloween.[44]

Thanks to McConnell's influence, after the Confederate flag was removed from the top of the capitol building, it was actually placed in a more prominent position, in a corral on a flagpole directly in front of the State House, next to the inevitable Confederate Monument.

Completing my circumnavigation of the State House I stand for a few minutes before the Confederate flag—Ben Tillman glowering to my right, the slave ship packed with nameless black masses to my left—and catch sight of a monument I'd missed the first time around, this one perhaps the most instructive of all. Flanking the front steps of the State House, a damaged statue of George Washington sits unrepaired more than a century after it was vandalized by Union troops. A plaque informs visitors that the statue was brickbatted by soldiers of Sherman's army, who wantonly defaced George and snapped off his walking stick during their occupation of Columbia.

For a century and a half now, the statue has remained in its damaged state. Rather than repair the fairly mild scratches and busted stick, the statue has been preserved as petty evidence that the dignified leaders of South Carolina can use to call attention to what a bunch of assholes those scared shitless, drunken, northern twenty-five-year-old soldiers were back in 1865.

Congratulations, South Carolina, you've made your point. Now could you fix the goddamn statue of the father of the country y'all are supposedly so proud of? The guy was from Virginia after all.

What We Got Here Is a Monumental Failure to Communicate

Civil War markers and various other monuments to white supremacists litter the South. Excepting Stone Mountain, Georgia, the most pompously defiant of these is located seventy-five miles northwest of Columbia in Abbeville, South Carolina. Walking past the granite obelisk dedicated to Confederate soldiery in Abbeville's historic town square, the casual visitor would likely not notice anything special. The gray monument looks like any of countless similar statuary in the centers of cities and towns throughout the South.

Take the trouble to read the carved inscriptions, however, and along with the usual odes to the bravery and valor of the Confederacy's battle dead, you'll find this blatantly treasonous declaration: "The world shall yet decide, in truth's clear far-off light, that the soldiers who wore the gray and died with Lee were right."

Unbelievable. Imagine statues of SS soldiers inscribed with quotes from *Mein Kampf* in every little town in Germany. The Civil War is the only conflict in history after which the losers were allowed to write the history.

I read the astonishing assertion for a second time, noting that the monument was erected not in the emotional aftermath of war in 1865, but in 1906 and then, in a ceremony replacing the original with a new one in 1996.

"The world shall yet decide, in truth's clear far-off light, that the soldiers who wore the gray and died with Lee were right." Not that the soldiers were patriotic. Or courageous. Or true to some ill-begotten sense of duty. They were right.

The only possible interpretation of this statement is that the cause for which the South fought—dissolution of the United States in order that the South might preserve slavery and, thus, the economic underpinnings and political clout of its privileged plantation class—was a morally righteous mission.

And, by the way, if you don't already know that slavery was the fundamental issue over which the South ripped the nation asunder, spend an hour with a slim volume by native southerner Charles B. Dew called *Apostles of Disunion*. Reviewing in 103 pages the major speeches and documents used by southern commissioners to argue the case for secession, Dew presents all the proof a sixth grader would need to conclude that to southern whites states' rights were a lot less important than the rights of southern states' whites.

Go ahead, read that again. It makes sense.

It wasn't until several months after my discovery of the Abbeville monument that I came to fully appreciate how completely its inscription distills the straitjacket of southern political orthodoxy that binds progress in the "country within a country."

Walking down Louisiana Avenue just north of the U.S. Capitol in Washington, D.C.—the majority African American city whose right to voting representation in the U.S. Senate has consistently been blocked in Congress by southern politicians—I stumbled upon the National Japanese American Memorial to Patriotism During World War II. With a center-piece sculpture depicting two cranes tangled in barbed wire, the monument stands as historic witness both to the valor of Japanese American soldiers who served in World War II, as well as the victimization of the thousands of innocent Americans of Japanese ancestry who were forced into wartime internment camps at home.

Attached to the monument, a bronze plaque bears the straightforward, powerful inscription: "Here we admit a wrong. Here we affirm our commitment as a nation to equal justice under the law."[45]

So striking. So honest. So liberating. Acknowledge a mistake, learn from it, and move on to create a better world.

How different this difficult but uncomplicated monument in the nation's capital from the one in Abbeville, and the thousands of other chunks of granite and poured concrete defiance that blight the South with a destructive architecture designed to keep ancient hatred alive. One might scour the world for a pair of monuments that represent more succinctly the ideologies of two nations moving in such completely opposite directions.

Yet in these monuments, separated by only a long day's drive, the observer can stand before the physical testament of one nation's willingness to assume what Robert Penn Warren called "the awful responsibility of Time," and another's determination to forever hide from that responsibility; to cower before the future so that it might careen ever backward into a fetish of loss and disaster, dragging all those unfortunate bodies caught within its orbit into the same gluttonous consumption of perpetual failure, forever working to, as Randy Newman sang, keep the niggers down, be they black, white, brown, or yellow.

The southern "traditions" of inflexibility and sabotage have for too long hobbled American political progress. It's time to unburden the country's future of a political race whose most powerful views, emotions, and ideas lurk forever behind them.

CHAPTER 3

Race: Alabama, Bigotry, Wildman, and the White Spike Lee

While prepping for the first stint in a near-two-year intermittent tour through the South, I'd asked a dozen or so southerners to help me put together a suitable itinerary. Finding Baptist churches, loony birthers, and half-cocked politicians was going to be easy. It was the traditionally more invisible parts of the South I'd been unsure about tapping into.

"As a black dude I can't tell you how to get to a Klan meeting, but I can tell you if you just operate in the southern way, if you just speak to people, say hello in the right way, everything will open up for you." This advice had come from Glenn Bracey, a recent Texas A&M doctor of sociology grad originally from North Carolina.

"It won't take long," he promised.

I'd been skeptical. "Race tourism," I assumed, has few tangible mileposts. Yet almost as soon as I crossed the Ohio River and ventured my first "Hey, y'alls," I found that avoiding race in the South is pretty much like avoiding sand at the beach.

As I was driving through North Carolina in 2011, Mississippi governor

Haley Barbour made national news for refusing to denounce a proposed Mississippi Sons of Confederate Veterans license plate design honoring Nathan Bedford Forrest, founder and onetime Grand Wizard of the original Ku Klux Klan. Forrest was also the Civil War general responsible for the cold-blooded massacre of several hundred defeated white and black Union troops, as well as women and children, at Fort Pillow, Tennessee.[1]

A military genius and savage white supremacist, Forrest has in the minds of many southerners in recent years surpassed gentleman general Robert E. Lee as the quintessential icon of the Confederacy. A profoundly disturbing fiberglass statue of a maniacally grinning Forrest on horseback sits off Interstate 65 near the affluent Nashville suburb of Brentwood, just a lazy afternoon drive east of Fort Pillow.

Several weeks after the license plate brouhaha died down, Public Policy Polling of Raleigh, North Carolina, released the results of a poll in which it was revealed that 46 percent of Mississippi Republicans believe interracial marriage should be illegal. Forty percent of Mississippi Republicans said interracial marriage should be legal. Fourteen percent were unsure.[2]

Stories and statistics such as these, which seem to slither out of the mouth-breathing South a few times every year, reinforce in my mind—and in the minds of millions of others—the prejudicial notion that the "dirty South" remains the most racist, or at least most racially fucked up, region of the country. A land whose people's romantic attachment to the days of ethnic prejudice places the entire region outside the principled bounds of the quasi-enlightened land of the free known as twenty-first-century America.

More simply put, a hell of a lot of people believe that the South is still a deeply racist place with more hard-core, culturally accepted, incorrigible bigots than anywhere else on earth.

This is a general idea that I grew up more or less accepting as common knowledge and self-evident fact. As an astonished junior high schooler I'd read about Harriet Tubman and Frederick Douglass. With my family, I'd watched in freaked-out awe as the twisted race-based hatred of *Roots* unfolded in weekly miniseries installments. Later, I squirmed in the face of the murderous southern racism depicted in countless films, such as *The Great Santini*. In real-world terms, the routine willingness of contemporary southern leaders such as Haley Barbour to pander to the lower ends of their constituencies simply confirms a lifetime of stereotyping southerners as unrepentant racists.

But are they really? Is there any way to quantify racism that might prove in real terms that the South's continuing inability to successfully deal with issues of race supports the argument for casting the region out of the federal compact in order that the rest of the country might get along with the business of becoming the multicultural, fusion-cuisine nirvana of which it likes to think itself worthy?

Racism is a pretty heavy charge to drop at the feet of a hundred million or so people. And if I'm being honest with myself, I have to admit that pretty much everything I know about racism in the South comes from third-party material. Books. TV. Movies. Loudmouthed southern boys who somehow made their way up to Juneau. Sources, in other words, whose fondness for hyperbole and false bravado is bred in the bone.

This chapter turns on two primary questions: Is racism worse in the South today than it is in the rest of the country? And, either way, how much does southern racism hurt the rest of the country?

Since "worse" is a subjective and malleable idea, it's necessary here to define my terms. For the purposes of this chapter, I'm concerned with racism as manifested in two classic ways.

First is systemic or institutionalized racism, the often invisible barriers through which minority populations must pass in order to gain equal access to jobs, education, housing, public programs, loans, and other means useful in the pursuit of profit, loss, and deep-fried cracklins. These barriers encompass everything from quasi-official efforts to disenfranchise black voters, to purposeful underfunding of schools with large minority populations, to a real estate agent not showing a house to a financially stable Hispanic family based on a tacit agreement with local residents that the prospective newcomers don't conform to the neighborhood's existing racial profile.

Second is the old-fashioned "No Nigras" redneck racism of the variety African American Talmadge Branch encountered in Perry, Florida, in 2001 when he stopped into the Perry Package Store & Lounge and ordered a beer. For Branch, walking in the front door of a bar and ordering a drink seemed like a perfectly normal thing to do. To the bartender, however, his brazen behavior amounted to an assault on local protocol.

The white female bartender told Branch he could only be served in a room in the back of the building, accessed through a separate entrance. Looking around at other patrons drinking at the bar, all of them white, Branch asked why he could not be served in the same room. The bartender told him these were "the rules." Someone else in the bar informed him that "coloreds" were served in the back.

This indeed turned out to be the arrangement at the Perry Package Store & Lounge. In 2001. More than half a century after Jackie Robinson scored the winning run for the Brooklyn Dodgers against the Boston Braves in his major league debut.

What the bartender didn't know was that at the time Branch was head of the Maryland Legislative Black Caucus. He'd come to Florida for a political meeting. The story made national headlines.

The bar and bartender were charged with civil rights violations and unfair trade practices. One can only speculate as to how much longer the segregated barrooms might have been maintained had a man of Talmadge's stature not wandered in.[3]

Because moral arguments feel good but are rarely persuasive with Americans, what I aim to do is pin down the material costs of southern racism—hard statistics, or at least a reliable financial calculation, that might show exactly how much southern racism costs the North. If racism really is worse in the South, and if it's possible to prove that as a country we simply cannot afford nineteenth- and twentieth-century attitudes affecting our twenty-first-century bottom line, these numbers will justify adding the charge of racism to the larger case for secession.

Meet and Greet with Johnny Reb in Monkeytown

My first stop on the southern race circuit is Montgomery, Alabama. Or, as my Pensacola pal Fred Garth tells me on the phone on my approach, "Monkeytown."

"That's what the truckers call it," Fred says in a good neighbor way, like a guy offering to help you open a jar or pick up your mail while you're out of town.

How times don't change. Montgomery is, of course, synonymous with the civil rights crusades of the 1950s and 1960s. Which makes it synonymous with racism. It's the city of Rosa Parks and the 1955 Montgomery Bus Boycott, an event many historians regard as the opening salvo in the modern civil rights movement. Here, as pastor of the Dexter Avenue Baptist Church from 1954 to 1960, Martin Luther King, Jr., worked out the kinks in his early civil rights material.

The Alabama capitol steps were the endpoint of the 1965 Selma-to-Montgomery March, in which 25,000 protesters walked for four days after an initial group of 600 marchers was repelled by police wielding billy clubs and tear gas at the Edmund Pettus Bridge outside Selma. In 1996, William Jefferson Clinton's federal government designated the road from Selma to Montgomery a National Historic Trail.[4]

The roots of resistance to quasi-fascist authoritarian whites in Montgomery, however, long predate the 1950s. At 644 Washington Avenue, directly across from the state capitol, stands the First White House of the Confederacy, the place where soon-to-be Confederate president Jefferson Davis and a passel of deep thinkers from the early secessionist states met to plot the bleak future of their agrarian peoples as blood enemies of a rapidly mechanizing, larger, and wealthier nation. Imagine Poland attacking Germany in 1939, instead of the other way around.

The First White House of the Confederacy is not to be confused with the White House of the Confederacy, the second official residence of Jefferson Davis and hub of southern social activity after the Confederate capital was moved from Montgomery to Richmond, Virginia. Throughout the short life of the Confederate States of America, Johnny Reb pretty much had to have his bags packed and be ready to scoot out the door at klaxon's notice, hence the South's redundantly confusing landmarks.

At the First White House of the Confederacy, I'm the only visitor on a moist afternoon in *Jew*-lie (as they say here). This means I get the full attention of a tour guide named Jean, an impeccably dressed woman in her early fifties who has retained the better part of her belle of the cotillion looks. Jean's white pantsuit is immaculate, her jewelry handsome, her smile gracious. The Aqua Netted silvery hair poof is flawless. This is a woman who gets her hair "done," not cut.

Somewhere between shuffling through the downstairs parlor and internalizing the news that Mr. and Mrs. Davis slept in separate bedchambers, I chance a Yankee ice-breaker.

"So, the whole time Jefferson Davis and men from the original seven Confederate states were framing their constitution, slaves were running this house?" I ask.

"Well, servants, yes," Jean replies, tilting her chin in a "Bless your northern heart" way. I do one of those moves from *The Office*, widening my eyes and staring blankly into a nonexistent camera just over her right shoulder.

"Now this was where the kitchen was," says Jean, soldiering on.

To my modern way of thinking, if you own a human being you own a slave. But the delicate slave/servant distinction remains in play at many southern historic sites.

In Natchez, Mississippi, guides and signs at Longwood Plantation (scenes from *True Blood* filmed here!) often employ the more genteel "servants." Signage at Monmouth cotton estate, however, unflinchingly refers to the former property owner's "slaves," or, in a stupendously awkward attempt to confer respect, "enslaved individuals." Everyone loves PC bashing, me included. It's nevertheless inspiring to be reminded of the endless capacity for manipulation of the English language, even in the service of small minds.

By no means is it all gray-jacket propaganda. During the First White House of the Confederacy tour, Jean enthusiastically touts the stunning, Maya Lin–designed Civil Rights Memorial located just a few blocks up the street. Rebel White House. State Capitol. Civil Rights Memorial. All's quiet now, but Washington Avenue in Montgomery has to be one of the most historically explosive streets in America.

Haters and the Haters Who Hate Them: Welcome to the Southern Poverty Law Center

A circular black granite table inscribed with the names of movement milestones and martyrs, Montgomery's Civil Rights Memorial is the brainchild of the Southern Poverty Law Center, yet another regional institution headquartered on Washington Avenue. Cofounded in 1971 by Morris Dees and Joe Levin—a pair of firebrand, white civil rights attorneys from Alabama— the SPLC's mission is "to ensure that the promises of the civil rights movement become a reality for all."[5]

Their efforts have been largely successful, if not always well received. Since 1978, the SPLC has prevailed in twenty-six court cases against rightwing extremists, helped bankrupt the Ku Klux Klan, and won convictions of criminals who are still serving up to thirty-year sentences. On the downside, there have been at least twenty-six attempts to kill Dees and other members of the organization, or to bomb the Monkeytown headquarters.

At the corner of Washington and South Hull, the SPLC headquarters stands in conspicuous contrast to the dilapidated anticharisma of old Montgomery. The hulking six-story structure has the look of an Atlantic Wall defensive bulwark built by the Third Reich along the western coast of Europe in the 1940s. The angled concrete setback from the street is designed to prevent explosive-laden vehicles from ramming the compound. Only narrow windows bearing the look of gun slits puncture the building's silver-steel exterior. If "siege mentality" were a design style, this building would appear in every architecture textbook in the country.

Once inside, the SPLC is less imposing. Hives of low-walled cubicles stretching across entire floors give the impression of a 1970s newsroom— papers and folders stacked in leaning towers, books and magazines spilling off of tabletops, break-out meeting areas, empty coffee cups, Chinese takeout containers with chopsticks poking out. Posters of Che Guevara, framed photographs of 1930s Klan rallies, and other signatures of liberal activism adorn the walls. Only the polite tik-tik-tik of keyboards breaks the silence.

My appointment on the fourth floor is with two of the SPLC's most celebrated targets of right-wing scorn. Mark Potok and Heidi Beirich monitor the activity of hate groups and extremist organizations around the world, then publish feature stories detailing their findings in the Southern Poverty Law Center's quarterly *Intelligence Report* magazine and *Hatewatch* blog.

The idea is to raise awareness of the racism still in our midst, apply the pressure of the media spotlight on hate groups, educate the public about the SPLC's efforts to fight racism within the legal system, and drum up donations for the nonprofit organization. Their articles bear such low-key headlines as "Crushing the Klan," "Behind the Noose," "Rebirth of a Nation," "The 'Synagogue of Satan,'" "Ready for War," "Arming for Armageddon," "Descent into Thuggery," and the ever-popular annual roundup, "The Year in Hate," sort of a Dubious Achievements Awards for the intolerant set.

"These boots were used as evidence in three murder cases in Phoenix," Beirich booms at me from across the floor, eager to make a good first impression. She flips over the soles of a pair of knee-high red leather boots to show me thick rubber treads stamped with raised swastikas.

"That's so they can leave their mark on the foreheads of their victims," Beirich says. "These were made in England. Real leather. Not like those made-in-China pieces of shit they sell on Aryan Wear."

Aryan Wear is an outfit in Texas that specializes in "white power T-shirts and nationalist clothing." When I visit the site a couple of days later they're celebrating Mussolini's birthday with a 15-percent-off-everything sale. Their knockoff swastika-soled Panzer boots are selling for $48.

Potok and Beirich say "fuck" and "motherfucker" a lot. From Vermonter Potok's graying beard and wire-frame glasses to Californian Beirich's T-shirt, baggy shorts, and dirty blond hair, their appearance screams Hippie Agitator. Nothing approaching the namby-pamby modernity of Harry Reid liberalism, these are two genuine 1960s throwbacks, unapologetic muckrakers, enthusiastic Freedom Riders, bloodthirsty Nazi hunters, and sworn enemies of unreconstructed nimrods. Everything about their audacious swagger invokes the iconic defiance of authoritarianism from the "Up against the wall, motherfuckers!" age.

I like them immediately.

"We've got some seriously fucked up politicians down here," Potok tells me. "A direct reason Alabama has [one of the] worst school systems in the country is no or low property taxes."

Potok tells me he pays about $500 a year in property taxes on a 3,500-square-foot house. In light of the two housing markets with which I'm most familiar, the tax assessment is a shocker. The annual property tax on my 1,900-square-foot house on a tenth of an acre in Oregon runs about $3,600. In Juneau, Alaska, with a mill rate of 10.51, you can expect to pay about $4,000 on a 2,000-square-foot house.

"What makes low property taxes a civil rights issue as opposed to just plain shortsighted?" I ask. "Don't underfunded schools hurt white kids as much as black kids?"

"If you ask people to vote for a raise in property taxes they think you're voting to give money to black schools and they won't do it. No white parent who can afford private school sends their kids to public schools here."

He's mostly right. Montgomery County's population is 53 percent black, 42 percent white. Meanwhile, the student population in Montgomery Public Schools is 78 percent black, just 15 percent white.

In 2009, local WSFA-TV traced the sad impact of school "desegregation" in Montgomery: By 1969, the city's flagship Sidney Lanier High School—an Ivy League–style "million dollar school" when it was opened in 1910 and whose alumni include Zelda Fitzgerald, Bart Starr, and Toni Tenille—had complied with a Supreme Court decision against the Montgomery County Board of Education and admitted thirteen black students. Forty years later, out of a student body of 1,600, only four white students remained at Lanier.[6]

The black-white, public-private school divide is hardly limited to Montgomery.

"If you want to see racism in the South, come to New Orleans," says Dr. Lance Hill, director of the Southern Institute for Education and Research at Tulane University. "New Orleans has the highest percentage of white people in private schools in America. Ninety percent of whites in New Orleans attend private schools. Every attempt to raise money to improve public schools has been defeated by white voters who show up at the polls ready to prevent any tax increase to a system that they don't use."

But unequal school funding is just a conversation starter at the Southern Poverty Law Center. The most attention-grabbing part of Potok and Beirich's work is the SPLC's infamous Hate Map, a state-by-state accounting of active hate groups in the United States. On the day I visit, the nationwide tally is up to an all-time high of 932. (By press time, the count was 1,002.)

Recent increases in hate groups are partly driven by politics. Membership in fringe organizations spiked dramatically following Barack Obama's election in November 2008.

You don't have to take the SPLC's word for that. Dr. Michael Hill, founder of the openly secessionist League of the South, told me that during George W. Bush's two terms in the White House, LOS membership *dropped* by a third or more. Immediately after Obama took office, membership nearly doubled, from about 13,000 to 25,000.

I want to find out if the SPLC's Hate Map supports my notion that racism is quantifiably worse in the South than in other parts of the country. On first glance, it looks as if I've opened Jim Crow's tomb. In a contiguous belt of states taking in Louisiana, Mississippi, Alabama, Georgia, South Carolina, and North Carolina, no state has fewer than 25 active hate groups. Tennessee has 35. Virginia has 29. Florida, a gaudy 49.

Hate group numbers from the conservative heartland are strikingly lower. Kansas: 6. Nebraska: 8. South Dakota: 2. North Dakota: 4. Wyoming: 5. Montana: 13. Idaho: 13. My home state of Alaska: 0.[7]

"Compared with the rest of the country, the South looks more like South Africa," I say.

Potok shakes his head.

"I think objectively it's true that racism is worse in the South, but it's not necessarily the Hate Map that tells you that," he says. "With few exceptions, it generally tracks population, not southern culture. It's gotten a little more southern, the high counts have moved south in the ten or twelve years I've been here. But zones where there is historic cultural conflict like Southern California always have high counts.

"The big exception is South Carolina, which is by far the number one state for hate groups on a per capita basis. We figure that every year and it's always South Carolina."

The chronically oppressed looking for places to retire might wish to avoid Amerikkka's top hate group states: California (68), Texas (59), Florida (49), New Jersey (47), Mississippi (40), and Georgia (39). The li'l hater that could, South Carolina, has a menacing 30. The heavy southern representation on the map doesn't surprise me, but the rankings of California and New Jersey show that the case against southern racism isn't as one-dimensional as many imagine.

The Hate Map is a lightning rod to those who consider the Southern Poverty Law Center a communist/soccer playing/vegan organization. A number of organizations and individuals with websites lambaste the map as a deceitful PR tool invented to help keep the SPLC and the "hate group industry" in business.

More strident groups take their anger beyond Internet screeds.

"Threats to the SPLC are constant," says Potok. "There are thirty or forty people in federal prison right now for trying to blow the place up."

"Mark and I live under basically twenty-four-hour surveillance from SPLC security," says Beirich. "We have cameras all around our houses, alarms, all of it. These are deeply racist people. They'll say, 'Fucking left-winger, you're making shit up.'"

Beirich hands me a copy of the spring 2010 issue of *The Social Contract*, a magazine out of Petoskey, Michigan. The cover features a color illustration depicting Potok, Beirich, and SPLC cofounder Morris Dees as witches stirring a burbling cauldron beneath the headline "Profiteers of Hate." The line is presumably a reference to the organization's $216.2 million endowment, amassed largely through thousands of private donations.[8]

I ask Potok and Beirich if they're ever concerned for their safety.

"You used to not tell people in town where you worked, but it's gotten better," says Potok. "A lot of people resent this place, but they also see that it's a business thing. With the Civil Rights Memorial Center and museum, we're the biggest tourist attraction in town."

A Thoughtful Counterpoint: "We're Not Racists. You're Just Gay."

Almost all southerners are incredibly touchy about the northern media's habit of trashing the South. This is especially true when blanket accusations of racism and quotes from SPLC vermin are used to besmirch the regional character and when anytime Hollywood needs an InstaRacist all it has to do is give him a southern accent.

As one Alabaman put it to me, "Southerners feel intensely the world-wide stigma of the South as a cesspool of racial hatred."

It's so bad that many southerners blow a musket anytime an outsider so much as raises the topic.

This I find out with acid recrimination when as part of my research on southern football, I make an appearance as a guest on the Paul Finebaum radio show to discuss the upcoming college football season.

Though his name is legend in SEC football territory, few casual fans outside the region know of Finebaum's preeminence. A frequent guest on ESPN and named by the *Orlando Sentinel* as the "SEC's Most Influential Media" member, Finebaum's rank on the southern sports scene has been touted by the *New York Times, Sports Illustrated*, and Columbia University, which honored Finebaum in 2008 as one of the winners of its "Let's Do It Better!" Workshop on Journalism, Race and Ethnicity.[9]

Apparently still basking in the three-year-old glow of big-time New York recognition, Finebaum pretty quickly steers our conversation away from football and into race. Having listened to the show in the weeks before my appearance, I wasn't completely taken aback by this. The social merits of "the black athlete" are an ongoing concern with the host and his listeners, so I'd come prepared to discuss Finebaum's favorite topic.

My on-air observation that college football being seen as akin to religion in the South might be related to the fact that the entire fantastically profitable business is predicated on an uncomfortably familiar economic model sets off an avalanche of angry calls and emails.

Specifically what I say is: "College football is a system that depends on an unlimited supply of free labor from young African American men and what used to be called yeoman class whites. And, yes, [college football] exists in all fifty states in the nation and everybody likes it, but only the South seems to attach a deep self-identity to this thing and is almost willing to go to war over it."

Despite what feels to me like obvious hyperbole, I quickly learn that southern football fans have absolutely zero sense of humor—or rational perspective on provocative observations based in fact. The primary lines of rebuttal are to call me a moron and racist and, predictably, to question my sexuality.

Finebaum giddily encourages the homoerotic abuse. When one toothless Jethro calls in to suggest essentially that I be taken into the dark hills of Tennessee and sodomized for having the gall to remark that racism might still exist in the South, Finebaum chortles, "Knowing Chuck, he might like that." So much for the pillar of southern sports thinking. Not to mention that "Let's Do It Better!" workshop.

The following response is typical of the 150 or so angry emails I received from Finebaum listeners, and from many other southerners with whom I get into race-related discussions.

> I was born in Alabama and have lived here all of my life. I can tell you from firsthand experience that the races get along as good, or better, here in the south as they do anywhere in the country (I have traveled a great deal). . . . Also, people in the south are not "thin skinned" and "sensitive." We couldn't care less about what you think about us. You are clearly biased and prejudiced towards the south and people from the south without knowing anything about the south or experiencing the south to a meaningful degree. You are seeing what you want and expect to see and nothing else.

And yet heartfelt emails and comments such as this pretty much make my argument for me. If I was seeing what I expected, it was only because I'd already seen the same misplaced outrage displayed over and over.

As it does everywhere else, racism in the South exists in many forms. And in some places not at all. Plenty of southerners work hard to fight racism. Still, for all but the most deep-fried simpletons, walking on racial eggshells has become a modern southern survival skill.

"Absolutely I treat black people differently," the white manager of a federal government office in South Carolina tells me. "Because if I don't I'm opening myself to all kinds of charges of racism. If a black person comes into work late or leaves early or takes a day off without telling me, I let it go in a way I never would for white employees. The black employees know that, too, and take advantage of it."

I don't doubt him. Neither does a black, twenty-year-old junior at South Carolina's Clemson University named Ahmad, who tells me, without a trace of animosity or gloating, "In this state, the whites are more afraid of the blacks than the other way around. . . . And I can say I've never been called a nigger in my life."

The whole thing feels like another Lost Cause. Even when people in the South go out of their way not to be racist, the results are limned with defensiveness, resentment, inequality, and fear.

It's not just local whites eager to deny the malevolence of southern racism. A number of blacks—a decided minority in my experience, but they exist—preach the harmony line. Countrified pace, cheaper living, and familial roots, they say, make the South a homier place for blacks than most northerners imagine.

At a barbecue restaurant on a dark, sweaty Memphis night, I have ribs and brisket with a middle-aged black woman named Jessica. She's a New Yorker who relocated to Oxford, Mississippi, several years ago and now works in the catfish farming business. When I ask why she's settled in the South, Jessica smiles, leans back on the outdoor picnic table, and says, "The cotton's high and the livin's easy."

"As a foreigner, it's great here," Jessica says, explaining that she's foreign both by her Trinidadian heritage and New York upbringing. "There are reminders every day that things are different. People say hi here. I don't say hi to people."

Jessica is no Pollyanna. Even if unintentionally, she acknowledges a multitude of regional ills.

"I love it here," she tells me. "I feel like a mental giant."

Perhaps not quite the endorsement many Oxford whites would hope for, but a minority endorsement nonetheless, so something of a liberal triumph.

Jessica personifies a notable demographic trend, a North-to-South migration that southern media in particular use to counter the idea of a region hostile to blacks. As many as 100,000 African Americans per year left other parts of the country to move south in the first decade of the 2000s.

"We have a lot of black students who come from outside the South and feel very comfortable here," says Dr. John Inscoe, a history professor at the University of Georgia in Athens. "We recruit black faculty and interracial couples and they initially worry about things, but they get here and feel very comfortable."

It's easy to be seduced by stories of color-blind progress. They make you feel good about the future of race relations, not just in the South but the entire country. Happy, prosperous African Americans working catfish farms. Interracial couples in Georgia welcomed with peach pies on the doorstep. Stereotypes met and refuted. Nothing to see here, folks, just keep moving along.

Trouble is, while these stories might comfort tourists ambling beneath the moss-draped live oak in Savannah's Forsyth Park (magnificent walk along Whitaker Street, by the way), as arguments for racial progress, they don't hold up under scrutiny. It turns out that despite plenty of evidence to the contrary, breathless predictions of a post-racial South have been deceiving the national media for more than a century.

In 2009, under the headline "Census: Blacks Are Moving to the South," the *News & Record* of Greensboro, North Carolina, pushed the ethnically harmonious South angle based on black migration patterns. A version of the same story can be found published nearly every year going back to at least 1974, when the *New York Times* ran an article beneath the headline "Blacks Return to South in a Reverse Migration." Citing "collateral evidence" and time-honored American believe-it-and-it-will-be-true self-delusion, W. J. Cash reported on the same phenomenon in his totemic *The Mind of the South*.

"Articles in the chief magazines hopefully announcing that the South was beginning to generate a wholly new attitude toward the Negro, were common even before 1910; commoner in the 1920's," wrote Cash. "And in 1929 so astute a social critic as Oswald Garrison Villard, writing in *Harper's*, could actually see the whole color line in the South as in the process of fairly rapid disintegration!" [10]

Just as social pathologies exist to some degree in every state in the country, northern racism surely exists. But I'm interested in southern racism; specifically the possibility that its unique history has embedded the raw material of prejudice in the psyche of the region in a way that it has not elsewhere. And that as a result southern racism constitutes an intractable problem that it's in the best interest of the rest of the country to jettison.

Of course, I still have to prove it.

Southern Racism: Not Just a Republican Thing

A professor of sociology at Texas A&M University, Joe Feagin has dedicated his life to studying race relations in America. As a result of this, or perhaps merely as the result of a lifetime spent in Texas, Dr. Feagin has arrived at some very depressing conclusions.

The worst of these is that every white person in America is a racist. Every single one. It's helpful to think of Feagin as the white Spike Lee, a likable pedant who nevertheless can't give his militancy a rest yet makes enough sense that you can't really discount him.

Feagin grew up in Houston during the Great Depression, graduated from Baylor University in 1960, and has since written or cowritten more than forty books. One of them, *Ghetto Revolts*, written with Harlan Hahn, was nominated for a Pulitzer Prize in 1973. The professor is given to ethnic print shirts and emotional outbursts about the perniciousness of racial jokes. His students love him.

"The South was the place where most enslaved Africans were brought, and this created the original American racist system," Feagin tells me. "Racism in the sense of a systematic institution was invented in 1619 in Virginia when the Jamestown colony decided to bring in twenty African slaves. The South invented institutionalized racism and expanded it dramatically."

"That was almost four hundred years ago," I say. "Does that necessarily mean the South is more racist today than other parts of the country?"

"You can argue that structural racism is much stronger in the South," Feagin says. "The South still has that underlying structure of slavery and Jim Crow. There are so many towns in the South where students tell me it's still like the 1950s. The South is where it's rooted most deeply and still is because it's got half the black population of the country."

Actually, more than half. According to 2011 U.S. Census figures, 57 percent of the country's 40 million African Americans live in the South. Atlanta recently replaced Chicago as the metro area with the largest number of African Americans after New York City. Of seventy-seven U.S. counties that are majority black or African American, all are in the South. On the Louisiana border, Claiborne County, Mississippi, has the highest percentage of blacks in the country, with 84 percent.[11]

"A lot of southerners tell me things are getting better," I say, hewing to my natural devil's advocate interview mode. "They have many success stories."

"A lot of white apologists like to play up these marginal stories to downplay white centrality to racism," Feagin says. "An important piece of this discussion is the 'white frame,' which rationalizes and legitimizes the structural system. That white frame moves as whites migrate to the Midwest and the West. And as blacks move, that white frame moves with them. That's why racist stuff is everywhere in the U.S."

Wow. This guy is tougher on southerners than I am. Not only did the South invent racism, it infected the rest of the country with it.

"Slavery did not start as a problem in Boston or New York City or Chicago, it started in Jamestown, Virginia," Feagin reminds me. "Then Charleston and New Orleans became main slave trading centers. A little later Houston. They were not in any northern state. Most whites here are in denial about that."

From what I've seen—and I don't mean what I "expected" to see—Feagin is right. When you get to their town or county, one thing people in the South often tell you is: "There weren't many slaves in this part of the state, so we escaped a lot of that bad racial stuff." I fell for this line the first ten or fifteen times I heard it, but after a while I realized that it's basically the equivalent of, "Well, yeah, I'm in a frat, but it's totally different from other fraternities."

Lance Hill of the Southern Institute for Education and Research says, "Racism in the South is alive and well, but it is not the slack-jawed, tobacco-chewing stereotype of old." He takes the white denial line a step further.

"The new practitioners are young, hip, and completely convinced that they don't have a prejudiced bone in their body," he says. "The greatest offenders in America today are the self-conscious and the consciously antiracist white liberals. They are the last to admit that anything they do can be harmful and discriminatory, and because of that they are often the first in line to engage in policies that are discriminatory."

"Give me an example," I say.

"You don't have to look any further than New Orleans in the post-Katrina recovery. There were endless policies implemented by well-intentioned, consciously antiracist liberals that have done more damage to African Americans displaced by Katrina than all of the organized racism throughout the South.

"Would it be possible for a conservative Republican elected official who is suspected of having racial prejudices to fire five thousand black teachers in one fell swoop and not have the nation react in horror to that? Because that is precisely what happened here in the name of [school reform], and the architects of that policy were primarily white liberals. Our major public housing projects after Katrina could have served as temporary shelters for displaced people, yet all but four were demolished. The leading advocates of that were white liberal social engineers in the urban renewal and planning sectors."

After talking to Feagin and Hill, the South bums me out even more than it did before. I mean, if you can't count on white liberals not to be racist, why bother getting out of bed in the morning?

• • •

"You know, people think we're all racists down here, but we're not," says Tony Smith. "We don't even think about it. We have white folks and black folks living together who are friendly with each other. Racism is not an issue here at all."

When Feagin and Hill talk about white denial of racism, Tony is the kind of guy they have in mind. A broad-shouldered, friendly guy from Picayune, Mississippi, Tony is a former punter and placekicker for the University of Southern Mississippi. After college, he parlayed his father's barbecue sauce recipe into a chain of eight Stonewall's BBQ restaurants. And, yes, the chain gets its name from famed Confederate General Stonewall Jackson, the oft-described "friend to the black man" who owned slaves and believed that institution had been ordained by the Creator.

Tony happens to be in the Picayune flagship store when I stop in with my weekend traveling companion and college pal, Dr. Bahr. When Dr. Bahr mentions he's from Arizona, Tony replies, "Arizona! I like your immigration law."

Starting with my usual, full-disclosure introduction, I tell Tony I'm at work on a book about the cultural dysfunction in the South, which I believe has put the brakes on national progress. This is when Tony tells me southerners aren't racist. Even though I never brought it up. This is typical in the South—people keep dropping the race card long before spades have been broken.

Tony does agree with me, however, that a sense of cultural and political malevolence is flooding the South.

"At PJ's coffee shop we all sit around and, I'll tell you, people think we're on the verge of a Civil War, that it's gonna happen."

"Between North and South?"

"Between conservative and liberal."

Like most people, Tony underestimates how closely the country's political divide is tied to geography, not merely hollow adjectives. For now, though, there's no point in pressing the issue.

Tony says entering the restaurant business was "as much a spiritual calling as a practical decision." He speaks sincerely about his commitment to serving the needy. A lot of Americans felt badly about Katrina victims—Tony spent months feeding them out of his own pocket.

"This is a very poor area," he says. "Eighty percent of the kids in this area are on free or supported school lunch programs. You go three blocks over that way and you've got whole roads of houses with no floors. Dirt floors. That still happens in America. Not black people. These are poor white people."

Tony is an incredibly nice man—the gratis bottles of barbecue sauce he lays on Dr. Bahr and me are the best we pick up in the South—but the implication that blacks would live in dirt-floor shacks and whites would not is quite an assumption for a guy who supposedly doesn't ever think about race, a rankling echo of what George W. Bush once called "the soft bigotry of low expectations." [12]

To be civil, I let Tony's comment slide—just as I hope my more dedicated readers will let slide my unironic use of a George Bush quote to support a point. I can't believe I just did that, myself.

"My wife isn't barefoot and pregnant," Tony assures us. "We got a website. We got technology down here. We're not all backward."

"I never said that I thought you were," I say.

In the lady-doth-protest-too-much habit of his brethren, Tony brings up all the southern stereotypes before anyone mentions them.

Dr. Bahr, who enjoys playing conscientious objector to my opinionated asshole, doesn't care for my snide reaction. He argues that rather than betraying an unhealthy preoccupation with race or cultural inferiority, by addressing these stereotypes Tony is employing a classic rhetorical tactic, raising objections he assumes I harbor as a way of disposing of them before I can introduce them. Having suffered through many similar discussions, Tony has no doubt learned to take control of uncomplimentary conversations about his homeland rather than sit back and wait to be put on the defensive.

I don't entirely buy the argument. And, just so you know, Dr. Bahr is the kind of guy who would argue with you about the time of day. But I acknowledge his point. Presenting Tony in a racial context—as part of Feagin's "white frame"—does feel a little lame. As every girlfriend and wife in the history of the world knows, it's easy to bank mental notes of conversational details that you can later twist to your advantage in an argument.

Tony is sweet, quick to laugh, intelligent, open, direct. The type I could see myself being fishing buddies with. I guess your barbecue chain doesn't grow to eight stores because you're not a genial guy capable of schmoozing with everyone.

In significant ways, though, he reminds me of two decent and intelligent Born Again white guys I met in Newberry, South Carolina. These guys swore up and down that the June 2010 local murder of a black man by a white man—after shooting him in the head in his trailer, the white guy tied the black man's body to the back of his truck and dragged it nearly ten miles down Highway 176—was not racially motivated.

What's more, the Born Agains insisted the crime's racial overtones, which attracted international media attention and brought the New Black Panthers to Newberry to demonstrate, were fabricated by agitators to incite local minority unrest. As if the local "good ones" needed a bunch of uppity out-of-town coons to convince them how wrong it is to tie a black corpse to a truck and drag it down a southern highway.[13]

Meet the KKKrazies

Before diving into my research, I'd decided not to focus on racial extremism. Everyone knows fringe weirdos are out there, you can find them in every country in the world. Shooting fish in a bathtub serves little purpose in an honest inquiry into mainstream values. But, goddamnit, the South's reputation for systemic racism sure isn't helped by the extravagant hate crimes and shocking offenses that explode out of the region year after appalling year.

> 2012: Math teachers at a suburban Atlanta school decide to mix in a little slavery history with a set of story problems written for third graders. Among the questions given to the students: "Each tree has 56 oranges. If eight slaves picked them equally, then how much would each slave pick?"

Another: "If Frederick got two beatings each day, how many beatings did he get in one week?" In Florida, the shooting death of an unarmed 17-year-old African American (carrying iced tea and a bag of Skittles at the time) by a white-Hispanic neighborhood watch volunteer (who claims self-defense) touches off a national firestorm over race relations and racial profiling.

2011: Captured on security camera footage, two white teenage boys and a twenty-year-old white male in a pickup truck in Jackson, Mississippi, are charged with (and in 2012 plead guilty to) assault, murder, and a hate crime for purposely running over and killing a middle-age black man in a hotel parking lot. The Jackson district attorney claims racial slurs are used during the attack and that one of the defendants later bragged that he "just ran that nigger over." In Pike County, Kentucky, members of the Gulnare Free Will Baptist Church vote to ban interracial couples from joining the congregation.

2010: Officials at Nettleton Middle School in Mississippi pass out a memo to students stating that only white children can be elected class president, while other, lesser offices would be reserved for African American students.

2009: Shortly after news of racially segregated high school proms being held in Montgomery County, Georgia, come reports of a Louisiana justice of the peace's refusal to issue a marriage license to an interracial couple.

2008: Federal officials in Tennessee arrest two white power advocates for scheming to assassinate presidential candidate Barack Obama and kill black schoolchildren. The affidavit says that as part of the killing spree the men had planned on "beheading 14 African-Americans." In Florida, an Orlando middle school teacher uses the word "nigger" in class to describe then candidate Obama.

2007: Six whites in rural West Virginia kidnap a twenty-three-year-old black woman. Over the course of a week she is forced to eat rat feces, choked, beaten, stabbed, made to drink from a toilet, sexually assaulted, and explicitly informed that she is being victimized because she is black.

2006: In central Louisiana, the Jena Six, a group of black teenagers, are convicted of beating a white student following escalating racial tensions at a local school and incidents that include nooses being hung from a supposed "whites only" tree. In Kentucky, a white public high school teacher attempts to discipline an African American freshman, Boy Scout, and honor roll student by telling the boy to "Sit down, niggah!"[14]

This stomach-churning annual checklist can be continued for as long as anyone needs.

No matter what my initial intentions had been, you can't spend time in the South and ignore the radicals. This is especially true when you're standing in a store on the historic downtown square in Laurens, South Carolina, while an active Ku Klux Klan member is trying to drape a white sheet over your head. You've probably never thought about it, but those pointy Klan hoods don't come with eyeholes—you have to cut them out yourself. Unless, like me, you've got a South Carolina Grand Dragon on hand to do it for you.

This is precisely the service that then sixty-five-year-old John Howard, owner of the Redneck Shop in Laurens and self-professed Klansman, tries to provide me after I buy a full KKK outfit—white robe, hood, insignia patch, rope belt—which sells for $125. In the South it's easy to find all sorts of Rebel-love merchandise—just up the road in Traveler's Rest, the Dixie Republic is essentially a Confederate megastore—but Howard's infamous Redneck Shop traffics in souvenirs with a more bare-knuckled message.

I arrive at the Redneck Shop with wallet open not because I want to contribute to the white power cause, but because I want to prove that it's possible to enter a store on a quaint town square in the South and walk out an hour and a half later dressed to lynch.

Howard cuts the price of the Klan uniform to $100 after I agree to buy $25 worth of other white pride shit. This includes an instruction booklet of secret rituals titled *Kloran: Knights of the Ku Klux Klan*; an embroidered patch featuring a swastika and the inscription "Master Race Member in Good Standing" and another reading, "We Must Secure the Existence of Our People, and a Future for White Children"; and bumper stickers that proclaim "I Endured a Year of Black History Month the First Day," "Never Apologize for Being White," "Forget Tibet, Free Dixie!," "Public Warning: Children Left Unattended Will Be Sold As Slaves," and "If I'd Known This I'da Picked My Own Cotton."

When you buy it off the rack, the hood of the Klan getup is just a piece of fabric, like a pillowcase. In the middle of my little 'Necks and the City shopping spree, Howard shows me how to make it stand up tall and proud.

"You just go down to Walmart and buy two pieces of white poster board and cut 'em to fit in here." Howard traces a line up the hem of the hood. "Then you gotta fold this little flap inside out and stick your poster boards in there. It's that simple."

When Howard tries to fit the hood over my head, I jerk away like a cornered badger.

"No fucking way are you putting that thing over my head," I tell him.

"How am I gonna know where to cut the eyeholes? I gotta measure it to your head."

"Measure it on Wildman."

Wildman is Howard's son, a devious-looking former carney in his thirties with gaps between all his teeth, a shaved, Rottweiler head, and a leather wallet with Klan insignia hooked to a chain on his belt. During the ninety minutes I'm inside the Redneck Shop, Wildman lurks in a corner and watches my every move. Pudgy, short, opinionated, and defiant, Howard's mouth works like an outboard motor. Meanwhile, Wildman says almost nothing. He's here as bodyguard for his father.

"His head is different than yours, everyone's head is shaped different," Howard says, gesturing to Wildman and trying to put the hood over my head again while I take another step back. This is easily the second most uncomfortable store fitting I've ever been a part of, just after my mother's annual check of the crotch displacement in my new jeans at Nugget Department Store, ages five through twelve.

Howard eventually places the hood on a table and guesstimates where the eyeholes should go. Once he's done cutting he folds the robe, sticks it in a clear plastic bag, hands it to me, and says, "Now just don't go wearing this on public property."

If you can ignore the creepy old recordings of KKK rally speeches playing in the background of his shop, most of the time Howard seems like just another loudmouthed redneck. But it's pretty easy to rile him up. When I ask if he can't see how his shop might be interpreted as an incredibly hostile gesture not just to blacks but to equality-minded whites, his face turns the color of a rotten plum.

"I ain't gotta go kissing no nigger bitches' asses! That's what they want you to do!" he roars from behind the cash register, a living avatar of xenophobic lynch-spirit.

"Is the Klan still active in this area?" I ask.

"Of course," he says.

"How often do you meet?"

"Every month."

"How many KKK members would you estimate are in South Carolina?"

"You can't count the different Klans on your fingers and toes, you've got so many lizards and gizzards."

"Seriously, how many? Twenty guys? Two hundred? Two thousand?"

"There is no one Klan. There is no central organization. You see what I'm telling you?"

Trying to pin down Howard on specifics is as frustrating as getting a teenager to tell you what they did in school today. Lots of deliberate obfuscation and vague comments.

"What do you do at meetings? What's the point of being in the Klan these days?" I ask.

"We keep the rituals alive. It's a fraternal organization."

"What rituals?"

This is when Howard hands me a copy of the *Kloran*. It's like a little guide to parliamentary procedure, only for guys with titles like Klexter and Klarogo instead of Senate Appropriations Committee Chairman and Republican Whip. I flip through the stapled pages and find a diagram showing Klansmen of different ranks where to stand in a circle during the opening of the klonkave. The accompanying text reads:

> "My Terrors and klansmen, make ready! . . . All present who have not attained citizenship in the Invisible Empire, Knights of the Ku Klux Klan will retire to the outer den under the escort of the Night-Hawk. The Klexter and Klarogo will take their posts and faithfully guard the entrance to this klavern." [15]

"I'll take it," I tell Howard, dropping the book on top of my pile of stickers and patches. "You do know that most people consider this stuff really fucked up, right?"

"It's gone, it's history," Howard says in his maddeningly inconsistent way. "Why the hell is everyone so afraid of it?"

The whole time I'm in the Redneck Shop, Howard yaps about the glory days of the Klan—"President Harding was buried in his Klan robe. It's common knowledge he was Klan!" The only way to get him to shut up is to ask him for specifics about modern KKK activity.

"Where does this stuff come from? The bumper stickers and T-shirts?" I ask.

"Most of that comes from China."

"How about the Klan robes and hoods? Who makes those?"

"It's made."

"By who? Local people? It looks like quality work."

"It's not your business to know where we get products we make money off."

Wildman takes a step forward during the last part of this exchange.

As I flick through the T-shirt racks, Howard compliments me on my complexion and guesses that I'm probably of "pure white extraction." When I tell him about my Norski ancestors washing up on the shores of Seattle in the 1880s, he congratulates me.

By the time my robe and stickers are tied up in the plastic grocery bag,

I'm afraid Howard and Wildman have pegged me for some sort of half-in-the-closet recruit to the cause, a curious mind wading into the reactionary pool even while shackled by the untruths of a liberal upbringing. The $125 cash I fork over seems to seal in their minds the existence of a budding kinship.

"I want to give you a gift," Howard says before I walk out the door.

He reaches into a glass case and hands me a bronze medallion with a die-cut KKK in the center ringed by the words "Member in Good Standing." I'd seen the same medallion in a Savannah antiques shop a week earlier with a $25 price tag, displayed in a locked glass case as though it were an exceptional artifact from a bygone era.

I ask if I can take a picture and Howard obliges (Wildman recedes into the shadows when the camera comes out), striking a pose next to a mannequin dressed in a ceremonial green satin Klan robe with pointy hood. It's strangely kimono-like in its feminine elegance.

"What's that say on the flag?" I ask. Behind the mannequin hangs a banner decorated with a Latin inscription and flying dragon.

"The Klan motto: Quod Semper, Quod Ubique, Quod ab Omnibus."

"What's it mean?"

"Forever. Forever more. For all times."

I press the shutter and wonder how much Howard represents the hidden conscience of small-town South Carolina—his shop is, after all, located on the city square, right across from the courthouse—and how much he represents the death throes of a fading power structure and ethnic ethos.[16]

A month earlier I'd visited with Rims Barber, the legendary white civil rights activist, in his office in Jackson, Mississippi. At seventy-three, as of July 2010, Barber was still feisty, still truckin'.

"Does the fact that 'nigger' is almost never used in public, and not much even in private, mean that things are improving in the South?" I'd asked.

Other than with people like Howard, many southerners had made the point to me that the N word is rarely used in the South anymore. Over the course of my travels, I heard it in casual conversation only a handful of times, far fewer times, for example, than one might hear it on a New York subway during the morning commute.

Barber thought for a moment, then tapped his forefinger on his desk.

"What that means is that the veneer on this wood is quite good," he said.

Barber remained silent, letting the thought sink in. Sizing up my bemused expression, he spread out his hand and ran it across the desktop.

"This desk looks nice, doesn't it?" he continued. "Like walnut or oak or something. I put a lot of coats of dark stain on it to make it look this nice. But, you know, it's still just plywood underneath."

An overwhelming sense of buyer's remorse washes over you when you walk out into the South Carolina sunshine holding a Klan robe in a see-through plastic bag—especially when the first person you see upon leaving the shop is a large black man smoking a cigarette and dead-eyeing you from in front of a barbershop. Wallace Creations is about five or six storefronts down the street from the Redneck Shop.

Prodded along by some massive, unnamed guilt complex—"Yo, my man, just dropped a C-note at the Klan shop. Whack!"—I stash the robe in the trunk of my car and walk across the street to introduce myself.

Christopher is a beefy, athletic twenty-six-year-old who works as a tool and die maker. He's lived around Laurens most of his life. As we exchange small talk, a thirty-year-old guy named Derrick ambles out of the shop. Derrick has Michael Cooper–style purple-black skin and dreadlocks halfway down his back. He's a welder who works for a large machine parts company assembling containers used for shipping car parts.

It doesn't take long for us to get around to the subject of Laurens's eight-hundred-pound gorilla.

"How exactly does a shop selling Klan gear stay in business here?" I ask.

Christopher tries to laugh. It comes out like an old man's dying breath.

"You're in the South, man," he says. "The South is still the South."

"The City Council members back him," Derrick says. "He had to go through the same approval process just like everyone else to get a business permit. They could have denied him any step of the way. . . . Instead of dogs and hoses, they use zoning laws and cut off money and act like we're not here."

Christopher and Derrick invite me inside the barbershop. For the next two hours I sit and watch barber Pee Wee (who, naturally, stands about six feet and probably weighs 250) preside over conversation from a steady stream of young guys getting Friday evening razor trims before the weekend gets rolling.

"What does it say when you got that Klan shit on display right across the street from City Hall and the courthouse, the place where you're supposed to go to get justice?" Derrick asks. He's the most militant of the bunch, but no one disagrees with him on this point.

"I know there have to be reasonable white people in this town," I say. "How much of the white sentiment does the Redneck Shop represent and how much is John Howard regarded as an embarrassment?"

"You know that movie *The Elephant Man?*" says a guy in the barber chair. "That's the white community here. So ugly it don't want to look at itself in the mirror."

After a while, Christopher and I get in my car for a tour of Laurens. He shows me the street that separates white and black sections of town—there's almost always a highway or railroad track dividing these southern towns—the place where the stately, well-manicured *Southern Living* mansions become Tijuana in the time it takes to run a red light.

As with the old saying about lovers' quarrels (there are three sides to every story—his, hers, and the truth), untangling the reality of racism between whites and blacks requires stepping back from extreme defensiveness on one side and an ultra-sensitivity to victimization on the other. No doubt, the truth lies somewhere in between. Still, for me, it's impossible not to be moved by emotional appeals from the underdog; appeals that seem to be born less out of anger and status quo entitlement and more out of the frustration of unrequited hope for justice.

"I've been waiting my whole life for this, to tell somebody like you about this," Christopher says as we drive. "If you tell the truth, I will support your book. I will buy a hundred copies and give them away. This is so important to let people know what goes on here."

The Audacity of Dopes—and How They Could Bankrupt Us All

On the website Occidental Dissent, a site dedicated to "racial conservatism in the American South," a young Alabama man named Hunter Wallace narrates numerous disturbing video clips in which he openly mocks "niggers" and regales his audience with "hilarious racial anecdotes."

Posted in June 2010, one of these recounts the details of an exchange at a gas station with an African American cashier who mistakenly undercharged Wallace at the computerized pump. The error leads to the assumption that the woman is unable to perform simple arithmetic and elicits the following mirthful exchange between Wallace and a buddy identified as H. Rock White.

WALLACE: It turns out I just got five free dollars in gas, courtesy of South Carolina Negroes and the existence of racial differences.
[Giggles and guffaws fill the car as Wallace drives while operating a flip camcorder.]

WALLACE: Okay, so now that we've had a little lesson in racial reality, we're on the way to the Confederate flag rally to . . .

H. ROCK WHITE: There's benefits, you know, to niggers living in your society. Small, yes.

WALLACE: Every now and then you luck up. Okay, we'll see everybody at the rally.[17]

Although websites such as Occidental Dissent contribute to my gut belief that it's true, I concede that I can't state unequivocally that racism in the South is *worse* than it is anywhere else in the country. My nearly two years of travel in the land of slave days nostalgics may have yielded plenty of horrifying anecdotes and historic facts to support such a view, but constructing a quantifiable measure of racism turns out to be nearly impossible.

Without hesitation, however, I believe it's fair to say that race consciousness is fundamentally different in the South than it is in the North.

There's a preoccupation with skin color below the Potomac River that exists nowhere else. On radio call-in shows, in impromptu conversations, bars, churches, parks, barbershops, coffee counters, in discussions that have absolutely nothing to do with race, southerners of all ethnicities introduce the topic as casually and as void of nuance as they might when bringing up the weather.

In Atlanta, sports journalist Spencer Hall explained it to me best: "Race is a topic of discussion in the South for the same reason unexploded ordnance is a topic of discussion in France and Belgium."

Though he functions as my southern sidekick only for a long weekend, Dr. Bahr—again, a man who would argue with you over how many letters are in the alphabet—tells me as we drive out of New Orleans that my generalizations about southern race obsession are overstated. If scientific method can't be applied to my blowtorch opinions, Dr. Bahr wants no part of them.

A few hours later in a bar in Jackson, Mississippi, we sit among sixty audience members for a show by the outstanding Mississippi folksinger Steve Forbert. Following his fourth number of the night, Forbert speaks through the applause.

"That was a Jimmie Rodgers song," says Forbert. "From Meridian, Mississippi."

Increased applause.

"Well, I know you're all prejudiced when it comes to Jimmie Rodgers."

Burst of applause, scattered hoots of approval.

"Oh, wait, you're all from Mississippi. I know I shouldn't use that word 'prejudiced'!"

Subdued laughter, instant energy suck, long, thoughtful pause.

"Partial!"

Exhale. Raucous laughter. Me elbowing Dr. Bahr in the arm and flashing shit-eating grin. See?

I know what you're thinking. Jackass homeboy just spent thirty pages telling me what I already know, which is that southerners live in a different racial universe from the rest of us, the Klan is still klanning (or is that "klaverning"?), and southerners make some damn fine barbecue sauce, even when it does come with Stonewall Jackson's endorsement.

So, why should you care? Put another way, how does southern racism adversely affect the country we all live in? I pose this question from a purely pragmatic point of view, which is to say, an economic one.

It's North Carolina native and doctor of sociology Glenn Bracey who finally provides me with the monetary argument I've been looking for.

"As the white population ages, their Social Security and pensions, the strength of the country at large, depends upon a young workforce," Bracey tells me. "Very soon, that young workforce will be a majority Latino and black. If current racial inequities continue, if white people continue to discriminate against people in education, jobs, housing, and other areas, whites are essentially impoverishing themselves in the long run."

I ask, "Are you suggesting minority populations will exact revenge on whites for years of discrimination by withholding monetary benefits once their numbers ensure them access to positions of economic and political influence?"

"It involves no animus or political ability on the parts of blacks and Latinos to punish whites or withhold earnings," Bracey says. "It's a matter of them simply not having the ability to contribute to such programs."

Bracey drives the point home with "See Spot run" clarity. Appropriate, since education and racism go together like desegregation and the National Guard.

"If we continue to educate black and Latino populations to the degree we do right now, they will not be able to compete for the education-intensive jobs in the global economy that bring in the kinds of wages a government can tax in order to secure the kinds of futures old white people might be expecting or be entitled to based on their own contributions to the Social Security system."

Census numbers illuminate Bracey's point. Assuming current levels of birth and immigration rates, half the U.S. population will be nonwhite by no later than the 2040s. By 2050, a substantial majority of a U.S. population of 439 million will be Americans of color. The Latino population is expected to grow from 15 percent of the population today to about 33 percent in 2050; blacks will account for 15 percent of the population; Asians will nearly double in percentage, from the current 5 percent to 9 percent.

More important is the forecast that by the mid-2020s, a majority of all U.S. elementary school students will be African, Latino, Asian, or other nonwhite American. That means we've got about ten years to fix schools for the students expected to pay the bulk of national taxes in the 2030s and 2040s.[18]

As the region that has consistently beset itself with the lowest emphasis on minority education and academic performance, the most niggardly (calm down, look it up) funding of public education, and the most ingrained convention of schoolhouse segregation, the South is by far the least likely part of the country to successfully address the issue of underperforming schools. The following story from Selma, Alabama, is one case of many:

Alarmed at the prospect of being swallowed up by predominantly black Selma, residents of a nearby and predominantly white, unincorporated community known as Summerfield hatched a plan in 2002 to keep themselves disconnected from the expanding city. By gathering enough local signatures, they would simply incorporate themselves into a new town, thereby separating their fortunes and futures from their more undesirable black neighbors. Thus was founded in 2003 the town of Valley Grande—complete with the presumptuous "e" on the end revealing all the élan of a Florida condo development.

"What they did was typical—they just made a new city so that Selma couldn't get its hands on the resources from this area," a local African American tells me.

Local whites, on the other hand, point to a decaying and downtrodden Selma and feel justified in their efforts to avoid being pulled into the obvious squalor. When I asked a longtime white Valley Grande resident why the town wouldn't want to be associated with historic Selma, he said, "You been to Selma? You seen Selma? All the empty buildings? That's the reason we didn't want in there."

Distancing itself from Selma's black population is not, of course, part of the city founders' party line. It doesn't take the white Spike Lee, however, to read between the lines of Valley Grande's official website (www.cityofvalleygrande.com) and arrive at some obvious conclusions. Noting the area's rich plantation history, the site goes on to explain, "In late 2002 it became evident that in order to preserve the quality of life people of the Valley Grande and Summerfield areas were accustomed to, and to maintain local control of their communities, it would be necessary to incorporate."[19]

"Today, southern states still reflect [their] racist heritage in many ways," writes Joe Feagin in the 2010 edition of *Racist America*. "As a group, these states not only have larger proportions of poverty-stricken citizens but also generally weaker public schools and universities . . . than do the northern states as a group."[20]

Justified or not, gerrymandered towns like Valley Grande help explain why this is so and why, without secession, the rest of the country is never going to escape the shadow of the South's most peculiar public institutions.

Not only does institutional racial enmity continue to bedevil southern education, it's poised to cause irreparable harm to American international diplomacy in ways it could not have ten or twenty years ago.

Alabama's 2010 gubernatorial primary campaign exposed this discomfiting reality when Republican candidate Tim James revealed the bizarre decision to make driver's license exams a major plank in his campaign. The policy was announced in a thirty-second television spot in which a painfully earnest James walks through a sunlit office while defining his jus'-folks position on the burning issue facing poll-going Alabamans:

> "I'm Tim James. Why do our politicians make us give driver's license exams in twelve languages? This is Alabama. We speak English. If you wanna live here, learn it. We're only giving that test in English if I'm governor. Maybe it's the businessman in me. But we'll save money. And it makes sense. Does it to you?"[21]

James may be a respected businessman, but in Alabama this doesn't necessarily imply that he's a particularly savvy one. If you're looking for a way to instantly fuck up the state's economy, alienating foreigners by forcing them to take a driver's license test in a language they don't understand would be a good place to start.

This is exactly what James's English-only exam would have done to managers and executives of Hyundai and its sister company Kia, people who happen to be investing $2.1 billion a year in Alabama. According to the Montgomery Area Chamber of Commerce, Hyundai's 2.3-million-square-foot Montgomery manufacturing facility and its thirty-five suppliers and related retail businesses account for twenty thousand jobs in the state. Not great jobs, as we'll see in Chapter 6, but the kind of jobs nonetheless to which Alabama has tied its future.[22]

It wasn't just the world-is-flat memo that James and his supporters didn't get. It was a two-by-four to the forehead emblazoned with the words "The United States needs Asia."

Inconveniently for some, this also means we need Asians. And, more frighteningly, Asian drivers. Maybe even female Asian drivers!

Having funded George Bush's wars in the Middle East—and don't believe for a second that Dubya would have been allowed within a hundred miles of Washington, D.C., without the support of the South—China now controls more than $1.1 trillion, or one-quarter, of the U.S. Treasury's debt. This makes China pretty much like the bank that holds the mortgage on that house that you don't really "own."[23]

According to the Indian Institute of Technology Bombay, in 2010 India surpassed China, Japan, and South Korea in percentage increase of graduating engineers—India saw a 10.4 percent rise and China posted a 9.9 percent gain, while the science-phobic United States recorded an engineering downturn of minus 1 percent. The same year, Boston-based Lux Research reported that "Japan, Germany, and South Korea surpassed the United States in terms of commercializing [the once American-dominated field of] nanotechnology and products."[24]

None of this has stopped elected southern politicians from going out of their way to bash Asians and Asian culture. You may already be familiar with southern stump favorites "raghead" and "macaca."

Gubernatorial hopeful Tim James's cluelessness isn't just run-of-the-mill, chauvinistic, "Learn some goddamned English, busboy!" crackpottery

from a Teabag dilettante. James is a member of Alabama's political estab-
lishment, the son of Fob James, a former two-term governor of the state. A
"businessman."

Fortunately for Alabamans who like to drive to work, Tim James did
not win the Republican primary. But the us-against-them approach he
employed has become a staple of southern political strategy because, more
often than not, it works.

I'll make the point again—racism exists in all fifty states. The South,
however, is the only part of the country with a constituency so large and
responsive to race-baiting that politicians can and do regularly appeal to it
on overtly racial terms, with a reasonable expectation of electoral success.

Southern politicians are often as not rewarded for racial slurs. As *The
Daily Show*'s Rob Corddry noted following then Virginia governor George
Allen's immortal put-down of an Asian man, "I don't know what 'macaca'
means, but it sure as shit sounds racist. Here in Virginia, I'm still not sure if
that helps or hurts a guy." (God, I miss Corddry on that show.)[25]

The Great Divide: How Secession Might Do for the South What Electing a (Half) Black President Could Not

When you're in the middle of indicting millions of people for being
blinded by their own prejudice, the last thing you want is to be blinded by
your own prejudice.

I entered into this examination of race holding the usual liberal conviction that any evidence of racist thought or behavior automatically dis-
qualifies a person for membership in the fraternity of the enlightened elite.
Interacting with good-hearted southerners who were nevertheless given to
the disappointing regional preoccupation with race forced me to revise that
position.

But accepting a certain level of inevitable racism doesn't erase the fact
that the South's continuing problems with race are a major obstruction the
rest of the country cannot abide if it is ever to overcome our shared legacy

of ethnic oppression. There's a reasonable chance, of course, that America never will transcend that sorry legacy. So long as the matter hangs in the balance, however, why should we allow the most regressive and racially engrossed part of the country to continue to pull us backward into history?

I'm not suggesting the South cannot possibly come to terms with its racist past. I'm not saying the rest of the country will come to terms with its racist past. I'm simply concluding that given their diametrically opposed approaches to the problem, it's unrealistic to think they'll do so in harmony.

The philosophy that America is "white man's country"—a view still fundamental to the South's intense political conservatism—was never really viable, not as long as Native Americans were living in traditional communities, black slaves were picking cotton, indentured Chinese were building railroads, and Spaniards and Mexicans were settling the Southwest. Positive superficial relations with minorities are no longer enough to safeguard the country's long-term interests. Overcoming a history of what might charitably be called "neglect" of minority education is vital to the country's long-term health.

Results—not "strides" or "hopes" or "improvements"—are the only things that will save us.

And African Americans aren't the only aggrieved population in the South. During my travels I was often told, "Hispanics are the new niggers of the South." Homosexuals were occasionally described in this way, as well, but as a concession to local etiquette I've already dealt with their plight the way southerners prefer to: in church. Refer to Chapter 1.

"The Latino population in the South has grown rapidly in recent years," Joe Feagin writes in *Racist America*. "As we move well into the twenty-first century, the Latino residents of a supposedly liberalized South still face much racial hostility and discrimination, most of it from whites thinking and acting out of an anti-Latino subframe of the white racial frame."[26]

The growth of the Latino population has caused consternation with certain groups across the United States. Again, however, my concern is with the uniquely southern ways the new minority population is being dealt with.

In Memphis, my liberal pal Stephen Usery expands Feagin's argument over beers in the P&H Cafe, the diviest barfhole I've been inside since

Little Louie's in South Carolina, and an apt symbol of the brooding, Third World weirdness of Memphis. The bar's pièce de résistance is a magnificent mosaic of bathroom graffiti, a national treasure that keeps me taking notes and pictures for far longer than anyone should inside a public head in Memphis. My favorite from the trailer park literati is "Your mother's cervis is shaped like my cock," with the obligatory rejoinder scrawled below, lambasting the original author's inability to spell.

"Memphis is probably 5 to 10 percent Latino now," Usery tells me, settling onto a stool at the bar. According to the 2010 Census Bureau's American Community Survey, Shelby County (Memphis is the county seat) is actually 4.5 percent Hispanic. But the perception that official figures grossly underestimate illegal immigrants, and thus the actual count of Hispanics living in the city, is common in Memphis. In an essay titled "Globalization, Latinization, and the *Nuevo* South," Raymond A. Mohl reported that local leaders in Memphis refuted the official 2000 census count of 23,400 Hispanics in the city by claiming "the real population is probably closer to 100,000 in the metro area."[27]

"Latinos tend to live in lower income areas because they're immigrants, so they have more contact with African Americans and less with white people," Usery continues. "A lot of times on TV you see crimes being committed against Latinos and most of the time it's African Americans taking advantage of them.

"The assumption is Latinos fear the police or their language skills are not good, so they're afraid to interact with authorities. Crime is easier against Latinos because they won't report it."

The dangerous implication here is that racial enmity in the South is so entrenched that it's being organically transferred onto new groups coming to the region. While America was predominantly white, it could live with a stepchild region broadly defined by systemic racism. With the ethnic profile of the country changing, it cannot. As the Brookings Institution reports, dramatic racial disparities particularly in scholastic attainment directly "threaten our future economic growth, as well as the broader promise of upward mobility in American society."

According to the U.S. Census Bureau, the average African American family earns two-thirds of what a white family does and has 10 percent of its net worth. The black median household income is $33,916. White median household income is $54,920. The black unemployment rate is about twice what it is for whites. The black family poverty rate is 24.5 percent. The white family poverty rate 8.2 percent.[28]

In some ways, these figures merely point out what everyone already knows, which is that NBA power forwards and Jay-Z aside, black people in America are generally less well off than white people. It's important to pay attention to these numbers, however, in order to understand how the country's future will be shaped by African Americans and other minorities, and how southern racism will adversely impact the economic well-being of aging Americans—specifically that final group of majority whites, i.e., most of the people likely reading this book.

The prosperity and sustainability of this country will very soon depend upon minorities, primarily blacks and Hispanics. What this means is that the country is in desperate need of healthy, prosperous populations of ethnic groups that have traditionally been relegated to the lower rungs of the social ladder. I, for one, am not comfortable leaving the movin'-on-up transition of these groups in the hands of the South.

It's a sociological axiom that displaced majority populations will respond to their new minority status with various strategies of social resistance. The ultraconservative politics, education, and hidebound religiosity of the South demonstrate that as the Caucasian numerical majority declines, the most aggressive and antisocial of these resistance strategies will likely be of southern origin.

We can no longer afford to wait on the South to get its racial shit together. It's time to move on, let southerners sort out their own mess free from the harassment of northern moralizers who won't even let them move their kids to decent schools without getting their noses all out of joint over it.

Cut loose from the relentless social shaming that unforgiving elements of the North can't let go of, and forced to a swim in the new world economy or become a North Korean–style pariah state, an independent southern republic might just surprise everyone with its ability to at last overcome. Or, at least, to at last come over to my side of the discussion with the realization that they, too, might be better off without 'em.

CHAPTER 4

Football: Louisiana State, ESPN, BCS, and the Gridiron Delusion of the SEC

Having remained alert through chapters covering matters of irrefutable national concern—religion, politics, racism, imaginary cave tots frolicking with giant prehistoric squirrels—some may now be moved to question the inclusion in this book of a section devoted to college football. Massive institution that it is, my less enlightened readers (few, imagined) might suggest that on the scale of "things I care about," football falls roughly between anal bleaching and Timothy Dalton–era James Bond films.

In any case, it could be argued, football hardly measures up to the weighty issues bandied about in a manifesto as earnest as this.

Such readers are therefore welcome to regard the pages that follow in the manner of lighthearted halftime entertainment, both reward for and respite from the grueling psychological fracas that has preceded and will follow. In the great tradition of halftime, they might choose to simply wander out of the arena for a few minutes, grab a beer in the parking lot, and return when the marching bands and baton twirlers and liver-spotted alumni being feted for long forgotten achievements have been ushered off the field and the real action resumes.

The rest of us know better. Fully indoctrinated in the holy crusade that is college football—especially as practiced in the South—we know that perhaps no argument offered in this book will do more to excite the passions and analytical resources of readers on both sides of the divide.

We know that when the *Washington Post* runs editorials calling for a complete overhaul of college football (2010), when the *Atlantic* magazine runs a cover story bemoaning the shameful state of college football and athletics (2011), and when President Obama, the U.S. Congress, and the Justice Department find time to address the inequities in the system for determining college football national champions, as they did in 2009 and 2011, that, like the bulk of their constituents, our cultural and elected leaders understand football as the peak expression of the national character. Tribal, violent, and cocksure, America's game is yet imbued with intellectual complexity, Manhattan Project levels of organization, teamwork among disparate ethnicities, and exploitation of virile young men and tanning salon strumpets tramping it up in color-coordinated undies in that peculiarly Yankee Doodle sideline mash-up of perky, hip-thrusting virgin-skank appeal. (Whenever people talk about jazz as America's only original art form and singular gift to world culture, I hasten to remind them of the cheerleader outfit.)[1]

Southerners already know that amateur football long ago crossed the Rubicon from mere Saturday-afternoon distraction to a concern of vital commercial and social interest.

As though there were any doubt, football's leviathan status in the South is regularly confirmed by bodies such as the Alabama Supreme Court, which in November 2011 ruled on which high schools would be allowed to participate in the state's Class 6A playoffs. The court's verdict banning the undefeated Clay-Chalkville Cougars from postseason play for having an ineligible player on their roster was, naturally, a front-page, top-of-the-fold story in the *Birmingham News*. (Sucks for you, Cougs, though it must have felt good watching your replacement, the undeserving pond scum of Gadsden City High, get rolled out of the first round of the playoffs by Mountain Brook, 21–0. Go Spartans!)[2]

As for northern football fans, we just want the game that's been hijacked since 1998 by the southern football cartel given back to us in all its former, semi-equitable glory. And even if a return to the days of level play-ing fields in college football is more or less a fantasy, secession would still produce what would become football's grandest extravaganza, an annual North-South gridiron border war between each country's champions that would dwarf even the Super Bowl for drama, spectacle, Miller Lite con-sumption, and thirty-second ad buys.

From a purely sporting point of view, the titillating possibility of a North vs. South Blood Bowl alone makes secession worth considering.

But I'm getting ahead of myself. First a bit of background. And booing. And boo-hooing.

Blinded by the Hype: The SEC, BCS, and 340-Pound High School "Juniors"

In *The Burden of Southern History*, famed historian C. Vann Woodward wrote: "The South has had its full share of illusions, fantasies, and preten-sions, and it has continued to cling to some of them with an astonishing tenacity that defies explanation."[3]

Few enduring southern delusions do more to illustrate Woodward's point than the region's storied devotion to college football. Although I've never bought into the widespread claims of southern football superior-ity, among sports fans and pundits across the South (and in much of the North), the prevailing wisdom is that the best football in the nation is played in Dixie.

At the collegiate level, where football matters most in the South, this belief is manifested at the highest level in the Southeastern Conference (SEC), a collective of university football teams almost unanimously pre-sumed to represent the pinnacle of college athletics. Of the 721 college football teams and seventy-five college football conferences in the United States, the twelve teams from the SEC are collectively regarded as whales to krill, the Beatles to Herman's Hermits, the iPhone to two cans and a length of string, jackhammer sex with Mila Kunis to dry humping your junior prom date standing up in her parents' garage.[4]

Gods among mortals.

Overlapping claims to general southern football strength and specifically to SEC superiority are based on a simple set of arguments.

First is the SEC's record in the Bowl Championship Series (BCS), the hazy apparatus through which college football national champions are crowned. Of the fourteen championships awarded since the 1998 advent of the BCS system, ten have been handed to schools from the South (eleven if you count Texas). Eight of those ten teams have come from the SEC, including, remarkably, the last six consecutive national champions—Florida, Louisiana State, Florida again, Alabama, Auburn, and Alabama again.[5]

Second: the tradition and pageantry surrounding college football in the South are considered more elaborate. The passion for the game greater. The tailgating tastier. The cheerleaders hotter. The stadiums more imposing. Transcending mere athletics, football in the South has in effect become a kind of religion followed by a devoted majority of the populace.

"SEC football is like the World Cup, a chance to pick up a flag and participate in ages-old grudges and engage in an ancient ritual," explains journalist Spencer Hall. "Thank God it is also violent."

A University of Florida grad, driving force behind the brilliant online football forum Every Day Should Be Saturday, and the best thing to happen to southern football media since Frank Broyles's torturous career as a national sportscaster finally ended, Hall makes this comment to me in East Atlanta's Midway Pub on a warm Sunday afternoon.

The meeting comes after I send Hall an email introducing myself with the open admission that I'm a stern resister to the SEC cult. Hall writes back very politely to say that he and a couple friends would be happy to disabuse me of my northern ignorance.

"The reason we get so much national hype is simple: we care more," Hall tells me in Atlanta. "Cheerleading here gets ruthless by junior high. There are people in Alabama named Paul Bear Bryant; like twenty of them now. You've got toothless hillbillies who will break down the intricacies of the skinny post and identify holes in cover-two defenses more accurately than anybody on ESPN."

"But hype doesn't necessarily mean you're good," I argue. "George Bush got a lot of hype in Texas. Toothless hillbillies loved him, too. It didn't make him a good president."

"The South is good at football for the same reason Brazil is good at soccer; there's a large underclass of blacks and whites who see sports as a way out," Hall counters. "I'm not a big fan of economic determinism, but we've got a huge, impoverished African American population."

"And wide receivers willing to get killed going over the middle," adds his buddy Michael, a University of Georgia graduate.

Michael and a third friend, Mike, form an amusing peanut gallery.

"In back-to-back Outback Bowls in 2001 and 2002, South Carolina beat Ohio State with a white tailback, which tells you all you need to know about Ohio State football," says Mike, taking a shot at the Big Ten's Ohio State Buckeyes, the favorite whipping post of SEC fans.[6]

"Ron Zook said, 'The primary difference between the SEC and the Big Ten is the SEC has more big guys who can run,'" says Michael of the former Florida Gators head coach. "That makes Zook an idiot who said something smart."

"SEC football is opera for southern men," concludes Hall.

College football dominates southern media. As a result, universities and their athletic departments have become frighteningly media savvy. When it comes time to fluff the national press, Hall tells me, SEC schools are three steps ahead of media backwater teams like Boise State or Wisconsin.

This is a vital skill to have since getting a shot at a BCS championship requires not only winning games on the field, but winning the even more pitched PR battle to convince college football's media agenda setters and poll voters to place your team high in the weekly rankings. Especially when your team's most impressive early season victory is a 63–7 drubbing of Div. II Southeastern Cornhole State. At home.

As Hall says, "College football is all interest-based politics and southerners do interest-based politics better than anyone."

What he means is that if you're a football school with aspirations of national recognition, you need guys like Colin Cowherd to buy what you're selling. Because he's one of ESPN's top college football experts, cohost of

ESPN's *SportsNation*, and one of the ten American males not named Vinny you'd most want to accompany you to a Vegas sports book, I call Cowherd after my meeting with Hall to get his take on SEC football.

"I have theorized for years on my show that the two things that make the SEC really good are poverty and obesity," Cowherd tells me, before connecting the dots between football and deficiencies in public education in the South. "They create enormous football players what with the unhealthy lifestyles and unhealthy eating habits. You can argue that California creates as many good running backs as any place in country, but nobody creates as many gigantic, 340-pound seventeen-year-olds. Educated parents don't let their kids get to be 340 pounds. That's not reasonable.

"One thing I've noticed with southern football is the enormity of the defensive lines. I covered it for a couple years in Florida. Florida public schools are atrocious. What always jumped out at me, you get these absurdly large defensive lines—in high school!"

My suggestion that SEC football isn't necessarily the best in the country is quickly slapped away by Cowherd. I'd hoped for a little more accord from a likable sports iconoclast who grew up in the Pacific Northwest. Not that I'd expected to go out beaver trapping with the guy, but when one of your tribe makes it to the big time you at least hope for a little of the old "I haven't forgotten where I came from" routine.

Cowherd is having none of that.

"The SEC puts more people in professional football than any other conference every year," Cowherd says. "That's a good barometer suggesting that they have better athletes and better teams. No other conference can compete with that."

"Yes, but college football isn't the NFL," I reply. "If it were, Tim Couch and Joey Harrington would still be enjoying long, successful careers as Hall of Fame quarterbacks."*

"It doesn't matter," Cowherd says. "Because they pay double and triple what everyone else pays for coaches, the SEC simply gets better coaches

---

* The first player selected overall in the 1999 NFL draft, Couch, a star quarterback at the SEC's University of Kentucky, is widely considered one of the biggest busts in NFL history. Taken number three overall in the 2002 NFL draft, legendary Pac-12/University of Oregon quarterback Harrington was unfairly expected to lift three of the NFL's most star-crossed franchises to greatness, and even if he did retire in 2007 with less than overwhelming stats, he'll always be Joey Heisman to me.

and, thus, better teams. The SEC pays their assistant coaches $700,000. UCLA barely pays that to [head coach] Rick Neuheisel."

Actually, Neuheisel was making about $1.4 million before being fired in 2011, but since Cowherd is to sports banter what Herschel Walker once was to stiff arms and sixty-yard touchdown gallops, I get out of the way and let him rumble for the goal line.

"Oregon defensive coordinator Nick Aliotti does well in the Pac-10, but he's not employable in the SEC," he says. "He would get eaten alive in the SEC. The bottom line is the conference is willing to pay much more because of the revenue they generate. You think money doesn't matter? The hell it doesn't."*

"Why are southern schools so obsessed with football that they pay head football coaches millions of dollars?" I ask, noting that University of Alabama head coach Nick Saban reportedly makes a little more than $4.7 million a year, Les Miles gets $3.9 million from LSU, and even Dan Mullen gets $2.5 million for coaching at Mississippi State. Meanwhile, Dennis Erickson, who won two national championships at Miami and has been a head coach with two NFL teams, made just $1.7 million at Arizona State for the 2011 season.[7]

"The South has often felt left behind or alienated or targeted by the North for their political and racial position," Cowherd says. "People mock the South. It's so damned important to the South because every region needs to be great at something. It's a way of saying 'we're number one.' The one way they can give a big F-you to the rest of the country is with college football."

Fixing College Football the Southern Way

That "F-you" is also born of a historic frustration on the part of southerners to get the results they want on the field. Though it's true that from the

---

* The Pac-10 added two teams and became the Pac-12 prior to the 2011–2012 season. For simplicity's sake, I'll use only Pac-12 in this chapter, even when describing teams and events posted under the Pac-10 banner. Direct quotes such as Cowherd's I'll reproduce as originally recorded.

southern Eden of halfbacks, hash marks, and hookers-as-recruiting-incentives, Crimson Tides from Alabama and Hurricanes from Miami have often ravaged the unworthy pigskin armies of the Pharisees, there have also been a number of championship disasters for southern teams. Most painfully, these have been meted out by the hated Notre Dame Fighting Catholics over Alabama in 1973, the much loathed Flesh-Eating Catholics over Texas in 1977, the repulsive, Madonna-Worshipping Catholics over West Virginia in 1988, and again by the dastardly, Boy-Fucking Catholics over Florida State in 1993.

In this last instance, it should be pointed out, the stain of defeat was so great for the South that the result of that regular season game was manipulated in such Wiccan fashion that light could be declared as darkness and darkness declared as light—meaning that despite a final score of #2 Notre Dame 31 and #1 Florida State 24, and both teams finishing the season with just one loss, Florida State was somehow handed the national championship by the media. This after a season in which the southern media continually pounded home the point that it was the Seminoles' much loved, good ol' boy head coach Bobby Bowden's "turn" to win a title. (Before the BCS, college football champions were chosen at the end of each season by rival media organizations such as the AP and UPI. Sometimes these bodies agreed with each other, sometimes they did not, almost always they pissed off half the country, as opposed to the 90 percent of the country the current BCS system manages to alienate.)

Yet even accounting for this type of bald-faced shamockery, all told between 1950 and 1997 only nine southern teams were crowned as undisputed national champions. From the southern "F-you, we're number one" point of view, a fix was clearly needed. (And, yes, 'Bama, I know y'all count fourteen national titles for the Tide alone, but I'm talking about documented undisputed title history, not the nonsense claims you print on your T-shirts.)[8]

And so a fix was created in 1998 by then Southeastern Conference commissioner Roy Kramer, who fashioned a national football championship system in cooperation with other conferences and major media. In 1998 the Bowl Championship Series was inaugurated with a title game between Tennessee and Florida State, thus guaranteeing the South a national football champion no matter the outcome on the field. The formula was repeated in 1999 so that the BCS championship game between Florida State and Virginia Tech again ensured a national champion from the land of the one true football faith.

Only 2004 and 2005 would produce a BCS national championship game in which a southern team did not participate. And even this defilement of reason was soon corrected, so that the title of the 2004 champion USC Trojans was revoked after an NCAA investigation into recruiting violations, and the 2005 title of the Texas kin was accepted. From this point and forever onward, by vagaries of the mystical BCS creed, a southern team would assume its anointed place in the national championship game, often against an undeserving opponent, so that from 2006 to 2012 teams from the Southeastern Conference were almost predestined to lay claim to all national titles.

By 2012, southern teams had hoisted ten championship trophies in fourteen years, triumphing in 71.42 percent of national titles in the BCS era, compared with a victory rate of 20.83 percent of undisputed titles in the half-century prior. Since the inception of the BCS, the SEC has been crowned champion 57.14 percent of the time compared with a victory rate of 10.42 percent in the half-century prior. Few fans these days question this abrupt shift of fortune or offer indiscreet comment on such academic concerns as statistical improbability, the consensus from coast to bayou to coast being that the South is to football what McDonald's is to two all-beef patties, special sauce, lettuce, cheese, pickles, onions on a sesame seed bun.[*]

Except for the heretics like me who still won't shut the fuck up about the fifteen-year, $2.25 billion (yes, with a "b") ESPN/SEC, and fifteen-year, $825 million CBS/SEC contractual con job being pulled on every sports fan in the country in the name of southern football mythology.[10]

---

[*] For an exhaustive explanation of how I arrived at these figures, the shameless load of championship caca peddled by Alabama boosters, and the rationale for beginning the count of national championships at 1950 (a start point that statistically favors the SEC), see note 9 in the Notes section for this chapter.[9]

"You're Great!" "No, You're Great!" "We're Both Great!" How Self-Fulfilling Prophecies, Not Games, Came to Rule College Football

Being of obstinate temper and committed to truth, reason, and empiricism, as opposed to conjecture, emotion, and belief in the scheming football madam known as the BCS, I decided to undertake a deeper investigation into the alleged superiority of southern football.

Here, incidentally, is where the diagnostic sledding may get a little rough for the nonfan. But stick with me, football haters, and you'll be rewarded with the most compelling reason you've ever had to justify your inborn loathing of football. This will come in handy the next time someone suggests meeting for drinks at a sports bar and you need a handy excuse for bailing out.

The first step in my inquiry was to look at head-to-head results of games played between schools from the SEC and conferences representing other parts of the country. The results confirmed a suspicion I'd long held. Judging by inter-conference records—that is to say actual games as opposed to media guesswork—the SEC plays other BCS conferences about equally. Witness the record since the start of the BCS era in 1998:

SEC vs. Pac-12 regular season:	10-12
SEC vs. Pac-12 bowl games:	1-0
SEC vs. Big 12 regular season:	6-10
SEC vs. Big 12 bowl games:	21-8
SEC vs. ACC regular season:	42-36
SEC vs. ACC bowl games:	16-9
SEC vs. Big Ten regular season:	7-4
SEC vs. Big Ten bowl games:	19-19
SEC vs. Big East regular season:	16-15
SEC vs. Big East bowl games:	3-8

The record is clear. In head-to-head matchups against other major conferences, the SEC has either a losing record or one that is generally only a little better than even, not counting the ACC, which is made up of mostly southern teams stocked with players passed over by SEC teams.[11]

To SEC boosters who claim that the SEC's overall winning record in bowl games is evidence of success in "games that matter" against "quality opponents," I offer the counterargument that because bowl game pairings are more easily manipulated than regular season games, and because SEC teams usually play in bowls at or near home stadiums, they often result in more favorable matchups for SEC teams. This tilt renders postseason play a less valid measure of strength than the more random sampling of results produced by regular season games.

In other words, imagine yourself taking a test and getting to choose ahead of time what questions you want to answer. And then being allowed to take the test at home and promising not to use your computer. That's roughly the advantage SEC teams enjoy in a number of bowl games.

In 2012, for instance, the SEC was able to even its BCS bowl record against the Big Ten at 19-19 when the Florida Gators beat Ohio State in the none-too-partisan Gator Bowl. The game was played in Jacksonville. No bowl games are played in Ohio.

Next I turned to the pros. As it happens, that oft-repeated, most-players-sent-to-the-NFL claim does favor the SEC, though not, as is commonly asserted, by an overwhelming margin. In the five NFL drafts from 2006 to 2010, SEC teams had 16.58 players per team drafted by the pros. The Pac-12 had 14.81 players per team selected. The Big Ten had 13.48. (Incidentally, I favor the players-per-team stat because looking at raw numbers of players drafted doesn't reflect the fact that the SEC has for most of its history fielded more total teams each season than other major conferences.)[12]

So, if the SEC plays other conferences about even, and doesn't produce an extraordinarily greater number of NFL-caliber athletes, why do SEC teams keep winning national championships?

That answer requires some background on the BCS and its corporate underwriters, which, being savvy to their own economic interests, have created a reliable business model for determining national champions that is in all respects a self-fulfilling prophecy.

The BCS business plan works like this: preseason rankings, which function like pole positions in an auto race, typically include two, three, or four SEC teams among the nation's top ten, more than from any other conference. From the outset, this bias for SEC teams builds into the system a near-insurmountable advantage. Start the season with two of the top four teams being from the SEC, as was the case in 2010 with Alabama and Florida, and in 2011 with Alabama and LSU, and the conference is virtually guaranteed to be represented in the title game—and this is an important point—*even if neither of those two schools ends up winning the conference.*

To be the best, so goes to the old sports adage, you've got to beat the best. But since only SEC teams are consistently declared the best, only SEC teams get the chance to prove themselves against "the best."

It's a chicken-or-the-egg situation. Does the SEC get favorable rankings because they're so good? Or is the SEC so good because they get favorable rankings? In light of their mostly even play against teams from other major conferences, I argue for the latter.

In 2010, for example, the Auburn Tigers began the season with a consensus ranking of #23, behind SEC rivals Alabama, Arkansas, Florida, and Georgia. The only way a team regarded so lightly early in the season can possibly climb into the national championship game—which Auburn did that year—is to beat a slew of highly ranked opponents, which Auburn also did that year. Because polls are arranged so that SEC teams will face the most highly ranked opponents over the course of a season—in the jargon of the BCS this is called "strength of schedule"—only teams from the SEC are time and again able to manage this feat.

Imagine Pizza Hut, Domino's, and Papa John's getting together to declare themselves the best pizza in the world and having a taste-off each year to determine which one ruled the pizza universe. In the end they'd satisfy a bloated chunk of the nation's most voracious and least imaginative eaters, but there'd be an awful lot of quality pizza out there left unaccounted for.

The trouble with the rankings is that college football teams don't earn their high spots the way race car drivers earn their pole positions, in road trials that measure actual performance. Instead, college football teams have their pole positions handed to them by media concerns with a massive interest in the performance of the teams and conferences in which they are most heavily invested.

Consider again that the BCS was created by then SEC commissioner Roy Kramer, also known as the "godfather of the BCS," a man who "attached plastic explosives to college football" and blew it up, according to ESPN. ESPN, of course, is the commercial entity that dominates the college football landscape, and which has a near-incalculable economic interest in promoting the nationwide perception of the SEC's elite status.[13]

Actually, you can calculate that interest.

In 2008, ESPN and the SEC signed that aforementioned fifteen-year, $2.25 billion agreement allowing the Worldwide Leader in Sports to televise the conference's football games. In addition, ESPN owns the rights to televise all BCS games, including the national championship game. In 2011–12, ESPN and its partner ABC broadcast thirty-three of the thirty-five college bowl games. Which is to say that for all intents and purposes ESPN, a subsidiary of the Walt Disney Company, the most successful spinner of dreams and fables in world history (not counting the Republican Party), owns college football as a commercial entity.

In a 2010 story titled "ESPN/ABC Has Monopoly over Bowl Games," Ryan Hogan of *Bombastic Sports* quite correctly noted that "ESPN/ABC has complete control over the images, statistics, and commentary associated with the college football bowl season. They alone will shape the narrative of college football's most important time of the year."[14]

Do I think direct economic interest is the motivating force behind ESPN's militia of pundits, including Colin Cowherd, who prop up the SEC as the paragon of football excellence week after week? I think Cowherd is an honest guy. But he also ain't a dumb guy. And as Cowherd himself would tell you, as Cowherd himself *did* tell me when talking about SEC expenditures on football, "You think money doesn't matter? The hell it doesn't."

I must assume that, like most others who work for ESPN, Cowherd is smart enough to know that if you get fired for shitting on your boss's doorstep, you've got no one to blame but yourself. Colin Cowherd does not want to get fired. Neither does anyone else who works for ESPN.

Because ESPN essentially owns college football, the SEC agenda it pushes invariably sets the tone that's followed by all other major media. In February 2011, more than half a year before the start of the football season, ESPN placed three southern teams in its top-five ranking for 2011 and published an Internet story beneath the headline "SEC Teams Dominate Early Look at 2011." The story referred to the rankings as though they were the result of some organic process.

A more honest headline would have been: "We've Invested $2.25 Billion in the SEC and We've Decided to Tell You, Yet Again, That SEC Teams Will Dominate College Football. Surprised?"

In its first official preseason poll, published in August 2011, ESPN listed seven SEC teams (more than half of the conference) in its top twenty-five. The national media followed suit—after all, who knows more about sports than ESPN?—elevating Alabama and LSU to top-four status, setting the table for another SEC national title run long before a single ball had been snapped or groin muscle pulled.[15]

Poll fabrications are perpetuated by like-minded sportswriters and coaches who cast weekly ballots. Although proven wrong in some fashion every single week of the season, these half-baked polls continue to function as the prima facie currency of college football, which, unlike any other sport, relies on opinions from people who don't even attend or watch the games to elect a champion. If you were as wrong at your job as often as football writers are wrong at theirs, you'd currently be cleaning out the grease trap at Wendy's, getting fondled by the night manager, and worrying about being late for your second job burning trash on the graveyard shift at the county landfill.

Sportswriters cannot possibly watch every game in the country, and end up casting poll ballots that follow the judgment of ESPN, so as not to appear out of step with the experts employed by the Worldwide Leader, whose ranks they would someday like to join.

Football coaches cannot possibly watch every game in the country and thus cast poll ballots based on reputation, friendships, and conference allegiance. They also follow the direction provided by ESPN, so as not to appear out of step with the experts employed by the Worldwide Leader, whose ranks they would like to join as soon as they're fired from their present jobs.

SEC football games not televised by ESPN, by the way, are televised by CBS, per terms of a fifteen-year contract between the conference and the network. Over the term of that contract, CBS will pay the SEC $825 million. In 2010, the SEC became the first conference ever to take in more than a billion dollars in athletic revenue in a single year, the largest chunk by far coming from football.

Economic debasement in the service of college football is a long-standing southern academic tradition. Writing in 1941 about southern universities, W. J. Cash stated that in a great many of them, "change was to be measured much less in the increase of knowledge and thoughtfulness and tolerance than in the reduction of the academic department to the status of an appendage of fraternity row and a hired football team."[16]

In more common language, what this means is that schools like Harvard and the University of Chicago and Cal-Berkeley measure success in terms of Nobel Prize recipients and patent awards. A large number of southern schools more often factor NFL rosters and rape acquittals into their equations for achievement.

A classic synthesis of academic subservience to financial interests and the southern penchant for willful self-delusion came before the 2007 football season, when LSU head coach Les Miles told a group in New Orleans that he "would like nothing better than to play USC for the title."

"I can tell you this, that they have a much easier road to travel," cracked Miles of the highly ranked Trojans' presumably weak Pac-12 conference schedule. "They're going to play real knockdown drag-outs with UCLA and Washington, Cal-Berkeley, Stanford, some real juggernauts. . . . The SEC provides much stiffer competition."[17]

Miles's LSU Tigers did end up being awarded the national championship in 2007. The team's "stiffer" road to the title included wins over such Herculean squads as Middle Tennessee, Tulane, Louisiana Tech, and SEC conference wins over Mississippi State (8-5, 4-4 conference), South Carolina (6-6, 3-5 conference), Ole Miss (3-9, 0-8 conference), and losses to Kentucky (8-5, 3-5 conference, a team whose winning record was secured only with victories over mighty Florida Atlantic, Eastern Kentucky, and Kent State) and Arkansas (8-5, 4-4 conference, and you don't even want to know the knock-kneed line of weak sisters the Razorbacks had to bully in order to achieve their winning record).

Lucky for Miles, or more accurately, thanks to a money-gamed system that favors the SEC, his LSU Tigers did not have to play a 10-2 USC team for the national title. The Tigers played Ohio State in the championship game. Essentially the SEC's version of the Washington Generals, Ohio State had most recently distinguished itself by losing eight consecutive bowl games to SEC opponents.

The game was played in New Orleans.

Here's how the self-fulfilling BCS prophecy breaks down in the SEC's favor over the course of a season.

The preseason top twenty-five is stocked with the usual high-profile teams from across the country—teams, not coincidentally, already scheduled for heavy broadcast exposure. (This is why NBC affiliate Notre Dame, which has pretty much been shit for a decade or more, continues to get good rankings and given automatic BCS berths anytime it manages to creep its record over .500.) Thanks to those gaudy ESPN and CBS contracts, many of these ranked teams come from the SEC. Their high rankings are based largely on name recognition and commercial value. The conference's history of national championships is offered as justification for SEC teams' advantageous rankings.

Once the season is under way, if a highly ranked SEC team beats another highly ranked SEC team, the winner rises higher in the polls than it might normally, based on the fact that it has just beaten a "top-tier" team from the country's "elite" conference. By the same coin, the losing SEC team in this scenario doesn't drop as far as it might otherwise, since, after all, it has lost to a presumably powerful "top-tier" team from the country's "elite" conference.

When "good" SEC teams suffer losses in league play, this allegedly proves how tough the SEC is from top to bottom. If an SEC leader wins all of its league games, this allegedly proves how great that team is, given that it somehow managed to go undefeated against a monster SEC schedule—ignored is the fact that SEC teams have pulled off this putative miracle for the last four straight seasons. For God's sake, it's tougher to go undefeated in the Colonial Athletic Association than it is in the SEC.[18]

If the same things happen in other conferences, however, the media and SEC boosters reverse the logic, claiming that if, say, a Mountain West Conference league leader loses to a lower-ranked Mountain West team, this merely proves how bad that losing team is, not how good the Mountain West is. In the same way, if a league leader goes undefeated in the Mountain West, the feat is said to merely demonstrate how weak the conference is, not accepted as proof of the strength of the unbeaten team.

Thus can a featured columnist like Brian Mazique of *Bleacher Report* (which calls itself the country's fourth-largest sports media site) get away with declaring that then undefeated Mountain West power Boise State had "bamboozled" the country into believing they were worthy of championship consideration. Like many compliant members of the national sports media, Mazique simply refused to accept the fact that Boise State opening the season with a 35–21 manhandling of the SEC's then top-twenty-ranked Georgia Bulldogs—*in fucking Georgia!*—was proof that the Broncos were any good.

"How long will Boise State be able to pull the wool over the eyes of the Associated Press, Harris, and the BCS in general?" Mazique whined, writing off that big Bronco win as a fluke with the esoteric bullshit that Boise State had prevailed "over a young Georgia team who had yet to find themselves."

Though its teams are rarely given the opportunity, the Mountain West, not the SEC, has the highest winning percentage of any conference in BCS bowl games (.750), even though its teams travel farther to play in BCS games than just about any others and with fewer supporting fans.[19]

The double standard also allows nonconference victories rolled up by "champions" such as the 2009 Alabama Crimson Tide against the likes of Florida International, North Texas, and Tennessee-Chattanooga to be regarded as evidence of gridiron distinction by those inside the solipsistic cocoon of the self-congratulatory SEC echo chamber.

The most capricious example of this pro-South pretzel logic occurred in 2008. When the Pac-12's #1 USC Trojans lost to Oregon State by six at Oregon State in the third week of the season, the loss was spun by pundits and fans across the country as a USC choke—as far as the national media is concerned, losing to the Beavers is like having your wife leave you for a marching band trombonist. After the week-three loss, USC's title hopes were dashed. Yet when the SEC's #4 Florida Gators lost to traditional door-mat Ole Miss *at home* the very next week, the result was cast as proof of the SEC's depth—"Ole Miss must be tougher than we thought!"—and Florida was allowed to remain in the title hunt.

Florida finished the season 12-1 and was awarded a shot at the national championship against the Oklahoma Sooners. USC finished the season 12-1 and was kept out of the BCS championship game. Ole Miss finished the season 9-4 and number fourteen in the polls. Oregon State finished the season 9-4 and number twenty-four in the polls.

The Sooners, by the way, weren't even the best team in their own conference (Big 12), making Florida's eventual road to the national championship that much easier. Oklahoma's regular season loss to Big 12 opponent Texas *by ten* on a neutral field conveniently forgotten, they were awarded the championship shot after finishing the season 12-1. Despite also finishing the regular season 12-1, and having kicked Oklahoma's ass in head-to-head competition, Texas, the demonstrably stronger team on the field, was denied the championship game, so as to protect the Florida/SEC chances of winning the title game.

Follow the logic? Neither does anyone else, but somehow an SEC team gets a shot at the title pretty much every year, no matter who wins and loses the actual games. I get so frustrated just thinking about this that I'm biting into the little stuffed Duck on my desk as I type.

In the same way that Bible literalists twist whatever meaning they want out of the Good Book, what college football really has in the ESPN/SEC/BCS fiscal alliance—and what it might feel compelled to change given a secession scenario—is an airtight business model with a self-affirming theoretical premise that cannot be affected by facts. Because any on-field outcome is simply spun to fit the original thesis, and because at season's end the champion of the SEC has always prevailed in a conference with more highly ranked teams than any other, SEC teams are "scientifically" awarded the chance to play for the national title per the BCS's byzantine computations.

With a participant in the national championship game nearly every year, the SEC is statistically more likely to win a disproportionate share of national championships.

I Attend the "Sham of the Century," in Which the Home Team Fails to Score a Touchdown, Commits Two Turnovers, Misses Four Field Goals, Yet Is Declared a Worthy Championship Contender... Even Before the Game Is Played and Then Again Right After!

The chicanery is only getting worse. The most bald-faced example of poll rigging occurred in 2011 when the Pac-12's then #3 Oregon Ducks lost a September game in Dallas to then #4-ranked LSU by a score of 40–27. Following the defeat, the Ducks dropped ten spaces in the polls, to #13. With the demotion, Oregon's championship hopes were essentially obliterated from the first week of the season.

When the SEC's then #2 Alabama Crimson Tide lost at home to #1 LSU in November, however, it dropped only one space in the polls, to #3.

I was in Bryant-Denny Stadium for that 2011 alleged "game of the century" between LSU and Alabama in Tuscaloosa. Having watched my Ducks hang twenty-seven points on LSU earlier in the season (the most any opponent managed to score against the stingy Tigers defense all year), I traveled to Tuscaloosa and paid out the ass for a scalped ticket because I was eager to see just how the mighty legends of the SEC take care of business at home.

It turned out to be a tough night for Alabama fans. The Crimson Tide's offense barely looked capable of tying its own shoes. The home team eked out only two field goals while converting on just three of eleven third-down opportunities and passing for a Pee Wee football–style ninety-one yards on nine total completions.

While LSU fans celebrated their 9–6 win in the Houndstooth Sports Bar in the hours after the game, I watched as pundits on ESPN went right to work setting up expectations of an LSU-Alabama title game rematch. The original "E" in ESPN stood for "entertainment," after all. Sports have always been a secondary concern.

Right there in the bar I started having Rodney King/Notre Dame/Florida State flashbacks. Did those abusive cops really walk free from that episode? Didn't anybody else see the same bullshit I just watched? Is ESPN really telling the nation that a team that fails to score a single touchdown, commits two turnovers, and misses four field goals *at fucking home in the biggest game of its season* deserves a shot at the national title? Teams from any other conference losing in such fashion would be escorted out of the top-ten club faster than a urine-scented hobo wandering into the Oak Room at the Plaza in midtown Manhattan.

Of course, I shouldn't have been shocked given that in the days leading up to the game ESPN shills had already spent hours talking up an Alabama-LSU rematch in the championship game, no matter the outcome in Tuscaloosa. I nearly ground my back molars into powder watching that televised charade from a hotel bed in downtown Birmingham.

When asked by a fan who he thought was going to win the game, for example, ESPN's Kirk Herbstreit, who has been called the "face of college football," reportedly answered, "Alabama. But I hope we get a rematch in the BCS title game." [20]

Within two weeks, just beaten Alabama had been scooted back up to #2 behind top-ranked LSU, and yet another SEC team (Arkansas) had been quickly installed at #3, thus ensuring that no matter what happened next, the SEC would be guaranteed a national title. The system of propaganda reached its torrid, circle-jerk climax with the 2012 BCS title game between two SEC teams, LSU and Alabama.

This time, Alabama won. In New Orleans. Convenient, by the way, that LSU manages to wind up in the BCS championship every time the game is played in Louisiana. That would be 2003, 2007, and 2012 for those keeping track.[21]

Computer programmers have a term for formulas that rely on flawed or biased original data: GIGO. Garbage in, garbage out. Relying as it does on a garbage premise from the get-go, the entire BCS formula is incapable of producing anything other than garbage results.

In the wake of the desultory 2012 bowl season and the lowest-rated championship game in the BCS's fourteen-year history, changes will inevitably be made to the system. Having succumbed to TV's dreaded "Fonzie effect" (charming role player becomes annoying lead, saturation fatigue ensues), even ESPN has to face the fact that every Goliath needs its David, every Laker needs its Celtic.

Tweaks will be made. These will be spun as improvements that facilitate an equitable selection process leading to the crowning of a "true" champion. As usual, the fixes will mostly be horseshit, the tweaks inevitably being invented for the sole purpose of protecting the investment.

This is neither the way I want my national pastime run, nor my societal mirror to reflect on our national scruples and professed commitment to equal opportunity.

Southern students of the game and even semi-sentient fans will by now be fairly boiling for my editor or anyone else involved in the publication of this book to point out that all of my whining comes down to nothing more than a pathetic, jumbo-size case of West Coast sour grapes. This owes to the fact that my own alma mater, Oregon, had its national title hopes destroyed on the field by the SEC champion Auburn Tigers in the January 2011 BCS national championship game (Auburn 22, Oregon 19), and then again in September 2011 on the field by the eventual SEC champion LSU Tigers in an early-season, 2012 championship table-setting game (LSU 40, Oregon 27).

There is perhaps some tannin of truth in this observation. I won't lie, SEC fans, I've had family deaths that hurt less than those losses, largely because your teams earned and deserved both victories. The fact remains, however, that the SEC con job was in full effect long before the University of Oregon became the University of Nike and started allowing its glue-sniffing designers in Beaverton to change our school colors every week.

My overall argument here is not that the SEC sucks. Clearly, it does not. Although the only reason that a two-loss LSU team got to play for the national title in 2007 is because it began the season ranked #2 in the country and God forbid the cashiers of college athletics allow something as inconvenient as wins and losses to get in the way of a good collective consumer delusion.

My argument is simply that if you look at results on the field—not guesswork from compliant writers, network suits, and BCS computers—teams from the major conferences, and some schools from smaller conferences, are actually a lot more evenly matched than the ESPN mouthpieces will have you believe. Despite being approximately equal to other conferences in most quantifiable categories, the SEC and other southern schools are unfairly presented with championship opportunities and favors on what should be a level playing field. This is heresy to the time-honored conventions of athletic competition, around which 82.6 percent of meaningful social interaction between American males revolves.

That southerners genuinely regard football as a religion in and of itself—go ahead, ask one, they'll tell you it's true—allows them to buy into any line of crap its high priests bother to come up with in between sessions of counting the collection plate and banging impressionable boys and devout ladies of the congregation. The SEC is better than other conferences at media manipulation and pretending that fiction is fact and fact is fiction. But as a top-to-bottom conference it is not better at football.

The Southern Killing Fields and a Not-So-Modest Proposal for a True College Football Championship

Over the 2010 and 2011 seasons, I continued my quest for southern football wisdom as the region commenced the annual orgy of hatred known as SEC conference play. The fraternal violence left with me a number of vivid impressions, as did many conversations with southern fans.

"We don't hate you guys, we barely know you guys," said a cheerful student named Brad after an Oregon vs. Tennessee game I attended in Knoxville. "Who we really hate is each other. Southerners are just a bunch of piranhas in a small pool, full of hate and out for blood."*

The ensuing weeks proved Brad right.

"That's an Ole Miss guy right there, I saw it right off that he was wearing a collared shirt," said a Louisville alum, who in unsettling ways of appearance and manner resembled Gary Busey. "I hate those fuckers. They're all fucking twats! Who wears a collared shirt to a bar like this?"

"There is special hatred in the hearts of LSU fans for Alabama," emailed a man from Louisiana.

"I wish you had spoken with some of the fan base of my beloved Auburn, instead of the inbred Bama Nation, you would have a different opinion of the SEC," emailed a fan from Alabama.

Strictly by my anecdotal count, by the way, the University of Alabama year in and out appears to field the most odious team and attract the most hated fans in the South.

My favorite quote came from a distressed southern patriot named Thomas Ray of Crystal Springs, Mississippi, who in a letter to the editor of Jackson's *Clarion-Ledger* complained of those forcing the retirement of Colonel Reb, the quasi-racist Ole Miss mascot: "If they want a new mascot, it should be the jellyfish and they should fly a white flag at all their games. . . . They need history lessons, or a ticket back North, not appeasement." [22]

I went back to Spencer Hall to help interpret the wrath.

"Because it's the South there's an irrational hatred of outsiders," Hall explained. "Southern psychology works in black and white. Everyone is imbued with the southern Us vs. Them mentality. Everyone is either enemy or friend. When they beat you down here they don't say, 'Nice game.' They chant, 'We just kicked your ass!' We just care more about destroying you."

"But the same bloodlust for football exists everywhere," I said.

"No! You would not shoot someone over this. You would not name a child after Rick Neuheisel. You've got people naming their children after

---

* Oregon 48, Tennessee 13. To the likely chagrin of Colin Cowherd, Oregon defensive coordinator Nick Aliotti was not eaten alive by the SEC.

coaches in the third year of their tenure and stabbing each other over the outcomes of games. I wish I was kidding about either of those, but I'm not." I did some research. Hall was indeed not kidding.

In 2005, a crazed Alabama fan screaming "Roll Tide!" rushed into an Auburn fraternity house and stabbed multiple Auburn fans on the night before the annual Iron Bowl.

In 2006, a man in Limestone County, Alabama, was arrested for attempted murder after stabbing a friend with a butcher knife over an altercation during a PlayStation video football game in which the victim's Tennessee team was beating Alabama. Not even a real game!

In 2008, after a drunken session of taunting that followed a real-life Alabama victory over LSU, supporters of both teams pulled guns on each other. The Alabama fan fired first, killing the LSU fan and his wife.

In 2009, in North Carolina, a man shot and killed a friend after the two got into an argument over a Texas-Nebraska game. Not even SEC schools and, still, homicide![23]

Because people actually killing each other over football games makes a huge impression on me, I eventually had to admit it—southerners do seem to be excessively devoted to college football in a way that the rest of the country is not.

But why?

Is football boosterism merely an easy and (relatively) safe way for southerners to project their seething "F-you" contempt for northerners?

Is SEC football an institutionalized funnel for a mass delusion of superiority—racial, religious, cultural, or patriotic, which, some might say, masks nothing less than a mass inferiority complex—that feeds into a never-ending, cyclical pathology of rancor and discord?

To elaborate on the point I made on Paul Finebaum's radio show, might the importance of college football in the South have anything at all to do with the fact that it is an insanely lucrative enterprise based upon free labor supplied predominantly by young black men and poor whites? Even unintentionally, can the fervor for college football be explained by a subliminal desire to affirm the peculiar institution through which the South rose to its apex in the same way of the lovingly restored mansions of the cotton barons of Natchez, Mississippi?

I'm not extending a definitive argument—just pointing out a curious and thought-provoking set of parallels. I mean, something beyond a deep academic interest in the spread offense and career-ending clothesline tackles has to account for people naming their children after an old man famous for wearing a houndstooth cap.

Or might the obsession have less to do with the South's plantation past than its numinous present? Is it possible that southerners cling to college football like no others because belief in a supreme being is a matter of faith, not proof?

Since there's no definitive system and never has been a definitive system for determining a Lord of Lords in college football, what's left is conjecture and faith. No group in the country, of course, is more primed than southerners to attach unyielding apostolic fervor to an unprovable equation. Explored by Alabama-bred Chad Gibbs in his 2010 book *God and Football: Faith and Fanaticism in the SEC*, this line of logic is followed by guys like Auburn head coach Gene Chizik, who in 2010 accounted for a missed field goal by a Clemson red-shirt freshman that preserved an Auburn victory by explaining, "It's a God thing."[24]

The blind acceptance that the SEC is the supreme being in college football follows the unthinking belief in the supreme being one finds at the Creation Museum; the openmouthed acceptance of fable; the hostility toward contradictory evidence.

Did dinosaurs and man live together? Yes. But what about the fossil record? Never mind, listen to this here passage some fellers wrote down in Genesis.

Is the SEC the most dominant football conference in the country? Yes. But have you looked at the stats? Never you mind all that fancy talk, just lookee here at this poll some fellers from ESPN put together.

As though recent history and record books were akin to fossils and inscrutable tree rings, it's as if no one in the South is capable of digging deep and copping to the evidence at hand: Since the beginning of the BCS era the SEC has losing records against the Pac-12 and Big 12 in regular season play. It posted a .500 record (5-5) in the 2010–11 bowl season, same as the Pac-12 and MAC, slightly worse than the Big East (4-2), and slightly better than the ACC (4-5). Those bowl results actually moved the wonks at esteemed but hardly entertainment-driven statistical aggregator SportsRatings to report, "In the end, no conference really dominated the bowl season, with most leagues overperforming [Big Ten] or underperforming [SEC] only marginally against expectations."[25] Yet despite this underwhelming performance, the 2011 preseason table was set once again for an SEC title run.

Viewed in this context, college football hypocrisy ties in perfectly with the dumb lug religious mind-set that functions as the foundation of southern society. No wonder the SEC bugs the shit out of me. It's a thinly disguised adjunct to evangelical hubris.

Football really is religion in the South. The notion of its southern covenant is entirely predicated on faith. Unwavering belief in shameless fakery helps keep it strong. Get rid of the South and I'll bet we have a real college football playoff system inside of six months.

Even better, upon secession, the greatest football conflagration ever conceived would feature an annual competition pitting the champion of the American conferences against the champion of the Confederate conferences. The game would be of such grotesque importance that neither side would allow a finagled champion to represent it. With the musky man-horn for victory trumping all other political and economic concerns, only legitimate, battle-proven warriors would be sent into combat.

So great would be the animosity on both sides that out of concern for public safety the Coca-Cola/Starbucks Blood Bowl™ would have to be played on an aircraft carrier in the middle of the Indian Ocean, surrounded by a nuclear-capable flotilla from a neutral third-party naval power, with only players, coaches, cheerleaders, and television crews allowed aboard the ship.

Wherever I traveled in the South, reactions to my northern football pros-
elytizing were predictable. Southern fans labeled me a moron, a jealous
Yankee, and, because it is the go-to rhetorical device for a certain type of
southern male when backed into an intellectual corner, a fag.

"In my part of the world," I replied to the outraged Dixie football
community in radio interviews, casual conversations, and emails, "we prefer to affirm civilization through logic and reason, not with the myopic,
exclusionary bias and anti-intellectual fanaticism that have been the twin
hallmarks of southern culture for going on parts of four centuries now. I
realize that years of Levitican literalism and fantasy computer titles have left
SEC fans with a casual relationship to reality, but please humor me a little
by allowing facts, not bought and paid boosterism, to drive the discussion.

"I know, I know, y'all still ain't convinced. The whole region's congenital
inability to trust schoolroom logic as far as Grandpa can spit a possum is
just too strong to resist. Ignoring facts is part of the program down here. As
avatars of poisonous West Coast liberalism, the Pac-12 is lame and limp-
dicked and in your minds barely more useful than Troy State as a tune-up
for a schedule loaded with such conference titans as Vanderbilt, Mississippi, Mississippi State, and Kentucky.

"As predictably as tailgaters named Dwayne and the Swamp Rat will
fly their slave-days flags y'all love so much in allegiance to some imagined
connection to historical greatness, you will retreat into the cold comfort
of make-believe championships gifted to your teams as justification for
your one-dimensional beliefs. And even reminders of a historical record of
mostly even play against teams from other parts of the country won't ame-
liorate the ulceric rage, narrow-minded hostility, and denial of reality that
comes with southern football fandom."

This approach did not win me many new friends. But even as fans
across the South bristled at my improvident and imbecilic oratory, on my
last point, the one about the Coca-Cola/Starbucks Blood Bowl™, they nod-
ded in unanimous enthusiasm and their eyes sparkled at the very possibility, as though the game were already on next year's schedule.

CHAPTER 5

Education: Arkansas, Mississippi, and the Three Rs of Southern Schools— Revenue, Resentment, Resegregation

The Little Rock School District needs a new superintendent.

This is not an unfamiliar situation for the school board, administrators, teachers, parents, students, and residents of the largest school district in Arkansas. The district has more trouble keeping superintendents than Bill Clinton once had keeping secrets. It's blazed through fifteen of them over the last twenty-five years.

Though superintendent of a large, well-funded district in a capital city should be one of the most coveted jobs for school administrators across the country, almost no one bothers to re-up at the end of their two- or three-year terms guiding Little Rock schools. Some, like Roy Brooks, in 2007, get pilloried in the press and then canned. After an acrimonious tenure fighting rival factions within the local education power structure, the school board decided not to renew the contract of its most recent superintendent, Dr. Linda Watson.

"Not really," Watson told Little Rock's FOX 16 news when asked if her spring 2011 termination surprised her, tacitly acknowledging what one Little Rock middle school principal described to me as the "poor man's politics" of local education in the South.[1]

"You get in and you get your friends jobs in the district, no matter how ignorant they are," the principal told me. "It's a complete political thing."

The man brought in to clean up Little Rock's latest education mess and find the district its new leader is Dr. Tom Jacobson, cofounder and CEO of the Omaha, Nebraska–based executive recruitment firm McPherson & Jacobson. Hired by the Little Rock School District, the company specializes in placing executives in government and public school positions.

A longtime public school administrator himself, and also a current full-time education professor at the University of Nebraska Kearney, the sixty-four-year-old Dr. Tom has the air of put-upon, schoolmarm authority built into his involuntary nervous system. Though his wire-frame glasses sit too tightly on his paunchy, pink face and pockmarked drinker's nose, his jaw remains firm, his eyes on the knife-edge of impatience. The minute he steps in front of a crowd you sense a man who has waged thousands of battles with divided boards, disgruntled unions, irresponsible kids, and yokel parents, and come away with a career winning percentage that's probably just above .500.

You also see a man in a dark pin-striped suit and tassled brown loafers on the verge of retirement who wonders what the fuck he's doing at six o'clock at night at a two-bit high school in Little Rock Fucking Arkansas leading the twenty-second of twenty-seven McPherson & Jacobson public forums to solicit community input on the new superintendent while his wife is at home doing needlepoint inside their cozy three-bedroom ranch house in Omaha with a roast steaming away in the Crock-Pot on the kitchen counter. Instead, Dr. Tom finds himself at J. A. Fair High School, an institution described to me two hours earlier by *Arkansas Times* editor in chief Max Brantley as "a genuine piece of shit."

"The student body test scores are terrible, it has demoralized staff, kids are getting away with murder," Brantley has told me.

Tonight's community meeting to discuss the hiring of the new superintendent is taking place in the school's "media room." Which means library.

Which also means that even socially conservative Arkansas isn't immune from the asinine mania to replace perfectly good, descriptive names with new ones every ten years. Anybody seen a "comic book" or "strip joint" lately, or have we all now somehow agreed to "graphic novel" and "gentleman's club"?

When I arrive I'm asked to sign a registration sheet that asks only for my signature, gender, and race. There will be no surprise as to the emphasis of tonight's discussion.

"You still have deep-seated racial issues here in all areas."

"There is a complete racial divide in the [Interstate] 630 corridor downtown—the west side and the rest side."

"The problem we have is the white corporate male has not stopped fighting the Civil War!"

These comments come about twenty minutes into the meeting in response to Dr. Tom's question: "What are the issues the new Little Rock superintendent should be aware of to be able to hit the ground running?" For the seventeen blacks and seven whites in attendance (the white count includes me and two Arkansas helpmeets who have provided me with numerous local contacts), this is by far the most emotional and volatile portion of the evening. Dr. Tom's request to hear "good things" about the district and "important qualifications" the new superintendent might possess have inspired only halfhearted replies or, in most cases, silence.

The solicitation to air grievances excites the crowd like a naked woman walking into a roomful of teenage boys.

The "white corporate male has not stopped fighting the Civil War" comment—which comes off as a pretty direct challenge to the very white-corporate-male-looking Dr. Tom—comes from a robust African American grandmother who prefaces her remark with the give-me-my-props note that she was a classmate of the Little Rock Nine, the supernaturally courageous African American students who in 1957 touched off a national desegregation shitstorm, defying Arkansas governor Orval Faubus and an Arkansas National Guard blockade by attempting to enroll in and enter Little Rock Central High School.

The Nine made it inside the school only after President Dwight Eisenhower intervened in the crisis, federalizing the Arkansas National Guard (thereby wresting it from Faubus's control) and having the students escorted into the school by the U.S. Army's 101st Airborne Division, the outfit historically called into action for motherfucker missions such as parachuting behind enemy lines in Normandy on the night before D-Day. A nation watched transfixed while the spectacle of pig-hearted southern racism standing in the way of the ideal of public education for all played out live on network television. The event became the defining moment in Little Rock's history.[2]

Dr. Tom has endured pretty much the same bellyaching about race at every meeting he's done so far. Blunt community appraisals from the executive summary McPherson & Jacobson issues at the end of its 2011 superintendent search will include:

"Little Rock is not a good place for black children."

"A number of children have . . . parents who can't read."

"The whites bring their special needs children to the district but take the other students to private school."

"We are losing students to charter schools."

"There is a growing involvement of the faith-based community in schools."

"Little Rock is the home of [the] 1957 crisis and some people are still in that place."

"Re-segregation [is] taking place."

"[The] system is sick and district is sick."[3]

My favorite comment from the J. A. Fair meeting—one that, sadly, will not end up in the executive summary—comes from an indignant African American man who stands up to express dismay that the current superintendent is not seen often enough at high school football games.

"The new superintendent should have concern for the student athlete and help them get good scholarships," the man says with the emotional southern regard for the healing synergistic powers of higher education coupled with sixteen-year-olds who run like antelope and $100 alumni handshakes.

Dr. Tom wants this meeting wrapped up on time. He keeps the discussion moving with the irritated, cut-you-off manner of a conservative talk-radio host. As soon as he senses a lengthy rant on the way he waves a hand and says, "Okay, let's stay on topic," or "That might be a good point, but it's not relevant to this discussion."

He doesn't much seem to like his job or the people in the room. When he calls his occupation "a commitment, a calling," the spiritual allusion feels manufactured for regional play with the crucifix crowd. His sour expression suggests that the only thing calling him are a couple leftover tabs of Pepcid AC back at the Days Inn. He's a smart guy and I'm sure he's got his own problems, but I dislike him and feel most of the people in the room share my feelings.

When the blessed end of the hour-plus forum arrives, I ignore the McPherson & Jacobson largesse (store-bought cookies and liter bottles of diet pop) and instead circulate around the room, chatting up various participants. The funniest moment comes after I interview a chrome-domed, man's man type—an African American from Louisiana who is actually here as a McPherson & Jacobson consultant—and I ask the guy for his contact information. He grabs the pen and notebook out of my hand, flips to a blank page, and jots his email address: johnshaft1@███████.com

When I finally get a minute with Dr. Tom, I ask if the national search he's conducting is likely to land Little Rock the kind of top-quality administrator who might actually have a chance to fix the district's evident problems. He shakes his head, perhaps already envisioning the first drip of vodka Collins hitting his bloodstream in the Days Inn lounge.

"They're paying $188,000 for the position," he says dismissively. "They should be paying about $250,000."

Why Can't Johnny Reb Rede? Or Spel?

Beyond accusing them of being racists, the fastest way to get under a southerner's skin is to reference the bumpkin stupidity that southerners think the entire world believes them guilty of. Hypersensitivity to the issue of the alleged dimwittedness of locals is a trademark of the southern persona.

To deny the notion of widespread hillbilly retardation, the righteous southerner will point out that no matter how silly it is, a larruping accent isn't necessarily an accurate barometer of intelligence. He will also bray at length about the region's brilliant scholars and writers—a few can actually name one other than William Faulkner and Ronnie Van Zant—as well as the highfalutin success of such academic bulwarks as North Carolina's Research Triangle Park, a seven-thousand-acre R&D center and home to university laboratories, multinational corporate operations, and start-up companies.

The problem with this line of argument is that no matter how fair and judicious one might want to be in allowing the South its due regarding matters of academic distinction, the overwhelming empirical evidence describes a much less peachy narrative. That southerners have always been less well educated (this doesn't mean stupid, yet) than other Americans is as statistically reliable a fact as the region also having the highest rates of obesity as well as the most homicides stemming from disputes over bass fishing territory.*

As clear as corn liquor, the historic achievement gap that has forever separated South from North has been scrupulously documented and remains a fixture of today's national education profile.

Explaining the scholastic inclinations of the Old South in *The Mind of the South*, W. J. Cash noted that "the South far overran the American average for (white) illiteracy . . . and that a very great segment of the [upper] class kept no book in their houses save only for the Bible." The official 1860 white illiteracy figures were 17 percent in the South versus 6 percent

---

* For those keeping me honest, the Death Penalty Information Center mentions nothing about bass fishing, but does helpfully inform the public that Louisiana leads the nation with 11.2 murders per 100,000 people—nowhere near lowball New Hampshire, which kills off just 1.0 per 100,000 citizens, though at least an improvement over the 17.5 people per 100,000 greased in Louisiana in 1996.[4]

in the North. According to University of Georgia history professor James Cobb, "Only 35 percent of the South's white children were enrolled in school in 1860 as compared to 72 percent outside the region, where the average school year was also 70 percent longer." H. L. Mencken reported in 1917 that even the South's leading light of Virginia "spends less than half upon her common schools, per capita, than any Northern state spends."[5]

While it's true that over the last half-century the South has pulled closer to national academic norms, the essential narrative of a southern region dragging down the nation's intellectual potential remains unchanged.

According to 2010 U.S. Census estimates, of the fifteen states with the lowest high school graduation rates, ten are in the South—eleven if you count Texas. No southern state appears in the top half of the rankings. Of the ten states with the fewest adults holding high school diplomas, seven are southern, eight if you count Texas. Per composite SAT/ACT scores, students in only two southern states score above the national average—and I'll be blowed if Tennessee and Kentucky ain't the two—though the rest of southern students languish nearer the bottom of the rankings. In a mild revelation to those new to national education statistics, upstart Arizona has recently displaced Mississippi with the lowest-testing kids in the nation.[6]

If you like, however, you can still beat Mississippi over the head as "dumbest state in the Union" by several measures, a compelling one being a 2006 report by Michael A. McDaniel of Virginia Commonwealth University assessing American IQ scores by state. In this ranking, Mississippi places brain-dead-last among all states. Not surprisingly, the South dominates the lower spectrum of the list with ten of the bottom fifteen states, though it's worth noting that, led by slow-charging Arizona, the Southwest has recently been making impressive strides in poor schooling, with the Grand Canyon state, Nevada, and New Mexico all playing spoilers in the race for lowest IQ average.

No southern state places in the top fifteen for IQ and only one—Virginia at sixteen—sneaks above the national average. Take away Beltway Virginians and the state very likely plummets into the cerebral ghetto occupied by its Rebel brethren.

Yes, the McDaniel study is six years old, but I find it worthwhile not simply because it's unusual—it takes balls to pin IQ scores on states in which a number of citizens can't even fill out the form—but for using its data to connect brainpower with community behavior and public policy implications.

"The correlation matrix shows that estimated state IQ has positive correlations with gross state product, state health, and government effectiveness," reads the study. "Estimated state IQ correlated inversely with violent crime. Thus, states with higher estimated state IQ have greater gross state product, citizens with better health, more effective state governments, and less violent crimes."[7]

In other words, remove the South and the United States instantly becomes more intelligent, healthy, safe, and financially sound.

One of my favorite though admittedly obscure measures of intellectual vigor comes from StateMaster.com (a treasure of state-by-state statistical breakdowns). In its ranking of public library visits per capita, Alabama checks in last, with the usual southern suspects dominating the bottom fifteen with ten entries, eleven if you count Texas. Not a single southern state, not even Virginia, places in the top twenty-five for library patronage.[8]

A number of factors play into the region's failure to attain educational equality with the rest of the country. These include religious dogma; a lingering, Confederate-odored, post-Reconstruction resistance to the system of free and universal public education that Yankee occupiers sought to impose upon the South; and, inevitably, racial inequality.

The main reason southern states fare so poorly in measures of education, intelligence, and intellectual curiosity, however, is that the states themselves place such a low value on public schooling. This stubborn refusal to support public education is in large part due to what Diane Blair and Jay Barth call the "common southern view that education was 'private, personal, and optional' and not public responsibility," in their book *Arkansas Politics and Government*.[9]

As was the case when Mencken was berating Virginia for its inadequate funding of schools, the historic norm remains fixed. According to U.S. Census Bureau figures released in 2011, southern states reflect their historic lack of commitment to education by doing less to gather funds for public education and collectively spending less on elementary and secondary public school students than any other part of the country.

This is particularly the case with property taxes, the traditional device through which funds for public schools are raised. The low property taxes Mark Potok from the Southern Poverty Law Center told me about in Alabama are consistent throughout the South. The average Arkansas property owner pays $512 year in property taxes. In Louisiana, it's $643. In Kentucky, $651. West Virginia, $683. Tennessee, $752. Compare that with states at the high end of the per capita property tax table—New Jersey ($2,625), Wyoming ($2,385), Connecticut ($2,381), New Hampshire ($2,317), New York ($2,009)—and you start getting some insight into those low southern test scores.

No southern state, not even Virginia, spends above the national average of $12,250 per year, per student. (New Yorkers spend the most on their kids' education at $20,645 per student, per year.) Even supposed federal-government-hating conservative states such as Louisiana manage to place relatively high (number 23 in annual student expenditures, at $11,967 per student, second-highest among southern states, after Virginia) because they happily accept more in federal education funds than almost any other state in the country. Yet again putting the lie to the myth of plain folk self-sufficiency honored in recent country music anthems like "Way Out Here," in which Josh Thompson proudly croaks of his dirt-floor kinfolk, "We won't take a dime if we ain't earned it, when it comes to weight brother we pull our own."

Turns out, not only do southern ruralites take those dimes, they slack off and statistically *don't* pull their weight once their snouts have been dragged out of the trough.[10]

The South's economic disregard for public education is incongruous with the rest of the country's determination to reestablish American schools as a standard-bearer for the world. The southern "approach" to education is nearly as dismal now as it ever was. The rest of us can no longer afford to drag the South's truant ass kicking and screaming into the world of twenty-first-century knowledge and discovery. Nor should we have to, given the way southerners take care of their own.

"When you compare test scores across the country and you look at Louisiana, Mississippi, Alabama, Arkansas, they are going to score in the lower part of the continuum and I think the culture of a state obviously has a distinct reflection on the education system," Dr. Tom tells me after the superintendent search in Little Rock is over. "I'm from Minnesota, a place where in any political election education is going to be one of the top three issues. It has to be about the kids.

"When we do work in the South it seems that students are not necessarily the number-one priority. A bunch of factors come into play before we talk about students."

"What factors?" I ask.

"Politics. Political motivations of board members seeking higher office. . . . This is a frustration of ours. When you go in and work with boards of education, you try to take them through a consensus decision-making process to focus on their top five or six criteria for what they are looking for in a new superintendent. For example, you might identify achievement issues, such as improving test scores or graduation rates. In all the meetings we did in Little Rock, I'm not sure those things were even mentioned."

Pride, Prejudice, and Cheetos-Infused Pickles at Forest Heights Middle School

I've come to Arkansas to give the South a fair shake on education.

Still beset by the dim stereotypes that resulted from the Little Rock Nine drama, and an unflattering 2007 HBO documentary, *Little Rock Central: 50 Years Later*, the state is, in fact, something of a rising star on the regional academic scene. Having taken more seriously than many the criminally impossible standards of achievement set by the federal government's 2002 No Child Left Behind Act, the state's public school teachers have yoked their students into measurable improvement.

"When I left the state we ranked forty-eighth for student achievement," says Dr. Charles Hopson, superintendent of Pulaski County Special School District, which takes in the fringes of Little Rock. After twenty years working as a school administrator in Portland, Oregon, Hopson has recently returned to his native Arkansas. It was Dr. Tom's firm, McPherson & Jacobson, that recruited him for the Pulaski County job.

"We're now ranked tenth in the nation in terms of student achievement," he tells me.

A serious-minded, loquacious intellectual, Dr. Hopson is also a natty dresser with a knack for smooth talk. His "ranked tenth" proclamation isn't exactly accurate. In its annual "Quality Counts" report on state-level efforts to improve public education, *Education Week* magazine ranked Arkansas sixth in the nation in 2011, up from tenth in 2010, for "efforts to improve the teaching profession, their standards, assessments and accountability systems." Arkansas's actual students fell well below the national average in measures of academic achievement, rolling in at number thirty-six and getting a D grade in the report—not exactly what's known as a résumé builder in the education racket.[11]

Still, thirty-six hardly makes Arkansas as deprived as Mississippi. And the state's increased emphasis on education is admirable. Gone, it would seem, are the days of 1921, when a state study concluded: "To [thousands of] children, to be born in Arkansas is a misfortune and an injustice from which they will never recover and upon which they will look back with bitterness when plunged, in adult life, into competition with children born in other states which are today providing more liberally for their children." Or even a 1978 study that reported, "By almost any standard the Arkansas system of education must be regarded as inadequate."

What's more, in Arkansas I'll mostly be giving a pass to the impoverished Delta Region, where the odd outsider can still wander around as I did for half an hour in towns such as Gould (population 1,129, median household income $14,906), be harassed by small gangs of decidedly unsociable mongrel dogs, and encounter nary a schoolhouse nor a human being willing to point you in the direction of one. "Delta" often conjures romantic images—lazy floats down bayou sloughs, ancient blues played on battered guitars from rustic wooden porches—but mostly it's flat and plain and dull and lifeless and hotter than Satan's taint sweat, a breeding ground for fourteen-year-old runaways who you wouldn't have the heart to send home if they turned up in your town.[12]

In Little Rock, I've chosen to visit the largest, most generously funded, highest-achieving school districts in the state. There's education money here, not just from the most affluent neighborhoods in Arkansas, but millions more from a 1989 federal court settlement stemming from desegregation battles that forced the state of Arkansas to pay about $70 million a year to the Little Rock, North Little Rock, and Pulaski County school districts.[13]

If any place can disprove my prejudices of negligent education in the South, it should be Little Rock.

First stop is Forest Heights Middle School, a large, single-story brick building spread across a hill filled with pretty, deciduous trees in a lower-income part of the city. Given that the school has been described to me as yet another Little Rock academy of despair—"Crime, fighting, drugs, discipline issues, nobody wants to send their kids there if they can help it," an administrator at another Little Rock school tells me off the record—the school's clean, smart exterior comes as a surprise.

I pull my rental car into the lot and park behind a beat-up Toyota Camry with an "Obama '08" sticker in the back windshield, a clue, perhaps, as to why "nobody" wants to send their kids to Forest Heights.

Inside the main office I receive an effusive greeting from principal Wanda Ruffins and Charlotte Brown, the school's literacy coach, parent facilitator, and the only black person I've ever met who hates Chris Rock. "His voice is so irritating!" Brown tells me.

Both women are smart, pretty, and impeccably put-together African American professionals. Both are products of Arkansas public schools. Both are outgoing and personable and accent their conservative businesswear with crucifix bling in the form of twinkle-y pendants and earrings.

"This school is 90 percent black, 80 percent of our kids receive free or reduced lunch, so we're entitled to state and federal funds," Ruffins tells me, adding with evident pride (like nearly everyone I meet at the school) that Forest Heights "made AYP" last year.

To spend ten minutes in the company of anyone remotely connected to education is to become an instant student of the acronymic jargon of the trade. ACTAP. NSLA. M-to-M. CTA. This is the buzz lingo that greases the wheels of modern education-speak.

AYP is the most important acronym in any public school in America. It stands for Adequate Yearly Progress and it's a measure of improvement in school test scores demanded by provisions in No Child Left Behind (NCLB). Schools that don't meet annual AYP goals are deemed to be "failing" and eventually subject to a series of reformation measures that in some states can wind up with the schools being turned into charter schools—tax-supported schools that private groups take over and operate without having to observe many local and state education regulations.

In April 2011, U.S. education secretary Arne Duncan seemed to set the table for public school Armageddon when he announced that 80 percent of American schools are "failing" under the guidelines of NCLB. In Florida, only 14 percent of schools made their AYP goals for the year.

Education experts such as Diane Ravitch, a New York University professor of education and U.S. assistant secretary of education from 1991 to 1993 under George H. W. Bush, warn that AYP has set "a timetable for the demolition of public education in the United States." The countdown will climax in 2014, when virtually all of the country's public schools will meet the legal federal definition of failure, thus setting them up for potential private takeover.

The most intense opponents of NCLB will tell you that the law—originally drafted largely by George W. Bush's Texas cronies and based on specious and now widely discredited achievement statistics of Texas students in the 1990s—was specifically designed to erode the power of public schools. The presumed intent was to diminish the role of "liberal" teachers in modern society and direct the vastly untapped market of private education into the hungry arms of soulless industrialists such as Rupert Murdoch. The ossified Aussified vulture is, in fact, becoming a major player in teacher union busting and the promotion and sales of Internet education. It's a conspiracy theory that's gained a surprising measure of adherents in public school circles.[14]

Arkansas, however, is playing the federal government's game, pushing its students and teachers to meet the nearly unattainable demands for improvement.

"The way we deliver education has changed," Principal Ruffins tells me. "We have a data board on every kid in the building. The board is divided into levels of proficiency. Every kid is tracked. Any time a kid fails a proficiency test, we look for root causes. We measure them every six weeks."

Jesus, talk about pressure. And surveillance! Junior high has become an even bigger gulag than when I went through it. No wonder so many kids get into drugs. It's a miracle they're not all junkies by the time they graduate.

Charlotte Brown leads me through Forest Heights's halls to Mrs. Higgins's sixth grade English class. We take up positions in the back of the room. After the bell rings signaling the start of third period the students take their seats, barely noticing me.

"They're used to having classroom observers," Brown says. "People are here watching them all the time."

Of the seventeen students in the room, fifteen are black, two are white. Mrs. Higgins is a pleasant, energetic white woman in her early thirties with a bob haircut, yellow and black print shirt, and black pants.

The classroom is standard-issue public school chic: flat green wall-to-wall carpeting covering a big, dull square room with the teacher's desk in front of rows of plastic chairs with laminated wood desktops. Fluorescent lights. White acoustic tile ceiling. Walls covered with inspirational posters, student papers, and handmade art.

A large section called the "Word Wall" is filled with vocabulary words, which appear in long rows. The choice of words strikes me as needlessly confrontational in that aggressive southern style I've almost grown accustomed to by now.

Juvenile delinquent	Intimidate
Numerous	Desperate
Apologize	Staffer
Deserve	Traitor
Imitation	Obvious

Nazi	Generous
Outhouse	Deformed
Electrocute	Tolerate
Motivate	Torture
Overthrow	Temptation
Hostile	

Mrs. Higgins introduces an exercise called "reader's theater," in which each student reads aloud a piece of dialogue from an ensemble scene out of a workbook. The scene is about a school election, with various kids running for class officer positions.

A pair of high achievers named Montrel and Kyesha get the best and longest parts. They read their lines with thespian élan, getting laughs from classmates and nods of approval from Mrs. Higgins. The rest of the kids read between a range of "get me the fuck through this as fast as possible" monotone and stuttering embarrassment.

As a grade schooler, I always found "read aloud" exercises excruciating to sit through. Breezing through a paragraph or two and dropping back into my seat was never a problem for me. Then as now, however, I found the public struggles of other kids forming words such as "education" and "exceedingly" both heartbreaking and a waste of my time.

Nevertheless, there's a positive vibe in Mrs. Higgins's classroom. Later, I'll chat with a couple of these kids at a lunch table with other students handpicked by Charlotte Brown. During this ad hoc "visiting old dude raps with the kids" session, I fire off a number of questions and get expected replies—"We hate the rule about keeping our shirts tucked in." "This school has a lot of lazy teachers." "Forest Heights has a bad reputation, we know what the rest of the schools think of us."

For me, the major revelation concerns a local delicacy called hot Cheetos and pickles. No less an authority than student body president Tonisha Grimes assures me this is a statewide favorite.

"You just stuff your Cheetos into a hollowed-out pickle and eat it," Tonisha tells me. "It's best with the Flamin' Hot Cheetos, those are the ones everyone uses."

About thirty minutes into her well-organized and largely peaceful class, the door to Mrs. Higgins's room abruptly opens. Two unhappy African American boys and one scowling mulatto kid are escorted in by the vice principal. The boys shuffle sullenly to desks at the back of the room and drop down like bags of wet cement. After the VP leaves—not a moment too soon, I can't help noticing—Mrs. Higgins reminds the threesome that they are not to sit next to each other. The boys mutter a response, then ignore several requests to split up.

Mrs. Higgins gets the rest of the class started on a team-reading exercise before returning to the malcontents and once more asking them to split up and read with different partners. The three don't bother to respond.

Mrs. Higgins and Charlotte Brown know exactly what I'm doing here—writer, observer, note taker, a guy who can make their shit-reputation school look as bad as he wants to. Clearly, I've been brought to a classroom of "good kids"—and in fact the level of order and all-around scholarship I find across the board at Forest Heights strikes me as impressive, much better than expected—but the scene with the boys is an embarrassment. Classroom observers aren't supposed to see this kind of disrespect for authority and, worse, authority's impotent response. I feel uncomfortable for Mrs. Higgins and Charlotte Brown, but Mrs. Higgins keeps at it, demanding attention and work from the three boys. She's got nerve.

The boys stare at their desks. One begins to doodle. The others do nothing in that genius way of doing nothing that kids have.

The rest of the class reads back and forth to each other. Mrs. Higgins walks around the room offering encouragement to various readers, but she keeps looking back to the three boys, painfully aware that she's lost a standoff not just in front of me, but in front of the whole room. Suddenly Montrel, star of the class, the handsome, outgoing jokester, breaks ranks and begins clowning around with a piece of masking tape over his mouth.

The kids erupt with laughter and chatter. Mrs. Higgins tells Montrel to return to his seat. He complies, but takes his time getting there. Order won't ever be completely restored before Charlotte Brown and I move on.

Charter Schools, Christian Academies, Homeschooling, and Other Ways of Undermining Minority Education in the South

The library at Forest Heights Middle School is clean. Its shelves are stocked with books with bright, crisp covers. Two rows of new Dell computers cover a set of sturdy tables that run end to end for half the length of the room.

"We're not lacking for state-of-the-art facilities," librarian Ken Sutton tells me. "We've got a lot of extra money in Little Rock because we won the desegregation lawsuit. The state has had to pour $4 million into this school."

Sutton is a casual, approachable, white male in Nikes, faded jeans, light-colored T-shirt, and glasses. His thinning hair and graying beard reveal a man not far from retirement age. Even so, he still enjoys the busy library. Kids come in and out, flip through books, work on computers, and talk just on the cusp of a little too loudly.

"I run a reading motivation program here. We try to get kids to read twenty-five books a year on their level," Sutton tells me. "For years, when black kids came into the library there were no books with African American characters in them. That's changing."

He points to a shelf filled with books from the "urban teen series" *Bluford High.*

"They love *Bluford High,*" Sutton says. "*Drama High* is another pop-lit series. It's aimed at girls."

He picks some *Drama High* titles off a rack: *Hustlin', Keep it Movin', Frenemies.*

"I don't have to direct them to *Sweet Valley High* or some lily-white Nancy Drew thing anymore," Sutton says. "This is just in the past ten years these series have come out. They've been a huge hit."

You look at Sutton's library—up-to-date, well managed, filled with energetic kids—and imagine a lot of community support backing it up.

The truth is more complicated.

Like many mostly black public schools in the South, Forest Heights Middle School remains a whipping post for angry critics of public education.

Many of these critics are proponents of charter schools who have abandoned the notion that quality public education is a viable cornerstone of the American promise. Across town, for example, strident courtroom appeals over that 1989 desegregation settlement continue even as kids check out *Bluford High* titles during lunch in the Forest Heights library.

A dangerous assault on the very idea of public education is taking place across the country, but it feels particularly virulent in the South. What kind of future society the defectors from the public school rolls envision I cannot say. However, having spent some time in the Democratic Republic of the Congo—a war-torn hellhole with one of those much coveted limited central governments, and, not coincidentally, a country in which fewer than half the school-age population goes to public school—I can say with certainty that I don't want to live there.

"What scares me is that it used to never be okay to say you don't care about public schools," says Max Brantley, editor in chief of Little Rock's weekly *Arkansas Times,* a man who has covered education in Arkansas for nearly thirty years. "Now it's not only okay to say you don't care about public schools, it's okay even to be hostile toward them.

"Public schools have been the great leveler of America. They were our great achievement. Universal education for all. Now we're ready to give up on all that."

Brantley is a brassy, heavyset, triple-chinned, six-three, no-bullshit, old-style newspaper editor in a white shirt and tan slacks. He looks like an overweight high school basketball coach. I meet him in his downtown Little Rock office, an open-floor, exposed-brick loft affair cluttered with secondhand furniture, piles of notes and papers and manila folders, and stacks of boxes with dates like "91–92," "95–96," and "01–02" scrawled on the sides in faded Sharpie.

Brantley sits in front of an ancient Dell desktop computer big enough to give you a hernia just thinking about moving it. Next to it, a giant, circular Rolodex bursts with thousands of cards.

"It's easy to demonize Little Rock because it's a majority black district," Brantley tells me. The district's student population is 68 percent black. "White people will flee black people in the South. The suburban ethos is part of the American narrative."[15]

• • •

Private schools and Christian academies—once known colloquially and more accurately across the South as "segregation academies"—are booming business in Little Rock and have been ever since popping up as legal ways for whites to get around the forced desegregation of the 1950s and 1960s. About 20 percent of Little Rock–area students now attend one of the metro area's thirty-nine private schools, up from less than 6 percent in the 1990s. According to the Arkansas Non-Public School Accrediting Association, those private schools account for an economic impact of $45 million. The largest private school in the area is Little Rock Christian Academy, which enrolled 1,327 K–12 students in 2011.[16]

Inspired by homeschool superstars such as Creation Museum founder Ken Ham, tens of thousands of other southern families have fled their public school systems in order to soak their children in the anti-intellectual sitz bath of religious denial. In Arkansas, many of these parents have found guidance in a rabble-rouser named Jerry Cox, a man who—wake me when this rerun is over—believes it's his duty to prevent you from having the right to abortion or gay sex.

After leading a successful effort to prevent the use of Arkansas public funds for abortions, Cox spearheaded a successful statewide campaign in 2004 to amend the Arkansas constitution to define marriage as the union of one man and another human being with genetically provided mammalian protuberances, to borrow one from Frank Zappa. The way these fanatics carry on about the proper use of genitalia, you'd think Thou Shalt Not Wank and Your Junk Belongs To Me were two of the Ten Commandments. Given that a good number of "Christians" can't name all ten, anyway, they might as well be.

Established in 1989 in association with James Dobson's radical "Christian" Focus on the Family outfit, Jerry Cox's Arkansas Education Alliance is the state's largest homeschool organization. The Arkansas Education Alliance falls under the aegis of the Cox-founded Family Council, whose website declares that it is "dedicated to upholding traditional values in accordance with biblical principles."

This means that a reasonable percentage of the 15,791 Arkansas children currently being homeschooled (the number has increased by an average of two hundred to seven hundred students per year since 1986) may be on track to graduate from high school unburdened by any knowledge of evolution or other global scientific consensus that can't be shoehorned into the origin fantasy of Genesis or the methed-up xenophobia and all-out genocide of Joshua.[17]

For those unfamiliar with this often overlooked gem of spiritual turpitude, the sharpened-stick murder sprees within Joshua include the indiscriminate slaughter of twelve thousand men and women (Joshua 8:25), roasting of a man on a fire (Joshua 11:11), hanging, baby killing, and city burning (pretty much all of Chapters 8 and 10), and some very pervy shit that goes down at a place called "hill of the foreskins" (Joshua 5:3). Critics of Bible-based ethics often focus their derision on the Dark Ages psychosis of Leviticus, but for unrelenting ammo to spray at KKKristian moralists, there's just as much madness and hypocrisy to mine in Joshua. (Tip for Ivy League education doctoral candidates: When searching for the headwaters of the southern achievement gap, try paddling up the river of biblical ignorance to the beachhead on which homeschool associations have established their modern-day confederacy of dunces.)

Most worrisome to the beleaguered local defenders of public schools, however, is that Little Rock is home to twelve of the state's seventeen taxpayer-supported charter schools. Each year, somewhere between 1 and 2 percent of Little Rock School District students transfer out of public schools into charter schools. Just as private institutions and homeschooling draw public resources, increasing enrollment in charter schools means less money each year allotted for those 68 percent black public schools. It also means that, more than ever, those public schools are populated with the least advantaged, most at-risk kids in the district.[18]

The most prominent of the charters, eStem Public Charter Schools, opened elementary, middle, and high schools under three separate charters in downtown Little Rock in 2008. The schools receive heavy financial and political backing from right-wing publishing magnate Walter Hussman, as well as the Walton Family Foundation, whose family founders have done fairly well with a little local business called Walmart. In the press and halls of legislature, Hussman and the Waltons have fashioned themselves as influential and bitter critics of Arkansas public schools and teacher unions.[19]

"The charter school movement is another big part of the problem," says Brantley. "It's being pushed hard by people like the Waltons and Hussmans who hate unions with every fiber of their being. A big part of charter schools is to bust unions. *Columbia Journalism Review* online did a piece on media coverage of the school reform movement. The money has co-opted the press without them knowing it. They get a free pass because they're rich and rich people's shit don't stink."

"Michelle Rhee's whole narrative was built on crap; she lied," Brantley says of the champion of school reform featured in the 2010 documentary *Waiting for "Superman."* "The Waltons, Gates, Hussmans, the thing that drives me crazy is all the mega-studies show that charters on balance get the same results as public schools."

Brantley is right about the studies, both nationally and in Little Rock. In *The Death and Life of the Great American School System*, her 2010 criticism of the current academic craze for performance testing, NYU prof Diane Ravitch cites study after study in smashing the myth that students in charter schools perform better on achievement tests than kids in public schools.[20]

Charter schools aren't unique to the South, but as Ravitch explained to me in an email, conservative states tend to respond most positively to their message. That makes the South prime ground for the further degradation of public schools.

In Little Rock, the tension between charter school advocates and public school teachers and administrators is regular front-page news. The toxicity of the debate is heightened by classic southern tinctures of union busting, congenital suspicion of the academic community, and, most corrosive of all, skin color.

"Desegregation isn't working," Ken Sutton tells me in the Forest Heights library, this more than fifty years after the federal government brought troops to Little Rock to enforce desegregation. "You can't make people put their child in a school they don't want them in. Little Rock has gone from mostly white to mostly black. I feel a little bit . . . (thoughtful pause) . . . I'm conservative but I feel like conservatives have abandoned the public schools for charter schools and private academies. They have no say here. It's all liberals. No offense."

"Why have conservatives quit on public schools?" I ask.

"We lost a lot of conservative evangelicals when it became common knowledge that there were lesbian and homosexual teachers on staff. This has been going on ten years or so when they came out of the closet or whatever you want to call it."

"I'm trying to pin some of these problems on a particularly backward southern outlook on education," I say. "No offense."

"I don't know how much being in the South has to do with it. I don't know. There's still that, you know, black-white . . . it's still an issue. I don't know how to say it specifically, but it's an issue."

"What's the issue exactly?"

"I was a librarian for an elementary school for two or three years. Two hundred and seventy kids. Two hundred and sixty-nine were black. Four-and five-year-olds. I had kids coming to me who had no concept of books. Didn't know what a book was. Literally had never seen a book!

"So you start with a gap in kindergarten or first grade, they start behind. No parent reading to them at night. You'd be amazed at the significant percentage of parents that just don't care that their kids are getting bad grades or get an F on a test."

"I'm sure there are plenty of criminally disinterested white parents, as well," I say.

"I used to be a ninth grade science teacher at a predominantly black school. Once, I asked how many African American students in here think I'm prejudiced toward you because I'm white and you're black. Out of twenty-five kids, sixteen raised their hands. That's the environment."

The Return of Dr. Charles Hopson, a Red Lobster Feast, and the Never-Ending Crusade for Minority Equality

In a suburb across town from Forest Heights sits the headquarters of the Pulaski County Special School District, one of three districts that serve the Greater Little Rock area. Inside the nondescript office building, new superintendent Dr. Charles Hopson moves between rooms with purposeful yet unhurried strides. He interrupts meetings to take calls or read texts, motions silently to a secretary to bring him a file, and, like a savvy politician, finds a few minutes to shake hands with every visitor, look them in the eye, and pay attention to their problems.

Dr. Hopson sees himself as a savior of education in the South, a visionary in a region famously lacking for vision. A rail-thin, charismatic African American who grew up in segregated Arkansas, he offers himself as a counternarrative to the common assumption of a system perpetually beating down the black man.

As Dr. Hopson will happily tell you, he applied himself in school, sweated through years of grad study, took advantage of the opportunity he'd earned, and moved to the green hills of the Pacific Northwest to help run schools for the children of enlightened whites. He enjoyed what he did in Portland, Oregon, so much that he decided to return to Arkansas armed with the kind of knowledge that will bring a brighter future—about which he is endlessly bullish—to his home state.

"I've had experiences in Oregon that, because of the liberal context there, allowed me to experience a global outlook and leadership that does not exist in this state," Dr. Hopson tells me. "A few years ago I was involved in getting Portland public schools, K through post-secondary, to provide Mandarin Chinese and other global languages in schools. Coming back to Arkansas it felt like being in an episode of *Star Trek* where you have lived in the future and now you've gone back to the past."

Not everyone is happy with Dr. Hopson's methods for school reform, which include publicly confronting issues of race. One of the first topics Dr. Hopson thrust into the faces of his neighbors was the disproportionate disciplining of African American males.

Since taking command of his district, Dr. Hopson has been a controversial local figure. In the fifty minutes I sit across from him at the large, oval conference table in his spacious office, I get a sampling of the black-man-with-a-degree tautology that has unsettled a number of Little Rockheads.

"We are now fifty-five years past *Brown v. Board of Education* and you see segregation re-created to the degree that existed before *Brown v. Board* was enacted," he says. "Systematically, we have re-created that.

"This new South we think has evolved is still rooted in the South of the past. We live in this illusory world where we think we're getting along. We're engaged in courageous conversations about race, but race is still at the heart of the Old South. Until we confront its impact on the narratives and paradigm for systemic inequity so much will remain entrenched and continue to re-create the Old South paradigm. The plantation mentality still has roots that still play a vital role in our society, and covertly in other states."

Ten minutes of exposure to Dr. Hopson's academic blam-blam-blam is enough to reduce segregation deniers to the level of Amway salesmen. There remains in the South, however, a sizable percentage of citizens who simply refuse to acknowledge major problems with their schools.

In an astonishingly out-of-touch 2011 editorial that appeared in the Hussman-owned *Arkansas Democrat-Gazette*, the state's largest newspaper, Andy Brack, president and chairman of South Carolina–based think tank Center for a Better South, described southern schools as something just short of a puppies-and-rainbows love fest. Brack's Betty Crocker absurdities were pillowed out beneath the headline "My, How Things Have Changed."

> These days, students across the South attend integrated classes with white, brown and black students. Although some schools may be more white or black than others, integration is accepted and has become part of our culture—so much so that news stories of racism are considered abnormal. Today, a black family or professional can travel—even at night—without worrying about being refused a hotel room or a place at a restaurant's table.[21]

Whoa! Even *at night* blacks can now travel in the South without worry of being lynched? I take everything back. I had no idea African Americans had it so cushy in the twenty-first century.

Several months before the publication of "My, How Things Have Changed," I'd actually met Brack in Washington, D.C., following a session he'd moderated on environmentalism at a "Future of the South" symposium sponsored by Little Rock–based *Oxford American* magazine. Brack had begun his session by bounding onstage with a hearty "How y'all doing?" and demanding from the audience "a big ol' amen!"

Brack seemed like a nice enough guy and he wasn't completely delusional about his beloved South—"People in the South are scared to think outside the box," he said—but I wish he could have attended the meal I had in Montgomery with two African American students from Alabama State University.

I'd met twenty-three-year-old Pierre at the Montgomery Embassy Suites, where he was working as a valet. When he told me he was a senior working toward his education degree at Alabama State, I invited him to dinner after his shift was over. I told him I'd pick up the tab at any place in town he wanted to go.

We meet at a Red Lobster at six o'clock. Pierre brings along DeShawn, a thirty-year-old schoolteacher working on his doctorate, also at Alabama State. Over a Fisherman's Platter and Admiral's Feast, the pair describe school conditions throughout the South that mirror what I'd later find in Arkansas—though with much less funding.

"The naked truth is that high schools are segregated everywhere I've seen," Pierre tells me. "The only white kids in public high schools are the ones from the children's home or who are just plain poor. Most of the white kids in Selma go to private institutions."

"I've taught in Tuskegee, at a suburban school in Atlanta, and here in Montgomery," adds DeShawn. "It's not the kids' desire that is lacking, it's that the resources and public support aren't plentiful enough."

In a red Polo shirt and pressed jeans, clean-cut, smiling Pierre wouldn't look out of place onstage at Eddie Long's church in Georgia. DeShawn is his revolutionary counterpoint, a short, slithery customer who doesn't take off his sunglasses the entire time we're inside Red Lobster—he's clearly suspicious of my motives.

"All the hatred toward Obama down here, it's not racism, it's placism," DeShawn says. "Obama is acting out of his place. An African American Negro is not supposed to be carrying himself as if he's better than white folk."

DeShawn tells me he's from a single- and sometimes no-parent home.

"My mother and grandmother used and sold drugs," he says. "My brother is doing twenty-five to life for that same story line."

"Why didn't you end up like that?" I ask.

"I saw the mistakes my brother made. If you know what the bottom smells like, you put yourself in a better position."

DeShawn is a "reading and writing ed specialist" (this sounds like a fancy way of saying "English teacher," but I keep my smart mouth shut) who spits out ideas and opinions in bundles. He's a genuine example of a once common and now vanishing species known as the working-class intellectual, a blue-collar champion who not only isn't afraid of books, but who embraces them with the religious conviction of self-improvement.

"Resources are our school's biggest plight," DeShawn says for the fourth or fifth time. "We can't compete in today's technical world with the resources we have to teach with and kids have to train with. Most of our kids have no computers. It minimizes everything we can do."

This mixture of frustration and hope I hear from educators—particularly African Americans—is consistent throughout my travels in the South.

"Old patterns of the South persist," Dr. Hopson tells me before I leave his Little Rock office. "But it's no longer valid to blame the oppression of the past for the failures of the present."

Dr. Hopson believes he is at the tip of a movement that will break the cycle of racism and close the regional and race-based achievement gaps. The problems he faces, however, seem so vast, too much a part of the DNA of the region. Having gone into our meeting thinking he might have the answers I've been searching for, or at least some optimism to impart, I end up shuffling out of Hopson's office feeling the prospects for change to be even more distant.

Dr. Hopson is intelligent and genuine and eager, and I wish him well. The man is trying. At the moment, though, he doesn't seem to have any more solutions than Pierre or DeShawn or the Waltons or Walter Hussman. Or even think tank dilettante Andy Brack, for that matter, who in Washington, D.C., memorably told me, "Fixing the South is like fixing a clunker—you know it's going to break down again."

African Americans' Second-Worst Enemy, and Closing the Best School in Biloxi

Given the obstacles it faces and the history that clings to its fabric like a cotton-eyed wraith, it's tempting for the liberal-minded out-of-towner to give the African American community a pass for its perpetual unwillingness to embrace education, and to accept as inevitable its sad fate at the bottom of the academic ladder. At that "Future of the South" symposium in D.C., I watched repeatedly as white speakers went to painstaking lengths to assure their audience that when they spoke about poor, uneducated southerners (i.e., blacks), they were being neither condescending nor judgmental.

"Uneducated does not mean unintelligent," they reminded the crowd, with academic condescension.

The trouble is, addressing southern academic inferiority in any honest way requires the well-intentioned whitey to flirt with racist stereotypes by admitting to generations of self-defeating behavior and egregious parenting by African Americans. And admitting that while the black community gives plenty of lip service to its sad lack of emphasis on education, on a large scale it does too little about it. More than just eerily reminiscent of W. J. Cash's denunciation of Old South planters who didn't keep a single book in their homes save the Bible, librarian Ken Sutton's story about African American children arriving at school without any concept of what a book was is as woeful an illustration of the endless cycle of black neglect of education in the South as one might muster.

At the African American Wallace Creations barbershop in Laurens, South Carolina, Christopher Williams told me, "There's a sad saying, I don't know if you know it, but all of us here do: If you don't want a black man to learn something, put it in a book."

Horace Smith, the African American director of board development for the Arkansas School Boards Association, tells a story highlighting the same black indifference toward perfect margins.

"I did a tour of our local schools with education delegates from eleven African countries," Smith tells me in his downtown Little Rock office. "They were appalled at how lazy and unmotivated our African American students were. These were education professionals in Africa. They could not believe that our students would complain to them about the amount of work they were expected to do, about studying, about the lack of materials. Can you imagine an American student sitting in front of a computer telling an African schoolteacher how tough he's got it?"

Fatalistic attitudes aren't the only thing that often make African Americans their own second-worst enemy. (If you can't guess who's number one, we'll get there in a minute.) Segregated schools might have been created by whites, but blacks have very much helped re-create the pre–*Brown v. Board* conditions that prevail in Arkansas and other areas of the South.

In one of the most frustrating scenes from that damning HBO documentary *Little Rock Central: 50 Years Later,* Minnijean Brown, one of the 1957 Little Rock Nine, visits a Central High classroom in 2006 only to discover that the room is neatly self-segregated on racial lines, all the whites sitting on one side, all the blacks sitting on the other. When she expresses horror over this arrangement—"My God, this room disturbs the hell out of me!"—it's the black students who immediately challenge her by defending segregation as a matter of "personal comfort." And it's a black student who is shown sleeping through Brown's emotional lecture recounting the Little Rock Nine's struggles for equality in the 1950s.[22]

Classroom apathy is an issue with all ethnic groups, but, not to get all Cosby here, should black students be more free of criticism than any other? Isn't the culture of low expectations for African American achievement in some ways just as insidious as more overt forms of racism?

The most outrageous accounts of incorrigible southern African American student behavior that I come across are from the Mississippi Teacher Corps. The MTC is a two-year program that recruits college graduates from around the country to teach in Mississippi schools, primarily in the African American Mississippi Delta. Wide-eyed liberal education majors are promised teacher certifications and "the opportunity to make a difference in the lives of students in one of the poorest areas of the country."

To anyone over twenty-five, this sort of language is a dead giveaway to a term of deprivation and misery, but college grads are an endlessly naive bunch who believe that suffering will transform them into the kind of well-rounded human beings their suburban upbringings failed to make them.

The MTC's website advertises an experience "modeled after the Peace Corps," but the painfully honest Web postings from valiant young educators recoiling from a taste of Delta life suggests something closer to survival school on Parris Island.

Mixed with the usual grumbling about shabby facilities, underfunded programs, and local administrators phoning it in is some truly entertaining venom directed at the students themselves. Every child may be precious, but Delta children appear to be by far the least precious in the world, a group that deserves not only the scorn heaped upon it in anonymous, three-martini teacher blogs, but the desperate adult lives of reeking poverty for which their lack of adolescent responsibility and crappy parents have set them up.

"My kids just bombed a really easy test and I'm glad," writes one unrepentant young instructor, who seems to have given up pretty quickly on making a difference in the life of anything except perhaps a bottle of Jack Daniel's. "They don't ever do anything, and they deserve to have failed. . . . I take no responsibility for the lack of learning that's happening here. I've done my job, am doing my job, and can't do anything more. I know that now, so F*** You 75% of my students. I love you, but F*** you."

"They threw my assignments on the floor," moans another broken soldier. "I'm not allowed to give detentions until tomorrow. . . . I hate what I'm doing in this fairly large, encompassing sense. They threw paper towels at me behind my back in the restroom."

"My district policy is a mandatory 80% pass rate on tests, and my Geometry classes had 28+ students in each," cries another. "They don't work. They don't care. They copy other people's work. They don't study. If I force them to do their own work they don't think on their own so I get driven completely f*** nuts doing and explaining everything. If I let them work in groups, no one works; no one does anything except the really motivated people, and everyone else just copies. They don't learn anything, then the test scores are bad. If tests are too bad, I have to retest. They'll fail on Monday because they won't study the study guide. Or maybe they will. F*** this."

Alarming as all this may sound to the lay observer, for anyone who has toiled a single day in the public schools trenches, it is pure cathartic gold.[23]

But don't think this sort of thing is confined to the impoverished backwaters. Every bit as sad as the Delta school blues is the report that came out in summer 2011 revealing that in order to raise its general competency test scores, principals and educators in nearly 80 percent of Atlanta Public Schools (which are three-quarters black and poor) didn't even bother to retest. They simply falsely inflated their students' scores.

Almost 180 principals and educators were involved in the cheating scandal that dated to 2001. Even so, months after news of the disgrace broke, the Atlanta school system's official website was still touting itself as "one of the top-performing urban school systems in America."

"When students pass through our doors," Atlanta Public Schools' site read, "we give them the confidence, social skills and intellectual capacity required to successfully compete in college and in the global marketplace."[24]

And then, just when you're about ready to call bullshit on every tired "white man keeping us down" excuse proffered by African American slackers, or roll your eyes at the Nat X militancy of scatterguns like DeShawn and his Jesse-esque "racism not placism" bon mots, you come across no-fucking-way stories about places like Nichols Elementary School in East Biloxi, Mississippi.

In 2010, the Biloxi Public School District voted to shut down Nichols and send all of its students to a lower-rated school for the 2011 academic year. This, despite the fact that Nichols was rated as Biloxi's top-performing elementary school that year: it ranked sixteenth out of 432 public elementary schools in Mississippi, was the only Biloxi school to earn the state's prestigious GreatSchools designation, and produced the state's 2009 Teacher of the Year.

Each of the school board's majority white members voted to close the school, citing budgetary concerns. Shuttering the city's top school, it explained, would save the district $400,000 a year. Despite public outcry, the board held firm to its decision, even when it was revealed that the school district was actually operating with a $10 million surplus.

Nichols Elementary's student body is—or, rather, was—90 percent black. The school is a landmark dating to 1886, the heart of a historic African American neighborhood, widely viewed as the social glue holding together a sense of pride and achievement within the East Biloxi community.

Livid, yet undeterred by the school board's decision to close the school, African American and other activists went to work to find a solution. Rather than waiting for their Superman, they went looking for one. Superman appeared in the form of the Kellogg Foundation, which offered the school district a $1.5 million grant to be paid out over three years, enough to keep Nichols in operation and out of the red.

The city's highest achieving elementary school had been saved. Except for one thing. The school board refused to consider the Kellogg proposal. Their decision was final. No further argument would be heard. Nichols was shut down for good at the conclusion of the 2010 school year.

"What kind of city closes its best school?" demanded an enraged Bill Stallworth, Biloxi's only African American member of the City Council, a body with no legal power to overturn school board decisions.

When Stallworth contended that Nichols was closed "to make sure that white schools in this district never have to be embarrassed by being outperformed by a black school again," it was difficult to reach any other conclusion. Uneducated may not always mean unintelligent, but as a great product of southern public schools once famously said, "Stupid is as stupid does."[25]

The same quote might be used to explain the conclusion of the search for a new superintendent in Little Rock.

Dickseedisfunkshun . . . But at Least the Floors Are Clean

In April 2011, after two and a half months of searching, Dr. Tom Jacobson forwarded to the Little Rock School District Board of Education the names of three candidates he and his executive recruitment firm of McPherson & Jacobson considered worthy of the position of superintendent of schools. The three finalists were a school superintendent from Springfield, Illinois, a deputy superintendent from Memphis, and the director of a school program targeting minority and low-income children in Seattle. Each was invited to travel to Little Rock in May to tour district facilities; meet with employees, parents, and students; and sit for a formal interview with the board.

Dr. Tom felt confident that each of the three fit the criteria he'd gathered from the exhaustive community meetings he'd chaired in Little Rock. Given their impressive collective experience with school reform, he believed any of the three would be up for the enormous task of repairing Little Rock schools. He was proud of the job he and his staff had done on behalf of the city. One night in Little Rock may have put Grand Funk Railroad in a haze, but Dr. Tom had kept his eyes on the prize, withstood multiple evenings of public outcry, and delivered a trio of committed, highly qualified candidates. Little Rock schools might yet have a shot at genuine reform.

On May 23, 2011, having taken the full measure of McPherson & Jacobson's eighty-three-page Stakeholder Input Report and the firm's candidate recommendations, the Little Rock school board announced its choice for new superintendent. He was Dr. Morris Holmes, the currently serving interim superintendent of the Little Rock School District, a local man who'd taken over when the previous superintendent had left the position before the end of her contract. In short, Little Rock rejected the recommendations of its consultant and did nothing to change the direction of the top post in its public education system.

Dr. Holmes gave a public address in which he outlined his strategic vision for Little Rock schools. Literacy and attendance would be his twin pillars of reform. Local media covered his mini-presser, but the news generated little attention and almost no public discussion.[26]

"There was virtually no reaction to Morris's selection except some scattered warm words for a guy who is well known here and enjoys a generally positive reputation," Max Brantley of the *Arkansas Times* emailed me after the announcement. "The consultant money was wasted, in the end. Internal board politics forced them to turn to Holmes as a compromise choice. It's somewhat complicated to explain, but it's a mixture of racial and gender politics and settlement of old scores."

The three McPherson & Jacobson candidates vanished from the news, presumably to pursue careers in more reform-minded districts.

Following the announcement, I called Dr. Tom in Omaha to ask what had happened behind the curtains in Little Rock. On the phone, I found him far more relaxed than he'd been when we'd met at the public forum at J. A. Fair High School. We talked for almost forty-five minutes and had such a pleasant conversation that I started to feel crappy about writing those dickish little comments about him in my notebook several months earlier.

"Politics very much came into play," Dr. Tom told me about the Little Rock hiring. "We lost good candidates because the Little Rock board meetings are video-streamed on the Internet and a couple of our final candidates watched some board meetings and chose to withdraw themselves for consideration as a result of viewing."

"Based on what?" I asked.

Dr. Tom hesitated. The superintendent search is a matter of public record, but it's still a sensitive topic and he's got a business to protect.

"Let it just be said that they were able to watch the board in action and based on what they saw chose to withdraw their names from the selection process. When we got down to the end there was only one candidate willing to interview and they showed up for the interview and had a good interview. When we started this search we were told that Dr. Holmes was not a candidate."

I asked what he thought of the hire.

"It's probably the best solution they had at the time. It'll give them a chance to regroup for two years."

"Is it disappointing to do all that work and then have your recommendations go to waste?"

"It's extremely frustrating to put that much time and effort into a service and then have the people who purchased your service ignore what you are telling them and not listen to you. It doesn't happen often, but it's extremely frustrating."

At about the same time as I was speaking with Dr. Tom, another mud-crusted shoe was dropping on Little Rock schools. In May 2011, a federal judge in Arkansas ordered the state to stop payment on most of the $70 million in annual funds the city's three school districts had been awarded in that 1989 decision stemming from desegregation battles dating to the 1950s.

Explaining his unanticipated decision in a 110-page ruling, U.S. District Court judge Brian Miller, who is African American, declared that Little Rock schools were now successfully desegregated, as defined by the federal court, and, thus, no longer entitled to desegregation funds. In a somewhat contradictory comment, Judge Miller, a 2007 George W. Bush court nominee, said that the funds intended to end desegregation were actually serving as an incentive not to achieve desegregation.

The loss of the $70 million immediately imperiled Little Rock's magnet schools and inter-district transfer programs, key components in efforts to bring minority and lower-income students into higher-performing schools.

"There is no way for the LRSD to adjust its budget to accommodate to [the] loss of $38 million,* more than 10 percent of its total budget, without a substantial negative impact on the education of over 25,000 students," Little Rock School District lawyers wrote in their appeal of the decision. "Teachers [will] have to be laid off and there is doubt the district could continue to operate magnet schools."

In June, a higher federal court issued a stay on Judge Miller's ruling, thereby allowing the desegregation funds temporarily to resume flowing into the districts, and bringing the promise that the school year would begin as planned in August. Nevertheless, Little Rock School Board president Melanie Fox acknowledged the certainty of bitter court battles to come in the nation's longest-running desegregation case, telling the *Arkansas Times* that the district was already planning "for the eventual loss of the money." You may be able to fight the status quo in the South, Fox seemed to be saying, but in the end, you know you ain't gonna win.

As Professor Jay Barth of Little Rock–area Hendrix College told me, "I don't think that much change happens over the long haul. State governments in the South have a lot of power."[27]

Incredibly, or perhaps predictably, depending on how much experience you have with southern education, the wheels kept coming off the old

---

* The other $32 million to be deleted from the budgets of Little Rock's two other school districts.

Little Rock schools clunker as spring baked into summer. On June 20, the Arkansas Department of Education moved to dissolve the entire Pulaski County Special School District and fired its crusading superintendent, Dr. Charles Hopson. The decision came after a legislative audit exposed a district in deep financial distress, due in part to more than a decade of mismanagement and a former high school principal's involvement in a bribery scheme that most likely lost the district part of its share of that same $70 million in desegregation funds.

Dr. Jerry Guess, a white administrator from Camden, about a hundred miles south of Little Rock, was handpicked by Arkansas education commissioner Tom Kimbrell to take over for Dr. Hopson.

"I have been an educator for thirty-four years in Arkansas, having spent thirty-three years in the same place, so I think I bring a message of stability," Guess told a small gathering of media in his woodsy, rocking chair drawl, before laying out his immediate priorities for the upcoming school year. "Bus routes, textbooks, desks, making sure cafeterias are prepared, and floors are cleaned."[28]

In barely more than a month, Little Rock schools had scotched the recommendations of one of the largest executive search firms in the country; tentatively lost millions in funding; dissolved a district; ousted its most charismatic campaigner for school reform; and replaced him with a paragon of southern status quo who promised to keep the floors mopped. I wasn't close enough to the action to know whether Dr. Hopson bore any measure of guilt for his school district's financial woes, but speaking in confidence, every Little Rock administrator near the situation told me some version of the same story.

"Dysfunction is the name of the game on the local boards," said one. "They are deeply divided between what I'd call 'pro–public school and pro–teacher union' members aligned with many grassroots community leaders and especially the African American community, and 'pro–charter school and anti–teacher union' members aligned with the white business community."

"Hopson became a victim of political pressures from both a dysfunctional school board and a zealous legislative audit committee," emailed another. "He was directly confronting some racial issues that needed to be addressed. However, that made a number of people very uncomfortable and contributed to his demise."

"Dr. Hopson is a quality person, we did that search that found him," said Dr. Tom, who by now I'd come around to seeing as a brother in arms in the work to expose educational deficiencies in the South. "He was fired for absolutely political reasons and by political forces."

When I finally reach Dr. Hopson by phone, I find him as upbeat and talkative as ever. He's already got feelers out to school districts in several other states—some in the South—and is confident that his record in Little Rock will help him land another job.

"Ninety percent of what the state asked us to do, we did it, but there were other interests involved that stood to benefit from the district being placed under state control," he tells me. "You mainly have one faction of the district that wants to secede from the current district and this new arrangement helps forward their cause."

"Did your outspoken stance on issues related to race in Little Rock play into your dismissal?" I ask.

"The race factor did play into it. I was not a status quo superintendent. When the board hired me I told them I was going to be a systemic equity leader and I was going to push for every student to be treated equally and it was going to be uncomfortable and it was going to be turbulent, but if we were able to stay the course we'd be better for it in the future."

"What was the toughest part of the year you were on the job?" I ask, impressed that a guy who just got very publicly canned doesn't sound sort of drunk. After getting fired from *Travelocity* magazine in 2001, I spent three contemplative months in my backyard listening to Belle and Sebastian and building a teahouse.

"For me it was the pain of looking at the inequality of the facilities and the way race and poverty were reliable predictors of the quality of facilities students had," Hopson says. "That was painful for me to witness and it became a moral imperative for me to take that on."

"What do you foresee for the future of students in Little Rock?"

"That is going to depend on the leadership. If the leadership is status quo, you're going to continue to get what you've gotten for the past thirty years."

"How does your experience in Arkansas compare with your experiences as an administrator in Oregon?"

"All boards have political elements everywhere you go, but what has happened with this board, there has been a southern flavor and context to how things happen in Arkansas.

"The sad thing is the students will suffer because, I will say it, the status quo is not working for black students in Arkansas. It is not working for white students in Arkansas. Our students have to be globally competitive and we're going to have to bring in opportunities and ideas from outside the borders of Arkansas so that those students are graduating with a global perspective and competitiveness that will allow them to excel for themselves and for this country. And the status quo here might not change for a long time."

Same as It Ever Was: Little Rock Central High School

Before leaving town, I pay a visit to Little Rock Central High School. Still a functioning school with approximately 2,400 students, Central High is also a National Historic Site, part of the National Parks Service. This means the first place you stop when you visit is the one-story Park Service Visitors Center, which sits kitty-corner from the school.

It's a strange way to enter a school. A uniformed ranger greets you at the front desk, the same type of employee who might direct you to the bathrooms in the Smoky Mountains or tell you not to feed the elk in Yellowstone.

"Of almost four hundred properties in the national parks system service, this is the only working school that is also a national landmark," the ranger tells me, before scuttling off to wrangle a busload of shouting and shoving black elementary school field trippers who have just arrived from Memphis.

I wander around the visitors center checking out displays on the "Three Weeks in September" that put Little Rock on the world's shitlist in 1957: accent-drenched audio testimonials from locals involved in the Little Rock

Nine drama; photos of U.S. Army troops wading through angry crowds; interpretive signage recounting the showdown between President Dwight Eisenhower and Arkansas governor Orval "Top Five Most Racist-Sounding Name Ever" Faubus; and black-and-white CBS News footage featuring an impressively hard-assed Mike Wallace reporting on the tumult and, phenomenally, looking and sounding not all that much different in 1957 than he did before he died in 2012. I'm going to go ahead right now and call Wallace the most underrated American journalist of the video age. Guy was a stone-cold, white-boy motherfucker long before Anderson Cooper got his hands on his first blow-dryer.

Statistically speaking, Little Rock Central High is today an exemplar of integration—the student body is approximately 54 percent black, 43 percent white. However, as most locals will tell you, and as Minnijean Brown discovered when she returned to the school in 2006, there are functionally two Centrals, one white, one black.[29]

Few officials in the district are eager to acknowledge the "two Centrals" system, but the awkward truth pops up in all sorts of unexpected ways. In 2008, a minor controversy arose when the committee organizing the Class of '98's ten-year reunion fixed a cost of $150 to attend the festivities. The ticket price effectively segregated the reunion between those who could afford to attend (whites, mostly) and those who could not (blacks, mostly). The back-and-forth between the two camps became nasty—a "meltdown," according to a former Central High student close to the situation.

Across the street from the visitors center, the large brown and white brick facade with towers, porticos, and Greek statuary makes Central High one of the most impressive high schools ever built in this country. Erected in 1926–27, the building itself is a commanding architectural testament to the civic centrality of education. Covering two city blocks and including 150,000 square feet of floor space, its imposing Collegiate Gothic style recalls flapper-era, art deco extravagance.

Inside, the school's period charm is meticulously preserved. Classic schoolhouse-shade light fixtures hang from ceilings. Large gray clocks—literally, old school!—hang on the walls. Square floor tiles are waxed to a brilliant tea-colored shine. The huge auditorium looks like an old Hollywood theater, with heavy wooden seat backs and ornate touches around an expansive proscenium. An enormous trophy case is stuffed with ribbons and hardware, evidence of Central's standing as the most prestigious academic and athletic high school in the state. No ankle-length wool skirts or ducktails are found roaming the halls, but students move between classes in the neat, orderly fashion of future community leaders.

I spend about twenty minutes inside the school—quite enough for me, I never really liked the oppressive vibe of these places—before heading back outside to take in the sharp spring air and vivid blue sky. With my back to the three sets of double doors at Central's main entrance, I look over a small reflecting pool and manicured lawn to the gas station directly across the street.

It's a gas station worth looking at—an immaculate, old-timey terracotta Mobil station painted white and crowned with red Spanish roof tiles. Like the school, every detail of the station has been lovingly preserved in its 1957 state, right down to the vintage red and white gas pumps with the old Pegasus logo below rotary pricer dials, and the large blue lettering above the service bay spelling "Mobilubrication." Not a stroke of paint, not a blade of grass, is out of place.

Standing on the steps of a school surveying the place where one of the most emblematic events in the history of the South took place, you can't help being impressed by the nostalgia of the scene. And the care and commitment the people have taken to see that everything here remains exactly the same as it ever was.

"You're Grounded . . . Forever!" The Scary Ramifications of Academic Failure

"Did you know that there are more people with genius IQs living in China than there are people of any kind living in the United States?"

Uttered by Jesse Eisenberg, playing Facebook cofounder Mark Zuckerberg, that line strikes the ominous opening note of 2010's *The Social*

Network, a movie that turns less upon the axis of social media than it does on the age-old human dread of being left crushed, broken, and humiliated by your former friends. (See also *Gone With the Wind*.)[30]

Lurking behind all of the hand-wringing about test scores, charter schools, Mississippi elementary schools, and the ability of Arkansas sixth graders to impress the visiting northerner during sessions of reader's theater, is a dark fear about the future of the country. The fear felt in all fifty states is typically expressed something like this: America is a declining power whose wealth, influence, and world leadership in the areas of commerce, politics, and all-around ass kicking face a mortal threat from ascending powers, upon whom the nation has become increasingly dependent for help with problems requiring technical or scientific solutions.

Chief among these threats is China—godless commies who have tricked us into emptying our national treasury in return for threadbare clothing, easily broken home appliances, chintzy trinkets, and iPhones (hey, at least we're getting something cool out of the deal). It doesn't help that the Chinese also happen to be better than us at things like math and capitalism, and in possession of terrifyingly motivated kids who probably now read more English-language books than our own. And with higher comprehension scores!

By out-mathing, out-computering, and out-fucking us—for by sheer dint of their billions the Chinese will inevitably demolish us, assuming their lead-based squirt guns don't do the job first—Chinese ascendancy foretells the dismal end of our carefree lives of fifty-five-hour workweeks and shitty health care ameliorated by high-def TV coverage of preemptive predator drone strikes and international wars that, to be glass half full, we still do rather well at producing, directing, and starring in.

In the face of this sort of synthesized media fearmongering, I'm generally able to keep my wits about me. I've recently spent some time in China and for all the irrational worry about that country "taking over the U.S.," it's comforting to remember that only on very rare occasions do established cultures ever get "taken over" by foreigners. The United States flattened Japan with two atomic bombs, rewrote its constitution, and occupied the country with its military, and sixty-some years later the Japanese are still eating sushi, dressing their schoolboys in quasi-military uniforms, and obsessing over godawful music squeaked out by prepubescent pop "idols" adored by fifteen-year-old girls and fifty-year-old men alike.

Even so, it'd be foolish to ignore the fact that dynasties fall and that it's never fun to be a part of one when that happens. I mean, who would you rather be, Mao Zedong or Chiang Kai-shek? Buster Douglas or Mike Tyson? Lady Gaga or whatever sparkle-titted, semi-talented, bondage-wear "maverick" hack in a conical bra that came before her captured our collective attention for forty-five minutes?

Unless we repair our rapidly Balkanizing education system, it's going to get harder each year to sustain the level of heating oil, air-conditioning, and spicy-nacho-meat-lover's-pizza consumption I've grown so attached to. I don't want the American Dream to die on my watch and I don't think it has to. Without a significant upgrade to our public education system, however, it very well might.

"It is clear from a demographic perspective that our future lies in our minority populations—success or failure in minority education means success or failure for the U.S."

These are the words of Dr. Steve Murdock, director of the U.S. Census Bureau from 2007 to 2009, former state demographer of Texas, and current professor of sociology at Rice University in Houston. I called Murdock to talk about the spooky prospect of the rapidly growing South educating a very large percentage of Americans in the coming decades. Murdock was willing to meet my southern paranoia only halfway. Still, coming from a Texan hearing criticism from a guy from Alaska, I felt like any concession to regional ineptitude constituted a small, personal victory.

"When you look at performance in education we're simply not succeeding, more so in the South because there are more African Americans and Hispanics in the South," Murdock said. "But African American and Hispanic education isn't being done well anyplace in America on a large scale. Los Angeles, Chicago, New York. This is an American problem, not a southern problem."

Murdock is right, education is a national problem, just like obesity, spiraling health care costs, and whatever hideous noncelebrity E! television is currently pumping into the national psyche. But after touring Little Rock schools and canvassing administrators, teachers, parents, students, and valets named Pierre across the South, I've come to the conclusion that the South is the least likely region of the country to solve the riddle of modern education. If you want to see the shadow that underperforming southern schools cast across the rest of country, take a trip to cities like Memphis or Little Rock and behold how much these places are arranged along the lines of Third World horror shows: wide streets lined with opulent, plantation-style homes sitting just around the block from apocalyptic Negro wastelands.

Because of its own self-defeating approach to the issue, the South simply won't come to terms with the North over matters of education anytime soon. The recent attempts of visionary southern governors to break historic cycles of parsimony by adequately funding public schools emphasizes the point.

Progressive efforts to overhaul education by the likes of Arkansas governor Bill Clinton (in office 1979–81 and 1983–92), Mississippi governor Ray Mabus (1988–92), and Alabama governor Bob Riley (2003–11) all failed before the immutable "political realities [that] put roadblocks in front of virtually any effort to raise money for the schools, outside of the regressive mechanism of a sales tax increase," to quote the 2011 book *Taxing the Poor* by Katherine J. Newman and Rourke L. O'Brien. In Arkansas, Clinton's experience was nothing new, reminiscent as it was of failed efforts at sweeping education reform by territorial governor John Pope in 1833 and governor Sidney McMath in 1949, among others.[31]

Southern states simply do not believe in funding education to the extent that northern states do. That's not a value judgment or insult—it's documented fact. The difference this makes in the ongoing concerns of society are enormous; the gulf it creates, significant. Unless we're willing to separate ourselves from our lowest common academic denominator, we'll forever be a nation sitting around waiting for the slowest kid in the class to catch up. Or at least learn to properly enunciate "education."

$$$

CHAPTER 6

Economics: Florida, Texas, the U.S. Military, and the Fiscal Future of Secession

January 1, 2017, Atlanta, Georgia

As a cloudless, blue-sky morning turns into an unseasonably warm Sunday afternoon, an estimated crowd of more than two million surrounds the Georgia state capitol. Martin Luther King Jr. Drive, Washington Street, Capitol Avenue, and all other roadways around Capitol Square have been closed to traffic since New Year's Eve, allowing revelers to dance, drink, sing, and emote in a semi-controlled corridor around the capitol's mammoth gilded dome.

Across the shoulder of the Statue of Liberty replica that stands on a stone plinth in front of the neoclassical building, some enterprising wiseass has draped a Confederate flag. Throughout the day, the Lady Liberty makeover draws chants of "C.S.A.! C.S.A.! C.S.A.!" and other intemperate remarks from passing rowdies.

Although inside the House of Representative chambers the crowd is more august and certainly better dressed—no "I Ride With Forrest" T-shirts or hats with beer cups attached—the mood is just as electric.

Massive Confederate flags hang in long, crimson columns around the room. The elbow-to-elbow crowd nearly spills out of the galleries.

On the floor, the ultra-privileged push close to the speaker's rostrum—this is the toughest ticket in the South since the 2016 BCS championship game between Florida State and Vanderbilt in the Louisiana Superdome—a tighter squeeze, as the saying goes, than a puppy passing a peach pit.

At precisely 1 p.m., a gavel bangs twelve times on the speaker's desk. The sharp reports ring through the chambers like a series of pistol shots, bringing the crowd to attention. After an opening prayer—for once mercifully short, even Jesus is impatient today—the sergeant at arms barks his historic line in the most regimental Citadel cadence he can muster: "All rise for the president of the Confederate States of America! The Honorable Robert Francis McDonnell!"

The order is unnecessary. The crowd has been on its feet since the chamber doors opened four hours earlier. Already half-crazed with anticipation and continuous belts from whiskey flasks, it now erupts in an avalanche of applause, whistles, and feral hoots of ecstasy. Many shed tears. News accounts will later report the fainting of at least two she-billies who have come to the presidential inauguration dressed in authentic nineteenth-century corsets and hoop skirts.

With what he'll describe in a few minutes as a smile that stretches from the banks of the Potomac River to the shores of Key West, President Bob McDonnell moves to the dais. Behind him, standing in line beneath a newly installed, thirty-foot-high golden crucifix that dominates the chambers, are the nascent southern government's principal figures: vice president and former Mississippi governor Haley Barbour; secretary of state and former South Carolina senator Lindsey Graham; and secretary of commerce and energy and former Florida governor Jeb Bush, McDonnell's chief rival during the yearlong Confederate States of America presidential campaign.

Raising both arms and spreading his fingers wide, a gesture of embrace to every sanctified soul inside and outside the capitol, McDonnell opens his inaugural address with long, dramatic bursts:

"My . . . fellow . . . Confederates!"

For ten full minutes, McDonnell is unable to speak above the avionic roar of approval. Watching the proceedings on massive Hisense video screens donated by the Chinese government for the occasion, the crowd outside does its best to stimulate an earthquake.

The delay gives television commentators one more chance to introduce Confederate States of America president Bob McDonnell to more than a billion viewers watching live around the world.

The Republican governor of Virginia until 2014, the trim, sixty-two-year-old McDonnell—with his CEO blond coif, tennis club smile, clear complexion, and dark, tailored suits, he could almost pass for fifty—possesses uncannily perfect credentials to lead the new nation carved from twelve former American states. Raised in Virginia, McDonnell played high school football and served twenty-one years in the U.S. Army, retiring as a lieutenant colonel. Earning a graduate degree in law from Regent University (formerly Christian Broadcasting Network University), he was elected to the Virginia House of Delegates in 1992 and became the state's attorney general in 2005.

A rabid opponent of abortion, gay marriage, and labor unions, the father of five (daughter Jeanine served as an Army platoon officer in Iraq) speaks with a pleasing southern drawl and enjoys an "A" rating from the National Rifle Association for his unwavering devotion to personal weaponry. Among his first acts as governor in 2010 was to declare Confederate History Month in Virginia, a written proclamation that briefly thrust him into the national spotlight for its omission of any mention of slavery.[1]

Continuing to fill applause time on FOX "News," Chris Matthews responds to a question about the choice of Atlanta as the C.S.A. capital.

"You ever driven through Richmond after six o'clock at night?" Matthews quips, before explaining that the Georgia capitol was constructed in the 1880s as an explicit symbol of the "New South" built upon the ashes of the Union Army's infamous 1864 March to the Sea that reduced it to rubble.

"The psychological history of the South, the symbolism here, made Atlanta the only possible choice," Matthews gushes to his audience. "Besides, this is where the money is. Atlanta wouldn't have allowed the capital to be located anywhere else."

Finally, the crowd allows McDonnell to speak. After thanking those around the speaker's chair and others who supported his candidacy, McDonnell addresses his new countrymen.

"The South has historically been defined, from Alexandria, Virginia, to Alexandria, Louisiana, as what it has been, rather than what it could be," he begins. "Today, I am pleased to be here to look in only one direction for a change: forward. This is a roomful of southerners who will use the windshield, not the rearview mirror."

Applause shakes the room. Barbour's face reddens, joy catching in his throat like a chicken bone. Holding up his hands like a fourth-and-goal quarterback begging for calm, McDonnell lays out his vision for the thirteen-hour-old nation. With nearly every sentence crafted as an applause line, the thirty-minute speech will take almost an hour and a half to plow through.

"Gone are the days of the Old South, when racism and prejudice were once a stain on our society," McDonnell half-shouts. "The South's future will be the story of a continuing growth in both population and diversity. Employers will prosper due to our pro-business climate. Workers will enjoy our great quality of life. Long a laggard in the American economy, the South is now leading the way.

"My interest is how we ensure that the future of the South is marked by the strong economy and good jobs our citizens need and deserve," McDonnell continues. "I believe one of the most important keys is education. The University of Virginia. The University of North Carolina. The University of Georgia. Ole Miss. These are not just schools; they are the factories of our twenty-first-century economy. They produce the human capital, attract financial investment, and incubate the ideas that power our states.

"The story of the future South will depend upon our commitment to promoting education in all forms. Improved K through 12 education will be one of the hallmarks of the South for the next forty years. Without a world-class system, from kindergarten to doctorate levels, the South will simply not be able to compete in this global economy."

If a few jaded public school teachers around the South cough out cynical guffaws, they go unheard above the incongruous din of rank-and-file southerners amenably applauding the notion of a permanent intellectual class. This is not a day for quibbling.

"Southerners compete in that interconnected global marketplace, and, frankly, we compete very well," McDonnell waxes on. "To use a boxing analogy, our region 'punches above its weight.' We have and will continue to have a great pro-business climate.

"Virginia has been rated the number-one state five years running for having the best environment for business, according to *Forbes*, CNBC, and *Fortune*. Charlotte and Atlanta have become major financial hubs. Agriculture and forest products remain a huge part of our economy. From the agriculture industry we generate $59 billion a year; $29 billion from the forest products industry. In Virginia, we've thought of changing our name from the Old Dominion to the Silicon Dominion to rival the Silicon Valley in the number of high-tech jobs we've got.

"We'll continue to rely on our great major military bases, such as Norfolk, the largest navy base in the free world. Charleston, Savannah, New Orleans, and Hampton Roads will increasingly rival New York for through-put maritime traffic. These ports are cheaper to use and closer to the Panama Canal, with fewer weather issues and strong right-to-work environments. They can expand and grow. They are not landlocked like northern ports."

Around the House chambers, the benefactors of the economic juggernaut described by McDonnell, many from overseas, launch into another lengthy cheergasm, discreetly soiling their silken undergarments in a collective climax of barbecue-scented profit-motive ecstasy.

With this portion of the address, McDonnell finds his rhythm, unabashedly revealing himself as the embodiment of a new southern political archetype. Far from the cigar-chomping, good ol' boy vote wrangler, he's a cash-flow technocrat, a dry-palmed facilitator of international business and its simple need for inexpensive, nonunion labor, minimal taxes, and generous government giveaways, such as free land and regulatory exemptions. He's a pragmatist more familiar with Asian boardrooms and European golf courses than Appalachian county office backrooms and ArkLaMiss polling stations.

"With abundant natural resources already providing 25 percent of North American production from Gulf oil rigs, the South will become the energy capital of North America," McDonnell motors on. "We'll drill for oil and natural gas off the coast of Virginia. With extensive fields in West Virginia, Virginia, Tennessee, and Kentucky, we'll become the Saudi Arabia of coal.

"We'll pursue hydrofracking for natural gas extraction. Virginia is poised to be the world leader in offshore winds. We're turning tobacco fields into sugarcane and switchgrass for biomass."

If amid the thundering elation any newly minted C.S.A. citizens of the Yellowhammer State are by this time wondering, "Has he said anything about Alabama? He sure seems to be mentioning Virginia a lot," their cares go unheeded. Incessant waves of approval are the order of the day and when they finally subside, it's for just enough time to let McDonnell wind up with the reliable money shot of regional political rhetoric.

"My administration will focus on family, hard work, faith, and good southern food," McDonnell says, waiting a beat for the appreciative laughter, and to allow Barbour to snort for breath one last time, before delivering the C.S.A. maxim, motto, and coup de grâce.

"God bless you all!"

Hog Farms, Assembly Lines, and Disability Checks: Revenge of the Confederate Dollar

This is the tricky part.

Even if up to now you've bought into my patriotic pissing and moaning about the degenerate influence of Dixie, even if you're a dyed-in-the-imported-wool hater of anyone who uses "y'all" more than once in a sentence, money changes everything.

You don't have to be Paul Krugman to grasp the economic implications of lopping off 25 percent of your population and 15 percent of your landmass.[2]

You don't have to be John Maynard Keynes to see financial suicide in the idea of stripping your national economy of a manufacturing base that puts together everything from biomass to Beemers.

You don't even need to have a mail-order Mississippi GED to recognize the problems associated with breaking up with a sprawling agricultural trove that includes, among other gigantic production centers, North

Carolina's Smithfield Packing Co., the largest hog butchering plant in the world; a Gulf's worth of oil refineries; immense deposits of coal and natural gas; corporate powerhouses such as Arkansas-based Walmart (the world's largest private employer) and Atlanta-headquartered Coca-Cola (the pre-eminent global brand, even above McDonald's); and dozens of key military bases and installations, including the aforementioned Naval Station Norfolk and Naval Air Station Pensacola, the country's primary training facility for all Navy, Marine, and Coast Guard aviators.

Although the Confederate States of America presidential inauguration and Independence Day ceremony depicted above is a work of fantasy, everything that Governor Bob McDonnell says in that imaginary speech is real. That's because the McDonnell quotes you just read were taken from the keynote address the governor delivered on October 5, 2010, at a Future of the South symposium held at the National Archives in Washington, D.C. I was in the audience, back row, scribbling notes.*[3]

To be fair to the governor, he was neither speaking about nor framing his comments in terms of a secessionist or independent South. Although as a side note, the regularity with which southerners demonstrate the need to conceive of themselves as having a future separate from the rest of the country remains highly suspect to me. People everywhere are proud of where they're from. Almost no one in the Northeast or Northwest, however, feels the need to organize symposiums and rally leading political figures to promote the idea of their own "otherness."

Regardless, McDonnell's comments underscore weighty and accurate points about the southern economy vis-à-vis the rest of the country. Long removed from being the "Nation's No. 1 economic problem," as famously declared by Franklin Roosevelt in 1938, the South is now, along with the West, one-half of America's twin economic spear tip.

Since World War II, its annual rate of economic expansion has surpassed the national average. According to a recent U.S. Census Bureau

---

* The only exception being McDonnell's "My fellow Confederates" salutation, the governor's company on the dais, and the imagined Chris Matthews quotes.

report, twenty-nine of the fifty fastest-growing metro areas in the country are below the Mason-Dixon line. (Eleven of these are in Texas.) The South, in many important respects, has already risen again.[4]

"The South and West have been the dominant sections of the country for twenty years now," former Census Bureau director Steve Murdock told me when I called him at his home in Texas. Murdock also wasted little time in telling me that, from a purely economic point of view, my idea for sawing off the bottom end of the country is madness.

"Look at population trends and employment by industry and you'll see very quickly where you would lose a lot of income if you lost the South," he said. "What's also different about the South is that its cities are newer. Its infrastructure is newer, and often superior to the rest of the country's."

Once almost entirely dependent on cotton, tobacco, and boll weevil defense initiatives, the diversity of the modern southern economy is remarkable: rubber, plastics, chemicals, electronics, energy, pharmaceuticals, metalworking, machinery, scientific research, automotive assembly, stone, clay, glass, and cement production, among many others, are industries that attract to the region both young Americans and immigrants. Taken as a whole and not including Texas, the South's annual GDP amounts to $3.138 trillion, or about 22.5 percent of the overall U.S. economy. An independent southern nation would rank as the world's fifth-largest economy, behind the United States, China, Japan, and Germany, and ahead of France and the United Kingdom.

What's more, under an independent South scenario, a truncated United States would likely be viewed as a market in severe decline, even if after losing the South its economy would remain roughly twice as large as China's. Meanwhile, with its increasingly disenfranchised middle class, the South might emerge as the model of the *en vogue*, Chinese-inspired twenty-first-century master-serf economy.[5]

"The population of New York doesn't look like a wonderful thing for the United States in fifty years," Murdock informed me. "It's going to be a very old state. Iowa's population is getting so old that in 2020, somewhere around seventy-two or seventy-three of their ninety-nine counties will have more people over sixty-five than under eighteen. That is an old, dying population.

"If the South disappears, the issues of an aging population in the United States and all the costs associated with that, and not having younger populations to offset them, would be tremendous. Problems of Social Security and Medicare and Medicaid increase dramatically if you ditch the South."

It's not just the number of jobs that make the South an economic beast. It's the people who do the work. Since the 1970s, international businesses have flocked to the South mostly for the cheap, nonunion labor and reliable quasi-fascist government/business circle-jerk guaranteed by "our orifices are open for business" state and county officials. A big reason they've stayed, according to the *Encyclopedia of Southern Culture*, is a labor pool that's become globally renowned for high productivity, low absenteeism, and stable employment. And moxie.[6]

Pay attention to the billboards as you drive the roadways of the Deep South and you can't help noticing all of the advertisements for personal injury lawyers. Rednecks may despise attorneys on principle ("There are two kinds of lawyers in the South, one who knows the law, and one who knows the judge."), but a hell of a lot of them eventually end up sitting across from one, greasy John Deere cap in hand. The reason so many southerners get hurt on the job is because they do so much demanding, dangerous work.

In Haile, Louisiana, retired oil worker James Tucker spent an afternoon on the front porch of his single-wide trailer on the banks of the Ouachita River explaining to me how his life has been shaped by a careless attitude with women and three major work-related accidents—including having his eye popped completely out of its socket and then popped back in at a hospital in Big Spring, Texas, after a high-speed collision with an oil tanker.

Even counting the three divorces, the worst of his personal calamities occurred when a length of metal pipe blew out of a well.

"It shot out of the well and split into two pieces in the air," Tucker told me. "One came to earth and bounces up at a crazy angle and hits me right in the back of my head. It went right through my hard hat and split my skull. Knocked my brain right out of its cage."

Tucker has endless stories of industrial mishaps.

"I'd had just left my shift when I get a call from my foreman asking if I seen this feller Rudy," he told me. "I said, 'Rudy's fine, I just left him not two minutes ago.' He said, 'Well, he's splattered all over the rig now.' I went back and Rudy was in bits and pieces. His last words were, 'Run! The rig's gonna blow!' I helped clean up the mess and the foreman calls me back and says, 'Well, you know his wife pretty good, don't you?' So that was my next job."

In ways you more readily associate with places like Bhopal, catastrophe and hazard are pretty much assumed on many southern job sites. My most memorable time with workers in the South was the ninety minutes I spent inside the security guard shack at the massive Angus Chemical Company plant in Sterlington, Louisiana. Among the chatty comers and goers, one introduced me to an exotic local elixir made by mixing Jim Beam whiskey with cherry Kool-Aid. The concoction reminded me of the Cheetos-stuffed pickles from Forest Heights Middle School in Little Rock. Hard places, I suppose, call for hard poisons.

In 1991, an Angus-owned plant operated by IMC Fertilizer exploded, killing eight, injuring 128, and forcing the evacuation of nearly half of Sterlington's 1,200 residents. Angus and the high-performance drag-racing world recovered from the blast (at the time, the IMC plant produced about 75 percent of the racing community's nitro fuel), but the explosion remains the town's touchstone event.[7]

These days, the Angus plant cranks out chemicals for cosmetics, rubber, medicine, and lots of other stuff you don't associate with the methane reek of synthetic cow shit, which is what Sterlington most often smells like.

"The odor changes depending on what's cooking," one affable "redneck and proud of it" worker told me. "There's a new smell a couple times a week, and it's always bad. Some days I have to put my head down in my shirt and hold my breath just to make it from the truck to the guardhouse."

"You ever consider wearing a mask?" I asked.

"I should, but I don't."

You can malign the South from tip to diagonal tip of that asshole flag, but you cannot deny the fundamental grit of its labor force. Even deep into the information age, we still need to produce shit, fix shit, and haul even more shit out of the earth. I may not trust the South with my vote, my kids' school curriculum, or the presets on my car radio, but, like most

Americans, I'm happy to let it go drill my oil, brew up my wife's makeup, and slaughter my hogs.

Is Growth Good? Not If It's Cancer. Or Brazil Nuts

So, done deal, case closed, chaw chewed, and hay baled, right? The preceding sections outlining the importance of the southern economy make the idea of an independent South even spookier than the idea of allowing the region to continue being "an abnormal growth on the national body," to borrow a term from historian Howard Zinn. Even the most cursory consideration of southern industry makes it plain that, no matter how much aggrieved lefties might wish to resist the increasingly influential tide of ill-educated, politically flat-footed, mouth-breathing evangelical banjo pickers hell-bent on leading this country down an Appalachia mineshaft, we pretty much need those banjo pickers and their mineshafts to survive.[8]

Or do we?

A more circumspect examination of the southern economic juggernaut turns up a rather different side of the story, this one exposing an economic system that, hand in glove with the region's religious, political, and educational polarities, is both dissimilar to and hostile toward the rest of the country. While by and large the South's economic gains are good for the South, they are not so good for the rest of the country. In fact, often as not, southern economic success comes at the *expense* of the rest of the country.

Indeed, one could make the argument that in terms of economic practice the South is profoundly un-American for the way in which it betrays our own citizens by prostrating itself to foreign interests and fat-cat traitors who sell out America's dwindling middle class for the short-term gain of a pocketful of euros and yuan; and that despite a few misleading statistics and specious political claims, northern citizens might actually be better off without the ball and chain of the southern economy.

By underscoring the three pillars of southern economic philosophy—abuse labor, fellate corporate interests (especially foreign ones), and fuck the environment—I intend to make that very argument.

It's common knowledge that the United States annually loses tens of thousands of manufacturing and service jobs to countries such as China, India, and Mexico. Developing nations take American jobs by attracting multinational companies with easily exploitable workers who, conditioned by years of native poverty, demand less money and expect fewer benefits than American workers.

What few Americans realize, however, is that for decades one of the most predatory and destructive of these "foreign" countries has been the South.

The most dramatic recent example of the southern taste for economic cannibalism is the fight that erupted in 2011 between Boeing and the National Labor Relations Board, which filed a complaint against the company on behalf of machine workers in the state of Washington. After Boeing announced that it was opening a 787 Dreamliner aircraft assembly plant in North Charleston, South Carolina—thousands of miles from its traditional manufacturing base in the Seattle/Puget Sound area—the NLRB accused the company of moving its facility as retaliation against the International Association of Machinists & Aerospace Workers for strikes the union carried out in 2008 in Washington.

Boeing had originally intended to build all of its Dreamliner aircraft in Washington, but changed its mind in 2009 when South Carolina lured an estimated 1,000 to 3,800 new jobs away from home with a reported $900 million corporate subsidy package (provided by the state's presumably socialism-hating taxpayers) as well as a much more, shall we say, "compliant" workforce. As Boeing executive vice president Jim Albaugh explained to the *Seattle Times*, not only would operating a plant in South Carolina be cheaper than doing so in Washington, "we can't afford to have a labor stoppage every three years."

Alleging union busting, the NLRB felt this was basically like Boeing saying, "We're sick of federal laws that allow workers a collective say regarding the terms of their employment. Far easier for us to relocate to the South where state governments allow us to get around pesky impediments to profits like 'wage protections for workers.'"

The Dreamliner plant in South Carolina ended up opening in June

2011. For most who caught the fleeting network news coverage of the imbroglio, the story passed by as yet another recession-days business downer. Industry experts, however, quickly assessed the situation for what it was: the latest major battle in a decades-long labor war waged by southern-based business interests against workers in the rest of the country.

According to *The Christian Science Monitor*, the NLRB complaint against Boeing represented "a stake in the ground for a brewing battle of political will between industrial, and largely union-friendly, Northern states and the 22 'right-to-work' states" ("right to work" being the Orwellian euphemism for "the right for companies to disregard the welfare of workers"), the majority of them southern and Plains states.

"The [Boeing controversy] really deals with some primal fears not just about competition between the U.S. and other countries for jobs, but between states for jobs," Clark University industrial relations professor Gary Chaison told the *CSM*.

Not even bothering to pay lip service to her state's own workforce at a CBS News town hall meeting staged to discuss the Boeing case, South Carolina governor Nikki Haley declared, "We are fighting the unions every step of the way. . . . That's what gives a company confidence to come and say, 'This is a state where we can make money.'"

By the way, any time you hear a politician or corporate head make a statement like this, you should substitute the words "worker" or "common man" for "union," because that's what it really means. Try it in the Nikki Haley quote above and you'll see what I mean.

Meanwhile, attendees at the Economic Development Association of Alabama's summer conference were told by experts that the Boeing situation could have long-term effects on their interests, given that in regard to its own acquisitive economic strategy, "Alabama is not that different from South Carolina."[9]

Sidestepping federal labor laws is an old Dixie trick, particularly in South Carolina. Disregarding the 1938 enactment of the Fair Labor Standards Act—a sweeping measure that protects Americans against such Industrial Revolution inventions as graveyard mill shifts for impoverished nine-year-olds—the Palmetto State repealed wage and hour restrictions for the textile industry in the same year. Wealthy industrialists might leave the state, its politicians explained, were they forced to acknowledge the basic rights of workers to fair pay, medical benefits, safe work environments, and the ability to get sick once or twice a year without immediately losing their spindle-minder job to some unfortunate urchin with a coal-smudged face and even more nimble hands.[10]

As noted in Chapter 2, unemployed autoworkers in depleted Detroit could look at the plight of Boeing's Seattle-area workers with bleak sympathy, they themselves having had their livelihoods systematically stripped away by the flight of the auto industry from the Midwest. Think all of those thousands of Michigan autoworker jobs have moved to foreign countries? They have, if you count the South as a foreign country.

Nowhere is this more evident than on the stretch of Interstate 65 dubbed "Auto Alley." Along this corridor are automotive factories and supplier outfits that include a General Motors Corvette plant in Bowling Green, Kentucky, a since-shuttered Saturn plant in Spring Hill, Tennessee, and Mercedes-Benz and Hyundai plants in Tuscaloosa County and Montgomery, Alabama. Other automakers that have opened shop in the past four decades in the famously nonunion South include Honda, Nissan, Toyota, Kia, BMW, and Volkswagen.[11]

The auto industry in the United States isn't dead. It's thriving. But it's doing so with cut-rate workers in southern states whose leaders have adopted the business tactics of banana republic despots who take jobs from American workers by shamelessly exploiting their own.

It wasn't just Japan and Korea and Mexican laborers that killed Detroit. Essentially operating as its own country with its own economic interests in mind, the "patriotic" South has done plenty to help wreck the Motor City.

According to a study headed by Grand Valley State economics professor Hari Singh, 2009 wages for autoworkers in Michigan averaged $74,498. In Tennessee, equivalent jobs paid $53,238; in South Carolina, $56,508; in Alabama, $56,579. In addition to lower wages, other drawbacks of the South's corporate-friendly and ubiquitous "right to work" laws include inferior health and pension plans, less job security, higher risk of being fired for trivial reasons, and diminished safety precautions resulting in more workplace fatalities and injuries.[12]

Think I'm exaggerating about the South as a Third World economy? Talk to a German autoworker. Taking advantage of a state-provided subsidy of $253 million, Mercedes-Benz opened an enormous assembly plant in Alabama in the early 1990s. As part of the deal, the great patriots of Alabama promised to buy $75 million worth of Mercedes cars to serve as state fleet vehicles. Its leaders also stood by, grinning, while Mercedes paid Alabama workers 30 percent less than it paid to its own German workforce. In all, by the middle of the decade, Alabama had doled out $874 million in taxpayer dollars to the executives of Mercedes, Honda, and Hyundai. German workers have since taken to calling the American South "our Mexico."[13]

Or you could talk, as I did, with Katherine Newman, coauthor of *Taxing the Poor: Doing Damage to the Truly Disadvantaged* (2011), widely published expert on poverty and the working poor, and James B. Knapp, Dean of Krieger School of Arts and Sciences at Johns Hopkins University.

"Yes, you've had job growth in the South, but they are low-wage jobs with poor benefits," Newman told me. "It's a very galloping economy that is based on low-wage labor and low levels of regulation. It is what the United States looked like in the heyday of the Industrial Revolution in the nineteenth century before we had muckrakers and people who were paying attention to health and safety issues for workers. Work-related injury rates are higher in the South, death rates are higher.

"It's very Brazilian in that way. It's a certain type of economic growth that is highly unequal. It's not necessarily the type of growth you want."

Bag Whores: How to Get Out-Progressived by Bangladesh and Uganda

The South's great unifying theme of exploitation doesn't stop with people. In the words of Florida novelist and screenwriter Connie May Fowler, "One of the things the South has always done is hurt this earth. We allow corporations like BP and others to just come here and exploit, exploit, exploit."

"We're good at mountaintop removal and mining and this stupid short-term view of things," says Diane Roberts, NPR commentator, Florida State University English professor, and eighth-generation Floridian. "The Florida legislature is filled with prize idiots. My favorite is the old boy [Charles Van Zant, Republican representative from Keystone Heights] who said, 'It doesn't matter if we drill out all the oil in the Gulf 'cause God'll make some more.' This guy was voted into office by supposedly sentient human beings."[14]

It's fine (sort of) if southerners want to continue shitting in their own beds. The problem is that in order to expand its sphere of influence, southern industry is primed to trash the rest of the country the way it has historically trashed its own backyard. Worse, it spends millions of dollars asserting its right to do so.

One exasperating recent case of southern business's evangelical eagerness to spread its sickness to the rest of the country involves those flimsy plastic shopping bags—"T-shirt bags," as retailers call them—that have come to represent the small-tragedy apex of global consumerist pollution. Made from petroleum-based, high-density polyethylene, the bags litter virtually every corner of earth and ocean, are nearly impossible to recycle, and will survive far longer than any remaindered copies of *An Inconvenient Truth*.

According to activist group Care2, the bags take five hundred years to decompose, and contain tiny toxic particles that contaminate water and soil. Long before they do that, they're a threat to wildlife. An estimated one million seabirds and a hundred thousand sharks, dolphins, turtles, and whales die each year from eating plastic bags. Warning that the bags are literally choking marine life around the planet, executive director of the United Nations Environment Programme Achim Steiner said in a 2009 UN press release, "There is simply zero justification for manufacturing [the bags] anymore, anywhere."

The world has taken notice. "Progressive" countries such as Bangladesh, China, Italy, South Africa, Uganda, and regions of India have issued outright bans on the bags, with stiff penalties for violators. Others have imposed fees on them, decreasing usage in countries such as Ireland by 90 percent.

Famed for their "wacky" and "moonbeam" and "granola-crunching" penchant for actually giving a shit about clean air and pure water, U.S. Left Coasties have also rallied against the bags, mounting vigorous anti-bag drives in California, Oregon, and Washington. The groundbreaking campaigns—West Coast states are often ahead of the curve in crucial areas of environmentalism, coffee flavoring, and athletic footwear—have garnered widespread local support.

In 2007, San Francisco became the first city in the country to ban plastic bags from large chains. In 2008, Seattle imposed a twenty-cent fee on the bags. A 2010 California bill to ban the bags statewide enjoyed the support of a coalition of retailers, grocers, environmentalists, and then governor Arnold Schwarzenegger. A statewide bag-ban bill was introduced in the Oregon legislature in 2011.

Incensed that a bunch of liberal kooks would have the temerity to take steps to ensure that their land and water be kept free of nonbiodegradable litter, the plastic bag industry flew into action. Its first step was to set up a lobbying group with the classic doublespeak moniker, Progressive Bag Affiliates (PBA), composed of leading plastic bag manufacturers Hilex Poly, Unistar Plastics, and Superbag.

The PBA was well funded. American shoppers roll through an estimated 102 billion T-shirt bags a year, more than 500 per U.S. consumer. Even at a penny a bag, that's more than $1 billion a year in shopping bags. A year.

According to a 2011 *Rolling Stone* article by Kitt Doucette, titled "The Plastic Bag Wars," in Washington state the PBA spent more than $1.5 million on a misinformation campaign that successfully brought the Seattle ban to a public ballot, where it was overturned by voters who'd been convinced that banning plastic bags would end up *costing* consumers more than $300 each per year. In fact, a ban would have cost PBA members a lot more than that. The $1.5 million "investment" from the PBA was the most ever spent on any Seattle city referendum.

In California, the ban was similarly defeated by an industry campaign that, according to Doucette, "spent $2 million on contributions to legislators, extensive lobbying and media ads that portrayed the ban as a 'hidden tax on grocery bills' that would create a new state bureaucracy." Caving to industry pressure, the state Senate rejected the ban by a vote of 21 to 14, despite the fact that, according to the *Los Angeles Times*, Californians alone use 120,000 tons of plastic bags each year and recycle just 5 percent of it.

Similar industry efforts and expenditures netted the same depressing result in Oregon. The legislature there eventually tossed out the proposed ban on plastic bags after what the Portland chapter of the Surfrider Foundation called "an epic battle against the goliath out-of-state plastic industry's various misleading ads, scare media and unrealistic recycling solutions."

"I'm blown away by the campaign to block this bill by out-of-state interests," state senator Mark Haas told *Rolling Stone*, adding that Hilex Poly had gone as far as suggesting to Haas that it might be willing to build a recycling plant in Oregon, provided he agree to drop his support of the ban. Haas rebuffed Hilex Poly.

The insidious thread that connects all of this interstate meddling is, of course, the headquarter locations of all of those Progressive Bag Affiliates signatories.

Hilex Poly: Hartsville, South Carolina
Unistar Plastics: Harahan, Louisiana
Superbag: Houston, Texas[15]

Country jakes are always whining about the sanctity of states' rights and individual freedoms. Yet when a couple of queers want to get married in Massachusetts, half the South goes apeshit with the homemade posters and fire-breathing sermons. And when a few million concerned residents of states thousands of miles away decide they want to stop destroying their landscape in the name of corporate mammon and consumer stupidity, the South sends out its greasy merchants of avarice to cajole, bribe, hector, lie, intimidate, and "lobby" until the seed of their plantation mentality is protected and their gluttonous mouths are once again filled with the jizz of the master caste before whom they kneel like Bourbon Street whores on Navy payday.

Think that's over the top? As today's trailer-dwelling tools of the modern southern aristocracy often reminded me, almost none of their ancestors who fought, died, and/or had their arms, legs, and dicks blown off in the

Civil War owned any slaves themselves, much less arable land. They were poor, disenfranchised schlubs then, just like they are today, and still obediently doing the deadly bidding of their elite.

As for the inevitable southern rejoinder that northern industrialists and carpetbaggers have been pillaging Confederate lands since the days of Reconstruction, I can only nod in agreement and reply that this is all the more reason true southerners should see that "better off without 'em" cuts both ways.

Who's Your Sugar Daddy? How the North Pays to Keep the South Afloat

If the economic rise of Dixie has been bad for the rest of the country, it's at least been a boon to southern workers; and since all's fair in love and capitalism, I should just keep my mouth shut and let southerners continue stacking jars of milk and honey on their long-delayed march to prosperity, right?

Yeah. And the sun don't shine in Hawaii, either.

According to the handbook *2011 Facts & Figures: How Does Your State Compare?* published by the Tax Foundation (a nonpartisan organization founded in 1937 to educate taxpayers about tax burdens borne by Americans), southerners per capita earn the least amount of money of any workers in the country. With the exception of Beltway-aided Virginia, residents of not a single southern state, including Texas, earn more than the national average of $42,539. The average worker in Mississippi brings home the smallest paycheck ($30,689), followed by those in West Virginia, Kentucky, Arkansas, and South Carolina.

So, what about the trickle-down implication behind that "great pro-business climate" talk, which insists that the South's corporate welfare system is a prerequisite to ensuring prosperity among the working class? Turns out, no matter how much guys like Governor Bob McDonnell would like to convince you otherwise, the numbers don't support this greatest of all right-wing economic fallacies.

For decades, South Carolina has been a favored glory hole of foreign investors, in part for having one of the lowest corporate income tax rates in the country. The state ranks forty-fourth in the nation for taking in an average of just $48 from businesses per resident. Top-ranked Alaska takes in $912 per resident, followed by New Hampshire, New Jersey, and Massachusetts. Yet South Carolina's minuscule corporate taxes, supposedly necessary for luring employers to the state, haven't come anywhere near translating to the overall well-being of South Carolinians, who rank forty-sixth in the country in personal income.

The explosion of economic investment and activity hasn't made southerners any happier, either. According to the 2011 Gallup-Healthways Well-Being Index, which assesses emotional and physical health, work environment, and access to basic necessities, among other factors, six of the ten least-happy states are in the South, including the bottom four of West Virginia, Kentucky, Arkansas, and Mississippi.

The good-for-business-bad-for-workers South Carolina model is typical of the region, leading to the central paradox of the southern economic miracle: for all of its undeniable industrial progress, why does the South continue to function as a financial drain on the national economy?[16]

According to the Tax Foundation, with the exception of Florida (and Texas, if you count it), no southern state contributes more money in federal tax revenues than it receives back in government assistance and entitlement programs such as Medicare, Medicaid, welfare block grants, disability payments, food stamps, housing assistance, and other programs. For every $1.00 Mississippians pay in federal taxes, for example, the state's residents receive back $2.02 worth of federal aid. West Virginians get $1.76 for every $1.00 they contribute to the national coffers. Kentuckians and Virginians get $1.51 return on their dollar. South Carolinians $1.35. Tennesseans $1.27. And so on.

Despite its collective caterwauling about government entitlements, the hard fact is that the South simply does not pull its own weight when measured against other states. Instead, it relies on the good people of New Jersey, Nevada, Connecticut, New Hampshire, Minnesota, and the like to carry its water. For every dollar they contribute to the federal treasury, those states receive back, respectively, $0.61, $0.65, $0.69, $0.71, and

$0.72. Even economically battered Oregon receives just $0.93 in federal programs for every dollar its residents contribute to the system.[17]

More unsettling is that, according to *Taxing the Poor* coauthors Katherine Newman and Rourke O'Brien, even as the southern economy has blossomed, the contributions-to-welfare ratio divergence has been *growing* over time in favor of the South.

"More than any other region, the South turns to the federal government," the authors write. "It exacts an enormous price in federal dollars that are flowing into a region that is both needy and, it would seem, unwilling to tax its own citizens to deal with the problem."[18]

The conclusion is as obvious as it is aggravating. In terms of contributions to the national economy, the South gets a free ride. And the ride is getting freerer every year.

All day long on front porches, café counters, bar stools, and talk radio, Dollar Store philosophers preach the gospel of self-sufficiency, congratulating themselves on a set of country-boy-can-survive skills with a counterfeit pride that presumably prevents them from accepting charity or assistance of any kind. The southerner's staunch belief that if you want to screw something up all you have to do is get the federal government involved conveniently ignores the fact that the great American triumphs "conservatives" often tout as "our" accomplishments—victory in World War II, moon landing, Cold War defeat of the Soviet Union, toppling Saddam Hussein—were all 100 percent federal government projects accomplished with federal government tax money and federal government employees and contractors sucking off the great federal government udder.

This to say nothing of the federally owned Tennessee Valley Authority, which illuminated half the benighted coonskin kingdom and continues to do so seventy years after its founding. The federal government meddling that northerners disproportionately pay for also does a pretty fair job of maintaining the Interstate highway system and keeps the amount of commercial air crashes pretty damn close to zero each year with a Federal Aviation Administration that gets blasted with far more criticism than deserved praise.

So, I'm sorry if the government—which, since southerners haven't noticed in a while, actually means "the people" in this country—does y'all such a terrible disservice. I'm more than anxious to see how the South gits along without it.

Throughout this persuasive little apoplexy of northern martyrdom, I've made efforts to cite the most recent studies, statistics, and quotes available. Mindful that the tax contribution figures noted above come from a 2007 report (for a variety of reasons, cost among them, the Tax Foundation has not repeated the study), I picked up the phone one afternoon and placed a call to Tax Foundation economist Mark Robyn in Washington, D.C.

Like many who spend their days in the company of spreadsheets and Google docs, Robyn speaks slowly and methodically, laboring over each answer in an effort to be as nonpartisan as possible.

I tell him right away what I'm up to. He's clearly wary of having his numbers used to paint him into a political corner, or being led by me down a controversial road. As a Dixie basher, I find his repeated disclaimers and long-winded explanations of methodology as frustrating as a graduate course on southern ethics. As a journalist, I gotta love him.

"The tax payments–versus–welfare study is from 2007," I begin. "Can I assume that the data in it remains fairly fixed and accurate through 2012? In other words, is it still true that as a bloc, southerners are taking more from the federal government than they are giving?"

"Well, if we were to update the study and not change the way we did the study at all, you might get similar results, probably fairly similar results. It probably hasn't changed a ton. If we were going to do it again, we'd probably update the methodology. We're always trying to improve our methodology."

The methodology used by the Tax Foundation in the study was pretty straightforward and seemed sound enough to me. Although, given that my sophomore Econ 202 final was the only test in my life that I ever felt the need to cheat on (Professor Felicidad Natividad, you seemed like a very smart person and I've always gotten along with my Filipina *hermanas,* but that accent of yours was as impenetrable as Manila rush hour. *Mabuhay!*), I invite readers to draw their own conclusions.

First, the Tax Foundation calculated all federal taxes paid by residents and businesses of each state, as reported by the IRS. Then it calculated federal spending programs and amounts doled out to each state—factoring for "public good" spending, such as national defense, which benefits all states—and came up with a total figure received by each state in federal aid. Then it subtracted one figure from the other and came up with its ratio.

"There are three or four thousand federal spending categories you have to allocate for, so it's a significant task," Robyn said. "Social Security and Medicare and Medicaid, those are the huge categories of spending."

Robyn then explained, in an excruciatingly detailed direct quote that consumed three full pages of my notebook, that the surging federal deficit, and how it eventually ends up getting paid off, could alter the results of the study. There's no way of knowing for certain what the results of a new study would be, but given the current inequity in federal tax burdens, it might just reveal a balance of payments-versus-allotments that tilts even further in favor of the South.

That treasury-draining war in Iraq that southerners disproportionately supported? Northerners already have and very likely will continue to pay a lopsided amount to underwrite that lunacy.

Robyn said something else that caught my attention, which is that by and large southerners pay less in state and local taxes than do residents of other states.

"That seems like a pretty canny way of supplementing your state budget," I say. "Southerners tax themselves less and make up for the shortfall by snaking a disproportionate amount of federal tax dollars from states outside their region."

"Some people do make that observation," Robyn said drily.

"I feel like a sucker here," I replied. "It's like I'm not just keeping up my own property value by mowing my lawn and repaving my driveway. I'm also paying for my asshole brother-in-law in Tennessee to fix his broken living room window and move his piece of shit Trans Am off the blocks in his side yard."

"Well, sort of," Robyn said. I could feel him fidgeting all the way across the country. "I would hesitate to say that somehow one state is getting away with that . . . (nervous laugh, long pause). But if states are providing services to their population and the population is able to shift the burden of the cost of those services onto people around the nation via federal grants or whatever, you could make an argument that is not an ideal situation."

"I not only could make that argument, I am making that argument."

"But federal policies are designed to address individual needs and where individuals are located geographically should be irrelevant from the federal government's perspective. It just so happens there are a lot of low-income people in certain states."

But why is this so? How is it that despite the supposed economic wonder that has graced the South, "it just so happens" that southerners remain the poorest and most unhappy people in the nation?

The answer is rooted in the traditional southern disregard for public education and a tenacious plantation mentality—you'll recall Dr. Charles Hopson in Little Rock told me the same thing—that suffocates reason out of the minds of its ill-taught masses. You don't have to take my word for that, by the way. Southerners are far more familiar with the story than I am.

"For all the economic benefits it may have brought, the courtship of foreign industry has so far done little to alter the traditional southern pattern of financing economic development at the expense of human development," writes James C. Cobb in *Globalization and the American South* (2005). "Despite Alabama's dead last standing in spending for elementary and secondary education, only a threatened lawsuit by an Alabama teacher's group prevented Governor Fob James from raiding the state's school fund to pay off a $43 million obligation to Mercedes in 1995, and the state cut $266 million from its education budget in 2001 before handing over $318 million in location and expansion incentives to Hyundai and Honda in 2002."

Cobb goes on to cite similar budget trade-offs favoring corporate welfare over public education in Mississippi, North Carolina, South Carolina, and Tennessee. No wonder southerners can't even be taught the definition of the word "socialism." [19]

The Stroke Belt: Where Every Day Is Fat Tuesday

One of the largest public costs associated with being southern, under-educated, and underpaid are gargantuan expenditures for gargantuans. An overweight population is expensive to maintain, and in terms of behavior, the South is a fat man at a county fair eating deep-fried ice cream while ambling toward the elephant ears.

On a personal level, I've got no problem with people who can't exercise self-control (much less exercise) or who consider yoga and pilates too homosexual to subject themselves to. But obesity is a national crisis. Related costs account for $150 billion a year (9.1 percent of all medical spending), of which taxpayers nationwide pay about $75 billion through Medicare and Medicaid disbursements, an over-representative share of which, remember, is doled out in southern states.

Fat, of course, is the new disabled, which is why you keep seeing so many suspiciously ambulatory-looking people chugging around grocery store bakery sections in stylish, candy-apple-red Rascal scooters. A 2004 study published in *Health Affairs* called obesity the key cause in the more than 50 percent increase in disability claims over the preceding two decades. Today, half of all disability claims made by those between ages eighteen to twenty-nine are obesity-related.[20]

This is why when some skinny community organizer who keeps himself in good enough shape to drop successive bombs from behind the three-point line gets himself into the White House, and his wife suggests that we all might want to watch our kids' weight a little more closely, and then all the fatties down south gather around to call her a whore (basically), it makes me want to choke Newt Gingrich with a KFC Double Down sandwich.

And don't imagine there isn't a political component to the fat cabaret. Listen to the Limbaugh "conservatives" and prosperity gospel preachers and you quickly see physical girth as a perversion of an American Dream theology that's somehow taken the promise of liberty, justice, and the pursuit of happiness and twisted it into a gluttony-is-good conviction that Americans deserve anything and everything they can get their hands and mouths on and to hell with anyone or anything that stands in their way.

And, okay, all of the nation's tub-o'-lards don't live Down South, but a disproportionate amount of them do.

According to a Centers for Disease Control and Prevention 2011 report, seven of the ten most obese states are in the South (eight, if you count Texas). The hungry hippo parade is led by porcine Mississippi and followed in order by West Virginia, Alabama, South Carolina, Kentucky, and Louisiana. A sebaceous 34 percent of Mississippians are obese, as compared with 21 percent of residents of Colorado, the least heavy state. West Virginia, of course, is the state in which TV chef and professional wanker Jamie Oliver stood in front of a first grade classroom in 2010 and failed to find a single student who could identify a fresh tomato or potato by name.[21]

I suppose it's naive to expect anything less from a region whose most famous grocery store is named after a pig, but the South's waddle-prone masses are nonetheless a startling feature for the tourist. I'm six-three and weigh in at a not-exactly-svelte 195 (that's what we call 205 in the Thompson house), but in virtually every southern restaurant I visited during my research, I was one of, if not the skinniest, guys in the room.

Trying to get into the swing of things at a belt-stretching Alabama meat-and-three—where feedbag devotees traded classic southern passive-aggressive barbs like, "How y'all been? We didn't see y'all in church on Sunday."—I followed my giant plate of meat and a Stone Mountain of potatoes with a dish of pecan cobbler. This delicacy was described to me by the sweet-faced grandmother behind the counter as being "just like pecan pie, only richer." As if that were somehow necessary.

Gasping for fiber at a New Orleans diner, I ordered an eggplant appetizer. It came soaked in grease and deep-fried batter. Leave it to the Stroke Belt to turn eggplant into heart attack food.

At Chester's Cypress Inn chicken joint ("If the colonel had our recipe he'd be a general") in Donner, Louisiana, everything is fried. Chicken, catfish, frog legs, gizzards, livers, shrimp. The dining room is filled with red-faced whales. On the day I visited, I stood and counted. Twenty-four people. All visibly panting. Even the kids.

The chicken oozes oil. The portions are too big. Six pieces of bird per order.

At an African American "trail ride" event (black southern cowboys, easily the most fascinating subculture I stumbled upon in the South) in Breaux Bridge, Louisiana, I spent an hour with thirty-seven-year-old Jason Bruno, a local accountant who sells Repicci's Italian ice treats on weekends at fairs and local events.

"Food is our big problem," Jason told me, referring to the African American community. "When I came back from school in Chicago I was in pretty good shape. Since April just this year I've gained ten pounds. You know what boudin is? Basically it's all the parts of the pig wrapped up in rice. We have that everywhere. I try to eat it only once a month."

This is not a healthy population. Or a culture with an optimistic life expectancy. Which makes the self-defeating "conservative" resistance to the idea of national health care incomprehensible to those of us who don't consider catfish tenders to be a lo-cal appetizer.

In fact, its willful stubbornness is just another example of the woe-betide Lost Cause mind-set that defines the region. So much of the South seems in a hurry to die, whether by biblical prophecy or the culinary Armageddon of gravy Big Gulps and deep-fried beer, a marvel of bloat-on ingenuity unveiled at the Texas State Fair in 2010.

Because southern identity is so wrapped up in its unhealthy eating habits, the blubber fest isn't going away anytime soon. Get rid of places like Chester's—or even cut the portions in half and mix in some steamed vegetables and a personal nutrition class or two—and the South just isn't the South.

As NPR *Splendid Table* host Lynne Rossetto Kasper explained to me, southern cooking uses all parts of the pig, including the fat for cooking. This makes its food and deeply ingrained eating rituals fundamentally different from those in societies whose agricultural and culinary traditions were built around healthier cooking oils derived from olives or corn.

Because you can't change history, reasonable people don't go to countries like Mongolia or Japan or Holland and lecture the locals on their yak-, seaweed-, or mayonnaise-heavy diets. In the same way, it's basically futile to tell southerners what not to eat and how much oil not to soak it in. Deny southerners their "down-home" cooking and you deny them one of their great pleasures and unique traits. You kill southerners the same way America killed the Comanche and other Plains Indians by massacring the buffalo, their primary food source and cultural point of reference.

From a "personal freedoms" standpoint, I don't care if southerners want to keep eating themselves into lard comas. As the great Texas philosopher and two-time gubernatorial candidate Kinky Friedman says, "We find what we love in this world and then we let it kill us."

If southerners don't want national health insurance coverage, if they want to whip out their muskets to defend a ten-year-old's right to morbid obesity every time someone in Washington suggests cutting down on the Little Debbie breakfasts, fine. Let 'em wallow in their paradise of wheelchairs and disability checks.

Just don't make me pay for it.

Set the South free to be as flabtastic as it wants to be. I'll come down to Louisiana once every few years to gorge for a week, then go back home to renew my gym membership and adjust the dial on my vegetable crisper for maximum crunchiness. Even if it is in the form of cholesterol and calories that I don't need, at least that way I'll no longer be subsidizing the South's inability to control its own piggish interests.

Secession: The First Easy Steps

Now that we've discarded superficial appearances and established southern economic practice as a negative influence on the rest of the country—it jilts workers, promotes poverty, sells out American interests to foreigners, wrecks the environment, makes trans fat pushers like Paula Deen and Paul Prudhomme into national heroes—the next step is figuring out exactly how to split apart a market that has been mostly conjoined for more than a couple hundred years. Waving buh-bye to a passel of religious fanatics, bloviating politicians, and Larry the Cable Guy will be easy. Lopping off millions of jobs, deep-pocketed foreign investors, and the nightly receipts from South Beach clubs will be a little more difficult to accept.

An important point to keep in mind when envisioning an independent Confederate States of America is that its relative economic strength is a good thing for a new streamlined America, not a bad thing. Sure, it'll be a bitch letting go of $3.138 trillion worth of southern GDP, but the last thing we want is another impoverished narco state on our southern border flooding the country with still more hungry, union-fearing, crucifix-clutching multitudes.[22]

We want the South to be strong, a neighbor more like Canada than Mexico. Following the economic trauma of separation—and despite any bluster about a sovereign South's ability to maintain itself on the world stage, there will be significant stress—future stability must be ensured through a series of military treaties and economic agreements that play both to southern strengths and American needs.

I refer primarily, of course, to guns and gas. Or, if you prefer the more publicity-minded terms of industry: national defense and energy.

Because of their love of uniforms, gunpowder, and the inalienable right of farmers with daughters to greet strangers at gunpoint, one of the first things an independent South is going to want to do is raise its own army. This is inevitable—trying to keep southerners away from guns and tanks is like trying to keep fourteen-year-old boys away from their peckers—but it's going to take time and money. Figure between ten and twenty years and a few gazillion yuan in loans before a neo-Confederate nation really gets itself set up to fly around the world dropping fragmentation bombs on brown people and pointing missiles at Washington, D.C., Havana, Mexico City, and San Francisco.

In the meantime, in a simple extension of the status quo, the South can continue to fatten itself at the teat of the military industrial complex. Beginning with huge federal investments following World War II and continuing at a fever pace through today, military spending has been the linchpin of southern economic vitality.

In the 1970s, the defense industry was the top employer in Georgia, Louisiana, Mississippi, and Tennessee. At times over the past few decades, nearly 50 percent of all American men and women in uniform have been located in the South and Washington, D.C. According to the U.S. Department of Labor's CareerOneStop website, the top three employers in

Georgia today are Fort Benning, Fort Stewart, and Robins Air Force Base.

To maintain American national security and southern financial stability, therefore, the United States (and, yes, the South-less North gets to keep the U.S.A. brand name) will need a series of Gitmo-like treaties on military facilities almost as badly as will the South, making a military alliance smart business for both sides.

To put the economic importance of the military into perspective, consider that of the 220 total "large" and "medium-sized" military bases and installations in the United States (as defined by the Department of Defense and including the Coast Guard), seventy-seven, or 35 percent, are located in the South. Lump in Texas's sixteen bases, and 42 percent are in the South. These include such heavyweights as Fort Bragg, North Carolina, and Fort Knox, Kentucky, as well as relative peashooters like Pine Bluff Arsenal, Arkansas, and U.S. Coast Guard Air Station Elizabeth City, North Carolina. And no offense to the fine men and women posted at either of those places, should I ever require your protective services. I'm sure whatever's going on in Pine Bluff and Elizabeth City is essential to national defense.[23]

By the way, I'm not one of these bleeding hearts who hates the military. My politics are libertarian where national defense is concerned. I like it. And I don't mind paying for it.

However, if you're one of those lefties who thinks our national sellout to defense contractors represents all that is wicked in American life, here's something that'll really make you spill macchiato all over your Sunday *New York Times*. The argument for getting rid of the South gets even stronger when you consider that without sixty years of government-coddled military expenditures in the former Confederate states, no one would have ever had any reason to print up those bumper stickers with the chilling Dwight Eisenhower quote warning about the nefarious influence of the military-industrial complex that adorns the back of your Subaru.

Without the military, the South collapses. This is because Florida and Virginia, the South's two leading economic drivers, are utterly dependent on military money. Florida is home to 181 total active and reserve military installations (including "small" and "other" installations, as classified by the Department of Defense) and three unified combatant commands. With

231 total active and reserve sites, anchored by that crucial Navy base at Norfolk, Virginia has been habituated into a similar preference for the taste of guns to butter.

The military's economic impact is staggering. In 2010, Florida governor Rick Scott announced in a come-hither meeting with defense contractors that, counting direct Florida expenditures of $27 billion, the U.S. military accounts for 10 percent of Florida's economy. This includes 732,300 direct and indirect jobs, as well as almost $1 billion in tax revenues. The research group PolitiFact later figured that Scott's estimate might actually be *low*, since the 2005 study the governor cited didn't include the impact of the Florida National Guard or Coast Guard, and that since 2005, Department of Defense spending "has risen substantially" in Florida.[24]

All of this, plus plenty more khaki-colored numbers I could bore you with, make military might the North's ultimate bargaining tool in separation negotiations with the South. (Seriously, does anything ever change in this world?) The first treaties drawn up between the North (U.S.A.) and South (C.S.A.), therefore, will logically provide for cooperative defense and co-ownership titles into perpetuity on major bases, especially at Norfolk, Pensacola, and all NASA facilities. Lease agreements on other bases around the region would sunset at increments of twenty-five, fifty, seventy-five, and a hundred years.

With these arrangements in place, an independent South is instantly assured of security, a reliable revenue stream, and an ample supply of dashing young uniformed plebes at cotillion balls. Sort of like the Philippines was until the U.S. Navy left its bases there in the 1990s. For its part, the North gets to keep Boeing, Lockheed Martin, and InDyne in business, and the People's Liberation Army Navy at bay.

Following secession, by the way, InDyne's corporate headquarters in Reston, Virginia, will remain part of the United States, per provisions of the Beltway Partition Agreement that will cede that section of Virginia to the United States. Sorry, Virginians, it's a lot of money and educated people to lose, but most of y'all don't consider that part of the state "southern" anyway, and neither do the rest of us.

•   •   •

Even with all the dire warnings about melting glaciers and earthquakes and hurricanes in New York, I can't help cranking up my thermostat in April and still sometimes drive my Buick to the Minit Mart five blocks down the street for Rainier beer and Tostitos. That means the second major piece of the U.S.A./C.S.A. Economic Separation Agreement ought to make the United States the guaranteed consumer of no less than 75 percent of all C.S.A. energy exports. This figure—which, unlike all other numbers in this chapter, I pretty much pulled out of my ass—makes sense inasmuch as it ensures northern energy needs will be met, while leaving the South with enough product to allow the new nation to nurture a healthy export economy.

In this cooperative scenario, former landowner United States is rewarded for decades of underwriting the welfare of southern workers with guaranteed access to oil refineries, coal, natural gas, and other developing energy sources. Southerners should already be familiar with this type of arrangement, which they might regard as a sort of updated sharecropper bond.

Because markets thrive on continuity, the next steps are relatively straightforward. Recognized by the United States, the Confederate States of America sets up its own national bank and stock exchange, probably in Charlotte. Open borders and existing interstate commerce laws are kept in place for a minimum of fifty years. In an agreement brokered with Canada and Mexico, the C.S.A. immediately becomes a signatory of NAFTA.

To be honest, I'm not sure what to make of NAFTA. You read the literature for two days and still can't quite figure out who's coming out ahead and who's taking it in the *pantalones*. For now, though, it's the system we've got, so it only makes sense to let southerners keep trading grits for tacos the way they've been doing for the past decade or two.

All of this talk of treaties and tacos and money finally forces me to deal head-on with an issue I've been skirting throughout this book: Texas. Ask ten Americans if they consider Texas part of the South and you can expect to get ten different answers. Ask ten Texans and you can expect a hundred different answers. All of which begin with, "That depends . . ."

My favorite answer to the "Is Texas part of the South?" question came from Coastal Carolina University history professor Dr. Charles Joyner, who advised me that for the purposes of my book I might consider the pragmatic approach other scholars have adopted when wrestling with the problem of Texas identity.

"Consider Texas part of the South when it suits your purposes," Joyner told me. "And declare it separate when it does not."

Although I have occasionally in this book provided parsed figures to show what the southern fraternity looks like with and without Texas, I've mostly taken pains to protect the ethic of Lone Star independence. While it's true that Texas is geographically connected to the South, was part of the original Confederacy, is batshit religious crazy, has a governor and onetime presidential candidate whose ranch was named "Niggerhead" and who once publicly sort of talked about thinking about the possibility of maybe perhaps seceding, and is in many significant ways culturally similar to the region as a whole, I have not treated it as part of "my South" for one reason: we can't afford to lose it.

Agriculture. Aeronautics. Computers. Energy. Research. Telecommunications. Transportation. Big-time college athletics. Texas is home to six of the top fifty Fortune 500 companies, including ExxonMobil, ConocoPhillips, and AT&T, as well as American Airlines and Dr Pepper. According to a 2011 *Economist* ranking, with a GDP of $1.224 trillion, Texas has an economy equivalent in size to Russia's. That makes it the fourteenth-largest economy in the world, second among U.S. states only to California.

For any serious secession plan to work, the South can't take with it both Texas (the second-largest state economy) and Florida (fourth largest). Like choosing sides in a pickup basketball game, the whole enterprise suffers without a fair distribution of top performers. In my secession realignment, Florida goes to the South for obvious reasons of history, geography, culture, per capita Molly Hatchet fans, appropriately dicklike appearance, and because every country needs at least one pocket of sensible liberal resistance, Florida's coming from retired Jews and Latin coke dealers.[25]

The North keeps Texas because we need the beef, because every country needs at least one pocket of gun-toting resistance to baroque hippie idealism, and because for no matter what else its sins, the state still produces the best cheerleaders we've got. Especially when they happen to be rooting for "USA! USA! USA!"

Closing the Curtain on the Great Southern Economic Swindle

Paraphrasing an 1866 account of post–Civil War southern economic policies, Edmund Wilson wrote in *Patriotic Gore*, "It is plain that Mississippi and South Carolina are already putting through new codes designed to restore serfdom." In 1942, historian, writer, Pulitzer Prize recipient, and longtime editor of the *Richmond Times-Dispatch* Virginius Dabney wrote an impassioned editorial calling for improved economic opportunities for the southern poor, particularly blacks. In 2011's *Taxing the Poor*, their exposé of the ways hidebound southern tax codes continue to perpetuate poverty among working southerners, Newman and O'Brien write:

> The legacy of the past—southern opposition to property taxation in the nineteenth century—continues to define the disparity in tax structure and revenue we see today. . . . That legacy has cost the southern states dearly [and] is placing a heavy burden on the rest of the country as well. . . . The pattern is distinctive and destructive. The problem is very much with us today in part because . . . very high barriers to change are in place throughout the South and have been for decades.[26]

In terms of uneven regional economics, it's not just that we've been here before. It's that we've been here all along. And things are getting worse. Divergence between North and South is growing, not shrinking.

What's more, southern "conservative" influence on federal fiscal policy is on the rise. Per Census-driven electoral reapportionment that will take effect in 2012, Texas will gain four seats in the U.S. House of Representatives. Florida will gain two. Arizona, Georgia, and South Carolina will add one each. Meanwhile, New York and Ohio will lose two seats each, with liberal and Rust Belt states Illinois, Massachusetts, Michigan, New Jersey, and Pennsylvania losing one each. The only southern state to lose ground, Louisiana, will get one fewer seat.[27]

I've included Texas and Arizona in the "southern gains" column above as a reminder that what have traditionally been regarded as southern "conservative" lines of attack on politics, education, religion, and economic policy have spread rapidly into the electoral bodies of the Southwest.

A bumper sticker I picked up in Georgia cheekily illustrates the contagion. It depicts a cutout map of the usual southern states against a red backdrop, but also includes contiguous Maryland, Missouri, Oklahoma, Texas, New Mexico, and Arizona as part of the "new" South. The text reads, "One nation indivisible with liberty and justice for all."

You can divine southern influence, of course, in any number of ways. Not all of them come off as pithy as a bumper sticker slogan.

Driving through rural Kentucky on Highway 460 just outside Frankfort one gray autumn afternoon, I passed by a large industrial complex in a field at the bottom of a hill. Enormous, slate-gray towers loomed over the usual sooty, fenced-off, modular warehouses. A tangle of corroded metal tubes snaked around the buildings. Massive silver storage tanks with tanker trucks lined up next to them stood nearby. By the look and smell of things, I figured the plant might be pumping out anything from rocket fuel to fertilizer.

Turning onto a narrow access road for a closer look, I passed a large wooden sign emblazoned with a familiar logo. This was no fertilizer factory. It was, surprise, the Jim Beam Old Grand-Dad plant, distiller of the liquid manifest recognized worldwide as the amber representation of sophistication, tradition, and southern charm.

From the roadside, it was about as sexy as hairs on a wart.

Pulling back the curtain on industrial production, of course, often reveals unsavory truths behind ad campaigns featuring oaken barrels, kindly old coots in suspenders, and napping hound dogs drooling on wooden porches. Driving past the ugly Jim Beam whiskey factory in the middle of

the green Kentucky countryside wasn't exactly on par with watching *Food,
Inc.* in the company of seething New Hampshire vegetarians. It was, nevertheless, a blunt reminder of how easily we all can be fooled into overlooking the bitter means used to achieve the illusion of a sweet end.

In operation since 1840, Jim Beam is a fixture of a booming South that,
as any economist will tell you, has enjoyed decades of billion-dollar investment and development. Yet for all of its growth, the South remains home
to nine of the nation's ten poorest states (including the top five) and nearly
40 percent of its impoverished people. It's a region that stands out from the
nation at large for its slavish devotion to economic policies that increase
the burdens on its poor, rather than allowing its lower and working classes
to share in the financial harvest that its politicians and business leaders are
so eager to tout in speeches, campaign debates, and keynote addresses at
symposiums designed to promote the notion of a southern-led future filled
with wine and roses, not Keystone Light and crabgrass.[28]

This time, I didn't bother to ease the car up the loose gravel road leading to the security guard shack at the front gate. There was no longer any
need for me to dig up more local stories of hard times and past-due disability checks. I'd seen enough of these places and talked to enough southern
workingmen and -women to know that I was done drinking their Kool-
Aid, no matter how much intoxicating bullshit they want to spike it with.

EPILOGUE

The South's Gonna Do It Again . . . and Again . . . and Again

One of the most surprising things about researching this book was how hard it turned out to be getting people to talk about secession. Even as a purely hypothetical thought exercise, the notion of prying the nation asunder genuinely intimidated people.

Many flat-out refused my invitations to talk about it. These included a number of high-profile political and social commentators who I'd initially thought would be fun to include in my survey, prominent figures who might have some interesting things to say on the subject. Among those who ignored multiple requests for interviews were CNN's loose Cajun cannon James Carville, *New York Times* economics guru Paul Krugman, and South Carolina senator and southern gunboat diplomat Lindsey Graham.

The snubs still surprise me. Associating with a secession advocate might be a spicy proposition for those in the media spotlight, but these are the types of publicity hounds who normally wouldn't shy away from a camera if it were planted beneath the john in a gas station bathroom.

One of the few brand names who replied to my dogged entreaties for a

secession interview was Michael Lind, policy director of the New America
Foundation's Economic Growth Program, author of such books as *Made
in Texas: George W. Bush and the Southern Takeover of American Politics*, and
a man who has practically made a living trying to convince people that the
South is a toothless lumberjack greedily chopping away at the mighty oak of
America. See the Lind quotes I used on pages 46 and 60 for typical examples.

But even Lind only emailed back to tell me that the idea of my book
was so repugnant that he wasn't going to dignify it with a quote. Quote: "I
disapprove of your project, which seems terribly snobbish, to judge by your
nasty title. The last thing we need at this moment is one group of Americans suggesting others belong in a different country. . . . Even as a joke, it
is not funny."

A fifth-generation Texan, Lind's reaction to my line of inquiry was typically southern: Angry. Hostile. Belligerent.

The stew pot of antagonism that simmers beneath the surface of many
pleasant southern countenances is something I met with often. As one
North Carolinian explained to me of his brethren's penchant for trip-
hammer indignity: "Southerners are super-well-primed to feeling misun-
derstood and underestimated and condescended to. They react to any sort
of criticism with aggression and anger. That is a huge psychological characteristic of the region and has been for over two hundred years."

If that sounds like some bong-hit observation by a turncoat southerner,
hang on. The southern tendency to rage more than others has actually been
quantified.

Among the more intriguing passages in Malcolm Gladwell's 2008 book
Outliers is the section that ties the South's nation-leading murder rates and
patterns of criminality to a University of Michigan study that measured
anger and loss of temper. Specifically, the study tested the short-fuse reactions of young males encountering a pushy stranger in a narrow hallway.
The key to the study was a trigger word—"asshole"—used by the stranger
to insult test subjects after he'd "accidentally" bumped into them.

Psychologists Dov Cohen and Richard Nisbett recorded facial expressions
and measured levels of testosterone and cortisol (the hormones connected to
arousal and aggression) to determine how quickly tempers flared following a

minor offense. The results were striking, though perhaps not surprising for anyone who has spent time in both parts of the country. Wrote Gladwell:

> Most of the young men from the northern part of the United States treated the incident with amusement. They laughed it off. Their levels of cortisol actually went down, as if they were unconsciously trying to defuse their own anger.
>
> But the southerners? Oh, my. They were *angry*. [Italics in original.] Their cortisol and testosterone jumped.[1]

Like those test subjects in Michigan, when southerners were willing to indulge me in discussions about secession, their words were more often than not imbued with anger. Mississippi-based civil rights liberal Rims Barber practically leaped out of his sensible red T-shirt and conservative gray slacks when I suggested splitting the country in two.

"It would be a disaster!" Barber shrieked. "We've got 800,000 black people in this state who want to be part of the Union. What are you going to do about them? The thing would get out of hand very fast. Black people would either have to leave or become serfs."

"That sounds a little extreme," I said.

"People always fear Reconstruction II will end like Reconstruction I. When the federal troops went away in 1875–76 that was the end. If we don't have federal rights we're dead. We have 47 black legislators out of 174 over in the capitol. If not for the federal courts we'd be lucky to have twenty. They'd be tokens. I would genuinely fear federal withdrawal. The price of liberty has to be fought for here every day."

From Apex, North Carolina, Baptist pastor James Alston was even more impatient with me.

"Even if one or two idiots wanted it, the South would petition for reinstatement within three years," Alston said, grimacing like I'd just shoved a yellow diaper in his mouth. "I don't even want to discuss this. It's not realistic. It's not helpful."

Not surprisingly, president of the League of the South secessionist organization Michael Hill was willing to speculate about an independent

South, though even he chose his words as though he were picking through a pile of unripe avocados.

"We have all the things necessary to be a strong country," Hill told me, taking on the issue from a southern survivalist perspective. "We would be resource rich, as far as energy goes. We would be able to provide for our own food. We have a reasonably well-educated workforce, and with less regulation and more true, free enterprise, the South could be an economic powerhouse.

"We certainly would be able to defend ourselves. The South has a tremendously rich military history. If not for southern participation in the military for the last 150 years, the U.S. military might not have been able to do some of the things it did."

I couldn't disagree with Hill on that last statement. And I appreciated his optimism. But his log cabin ruminations weren't exactly the voice of mainstream reason I was after—at least not as expressed aloud in decent society.

Although he was one of the few northern or southern politicians ballsy enough to take my call, my conversation with South Carolina congressman Joe Wilson, the man who became infamous for shouting "You lie!" during President Obama's 2009 State of the Union address, was a disappointment. Displaying the veteran pol's celerity with misdirection, Wilson deflected questions such as "Would the South be better or worse off if it seceded?" by providing long-winded discourses on the history of the Republican Party in South Carolina (an area of special interest for him, as it turns out) and, predictably, refuting phantom charges of racism, even though I never brought up the subject in any way.

After I suggested that southerners might appreciate the right to decide for themselves on the legality of abortion and how to handle immigration, Wilson replied, apropos of nothing, "South Carolina had the very first Jewish elected official in the United States; his name was Francis Salvador."

Salvador was a London Jew who came to Charles Town in 1773 and indeed served as deputy to the Provincial Congress of South Carolina in 1775 and 1776. Wilson followed this bizarre observation with another one apparently meant to head off some imagined pattern of Palmetto State anti-Semitism.

"South Carolina's speaker of the house [for thirty-two years] starting in the 1930s was Solomon Blatt, who was a person of Jewish heritage,"

Wilson informed me. "I know from the liberal perspective we're perceived as being intolerant, but that has not been the case." [2]

"Why does the southern-led conservative coalition in Congress seem so unwilling to negotiate with northern liberals?" I pressed on, ignoring all the disconnects. "Isn't politics about the art of compromise? Might it be that southern politicians would simply prefer not to deal with the other half of the country altogether?"

"That's a misperception. The very first year I was in Washington, D.C., I think I was rated the most conservative member in Congress. That same year Diane Watson of California might have been the most liberal member. We had offices right across from each other and we were the best of friends."

Only once did Wilson relent and address secession, and then only in a historical context.

"I know the consequences of secession; it's called turning the state into ash," he allowed of the Civil War. "It was not good."

The twenty-minute conversation with Wilson left me feeling as though I'd been granted an audience with the riddler Sphinx. The points I was trying to make simply weren't registering with him.

Regarding his apparent assumption that charges of bigotry are behind every northern criticism of the South, Wilson did strike me as an absolutely flawless representative of his people. Nice man. Smart enough to rattle off a bunch of facts. But worlds apart in sharing my understanding of the central issues affecting the country.

This was typical of my conversations with southerners. Either these people were living in complete denial of reality, or I'd become consumed by a paranoid pipe dream. Given what I'd seen at places like the Creation Museum, I was inclined to go with the former.

The Southern Rebuttal: Seven Wise Men and a Facebooking Chick I Hope Gets Flunked

Toward the end of the very first interview I conducted for this book, Coastal Carolina University history professor Charles Joyner told me, "If you're really serious about this project, you're eventually going to have to speak with Jim Cobb."

Jim Cobb—it's James Cobb on the covers of the thirteen books he's written or edited, several of which are quoted in this book—is widely considered one of, if the not *the*, preeminent living scholars on the South. Neither Dixie apologist nor hater, the much-awarded University of Georgia professor's influence on southern scholarship has made him a beacon among those who think and write about the South for a living. He's a former president and still leading member of the Southern Historical Association. If Ken Burns were making his Civil War documentary today, Cobb is likely the man he'd call on to fill in for the deceased Shelby Foote.

Cobb proved easy to track down by phone. To my eternal appreciation, he was not only willing to discuss secession with a stranger, he was, after a bit of explanation, even willing to give my twisted exercise his blessing.

This is not to say he was ready to take my cold-country opinionating lying down. From the start, Cobb's attitude toward me felt less like professional rapprochement than the lip-smacking "give him enough rope" air of encouragement associated with prosecuting attorneys when bumbling murder defendants choose to take the stand in their own defense.

"Tell me again why you're not including Texas in your plan for partition?" Cobb asked calmly after I'd hit him with two smoking barrels of Yankee secession logic.

"Because it's too valuable to give up," I said. "Southerners can complain all they want about how they're the 'real Americans' and defenders of the true American tradition, but if they want to escape the tyranny of Washington, D.C., they're going to have to make concessions."

"What about Ohio?"

"We're keeping it."

"Good. You can have it. Talk about a bunch of crazy people."

Shit, did we really want Ohio? Cobb had a magical facility for placing doubt in my mind.

"Actually, maybe we can kick that around a little," I said. "You interested in all of Ohio south of Franklin County?"

"What's fascinating about your model is that you are presuming it's going to be northerners who are going to draw up the blueprint," he replied. "'We'll let you have this, we'll let you have that.' Why should southerners settle for losing Texas? They are probably more influential in Congress than any northern bloc. Where have you been, son?"

Finally! A southerner willing to engage. And not with faith and fallacy, either, but with analysis and brainpower. And gay-bash-free sass. I hung up the phone and booked a flight for Athens.

The idea behind my trip to the University of Georgia, one of the South's largest academic communities, was to convene a roundtable secession forum with a select group of southern academics and students. For going on two years I'd been formulating my arch-plan for secession. Now I wanted to present my ideas to a panel of qualified southerners interested in responding to it.[3]

The trip would finally give me the chance to find out if any thinking person outside of Michael Hill would agree with the notion that both sides of this nation might be after the same thing: freedom from the other's senseless and seditionist tendencies. I'd bounce around ideas, let learned southerners shoot a few holes in my theory, figure out which spots needed patching up. Best-case scenario: I'd find common ground with southern scholars, young and old, who couldn't help but acknowledge the mutual benefit of North and South parting ways.

The plan gets under way on a sunny November morning with me taking a wooden-backed, fold-down seat in the rear of "Understanding Southern Culture," Jim Cobb's Tuesday-Thursday undergraduate course. In his sixties, Cobb enters the room slowly, with a bit of a limp. He wears silver, wire-rimmed glasses. His full head of white hair is brushed back. He carries two pens, one black, one blue, in the pocket of his long-sleeved checkered dress shirt.

From a small Georgia town near the South Carolina border—his favorite Faulker novel is *The Hamlet*—"Cobby" is not so much a dynamic lecturer as he is a thoughtful presenter. Like the sun poking in and out of the clouds on a stormy day, his wry humor shows up in flashes, drawing laughs and keeping the class on alert for the next sardonic aside.

"I assume everyone's calmed down from our incredible victory over the hated Florida Gators," Cobb says to open the class. He flicks on an overhead projector—the red and blue presidential electoral map of 1924 appears on the screen—and commences a discussion of the civil rights movement's role in the demise of the Democratic Party in the South.

Though I haven't been on this side of a college classroom in more than twenty years, muscle memory and test anxiety instantly kick in. Even though I'm pretty sure Cobb isn't going to make me sit for the midterm (but he's a crafty one, so who knows?), I begin scribbling in my spiral-bound Mead notebook so fast my hand cramps up. I was a heroic note taker in college, a front-row sitter capable of filling entire notebooks in the space of a week, while friends shambled back from class with only empty pages and plans for the weekend.

As it did then, it occurs to me in Cobb's classroom that somebody somewhere needs to teach college kids a class in note taking. Maybe I'd just forgotten how disengaged or hungover twenty-year-olds can be at 11 a.m., but these kids are pathetic, especially the blond chick in front of me who spends the entire lecture scrolling through Halloween party photos of herself on Facebook.

From Cobb I'll not only finally get the answer to the question of those two extra stars on the Rebel flag (the optimistic Confeds added stars for Kentucky and Missouri, whose state legislatures were divided on the issue of secession), but classic examples of the poetic rhetoric southerners of yore could muster even in the service of their heinous prejudice. Reacting to a black minister brought in to give the invocation at the 1936 Democratic National Convention in Philadelphia, Cobb tells us that appalled South Carolina senator "Cotton Ed" Smith described the man as being "as black as melted midnight" before storming out of the convention with the declaration, "Get outa my way. This mongrel meeting ain't no place for a white man!" How do you not pay attention in a class like this?[4]

Blondie aside, most of the students do seem engaged in the lecture. Several casual discussions I have after class—from this group I plan to recruit a handful of students for my ad hoc secession forum—only enhance my estimation of their professor.

"Cobb is the next legend of southern academia," says a young man in unlaundered sweatpants with a Big Gulp glued to his paw. "He understands the southern experience without apologizing for it."

"I dropped my religion major just so I could take this class from Cobb," says an earnest twenty-two-year-old named Dylan.

"I waited three years to take this class," chips in a large, thick-boned kid named Wade. "Cobb is the vast majority of us. Other professors here are more of outside observers. They're just going to make you feel bad for being a white southerner. I don't need that this semester."

"You're at the mecca of southern understanding right now with Cobb, Inscoe, and Bullock all here," adds Dylan.

In addition to southern history's star player, Dylan is referring to UGA history professor John Inscoe, who has written about the importance of southern memoir and multiculturalism, and Charles Bullock, a UGA political science professor who has become a national authority and talking head when the media needs pinpoint analysis of southern politics and voting patterns. Along with retired UGA sociology prof Woody Beck, who made his name studying southern lynchings, these four tenured academics have agreed to make up the fearsome foursome on the professorial side of my secession roundtable.*

From the "Understanding Southern Culture" class I attract three students, thanks largely to the standby collegiate enticement of free beer. All are male, all are white, all are upperclassmen, and all, happily, are of age, meaning my six-strong panel of southern spokesmen can retreat to the Globe, an atmospheric pub with a large, curved brass bar on the north end of the sprawling campus.

The student section of my secession panel is made up of three Cobb students: Georgia-born Dylan, North Carolina native Matt, and Made in Georgia Wade. Though all three "die-hard southerners" have that

---

* Bullock was unable to attend the actual roundtable. I interviewed him in his office an hour before meeting with the rest of the panel and have included some of his observations as part of the larger discussion presented here.

recognizable fraternity bearing, it doesn't take long for distinguishing features to become evident.

With a well-worn Atlanta Braves cap pulled low over his forehead, dark-haired Dylan is the most introspective and equivocal. I size him up fairly quickly as the most likely defector of the bunch, a natural skeptic who in two or three years will probably be living in New York or Seattle or Shanghai.

With an athletic build, strong jaw, and crew cut, Matt could easily be cast as the guy in cut-off sleeves driving a tractor in a country music video. Raised on a cattle farm in North Carolina, he's got the pedigree. Not that he's some kind of country-hunk meathead. Of everyone at the table, including the professors, Matt presses his points on southern culture with the most precision.

By outward appearances the product of money, Wade's curly blond mop is a perfect complement to the type of engaging youthful truculence that springs from an upbringing of comfort and the confidence that financial needs will never be a great concern in life. Wade is intelligent, easygoing, and likable, but the outspoken, bully-pulpit charge in his voice is unique at the table.

Red, White, and Patel: These Colors Don't Run. But They Do Sometimes Mix Uncomfortably

Cobb, Beck, Inscoe, and I arrive first, and settle into a large semicircular booth next to the front window facing the street. Over a first round of beers, I recap my research for Beck and Inscoe. The ice cream socials, the redneck bars, the epic, personal meltdowns on election nights 2000 and 2004. When the three students arrive and take up seats around the table, Cobb says, "Now don't be fooled by this fast-talking Yankee, he's just as full of bullshit as the rest of them."

Assuming no grander introduction forthcoming, I order another round for the table and lay out my scenario for secession. Starting with the political and economic plans outlined in the previous chapter, I weave in details of a sovereign paradise for everyone from Foghorn Leghorn to Guatemalan immigrants.

"Imagine a South free to run its business according to the will of its people," I say. "Abortion. Illegal. Gay marriage. Gone. Trade unions. Abolished. Ten Commandments. Carved in granite on the capitol steps in Atlanta and posted at the front of every classroom. Confederate dollars. Issued by the C.S.A. Treasury in Charlotte with Jeff Davis on the one, Nathan Forrest on the five, Robert E. Lee on the ten, and Dale Earnhardt on the twenty."

The panel is intrigued. Or at least polite enough to allow me to continue as long as I'm footing the bar tab.

I explain provisions of the U.S.A./C.S.A. Treaty of Secession that mandate a ten-year open border and automatic citizenship in either country for those left on the wrong side of the national divide. Thus might everyone from tofu-snarfing liberals trapped in Arkansas to God-fearing survivalists holed up in the mountains of Washington be allowed unencumbered passage and legal residence in the social homeland of their choosing. With no zealot left behind, both sides finally assume the shape of the cohesive cultural units they were always destined to be.

At last able to send children to schools that reflect their ethnic values, the guilt-free Confederate man and wife come home from their second jobs at the Dongfeng plant (work is plentiful, living wages are a different story), crack open cans of Dixie Pride beer, and flick through channels on Satellite South, the country's sole communications provider—"The only information you need," goes the system's operating slogan.

After a few minutes of *Confederate Idol*—Faith Hill is a godsend panel counterpoint next to that asshole Jew record producer from L.A., who nevertheless does get off a good line or two each week—they stop on Stars and Bars News.

In Atlanta, President McDonnell and Secretary of Commerce and Energy Bush are preparing to welcome a delegation of ASEAN country representatives. Tomorrow's economic summit meetings are expected to be less congenial than tonight's state dinner—hoisin-glazed pork belly, confit of crawfish, and jalapeño-infused cornbread are on the menu—with representatives from the Philippines, Laos, and Myanmar already accusing the C.S.A. of using lowball labor bids to undercut their own existing trade agreements with China and Unified Korea.

As always, Taiwan is boycotting the meetings in protest of the C.S.A.'s refusal to recognize its political autonomy. From the very beginning of its independent history, the C.S.A. has used Taiwan to drive a wedge between the United States and China, cannily exploiting America's increasingly untenable position vis-à-vis its long-standing Taiwanese ally and mounting economic dependence on China. Beijing has been only too willing to play the two countries off one other, giddy to finally have significant leverage in the South China Sea against the world's greatest military power. The C.S.A.'s most important diplomatic coup often leaves the United States and Taiwan twisting in the wind on numerous issues involving China.

In domestic politics, the liberal minority Republican Party is threatening to filibuster the vote on the Senate majority Fundamentalist Party's proposed tax cuts. The Confederate GOP is forecasting doom if its own plan for federal tax increases isn't adopted in time to be implemented for next fiscal year.

The religion news is brighter, with the national Bureau of Spiritual Services releasing statistics that show an all-time low in illegal abortions. The decrease is due largely to the imposition and enforcement of even stiffer prison sentences for offenders in Florida and Georgia. The Lord and Savior Jesus Christ remains a loving and nurturing close personal friend to all of his Confederate charges.

In international news, the American Atheist Party is celebrating victory in the Vermont gubernatorial campaign. The win gives the party control of its first major elected office.

Joining existing New York–Philadelphia–D.C. and Los Angeles–San Francisco–Seattle lines, the United States' third high-speed rail route is set to link Chicago, St. Louis, and Dallas. Traveling at speeds of 235 mph, the train is part of an American-Chinese-Japanese-French rail consortium whose multiple projects are all deeply in debt and several years behind schedule.

In sports, while Diesel McCabe, the C.S.A.'s top-rated prep quarterback, has outraged the nation by committing to play football at Ohio State, all nine of the nation's remaining top ten recruits have signed letters of intent with Confederate schools. Vegas oddsmakers have installed the

University of Nokia at North Carolina CellNet™ Tar Heels as prohibitive favorites to bring home the C.S.A.'s third consecutive Coca-Cola/Starbucks Blood Bowl™ trophy.

I blurt it all out in ten minutes—the dubious Blood Bowl winning streak being a curry-favoring olive branch—then sit back and take stock of my mesmerized audience.

"What do you think?" I say.

Hands wrapped expectantly around pint glasses, the panel defers to the celebrated font of southern wisdom, waiting for judgment from the very seat of Dixie acumen.

"Well," Cobb finally allows. "I think you-all will be dull as shit without us. You won't be much fun to be around."

Cobby's students pick up the thread.

"There's a reason we study southern history and not midwestern history or northeastern history," says Dylan.

"Because we're more interesting," kicks in Wade.

"Would we keep having to take so many immigrants from you guys?" Cobb asks. "Because some of us are getting a little sick of it."

Not precisely the reaction I'd expected. But no disaster. No one seems overly outraged by my plan. In fact, they seem to be taking the breakup surprisingly well.

As the conversation rolls forward, Cobb naturally assumes the point position. He starts a lot of sentences to me with phrases like, "The thing you don't understand is . . ." and "The issue I have with your gross oversimplification is . . ."

Pretty soon, everyone is chipping away at my key points.

First is religion. I roll out my now well-rehearsed beef about evangelicals, and forecast the church playing an even greater role in southern society once the South is freed from all that annoying "separation of church and state" drivel. The back-and-forth goes on for thirty or forty minutes.

"*Roe v. Wade* would go out the window, but other than that I don't know how much things would change," Professor Beck says.

"You're playing into the theocracy thing too hard," Matt protests. "It's not as religion-based as you think down here, especially among my generation. Nobody I know is adamantly protesting against civil unions."

"You're talking about the older generation of southerners, that's not us at all," adds Wade.

"That excuse has been repeated for a hundred years," I say. "Things are always supposed to be getting better in the South, the younger generation is always changing things, but things never change."

I ask the students about their religious upbringings. Dylan is Catholic. Matt grew up attending Presbyterian services every Sunday. Wade proudly proclaims he attends the same church as his great-great-grandfather.

Like most twenty-somethings, this group doesn't understand that they won't be the same at forty-something, after jobs have become careers, and kids, mortgages, and retirement investments have given them a larger stake in the game. That's when they'll become nostalgic for the halcyon days and turn to the conservative lessons of their youth for guidance.

People spend their teens and twenties rebelling against their parents. They spend their forties and fifties becoming them. That's also when they start to vote in reliable numbers, and begin to exert genuine influence on society.

"Don't tell me this isn't formative, that this isn't the institution through which social conservatism is still passed down," I argue. "Superficially things might look slightly different. Sure, Jim Crow no longer exists. But the South keeps voting the same, it bends over forward for business the same, it educates its kids the same, its college football programs still feel just as crooked as its elections, and, at the core, its hypocritical hyper-religiosity bleeds into every aspect of society. The South doesn't get less Bible thump-y with independence, it gets more so."

This little screed nearly brings West Virginian Woody Beck out of his seat.

"Things haven't changed? Are you kidding me?" Beck sputters into his glass. "On the way over here I saw a young white boy and black girl hugging and kissing. For someone who grew up in the South that's a fucking revolution! It's a REVOLUTION!"

To me, this is just southerners doing out in the open what they've always done in the butler's pantry. What I feel like saying is that banging black girls ain't nothing new for white boys in the South. But Beck's outburst is so impassioned I hold back my intuitive dickishness.

"Show me another population of two juxtaposed races that have seen as much change for the better—and, yes, some for the worse—over fifty years," says Cobb.

"I have a friend from Italy," Beck continues. "He says, 'I can't believe how many Confederate flags I see on bumpers.' I say, 'Roberto, I can't believe how few Confederate flags I see compared with what I grew up with.'"

"My father died in 1968," says Cobb. "If he came back now he'd probably die again."

"He'd probably commit suicide," adds Beck.

"It's easy to bring the quick hammer down on the South," says Cobb. "But no one said how long this was supposed to take."

"Well, how long is it supposed to take?" I ask, moving on to address racism in the South. "Social rights activist Rims Barber told me an independent southern nation would amount to Armageddon for African Americans because they still rely on federal protections to ensure things like access to the political process, fair housing, and public schools. What happens to African Americans in an independent southern state?"

"How old is Barber?" Beck asks.

"He was seventy-three when he told me that last year," I say.

"That figures," Beck nods. "That's a typical attitude of people who faced the truncheons of the civil rights era. But blacks are not going back to Jim Crow. There would be a race war."

Not everyone is so confident. Earlier, Charles Bullock had told me that secession might endanger provisions of the Voting Rights Act. When I asked what parts of the Voting Rights Act are important to African Americans, Bullock raised his eyebrows and sighed the deeply distressed sigh of the put-upon professor saddled with a never-ending supply of retard undergrads. Tough guy to have as your adviser.

Signed into law in 1965 by President Lyndon Johnson, Bullock explained, the Voting Rights Act abolished literacy tests and other unfair measures used to determine voter eligibility. It's hailed as the key piece of legislation that allowed large numbers of blacks and non-English-speaking Americans in the South to finally go to the polls.

"Without federal enforcement," Bullock told me, "there could be a lapse of compliance."

"I don't think I'd go that far," Cobb responds in the Globe. "In your scenario, there would be a lot of risk involved for lower-income blacks because a lot of what has been done for them comes from the federal government. But by far there have been more black businesses created in the southern states than the North. Atlanta, Dallas, there are more affluent black people in the South than anywhere else in the country. You're going to be losing a lot of wealthy, educated black people."

"Maybe federal protections have helped some southern blacks prosper in an environment that's historically been tilted against them," I posit.

"What broke the back of segregation in the South was that the economic cost was too high," counters Cobb. "There isn't any evidence of southerners practicing discrimination to their economic detriment. Woolworth's was just fine with Jim Crow as long as it wasn't causing any problems. When the lunch counter sit-ins began [in Greensboro, North Carolina, in 1960], that's when they got uptight about it."

"If your effort is to prove the South is more racist than the North, you're doomed to fail if you're being intellectually honest," says Beck.

"But you might be on to something," Dylan says to me. "I can't get over the fact that we've sat here discussing the South for an hour and haven't talked about the African American experience once until now. That deeply troubles me."

"I used to work in a hunting club in South Carolina," says Matt. "I worked with four older black men. I had this longing to know where they were from. It was the most southern experience I've ever had. One was a farm manager whose great-great-grandfather was a slave. That's southern right there."

"I had the same experience on a construction job last summer in Georgia," says Wade. "My best friend on the site was a black guy."

"May I then take this opportunity to make an asshole observation?" I say, waiting for the hesitant nods. "I was in Cobb's Understanding

Southern Culture class this morning and did a head count. Out of thirty-two students in the room, thirty-two were white."

"It's a problem, but do you know what the most common last name at the University of Georgia among incoming freshmen is this year?" asks Inscoe. "It's Patel. You don't see a lot of Jim Williamses or Susie Davises. In southern history and culture topics, it's still hard to lure African American undergraduates, who are not going to be confident about the comfort level of the class."

"African Americans in the South might not have it as bad as people like Rims Barber predict," I say. "But I'm guessing a lot of them would be happy to take advantage of my open emigration and citizenship policy."

"We are a hundred years away from equality," agrees Matt. "People who think otherwise are fucking idiots."

Colonized by Texas! A Secession Plan Gone Awry

Next up, another round from the bar. Then business and politics.

"Set free from the North, how does the South pay for itself?" I ask once the gang has settled back into the booth. "Would the South finally sack up and pay for its own social services?"

"The South has always hated the federal government, so with secession they'd become their own worst enemy," says Beck. "They'd be faced with the devil. They'd have to establish a federal government. Impose taxation at a federal level. They'd need to spend taxes for military."

"You'd see a severe shrinkage of the welfare system," says Cobb. "We're going to give all of them [welfare recipients] cheap bus tickets to your part of the country. That's what they did in Mississippi in World War II. Gave them all bus tickets to Chicago and information on how to get on welfare."

"Deporting poor people sounds like a Cuban solution to the problem," I say, acknowledging Cobb's half-joke.

"Southerners don't mind spending if it's on defense," responds Cobb. "The Department of Southern Defense would be the largest employer in the South. The fact is, there is a general willingness to operate on a small tax base. Part of that is because we're living too much now off the federal government."

Earlier I'd asked political science professor Bullock if an independent South would be obliged to reverse its traditional antipathy toward federal taxation.

"It would have to, yes," Bullock said without hesitation. "It would want to do even simple things like opening embassies all over the world. That requires public money."

"So, after centuries of hostility toward federal governance, *now* southerners would be willing to say, 'Okay, with Uncle Sam no longer around to take care of us, we've changed our minds, we'll contribute to a federal government, just as long as it's *our* federal government?'"

"They'd let some functions lapse," predicted Bullock. "They'd let the EPA or OSHA or things like this lapse. They wouldn't provide every function. But at the very least they'd need some form of armed services."

"How would southern politics evolve?"

"Initially, you'd have the Democratic and Republican parties continuing on, with a helping of Dixiecrat or Tea Party types."

"In other words, the same system we have now?"

"The ones being squeezed out of southern politics right now are white Democrats," Bullock told me. "Only one white Democrat is left in Congress from the Deep South—John Barrow of the 12th District of Georgia. That trend would continue. The state legislative chambers have far more black members who are Democrats than whites. Whites equal Republicans. Blacks equal Democrats. The Republican Party in the South is the white person's party. Latinos and African Americans are growing populations. Not too far down the road, there will not be enough whites even for Republicans to hold on to their seats.

"I think if there were a secession movement it would extend to Texas, Oklahoma, New Mexico, and Arizona," said Bullock. "It would become the Sun Belt against the Rust Belt. Where is the growth in this country? The Sun Belt. The South. The remainder of the nation is losing an awful lot of its dynamic. It would be the Rust Belt that would continue to rust."

When I repeat it at the Globe, Bullock's "rust" comment draws a big laugh. After Cobb predicts that the major political conflict to come in the

South will be between African Americans and Hispanics—"People are dead wrong to assume that blacks and Hispanics are a natural coalition"—the discussion takes a sharp right turn to consider the effects of secession on my side of the divide.

"When y'all secede from the South you're going to have the Republican homeland in Idaho to contend with," notes Cobb.

"That's okay," I respond. "My problem isn't with Republicans. It's with hyperventilating ideologues and extremists who want to conflate Bible law with U.S. law. When they're behaving like reasonable negotiators, the Republicans are fine."

"You'll reach a point where you'll be sorry you didn't give us Texas, they'll be a pain in the ass," Cobb continues. "My prediction? Texas is liable to take over the whole damn place. It'll have more people than California."

"You may become an extension of Texas," agrees Beck. "You'll regret not giving that to the South."

One of the students makes the observation that the Texas flag is the perfect symbol of the Texan outlook—it's just like the American flag, only without any of the other states. Laughter spreads across the table.

"Another thing you liberal boys will have to deal with is Utah and Montana and other states wanting to be part of the South," continues Cobb, now positively warming not just to the idea of secession, but secession with noncontiguous southern anschluss. "It'll be like college football conference realignment. Everybody wants to be part of the SEC."

"Everybody doesn't want to be part of the SEC," I mutter unconvincingly. "Even the University of Texas didn't want to join the SEC because it didn't want to lower its academic standards in order to compete. The university president once said as much."[5]

To my disappointment, no one takes this bait, maybe because it hits too close to home. Or maybe because it's getting harder and harder to get a word in with the beer-fueled debate now reaching a volume that attracts attention from other tables around the bar.

"Why is it all these people from other parts of the country decide to move to the South?" demands Cobb. "Maybe the public schools aren't as good, but people look at things here and make a decision and decide they prefer lower taxes to good schools. There's something here they like. What you represent is a minority. People outside the South aren't as liberal as you think."

I tell Cobb he might well be right, but repeat that the issue I have is with mainstream southern radicalism, not heartland-style conservatism.

"The ultimate question, I suppose, is whether or not you see the North and South as fundamentally different places," I say.

The table ponders this for a moment, once more deferring to Cobb.

"I never met anybody who spent any time down South who came from elsewhere in the country who didn't get a different feel from the South," he says. "I don't see that fading."

I don't either. If nothing else it was worth coming to Georgia to get professional verification.

When I'd asked Bullock if he thought North and South might separate culturally after secession, he'd answered quickly.

"I would assume the two sides would drift apart," he said. "The competition to recruit business from around the world would factor into that. It would not be a hostile relationship, but I would assume a degree of rivalry."

"The South today is much more obsessed with economic development than any other issue," says Cobb, affirming Bullock's position.

"You don't have to tell me that," I reply, bringing up the story of the poached Boeing plant in South Carolina and my litany of gripes about the South's role in the decimation of Detroit.

"You haven't been watching closely when there is a bidding war for one of those big factories," Cobb says. "What northern states now give to industry is very comparable to what is offered in the South."

"That's part of my point," I say. "The rest of the country is increasingly adopting southern tactics. It's just like Texas trying to resist lowering its standards in order to compete with the SEC. You know they won't hold out forever. We're all being forced into this Third World business model because we're being undercut by the Third World southern market inside our own country."

For some reason, people get upset when you start describing their homes as "Third World." The intensity of the debate ratchets up instantly. After all the bashing away at the South I've been doing, it's only fair to let the guys discharge some spleen at my people. Dylan tells a story about working as a lifeguard at Sea Island, Georgia, the hoity-toity resort that for nearly a century has been the retreat of choice for the South's filthy wealthy.

"After the G8 Summit was held there [in 2004] the resort began appealing to outside travelers," Dylan says. "We went from seeing clientele that was genteel and patriotic to all of a sudden there's all of these Chicago and Ohio and Boston and New Jersey and Pennsylvania accents. The whole culture of the place has changed for the worse."

"Jeans at bingo! That was the worst!" interjects a scandalized Wade, whose family have been Sea Island visitors for several generations. "In the last five or ten years it's just a bunch of Yankees complaining that you can't wear jeans to bingo. 'Oh, but they're $200 jeans!' You never heard such a stink."

"I have more animosity toward Yankees than to other people," Dylan admits. "That rate of talk. The amount of words Yankees use. I have a wariness of northerners. I do."

"Carpetbaggers!" Wade exclaims.

"You still use that word?" I ask.

"We have carpetbaggers up the ass," Wade says.

"This afternoon John [Inscoe] told me about an instructor at The Citadel who is proposing to teach a class on the Civil War called 'The War for Southern Independence,'" I say, gesturing to Inscoe across the table and giving in to the unavoidable Yankee-Rebel conflict these discussions always devolve into.

"That's the first time I've seen that sort of language at the college level," Inscoe confirms.

"Where does all this nonsense about the Civil War not being about slavery come from?" I ask. "And why does it gain such currency with so many educated people? It's an embarrassment to the South."[6]

"It becomes a way of dealing with race and class discontent and the lingering inferiority complex," says Inscoe. "It's been going on since at least the 1980s. A lot of it is resentment over the Civil Rights Act and affirmative action."

"We have this chip on our shoulder from growing up down South," Matt says, relating a version of a story I've heard hundreds of times. "I grew up hunting and fishing. When I was a high school freshman at a boarding school in Orange, Virginia, my roommate was from New York. I went to New York and stayed with his family for a week and I have never been so bombarded with questions and comments about the South.

"I had no idea there was such a disconnect. The first question I got was, 'Do you own a gun?' They kept talking about my accent."

"So what?" I say. "When I came down from Alaska I got the same thing. Is it dark all the time? Do they use American money there? Do you live in an igloo? Who cares? Why be so sensitive to this stuff?"

"I realized when I went up there they thought I was one of those rednecks I'd always disassociated with," Matt continues. "From then on I started becoming more southern."

"For sure!" Wade erupts, clearly now feeling his oats. Not to mention his hops and barley. "I don't give a shit about abortion, but don't try to take away my guns."

"Who the hell is trying to take them away?" I ask. "I'll never understand this paranoia about gun control. Where does it come from? Please listen to me: no one is trying to take away your guns. People like shooting shit in the rest of the country just as much as you do. Come to Oregon, I'll show you where to blast all the pheasant and elk and Bambis you can fit on the hood of your car."

"The most fundamental flaw I see in your scenario is the South has come to really embody the real patriotic America," counters Wade. "If we secede, the U.S.A. would become Canada South. We are the real U.S.A."

In Which Our Intrepid Reporter Survives Butterscotch Shots and Summons the Ghost of Rhett Butler for Analytical Support

No matter how noble the original intentions of its participants, the inviolable rule of debate is that standards of academic rigor have an inverse relation to the amount of alcohol consumed. As an Arkansas friend of mine likes to say in bars, "There's a whole lot of talking going on here, but not much saying."

"Would secession be detrimental to the North?" I ask, making a final bid to draw insight from the elder statesmen before the mawkish, Faulknerian soliloquies about Granpappy's hand-me-down deer rifle and Skynyrd and old black men inevitably start gushing from the intoxicated young rabble.

"It depends on the ground rules you lay down," says Cobb, noting for the record that in the event my ludicrous fantasy were to ever come true he'll be staying in Georgia. "You guys might be putting up a Berlin Wall because you're losing so many people. We might put one up because we're gaining so many."

"If you don't have the South to look down on who would you look down on?" asks Beck.

"I don't want to look down on anybody," I say. "I'm not here to look down on the South. I'm merely suggesting that the region's core social values and collective political will are incompatible with the prevailing attitudes and institutions in the rest of the country. Is that wrong?"

"You'd have to look at yourself in the mirror and you might not like it," says Cobb, brushing aside my argument. "A big part of the country's idea of the South is static. It's hung up on Selma and it's not going to see the South as anyplace else. To them, the South hasn't changed. My point isn't that the South doesn't deserve a hellacious amount of criticism. It does—even more sometimes than it gets. My objection to what you're doing is using the South to wink at all the stuff in the rest of the country that needs addressing."

Professors aren't professors for no reason. When my three wise men see the slushy, truth-serum effects of beer and political talk with a loudmouthed Yankee descending upon the evening, each bids a polite farewell and makes a hasty exit.

Less wise, I remain bolted to the booth—another round of beer is on the way and we mustn't leave dead soldiers. After more ardent, dead-end discussion, Dylan, Matt, Wade, and I end up lurching into the night for another campus bar—at this point my notes become illegible, so don't ask me the name of the place—where I end up breaking two of my cardinal drinking rules: shots, frat boys.

This is a combination even more lethal than red wine and tequila. Especially when the shots come in waves and taste like butterscotch anus. Within an hour I'll be zigzagging down an Athens sidewalk trying to remember if I'm staying at the Holiday Inn or the Holiday Inn Express four blocks away.

Even the conviviality of last call can't bring the roundtable together. The discussion to decide the future of South and North ends in stalemate. In some ways, I'm back where I'd started with this project, destined to dissent.

Nothing really new there. As Abe Lincoln said of slavery in the run-up to the Civil War, "Their thinking it right, and our thinking it wrong, is the precise fact upon which depends the entire controversy."

It takes little imagination to apply that statement to many of the fundamental divisions still hamstringing the country: religion, abortion, federal governance, taxation, education, health care, assistance for less fortunate neighbors, distribution and ownership of public wealth and resources. These are philosophical and moral problems with no definitive answers, issues that simply come down to one side thinking them right, and the other side thinking them wrong.

In his "House Divided" speech, Lincoln also said that he did not believe the American house would fall. "I do expect it will cease to be divided," he said. "It will become all one thing, or all the other."[7]

But Lincoln was wrong about that one. Unity hasn't ever really come. Slavery is gone, but the cultural milieu that produced it and a raft of other cultural toxins still exists. After more than 150 years of contending with the national divide, I think even persevering old Abe by now might be moved to toss in his cards and say, "Fuggit, this fight ain't worth it anymore, let 'em go already."

Although the night hadn't produced the secession quorum I'd be angling for, in an unexpected way it did provide a glimpse into how the future of the South might play out, with or without separation.

In the same fashion that people across the South had denied culpability to me, had winked at all the issues that needed addressing in their own part of the country, every one of those who'd gathered at the Globe had in some form or other insisted that they themselves did not embody the predictable characteristics and behaviors (I'm not calling them stereotypes, I believe I've provided enough evidence to back up my contentions) that I was using to portray the less attractive side of Dixie.

We aren't crazy religious—*that*'s just a small percentage of southerners who you're thinking of.

We aren't dedicated political obstructionists—*that*'s just a small percentage of southerners who you're talking about.

We aren't racist—*that*'s just a small percentage of southerners who have a problem.

We aren't the ones keeping public school budgets at barely functional levels—*that*'s just a small percentage of southerners that don't appreciate the inequities in the system.

We aren't against basic rights for workers—*that*'s just a small percentage of southerners who you have an issue with.

We aren't single-issue abortion voters or the ones who have a problem with gays—*that*'s just a small percentage of southerners who the media unfairly fixates on and uses to vilify the rest of us.

All of these statements may be true. The majority of southerners are not loudmouthed, uneducated, redneck fuckwits flying Confederate flags from the backs of their Kia and Mercedes lynch wagons. To what extent they were ever true many of these notions are comically outdated. Operative word "comically," which is why I've employed them from time to time in this book, since few things are as hilarious to the northerner as a well-placed Snuffy Smith zinger.

What the majority of southerners are, and have always been, however, is willing to allow the most strident, mouth-breathing "patriotic" firebrands among them to remain in control of their society's most powerful and influential positions. This is true whether they operate in the realms of religion, politics, business, education, or just basic day-to-day civic operations, like the hamlet nabobs in Laurens, South Carolina, who, knowing it's wrong, still grant a business license to a guy who sells Klan shit from a shop in front of their picturesque little courthouse.

Just as it was southern zealots who pushed the country into the Civil War, it was southern zealots who, while the rest of the South turned its back, were allowed to construct and maintain the legal foundations of Jim Crow; who were allowed to turn the Scopes Monkey Trial into a humiliating circus; who were allowed to subvert federal laws protecting downtrodden laborers; who were allowed to circumvent *Brown v. Board of Education* and school desegregation by calling out the National Guard and building segregation "academies"; who were allowed to resist civil rights with dogs and water cannons; who are still allowed to sidestep equitable school funding and proclaim without ridicule that a black president's birth certificate is fake; who throw secessionist balls and insist that slavery had nothing whatsoever to do with the War That Did Not Have to Happen, and who swear that all of this was and is somehow being done in the name of a liberty to which they feel deprived due to their miserable lives of oppression and persecution beneath the Stars and Stripes.

Maybe the fanatics do represent a minority, say one in three southerners—that's a fair guess, in my estimation. That's still an extremely potent one-in-three that the rest of the South enables—or succumbs to—or aligns with—or votes for—year after year, decade after decade, century after century. Theirs are the voices that perpetuate the agenda because theirs are the voices that ring with the most sincerity, that are most bereft of apology, that in their bellicosity resonate as the most authentically "southern." If there's one thing about the South that hasn't ever changed it's the hypnotic influence of the angry crusader.

Shots shooted, bar tabs settled, bro hugs administered, I said good-bye to my new college buds—three intelligent, thoughtful, ambitious guys on the campus of a major university that pulls 60 percent of its student population from metro Atlanta, the most important city in the South. Three likely leaders of tomorrow.[8]

Dylan, I was more certain than ever, would soon find his way out of the South to join the hundreds of thousands of southern expats scattered around the country and world. He was the only one of the bunch, after all, who'd bothered to give me his email address.

Matt would just as certainly stay and, whether back on the farm or in a business park in Raleigh-Durham bootstrapping some tech company into profitability, become a stalwart man of the community in North Carolina.

Arguably the most interesting of all, surely the most deafeningly southern, Wade wasn't going anywhere. Whether on the bumper of his truck or simply in his heart, he'd plant the Confederate flag, put on a few pounds and few extra degrees of certitude with age, pull the names of his kids out of the same Bible his great-great-grandfather had used to memorize scripture, and teach them how to hunt, fish, and never back down from anybody, especially no fast-talking Yankee trying to tell them what to do or think.

Of the three—Dylan, Matt, Wade—if I had to choose in twenty or thirty years which one was going to be exerting the most influence on southern society, I have no doubt at all who I'd pick. If you can't figure out which of the three I'm talking about, you haven't been reading very closely.

I'm not blind to the difficult issues this book attempts to address. Splitting the country apart feels unnatural; at the very least, a crime against manifest destiny. Americans have become so accustomed to their hard divisions—conservative-liberal, black-white, Roe-Wade, red-blue, call them what you like—that the chasm separating North and South feels ordained, an organic, even integral part of the national tradition.

Just because spiritual, political, racial, and commercial divides have always been with us, however, doesn't mean they have to continue to define us.

Though southerners inevitably lionize the out-with-a-blaze-of-glory impudence of his frankly not giving a damn, the greater wisdom proffered by Rhett Butler, that most famous of all American fence riders, always did tilt in a more northerly direction. Heralding his optimistic entry onto the scene, not his bitter, defeated departure, the Butler sentiment that became my go-to rejoinder in debates with southerners is the same one that fills the white divide between every black word of this book: "I'm sorry if the truth offends you."

ACKNOWLEDGMENTS

Aside from contemplating the consequences of antagonizing a fair portion of the country's Second Amendment enthusiasts, the most gut-wrenching part of doing a book like this is deciding, as Bob Seger once sang, what to leave in and what to leave out. The experiences documented in these pages represent only a small sample of the enlightening and often entertaining encounters I had while conducting research. After thanking all of those who appear herein (some with names changed), my next task is to express gratitude to all of those unnamed figures who took the time to speak with an overly curious stranger. I'll let a funny story I struggled unsuccessfully to find a place for in this book stand as an emblem for all the other interesting characters whose stories will have to wait for another day to be told.

In Mississippi, I made a point of seeking out George County, a place that, due in part to its onetime enthusiastic electoral support of David Duke, has been described by several Internet commentators as the most racist county in the South.

The answer to the obvious question—"What could the most racist county in the South possibly look like?"—seemed to come to me in the form of two African American men dressed in the unmistakable green-and-white-striped wardrobe of convicts. Appearing outside the window of my car just as I wheeled into the county seat of Lucedale, the pair was doing yard work in front of City Hall. For symbols of southern racial oppression, the visiting writer can't ask for much more than black men in horizontal-striped prison garb straightening up the lawn in David Duke territory. I screeched to a halt, parked the car, walked across the street, and introduced myself. About twenty yards off, a white guard carrying a shotgun watched closely but did not intervene.

As with George County itself, neither convict lived up to expectations, much less supported stereotypes. The older of the two declined to give his name or say much of anything. The younger man, a forty-one-year-old named Marcus, spoke freely about his experiences. He was on the last ninety days of a six-year stretch.

"It ain't so bad," Marcus told me after I'd suggested that for a black man life in a Mississippi state prison must be a daily horror show. He had no complaints about the treatment he'd received. "We're actually seeing more whites coming in prison now 'cause of this meth thing. It's getting more balanced out. I got no excuses. My mother is a doctor. I went to college in Illinois."

Marcus was doing time for stealing ATMs. Allowing that he was guilty as hell and rightly convicted, he merrily outlined for me the particulars of ATM theft.

"It's not hard, you just gotta have the right tool," he said. "You just unbolt the ATM from the ground—there are only four bolts most the time—put it in the back of your truck, take it home, cut it open, and watch the twenties come out."

Marcus's larceny spree had taken him from Boston to Texas. By the time he was apprehended in Mississippi, he'd stolen $340,000.

When I asked why he needed $340,000, why he didn't just stop at $100,000 or even $200,000, Marcus grinned.

"Because I like to buy pussy and other fine things," he explained.

Like so many others, Marcus reaffirmed the good nature and humor of most southerners I dealt with, but if any individual embodied the spirit of Old South class and generosity it was Mr. Bud Ford, the longtime media relations director for the University of Tennessee. Bud's (I'd call him Mr. Ford, but he insisted on "Bud") handling of my visit to Knoxville for the 2010 Oregon vs. Tennessee football game made it one of the more pleasant trips I undertook in the South. In no way should he be held accountable for or regarded as an accomplice to my work. Bud and I dealt with each other openly—querulous Duck to upstanding Vol—but that doesn't mean he agrees with a single point I've made in this book.

As for the UT supporters in Knoxville, even in their tipsy condition and sweatshirt-and-pant combos the color of circus peanuts, they were almost unanimously kind and gracious with our visiting group of Ducks. Though, let's be honest, people are by and large kind and gracious everywhere you go. Sorry, I know this isn't going to earn me any more positive reviews down South than I've already not earned, but this whole myth of southern hospitality really is overblown.

Generosity toward strangers is not novel behavior and is practiced no more or less in the South than anywhere else in the country, and with nothing close to the zeal with which one finds it extended in countries such as Cambodia, Botswana, and Turkey. When it's accompanied by one of those buttery southern accents, I guess it can be intoxicating for some, but there's no reason for the South to keep patting itself on the back for normal displays of plain human courtesy.

As with so many other observations in this book, the evident libel here is nothing new. Traveling the South in the 1850s on a mission much like my own, writer and famed landscape architect Frederick Law Olmsted (he designed Central Park, which I suppose gives him almost as much credibility as me) also swore that the notion of southern hospitality was greatly overstated. More than 160 years later in South Carolina, I was informed that the more "natural" southern character was, in fact, one of coven suspicion and standoffishness, as typified by the shotgun-next-to-the-front-door, arsenal-in-the-gun-cabinet hillbilly stereotype.[1]

If a "nicest people" trophy were to be awarded to one state, it'd have to go to Utah. Fucked up as that place can be.

The most unfortunate casualty of my southern adventures was without doubt Trevor Childress, a gentleman in all senses of the word who suffered the consequences of showing me kindness and hospitality in Chattanooga. About two-thirds the way through this project, voters in an *Outside* magazine Facebook poll named Chattanooga as the "best town ever," in the hyperbolic style of modern magazines. *Outside* dispatched me to Tennessee to profile the town. For two days, Trevor showed me the best of his city—including piloting me on a memorable, and stomach-turning, hang-gliding flight over the scenic Sequatchie Valley.

I returned from Chattanooga thoroughly impressed by Trevor, but still mildly skeptical about the curiously weighted opinions of Facebook voters.

The mildly skeptical story I wrote outraged predictably touchy locals. Not satisfied with being named ever's "best town," scandalized residents also apparently expected me to fluff their city as though I were writing brochure copy for the local CVB. A victim of guilt by association, Trevor was regrettably caught in the righteous Internet crossfire. Trevor: You remain one of the most impressive outdoorsmen I've ever met—and I've met many. Chattanooga: They held the Scopes Monkey Trial in your backyard, you're so politically spiteful that half of you bragged to me about not allowing Al Gore to carry his home state in 2000, and every fucking two-bit burg in the country has a "really cool brew pub where they make their own beer." Get over yourself.[2]

For being named best town ever and still bitching, Chattanooga reminded me of my buddy Roderick Moore. After Roderick's beloved Auburn Tigers beat my Oregon Ducks, 22–19, in the 2011 college football BCS championship game, I dropped in on him and his wife for a magnificent, Thanksgiving-sized, home-cooked meal at the Moore residence outside Selma, Alabama. After dinner, Roderick led me to his video room where he told me he'd replayed the championship game film no fewer than twelve times.

"I'm still mad at [Auburn head coach] Gene Chizik for his offensive game plan," Roderick told me. "Had we run the ball ten or fifteen more times, we would have beaten you guys by two touchdowns. We passed way too much."

This sort of observation is made every day in the South, and tells you all you need to know about what it takes to be a football coach there. A Heisman Trophy quarterback leads your team to an undefeated season, you bulldoze through the SEC unscathed, beat a pretty flashy University of Nike team to win the national title, and your most faithful fans are still criticizing the job you did.

Despite his rabid support of the Scam Newton regime, Roderick and I struck up an email friendship after my lightning rod appearance on the Paul Finebaum radio show, one that I'm sure will continue. As for Finebaum, he brought the hayseeds in his audience out to play and I ended up meeting a few of the intelligent ones, so I guess we both got what we wanted out of my appearance on his show.

Among many others, Frank Cantrell of Memphis wrote an entertainingly apoplectic email that helped inform the part of my own SEC breakdown that appears on pages 140–141.

Again without implying fault for any of my editorializing, I owe thanks to a number of people in Little Rock, including *Oxford American* publisher Warwick Sabin, *Arkansas Times* editor Max Brantley, Hendrix College political science professor Jay Barth, and Debbie Milan of the Little Rock School District.

Appreciation to Phil Bailey and Wesley Donehue in Columbia, South Carolina, for agreeing to hold a personal *Pub Politics* night with me.

If anyone has a great southern book in them waiting to be written, it's the way-too-smart-for-his-own-good Stephen Usery, who performs many noble services for the Memphis Public Library and itinerant writers.

Mississippi native, Vanderbilt University grad, and author of *The Eyes of Willie McGee: A Tragedy of Race, Sex, and Secrets in the Jim Crow South*, Alex Heard was a reliable source of ideas about the South and conversation about the book biz in general.

My good friends Dave Malley and Shanghai Bob kept me updated on southern news by emailing helpful links and observations, often with subject lines like "Check this shit out!"

Virginia Commonwealth University Bible scholar Kristin Swenson kindly talked me through several sections of the chapter on religion.

Following two weeks of Baptist church services and a general onslaught of evangelical orthodoxy, John and Margaret May graciously allowed my beleaguered soul a few days to recuperate in their home and swimming pool in Grapevine, Texas.

To the aspiring humorists behind all of those pithy church marquee messages: Don't give up—Moses was once a basket case.

Greetings to the fourteen-year-old, high school wide receiver I met on the hike up Stone Mountain, who told me he hoped to play ball either at Alabama or Oregon, then two minutes later recommended the best strip club in Atlanta for my evening's entertainment. Jarius, I never did make it to Magic City, but I have a feeling you're going to do very well playing football.

In Atlanta, Spencer Hall proved himself not just a leading authority on football, but one of the sharpest, funniest guys in the South. In the country, for that matter.

It was my and Dr. Bahr's great fortune to run into the seventeen-year-old Leosha on her shift working the front counter of the Holiday Inn Express in Breaux Bridge, Louisiana. It took several minutes to wade through that Cajun accent—Chaffre Roinge? Coffee Raunch?—but without her, we would never have found the Caffrey Ranch trail ride and zydeco event, easily the best party in an unlit country field either of us have ever had the nerve to crash.

Because I'm susceptible to the types of arbitrary rankings that occasionally incite bar fights and email wars, and because try as I might I could find no plausible way of shoehorning this into the chapters on education or religion, herewith my list, in order, of the top twelve southern-fried rock bands of all time: 12. Sanford-Townsend Band 11. Blackfoot 10. Black Oak Arkansas 9. Drive-By Truckers 8. Outlaws 7. The Black Crowes 6. .38 Special 5. Molly Hatchet 4. Atlanta Rhythm Section 3. Allman Brothers Band 2. Marshall Tucker Band 1. Charlie Daniels Band.

And calm down with the Skynyrd outrage. I said rock bands, not American deities.

It seems that all of my books end up including at least one epic hangover story. I'll withhold details of the worst one I endured in the South—though any aggrieved southerners who've made it this far into the book might be happy to learn that in Pensacola, publisher Fred Garth exacted some measure of revenge on your behalf by introducing me to the Flora-Bama Lounge and a filthy local concoction known as a bushwacker. To the best of my recollection, the drink consists of a toxic lode of ice cream or dairy-like product laced with enough Kahlúa, rum, and fermented ass hair to subdue a great white shark. I bought three or four rounds. In his gracious southern manner, Fred bought two or three times as many. He was also good enough to provide an incredibly comfortable bed in his home overlooking the water on Perdido Key—there are far worse places to wake up with cotton mouth and a T-shirt you swear to Nathan Bedford Forrest you didn't buy, much less put on yourself.

Though the recovery time was less severe, the night out in New Orleans in the company of Ted Sullivan was similarly memorable. I'd been to Frenchman Street on several prior occasions, but never with such outstanding company.

Thanks also to Brent Kovach for hosting me at my new favorite hotel in New Orleans, St. Peter House Hotel in the French Quarter.

Though I can't give such a ringing endorsement to many of the places I stayed during my travels, I'd like to extend profound admiration to the inventor of the parabolic ARC Shower Bar, the curved rod that prevents mildewy shower curtains from rubbing against your naked body in cheap motels across the country. Finding that little miracle of service-industry engineering pretty much saves the day in places like the Fulton, Mississippi, Days Inn.[3]

As with hangovers, John DeVore somehow manages to pop up in the Acknowledgments section of every book I write. This time he gets the nod for convincing me to read Edmund Wilson's magnificent *Patriotic Gore: Studies in the Literature of the Civil War*. As usual, I remain grateful for the presence of a token, theatergoing, reactionary, splatter-gun Texan in my life.

Dai-sized gratitude to Andrew Demaria for his unwavering support and patience with me while I tried to balance a southern travel schedule with Hong Kong dim sum edits; also to the entire CNNGo staff for putting up with my loud typing and louder emailing.

Enduring thanks to Dana Joseph for introducing me to Texas, regular writing gigs, and so much more.

Defender of good causes, publisher Alan Davis is owed undying gratitude for being an honest and generous exemplar in a very tough and nonsensical business.

I undertook most of the travel for this book alone, though the occasional company of temporary companions made things a lot more fun. Of Dr. Bahr, Kevin Hiestand, Dave Swansborough, and my brother Mike, only Dr. Bahr made it into the pages of this book, but all are here in spirit. As with so many other anecdotes, I regret the omission of the 100 mph, Bo and Luke Duke charge from the Dixie Republic in Travelers Rest, South Carolina, to the Charlotte airport. I'll trust the One Man Frat and Speedster to keep its heroic memory alive.

Long before I met him, I was lifting quotes from James Cobb, superstar of southern academia. "Cobby" turned out to be even more impressive in person. Without his help, this book may never have found its ending.

Thanks also to everyone who helped me at the University of Georgia, particularly my courageous "secession panel," professors Woody Beck, Charles Bullock, John Inscoe, and "Dylan," "Matt," and "Wade," three guys who reminded me why I barely survived college.

Professional thanks are extended to Joelle Delbourgo, who remains a class act and great agent.

Patrick Clark, Tom Colligan, and Paul Zemanek all contributed stellar research to various sections of this book.

Judd Harris acted as backup reader, invisible conscience, and mystical New Orleans presence.

The first step in getting this project off the ground was securing the enthusiastic support of indubitable agent David Patterson. It helped to get the endorsement of a native southerner, though I'll withhold the name of David's home state lest angry residents there see fit to tar his heels for aiding and abetting such treason as has occurred in these pages.

Starting with the extraordinary Jonathan Karp, everyone at Simon & Schuster sets the bar of professionalism impossibly high. Special thanks goes to associate publisher and tolerant Kentuckian Richard Rhorer, publicist Kate Gales, marketing specialist Jessica Abell, and editorial assistant Molly Lindley.

I like to forewarn people meeting me for the first time that in print I come off two inches taller, ten pounds lighter, and twenty IQ points smarter than I do in real life. The principal reason for this discrepancy is Sarah Knight, my editor and fellow picky eater/person of discerning taste. If Sarah outdid herself with this book, it's not just because my writing forced her to, but because she never fails to make any book better than its author deserves to take credit for.

Thanks to Mike, Evie, Erik, Chuck 2.0, and Dylan for allowing me to use their home (and Evie's kitchen) as an occasional base of operations for southern expeditions. Carlene and Amy are the world's best sisters, even if, with great apologies, I've hardly seen them for the past year or so. Kyle, Carlos, Jake Jai, Gracie, Junior, and their parents also merit much love and fawning praise.

Whether in books or on the radio, I've never been a big fan of dedications. If I were to cite one person who I thought of most often while writing this book, however, it certainly would be Jay Easley. A big, bearded, charismatic Georgia boy who could fix anything from a universal joint to a cockfight, Jay and I became friends in Juneau through his wife and my then-coworker and the Pride of Sitka, Maria Easley. I can't recall now exactly what brought Jay to Alaska, but no doubt it was something to do with difficult work and heavy machinery. Jay had a man's man way about him that, of course, charmed all females within a twenty-mile radius, including my mother, who never did get over Jay's "gift of gab."

The first night I met Jay was at a barbecue at his and Maria's place. Jay had spent the afternoon cooking a pig in a pit he'd dug in his side yard (surely in violation of trailer park rules). Jay served the best pork I've ever eaten, listened to my flood of jackass opinions, laughed at half of them, deftly proved the other half wrong, and pronounced me "an actual human being," which was damn nice of him considering that I drank most of the beer in his fridge.

I embarked on my travels through the South, and Georgia in particular, looking forward to running into a few southern gems like Jay. The many miles I logged and many southerners I spoke with, however, only confirmed for me what those closest to him already knew—that Jay Easley was one-of-a-kind and nevermore to be seen on this earth.

Jay died far too young, the victim of the hurt sustained over the course of his many impossible jobs, but he is survived by Maria and his son, Clay, who is as fine a gift to the Pacific Northwest as the South could ever hope to give.

The only thing I can imagine being more mentally draining than finishing a book is living with someone who is constantly whining about the mental drain of not being able to finish his book. The one and only Joyce not only bore that burden with the equanimity of a guardian sea turtle, but with the kind of love and supernatural friendship no one who spends as much time as I do rewriting copy at 2:30 in the morning is worthy of. Joyce can down an entire plate of Piggie Park barbecue in South Carolina, then eat at Paula Deen's butter-soaked Savannah restaurant twice in a twenty-four-hour period without moving the needle on the scale even a fraction. Her most magical power, however, is the ability to remain invisible while dancing across every single page of every single thing I've ever written.

NOTES

Introduction: Divided We Stand (Sort Of)

1. The Republic of Cascadia site provides population and GDP estimates based on 2005 and 1996 estimates, respectively, at http://zapatopi.net/cascadia/. I updated Cascadia GDP amounts using 2010 figures from Suzanne Stevens, "Oregon GDP Down 2.8 percent," *Portland Business Journal*, November 18, 2010, http://www .bizjournals.com/portland/news/2010/11/18/oregon-gdp-down-24-percent.html; and http://www.bcstats.gov.bc.ca/data/bus_stat/econ_acct.asp. Updated 2010 population statistics for Oregon from http://quickfacts.census.gov/qfd/states/41000.html; for Washington 2010 from http://quickfacts.census.gov/qfd/states/53000.html; for British Columbia 2011 from http://www.bcstats.gov.bc.ca/data/bcfacts.asp.

2. Mason-Dixon line and Penn-Calvert history from Kathryn DeVan, "Our Most Famous Border: The Mason-Dixon Line," Pennsylvania Center for the Book, Penn State University Libraries, Fall 2008, http://www.pabook.libraries.psu.edu/ palitmap/MasonDixon.html. Jeremiah Dixon as "ethically weak" and background on Charles Mason and Jeremiah Dixon from Edwin Danson, "Mason, Charles, and Jeremiah Dixon," *American National Biography Online*, Oxford University Press, January 2002, http://www.anb.org/articles/13/13-02640.html.

3. "Stand Watie," Civil War Home, http://www.civilwarhome.com/watiebio.htm.

4. Delvin R. Berg, "Biography," Lyndon B. Johnson Online Museum, 2008, http:// lyndonbjohnson.org/Biography.html.

5. Population statistics calculated from "State & County QuickFacts," U.S. Census Bureau, October 13, 2011, http://http://quickfacts.census.gov/qfd/states/41000 .html.

6. Rick Perry discusses Texas secession from Hilary Hylton, "What's All That Secession Ruckus in Texas?," *Time*, April 18, 2009, http://www.time.com/time/nation/ article/0,8599,1891829,00.html. Maggie Haberman, "Rick Perry Critics Unearth Another Secession Comment," *Politico*, August 10, 2011, http://www.politico.com/ news/stories/0811/61030.html.

7. Gulf Coast capacity statistics from "Refinery Facts" report, National Petrochemical & Refiners Association, January 1, 2011, http://www.npra.org/ourIndustry/refinery Facts/?fa=refineryStatistics.

8. Rutledge background from "John Rutledge," Colonial Hall.com, January 1, 2004,

http://colonialhall.com/rutledgej/rutledgej.php. Edward Rutledge's "no wisdom" quote from Valeria North Burnet Orr, "Edward Rutledge," Descendants of the Signers of the Declaration of Independence, 2008, http://www.dsdi1776.com/Signers/Ed%20Rutledge.html. League of the South "bastardisation" quote from League of the South, 2011, http://dixienet.org/rights/verbal.shtml.

9. John C. Calhoun and doctrine of nullification background from "John C. Calhoun Statement on Nullification," Public Broadcasting Service, pdf available at http://www25.uua.org/uuhs/duub/articles/johnccalhoun.html. Holley Ulbrich, "John C. Calhoun," Unitarian Universalist History and Heritage Society, 1999–2011, http://www25.uua.org/uuhs/duub/articles/johnccalhoun.html.

10. James C. Cobb, *Away Down South: A History of Southern Identity* (New York: Oxford University Press, 2005), 3, 14.

11. Edmund Wilson, *Patriotic Gore: Studies in the Literature of the American Civil War* (New York: Oxford University Press, 1966), xv.

Chapter 1: Religion: Georgia, Kentucky, End Times, and the Rise of KKKristian Zombies

1. Dr. Michael Hill, "What Is the League of the South?," League of the South, 1995–2011, http://dixienet.org/rights/whatisthels.shtml.

2. Samuel S. Hill, "Religion," *Encyclopedia of Southern Culture* (Chapel Hill and London: University of North Carolina Press, 1989), 1269.

3. Ibid.

4. Wilson, *Patriotic Gore: Studies in the Literature of the American Civil War*, 336.

5. "New Barna Report Examines Diversity of Faith in Various U.S. Cities," Barna Group, October 11, 2010, http://www.barna.org/faith-spirituality/435-diversity-of-faith-in-various-us-cities.

6. Ibid.

7. "How Religious Is Your State?," the Pew Forum on Religion & Public Life, December 21, 2009, http://pewforum.org/How-Religious-Is-Your-State-.aspx.

8. "U.S. Religious Landscape Survey," the Pew Forum on Religion & Public Life, 2010, http://religions.pewforum.org/portraits. Jeffrey K. Hadden, Charles E. Swann, "Broadcasting, Religious," *Encyclopedia of Southern Culture*, 1279.

9. Cobb, *Away Down South: A History of Southern Identity*, 49.

10. I first began making notes of Christian hate mongering while driving through the Arizona desert outside Phoenix on November 4, 2004, and being astonished enough by this inflammatory quote to record it in my notebook. Broadcast archives unavailable.

11. "Exemption Requirements—Section 501(c)(3) Organizations," IRS, November 15, 2010, http://www.irs.gov/charities/charitable/article/0,,id=96099,00.html.

12. Scott Thumma quote from "Mega Churches Mean Big Business," CNN World, January 21, 2010, http://articles.cnn.com/2010-01-21/world/religion.mega.church.christian_1_mega-churches-worshippers-joel-osteen?_s=PM:WORLD. Major League

Baseball revenue from Maury Brown, "MLB Revenues Grown from $1.4 Billion in 1995 to $7 Billion in 2010," Yardbarker.com, Foxsports.com, April 14, 2011, http://network.yardbarker.com/mlb/article_external/mlb_revenues_grown/from_14_billion_in_1995_to_7_billion_in_2010/4560405. Cotton industry revenue from "Cotton Farming in the US: Market Research Report," IBISWorld, December 2010, http://www.ibisworld.com/industry/default.aspx?indid=37.

13. "Percent of People 25 Years and Over Who Have Completed High School (Includes Equivalency): 2005," U.S. Census Bureau, http://factfinder.census.gov/servlet/GRTTable?_bm=y&-geo_id=01000US&-_box_head_nbr=R1501&-ds_name=ACS_2009_1YR_G00_&-redoLog=false&-mt_name=ACS_2005_EST_G00_R1401_US30&-form at=US-30.

14. "Julian Bond: I Boycotted King Funeral Because Eddie Long Is a 'Raving Homophobe' [video]," MAJIC 107.5 and 97.5, 11 Alive News, 2006, http://majicatl.com/videos/glennwoods/julian-bond-i-boycotted-king-funeral-because-eddie-long-is-a-raging-homophobe-video/. Brentin Mock, "Bishop Eddie Long," *Southern Poverty Law Center Intelligence Report*, Spring 2007, http://www.splcenter.org/get-informed/intelligence-report/browse-all-issues/2007/spring/face-right/bishop-eddie-long. Edeclo Martinez, "Bishop Eddie Long (pictures): Who Is the Pastor Accused in Sex Scandal?," CBS News, September 23, 2010, http://www.cbsnews.com/8301-504083_162-20017430-504083.html. Boyce Watkins, Ph.D., "Bishop Eddie Long Update: Trial Date Now Set for Next Summer," *BlackVoices*, November 22, 2010, http://www.bvblackspin.com/2010/11/22/bishop-eddie-long-has-his-first-day-in-court/. Elena Garcia, "Bishop Eddie Long Reaches Settlement Out of Court," *Christian Post*, May 26, 2011, http://www.christianpost.com/news/bishop-eddie-long-reaches-settlement-out-of-court-50561/.

15. James Sessions, "Civil Rights and Religion," *Encyclopedia of Southern Culture*, 1282–83.

16. B. A. Robinson, "Christian Reconstructionism, Dominionism, Theonomy, Dominion Theology, etc.," Religious Tolerance.org, August 13, 2009, http://www.religioustolerance.org/reconstr.htm.

17. B. A. Robinson, "Christian Identity Movement," Religious Tolerance.org, May 30, 2006, http://www.religioustolerance.org/cr_ident.htm.

18. "Jerry Mitchell's Entry and Biography," *Clarion-Ledger* (Jackson, Mississippi), October 22, 2009, http://www.clarionledger.com/article/99999999/SPECIAL17/60416008/Jerry-Mitchell-s-entry-biography.

19. Congress of Racial Equality protest from Macel Falwell, *Jerry Falwell: His Life and Legacy* (New York: Howard Books, 2008), 99. Jerry Falwell depiction on *Queer Duck* from "Queer Duck," the Titi Tudorancea Learning Center, October 20, 2010, http://www.tititudorancea.org/z/queer_duck.htm.

20. Reproduced faithfully in the text, John Howard's original quote to me referred to bankruptcy proceedings against the Ku Klux Klan in 1948. Presumably, he was referring to Klan-crippling federal tax delinquency proceedings of 1944. R. A. Guisepi, ed., "Ku Klux Klan," History World International, World History Center, http://history-world.org/ku_klux_klan.htm.

21. http://www.westmobilebaptist.org/.

22. Kristin Swenson, *Bible Babel: Making Sense of the Most Talked About Book of All Time* (New York: Harper, 2010), 87.

23. "Bristlecone Pines," National Parks Service, August 29, 2006, http://www.nps.gov/grba/planyourvisit/identifying-bristlecone-pines.htm.

24. Laurie Goodstein, "In Kentucky, Noah's Ark Theme Park Is Planned," *New York Times*, December 5, 2010, http://www.nytimes.com/2010/12/06/us/06ark.html. Ken Ham, "International Press on the Ark Encounter," *Answers in Genesis*, September 7, 2011, http://blogs.answersingenesis.org/blogs/ken-ham/2011/09/07/international-press-on-the-ark-encounter/.

25. Mario Livio, *Is God a Mathematician?* (New York: Simon & Schuster, 2009), 82.

26. Scopes Monkey Trial overview from Noah Adams, "Timeline: Remembering the Scopes Monkey Trial," National Public Radio, December 20, 2005, http://www.npr.org/templates/story/story.php?storyId=4723956. W. J. Cash, *The Mind of the South* (New York: Alfred A. Knopf, 1941; Vintage, 1991), 45.

27. Information in the three preceding paragraphs from: Brian Montopoli, "Va. Lawmaker: Disabled Kids Are God's Punishment for Abortion," CBS News, February 22, 2010, http://www.cbsnews.com/8301-503544_162-6232759-503544.html. Joshua, "Exodus 13: Abortion, Virginia Politics, and the First-Born," *Eat the Bible*, February 23, 2010, http://eatthebible.blogspot.com/2010/02/exodus-13-abortion-virginia-politics.html. Amy Gardner, "Va. Candidate McDonnell Says Views Changed Since He Wrote Thesis," *Washington Post*, August 30, 2009, http://www.washingtonpost.com/wp-dyn/content/article/2009/08/29/AR2009082902434.html.

28. "Our Doctrinal Church Statement: We Make No Apologies for Our Stand!," Freedom Baptist Church, 2009, http://www.freedombaptist.net/whatwebelieve.html.

29. John Collins Rudolf, "Climate Skeptic Seeks Energy Committee Chairmanship," *New York Times*, November 16, 2010, http://green.blogs.nytimes.com/2010/11/16/god-man-and-congress-on-climate-change/. John Shimkus background and efforts to thwart EPA mercury emissions controls from Michael Barone with Richard Cohen, *The Almanac of American Politics 2006* (Washington, D.C.: National Journal Group, 2005), 610–11.

30. Samuel S. Hill, "Religion," *Encyclopedia of Southern Culture*, 1274.

31. *Left Behind* 65 million sales from "Plans for Big Budget Left Behind Remake," Cloud Ten Pictures, October 13, 2010, http://www.cloudtenpictures.com/site2/news_article.php?id=42.

32. U.S. Religious Landscape Survey, the Pew Forum on Religion & Public Life, 2010, http://religions.pewforum.org/maps#.

Chapter 2: Politics: South Carolina and the Seven Deadly Sins of Southern Gub'mit

1. James McBride Dabbs, *Who Speaks for the South?* (New York: Funk & Wagnalls Company, 1964), 320.

2. Paul Krugman, "The Real Story," *The New York Times*, September 2, 2010, http://www.nytimes.com/2010/09/03/opinion/03krugman.html; Michael Lind, "The South vs. Obama," *The Daily Beast*, January 29, 2009, http://www.thedailybeast.com/articles/2009/01/29/the-south-rises-again.html.

3. Dr. J. H. Thornwell quote from Cash, *The Mind of the South*, 45. Theodore Bilbo quote from Hugh Davis Graham, "Demagogues," *Encyclopedia of Southern Culture*, 1163. Newt Gingrich quote from Dan Gilgoff, "Gingrich at Liberty University: Obama's a Secular Socialist," CNN, October 27, 2010, http://religion.blogs.cnn.com/2010/10/27/gingrich-at-liberty-university-obamas-a-secular-socialist/.

4. Charles B. Dew, *Apostles of Disunion: Southern Secession Commissioners and the Causes of the Civil War* (Charlottesville and London: University of Virginia Press, 2001), 50.

5. Paul Broun quote from Maryann Tobin, "Rep. Paul Broun Calls CDC Phone Survey 'Socialism of the Highest Order,'" Examiner.com, October 2, 2010, http://www.examiner.com/political-spin-in-national/rep-paul-broun-calls-cdc-phone-survey-socialism-of-the-highest-order. Jabez Lamar Monroe Curry quote from Dew, *Apostles of Disunion: Southern Secession Commissioners and the Causes of the Civil War*, 57. Paul Reynolds quote from Phillip Rawls, "Turnout Key in GOP Gubernatorial Runoff," *Montgomery* (Alabama) *Advertiser*, July 12, 2010, 3A. Robert Bentley quote from ibid. Alabama gubernatorial history from http://www.archives.state.al.us/govslist.html and Phillip Rawls, "Turnout Key in GOP Gubernatorial Runoff," *Montgomery* (Alabama) *Advertiser*, July 12, 2010, 1A. No Alabama Democrats in U.S. Senate since 1997 from U.S. Senate, http://www.senate.gov/pagelayout/senators/one_item_and_teasers/alabama.htm.

6. Day of Prayer approved unanimously by Louisiana Senate and Day of Prayer decree from "Louisiana Oil Spill Day of Prayer: Bobby Jindal Orders June 27 as Day for Religious Perseverance," *The Huffington Post*, June 27, 2010, http://www.huffingtonpost.com/2010/06/25/louisiana-oil-spill-day-o_n_625757.html. Robert Adley "miracle" quote from "Louisiana Lawmakers Propose Prayer to Stop Oil Disaster," CNN, June 20, 2010, http://articles.cnn.com/2010-06-20/us/gulf.oil.spill_1_gulf-oil-spill-oil-disaster-discoverer-enterprise?_s=PM:US. BP oil spill stop details from Bradley Blackburn and David Muir, "Gulf of Mexico Oil Spill: Well Integrity Test Shows Oil Stopped," ABC News, July 15, 2010, http://abcnews.go.com/WN/gulf-oil-spill-bps-cap-success-oil-stops/story?id=11173330#.TuPQsErmvM9.

7. Wilson, *Patriotic Gore: Studies in the Literature of the American Civil War*, 99–100.

8. Rosalind S. Helderman, "Delegate Proposes Va. Mint Its Own Money," *Washington Post*, January 5, 2011, http://voices.washingtonpost.com/virginiapolitics/2011/01/delegate_proposes_virginia_min.html#more. House Joint Resolution No. 557, Virginia's Legislative Information System, 2011 Session, http://lis.virginia.gov/cgi-bin/legp604.exe?111+ful+HJ557.

9. "Never entirely recognized the authority" quote from Wilson, *Patriotic Gore: Studies in the Literature of the American Civil War*, xxi. Twenty-three percent of Republicans believe their state should secede from "Harper's Index," *Harper's Magazine*, May 2010, 15.

10. Senator Jim DeMint's "Waterloo" quote from "White House Plans to Use DeMint's 'Waterloo' Quote to Rally the Troops," ABC News, July 19, 2009, http://abcnews .go.com/blogs/politics/2009/07/white-house-plans-to-use-demints-waterloo-quote -to-rally-the-troops/. Senator Lindsey Graham censured for "tarnishing the ideals of freedom" from Robert Behre, "County Republican Party Leaders Censure Sen. Graham," *The Post and Courier* (Charleston, South Carolina), November 11, 2009. Graham censured in 2010 from Kate Phillips, "Senator Graham Censured Again," *New York Times*, January 5, 2010, http://thecaucus.blogs.nytimes.com/2010/01/05/ senator-graham-censured-again/.

11. Vicksburg Fourth of July celebration history from "Fourth of July," DC Pages.com, http://www.dcpages.com/Tourism/Fourth_of_July/. "Keep our anger alive" quote from Cobb, *Away Down South: A History of Southern Identity*, 300.

12. Jonathan Tilove, "Obama Made Inroads with White Voters Except in Deep South," *The Times-Picayune* (New Orleans), November 8, 2008, http://www.nola .com/news/index.ssf/2008/11/obama_made_inroads_with_white.html. Obama/ McCain platform comparisons for tax cuts from "Obama and McCain Tax Proposals," *Washington Post*, http://www.washingtonpost.com/wp-dyn/content/ story/2008/06/09/ST2008060900950.html. Obama/McCain platform comparisons for education from Greg Toppo, "Where They Stand: McCain, Obama Split on Education," *USA Today*, October 14, 2008, http://www.usatoday .com/news/education/2008-10-13-obama-mccain-policy_N.htm. Obama/McCain platform comparisons for health care from "Obama vs. McCain Health Care Policies," *Healthcare Economist*, August 18, 2008, http://healthcare-economist .com/2008/08/18/obama-vs-mccain-health-care-policies/.

13. Associated Press business staff, "Korean Company Announces South Carolina Electric Car Plant," Cleveland.com, July 1, 2010, http://www.cleveland.com/business/ index.ssf/2010/07/korean_company_announces_south.html.

14. Republican majority overrides Woodrow Wilson's veto of Prohibition from Andrew Glass, "Congress Overrides Prohibition Veto, October 28, 1919," *Politico*, October 28, 2009, http://www.politico.com/news/stories/1009/28790.html. Republican Richard Nixon signs 55 mph national speed limit into law, "Connecticut Enacts First Speed-Limit Law," History.com, http://www.history.com/this-day-in-history/ connecticut-enacts-first -speed-limit-law.

15. Alan Brinkley, "Long, Huey P.," *Encyclopedia of Southern Culture*, 1191.

16. Michael Lind, "The South vs. Obama," *The Daily Beast*, January 29, 2009, http:// www.thedailybeast.com/articles/2009/01/29/the-south-ri ses-again.html.

17. Nancy Crawley, "Nancy Crawley: How Long Will Right-to-Work Law Be a Real Issue?," *Grand Rapids* (Michigan) *Press*, September 5, 2010, http://www.mlive.com/ business/west-michigan/index.ssf/2010/09 /how_long_will_right-to-work_la.html. Dr. Hari Singh, "Right to Work and Economic Impact: What It Means for Michigan," academic paper, Seidman College of Business, Grand Valley State University, 2010, pdf available at media.mlive.com/news_impact/other/RTWHari4word.pdf.

18. Jimmy Lea, "National Politics," *Encyclopedia of Southern Culture*, 1169.

19. Ben Evans, "White Southern Democrats Nearly Extinct," Associated Press, November 5, 2010, http://www.huffingtonpost.com/2010/11/05/white-southern-democrats-_n_779345.html.

20. C. Vann Woodward, *The Burden of Southern History*, 3rd ed. (Baton Rouge and London: Louisiana State University Press, 1960, 1993), 257.

21. Evans, "White Southern Democrats Nearly Extinct."

22. Jimmy Lea, "National Politics," *Encyclopedia of Southern Culture*, 1169.

23. Mary Orndorff, "Spencer Bachus Finally Gets His Chairmanship," *Birmingham* (Alabama) *News*, December 9, 2010, http://blog.al.com/sweethome/2010/12/spencer_bachus_finally_gets_hi.html.

24. Dixie politicians control 60 percent of congressional chairs in 1950s from Jimmy Lea, "National Politics," *Encyclopedia of Southern Culture*, 1169. Southern population nearly doubles from 1960 to 2000 from James M. Glaser, *The Hand of the Past in Contemporary Southern Politics* (New Haven and London: Yale University Press, 2005), 3. More than one-third of U.S. population in South (including Texas) from Paul R. Campbell, "Population Projections for States by Age, Sex, Race and Hispanic Origin: 1995–2025," U.S. Census Bureau, Population Division, 1996, PPL-47, http://www.census.gov/population/www/projections/pp147.html.

25. Glaser, *The Hand of the Past in Contemporary Southern Politics*, 6–7.

26. Cobb, *Away Down South: A History of Southern Identity*, 325 (first part of quote), 58 (second part of quote).

27. Dew, *Apostles of Disunion: Southern Secession Commissioners and the Causes of the Civil War*, 51–55 ("arming their emissaries" quote from page 52). Stephen Fowler Hale biography and details of death from "Famous Greene County Residents," Al-GenWeb, part of U.S. GenWeb Project, Greene County, Alabama home page, June 27, 1997, http://home.earthlink.net/~rodbush/GALFamou.htm.

28. John A. Lupton, "Abraham Lincoln and the Corwin Amendment," Illinois Periodicals Online, Northern Illinois University Libraries, 2006, http://www.lib.niu.edu/2006/ih060934.html. Fort Sumter attack details from Geoffrey Perret, *A Country Made by War: From the Revolution to Vietnam—The Story of America's Rise to Power* (New York: Random House, 1989), 175. Fort Sumter attack details (eighty-five Union defenders) from "Fort Sumter National Monument," National Parks Service, April 20, 2006, pdf available at www.nps.gov/fosu/planyourvisit/upload/FOSU12043F01.pdf.

29. Cobb, *Away Down South: A History of Southern Identity*, 17–18.

30. William Gilmore Simms quote from Wilson, *Patriotic Gore: Studies in the Literature of the American Civil War*, xiv–xv. Mary Chesnut quote from David Colbert, ed., *Eyewitness to America: 500 Years of American History in the Words of Those Who Saw It Happen* (New York: Pantheon, 1997), 207. Southern support for the Vietnam War from Woodward, *The Burden of Southern History*, 236. Two-thirds of southerners favor invasion of Iraq, and southern majority continues to support Bush policy from Cobb, *Away Down South: A History of Southern Identity*, 325.

31. Tony Horwitz, *Confederates in the Attic: Dispatches from the Unfinished Civil War* (New York: Vintage Departures, 1999), 34.

32. "Alvin Greene Wins the South Carolina Primary," *The Daily Show with Jon Stewart,* June 14, 2010, http://www.thedailyshow.com/watch/mon-june-14-2010/alvin-greene-wins-south-carolina-primary.

33. Andrew Bauer compares kids to stray animals from Andy Barr, "S.C. Lt. Gov.: Poor like 'Stray Animals,'" *Politico,* January 25, 2010, http://www.politico.com/news/stories/0110/31959.html. Ken Ard resigns from Robert Behre and Schuyler Kropf, "Lt. Gov. Ard Resigns from Office; Pleads Guilty to Ethics Violations; Receives Probation," *The Post and Courier* (Charleston, South Carolina), March 9, 2012, http://www.postandcourier.com/news/2012/mar/09/lt-gov-ard-resigns-office. Thomas Ravenel sentenced to federal prison from Schuyler Kropf, "Ravenel Sentenced on Federal Drug Charge," *The Post and Courier* (Charleston, South Carolina), March 15, 2008, http://www.postandcourier.com/news/2008/mar/15/monthsravenel_sentenced_on_federal_drug_33970/. Rusty DePass "gorilla" comment from David Knowles, "SC Republican Compares Michelle Obama to Escaped Gorilla," *Politics Daily,* June 15, 2009, http://www.politicsdaily.com/2009/06/15/south-carolina-republican-compares-michelle-obama-to-escaped-gor/. Senator Jim DeMint praised for acting like a "Jew" from Oliver VanDervoort, "S.C. GOP Chairmen: DeMint like a 'Jew' Who Is 'Watching Pennies,'" *Ground Report,* October 20, 2009, http://www.groundreport.com/Business/S-C-GOP-chairmen-DeMint-like-a-Jew-who-is-watching/2909623. Representative Joe Wilson "You lie!" from "Rep. Wilson Shouts, 'You Lie' to Obama During Speech," CNN, September 9, 2009, http://articles.cnn.com/2009-09-09/politics/joe.wilson_1_rep-wilson-illegal-immigrants-outburst?_s=PM:POLITICS. Senator Jake Knotts refers to Nikki Haley and President Obama as "raghead" from John O'Connor, "Knotts' Slur Stirs the Haley Storm," *The State,* June 3, 2010, http://www.thestate.com/2010/06/03/1315978/knotts-uses-slur-to-describe-haley.html. Alvin Greene likely plant from Kate Phillips, "Investigation Is Sought into Primary in S. Carolina," *New York Times,* June 10, 2010, http://www.nytimes.com/2010/06/11/us/politics/11greene.html.

34. Jennifer Steinhauer, "Confronting Ghosts of 2000 in South Carolina," *New York Times,* October 19, 2007, http://www.boston.com/news/politics/president/articles/2004/03/21/the_anatomy_of_a_smear_campaign/.

35. John Heilemann and Mark Halperin, *Game Change: Obama and the Clintons, McCain and Palin, and the Race of a Lifetime* (New York: Harper, 2010), 375 ("right-wing freak show"), 205 ("boiled down to race"). John McCain wins 2008 South Carolina Republican primary from Michael Cooper and Michael M. Grynbaum, "McCain Wins South Carolina Primary," *New York Times,* January 19, 2008, http://www.nytimes.com/2008/01/19/us/politics/19cnd-repubs.html?pagewanted=all.

36. Jack White, "Lott, Reagan and Republican Racism," *Time,* December 14, 2002, http://www.time.com/time/nation/article/0,8599,399921,00.html. Bob Herbert, "Righting Reagan's Wrongs?," *New York Times,* November 12, 2007, http://www.nytimes.com/2007/11/13/opinion/13herbert.html.

37. Lee Atwater quoted in Alexander Lamis, ed., *Southern Politics in the 1990s* (Baton Rouge & London: Louisiana State University Press, 1999), 8.

38. Maurice Bessinger, *Defending My Heritage: The Maurice Bessinger Story (Growing Up Southern)*, (West Columbia, South Carolina: Lmbone-Lehone Publishing Company, 2001), 148.

39. Bessinger's Supreme Court ordeal from ibid., 97–109. "White people are the best friends" from ibid., 212.

40. Chandler Davidson and Bernard Grofman, eds., *Quiet Revolution in the South: The Impact of the Voting Rights Act, 1965–1990* (Princeton, N.J.: Princeton University Press, 1994), 194.

41. Thurmond's illegitimate daughter from David Mattingly, "Strom Thurmond's Family Confirms Paternity Claim," CNN, December 16, 2003, http://articles.cnn.com/2003-12-15/us/thurmond..paternity_1_thurmond-family-essie-mae-washington-williams-carrie-butler?_s=PM:US. Rebecca Leung, "A Burden Lifted," CBS News, *60 Minutes*, December 5, 2007, http://www.cbsnews.com/stories/2003/12/16/60II/main588945.shtml.

42. William J. Cooper, "Wade Hampton: Confederate Warrior, Conservative Statesmen," *The Journal of American History* 92, issue 3, 1006–1007, http://jah.oxford journals.org/content/92/3/1006.extract.

43. Ken Hawkins, "Don't Like Sanford? Get a Load of Gov. Coleman Blease, Known as 'Pardoner of Criminals,'" *Digital Charleston*, October 12, 2009, http://charleston.thedigitel.com/politics/dont-sanford-get-load-gov-coleman-blease-1915-know-6579-1012. "Startled gaze" from Cash, *The Mind of the South*, 284.

44. Carol Sears Botsch, "The African-American Monument," University of South Carolina Aiken, 2003, http://www.usca.edu/aasc/African-AmericanMonument.htm. Glenn McConnell in Confederate dress from Frank Beacham, "Why the Confederate Flag Still Flies in South Carolina," *Frank Beacham's Journal*, April 12, 2010, http://www.beachamjournal.com/journal/2010/04/index.html. Glenn McConnell in Confederate dress from "How Republicans Party," *Fitsnews*, September 14, 2010, http://www.fitsnews.com/2010/09/14/how-republicans-party/. David Firestone, "S. Carolina Senate Votes to Remove Confederate Flag," *New York Times*, April 13, 2000, http://movies.nytimes.com/library/national/race/041300race-ra.html.

45. National Japanese American Memorial Foundation, 2011, http://njamf.com/.

3: Race: Alabama, Bigotry, Wildman, and the White Spike Lee

1. Barbour refuses to denounce license plate from Peter Beinart, "The GOP's Race Backslide," *The Daily Beast*, February 17, 2011, http://www.thedailybeast.com/articles/2011/02/17/haley-barbour-gaffe-drags-republican-party-backwards-on-race.html?om_rid=NsgLCq&om; sfmid=_BNXnXJB8ZBrfNl. Fort Pillow massacre from John F. McClymer, "What Happened at Fort Pillow?," Assumption College, http://www1.assumption.edu/users/mcclymer/his130/p-h/pillow/default.html.

2. "MS GOP: Bryant for Gov., Barbour of Huckabee for Pres.," Public Policy Polling, April 7, 2011, pdf available from http://www.publicpolicypolling.com/pdf/PPP_Release_MS_0407915.pdf.

3. "Perry Liquor Store Owners, Bartender Charged with Civil Rights Violations, Unfair Trade Practices," Florida Office of the Attorney General, February 28, 2001, http://myfloridalegal.com/newsrel.nsf/newsreleases/0D0CE4F637EC15D685256 A01004AB2F0. Robinson scores winning run from "Box Score of Jackie Robinson Major League Debut," *Baseball Almanac*, http://www.baseball-almanac.com/boxscore/04151947.shtml.

4. "Selma-to-Montgomery March," National Parks Service, http://www.nps.gov/nr/travel/civilrights/al4.htm.

5. "SPLC History," Southern Poverty Law Center, http://www.splcenter.org/who-we-are/splc-history. Other SPLC details (which I have since updated) from interview with Mark Potok and Heidi Beirich at SPLC headquarters, Montgomery, Alabama.

6. Montgomery County and public school populations by percentage from "Public vs. Private: A Parent's Decision," WSFA-TV 12 News (Montgomery, Alabama), November 19, 2009, http://www.wsfa.com/Global/story.asp?S=11542597. Sidney Lanier High School information from "History" and "Notable Students," Sidney Lanier High School, http://sidneylanier.org/the-school/School-History/.

7. Hate Map from Southern Poverty Law Center, http://www.splcenter.org/get-informed/hate-map.

8. *The Social Contract* 20 no. 3, Spring 2010, from the Social Contract Press, spring 2010, http://www.thesocialcontract.com/artman2/publish/tsc_20_3/index.shtml. SPLC $216.2 million endowment from "Financial Information," Southern Poverty Law Center, http://www.splcenter.org/who-we-are/financial-information.

9. Paul Finebaum bio from Finebaum.com, 2011, http://www.finebaum.com/Article.asp?id=1952141.

10. Lorraine Ahearn, "Census: Blacks Are Moving to the South," *News & Record* (Greensboro, North Carolina), March 22, 2009, http://www.news-record.com/content/2009/03/21/article/census_blacks_are_moving_to_the_south. B. Drummond Ayers, Jr., "Blacks Return to South in a Reverse Migration," *New York Times*, June 18, 1974, http://partners.nytimes.com/library/national/race/061874race-ra.html. Cash, *The Mind of the South*, 300–301.

11. Bobby Bowman, "A Portrait of Black America on the Eve of the 2010 Census," *The Root*, February 10, 2010, http://www.theroot.com/views/portrait-black-america-eve-2010-census. Sabrina Tavernise and Robert Gebeloff, "Many U.S. Blacks Returning to South, Reversing Trend," *New York Times*, March 24, 2011, http://www.nytimes.com/2011/03/25/us/25south.html.

12. Chuck Noe, "Bush Decries Democrats' 'Soft Bigotry of Low Expectations,'" NewsMax.com, January 9, 2004, http://archive.newsmax.com/archives/articles/2004/1/9/110923.shtml.

13. Tony Santaelia and James Gilbert, "Killing of Anthony Hill in Newberry County Could Be Hate Crime," WLTX-TV (Columbia, South Carolina), June 2, 2010,

http://www.wltx.com/news/story.aspx?storyid=88178. Shaila Dewan, "Call for Justice Sets Off a Debate," *New York Times*, July 18, 2010, http://www.nytimes.com/2010/07/19/us/19panther.html.

14. Math slavery story problems from "Georgia teacher resigns over slavery math question," Associated Press, January 18, 2012, http://www.foxnews.com/us/2012/01/18/georgia-teacher-resigns-over-slavery-math-lesson/. Daniel Trotta, "Friends Fear for Safety of Man who Shot Florida Teen," Reuters, March 25, 2012, http://www.reuters.com/article/2012/03/25/us-usa-florida-shooting-id USBRE82O0F820120325. Jackson, Mississippi, murder from Holbrook Mohr, "Mississippi Killing Sparks Internet War of Words; Did Case Involve Race? (video)," Associated Press, August 13, 2011, http://blog.al.com/wire/2011/08/mississippi _killing_sparks_int.html. Kim Severson, "Three Plead Guilty to Hate Crimes in Killing of Black Man in Mississippi," *The New York Times*, March 22, 2012, http://www.nytimes.com/2012/03/23/us/three-plead-guilty-to-hate-crimes-in-killing-of -black-man-in-mississippi.html?_r=1&adxnnl=1&src=recg&adxnnlx=1332590413 -WMll3K9M3yeUf0pTQuHJfQ. Kentucky church bans interracial couples from "Ky. Church Revisits Ban on Interracial Couples," Associated Press, December 3, 2011, http://www.usatoday.com/news/religion/story/2011-12-03/church -interracial-ban/51607194/1. Nettleton school student elections from "Class Officers Segregated by Race," *The Smoking Gun*, August 26, 2010, http://www .thesmokinggun.com/documents/fail/class-officers-segregated-race. Segregated prom from Sara Corbett, "A Prom Divided," *New York Times*, May 21, 2009, http://www .nytimes.com/2009/05/24/magazine/24prom-t.html?pagewanted=all. Louisiana justice of the peace refuses to marry interracial couple from Amanda Terkel, "Louisiana Justice of the Peace Denied Marriage License to Interracial Couple, Worried They Might Have Children," *Think Progress*, October 15, 2009, http://thinkprogress.org/politics/2009/10/15/64740/interracial-couple/. Obama assassination attempt from Eric Lichtblau, "Arrests in Plan to Kill Obama and Black Schoolchildren," *New York Times*, October 27, 2008, http://www.nytimes.com/2008/10/28/us/politics/28plot.html. Florida teacher uses N word from "Teacher Suspended for Using N Word to Describe Obama," *The Daily Voice*, October 3, 2008, http://thedailyvoice.com/voice/2008/10/teacher-fired-for-using-n-word-001200.php. West Virginia kidnapping from "Officials Consider Hate Crime Charges in Week-Long Kidnap, Torture of West Virginia Woman," FOX News, September 11, 2007, http://www.foxnews.com/story/0,2933,296429,00.html. Jena Six from "The Case of the Jena Six: Black High School Students Charged with Attempted Murder for Schoolyard Fight After Nooses Are Hung from Tree," *Democracy Now!*, July 10, 2007, http://www.democracynow.org/2007/7/10/the_case_of_the_jena_six. Teacher calls Kentucky freshman N word from Tamia Booker, "Ixnay on the N-Word Already," *Campus Progress*, March 9, 2006, http://campusprogress.org/articles/ixnay_on_the_n-word _already; also from WHAS-TV (Louisville, Kentucky), http://www.youtube.com/watch?v=VY16_nKORb8.

15. *Kloran: Knights of the Ku Klux Klan* (Lodi, Ohio: The Knights of the Ku Klux Klan, Inc., copyright Dale Reusch, Imperial Wizard, 1975), 7.

16. The Redneck Shop, 108 West Laurens Street, Laurens, South Carolina, http://www
    .theoriginalredneckshop.com/index.html.

17. "South Carolina: Confederate Flag Rally," *Occidental Dissent*, June 28, 2010 posted
    by Hunter Wallace, http://www.occidentaldissent.com/2010/06/28/south-carolina
    -confederate-flag-rally/.

18. Ed Pilkington, "US Set for Dramatic Change as White America Becomes Minor-
    ity by 2042," *The Guardian* (U.K.), August 14, 2008, http://www.guardian.co.uk/
    world/2008/aug/15/population.race. "Minorities Expected to Be Majority by
    2050," CNN, August 13, 2008, http://articles.cnn.com/2008-08-13/us/census
    .minorities_1_hispanic-population-census-bureau-white-population?_s=PM:US.

19. "About Valley Grande," City of Valley Grande, 2011, http://www.cityofvalley
    grande.com/index.php?option=com_content&task=view&id=39&Itemid=55.
    "History," City of Valley Grande, 2011, http://www.cityofvalleygrande.com/index
    .php?option=com_content&task=view&id=40&Itemid=56.

20. Joe R. Feagin, *Racist America: Roots, Current Realities, and Future Reparations*, 2nd
    ed. (New York and London: Routledge, 2010): 216.

21. Charles J. Dean, "Tim James Has Come Under Criticism for Ad Espousing English-
    Only Driver's License Testing," *Birmingham* (Alabama) *News*, April 26, 2010,
    http://blog.al.com/spotnews/2010/04/tim_james_has_come_under_criti.html.
    Video of Tim James's driver's license campaign ad available at http://www.youtube
    .com/watch?v=eEPh_KITyII.

22. David Zaslawsky, "Investor Profiles: Hyundai Motor Manufacturing Alabama,
    LLC," *Montgomery Business Journal*, July 2009, http://www.montgomerychamber
    .com/Page.aspx?pid=765.

23. "US Debt: How Big Is It and Who Owns It?," *The Guardian* (U.K.), July 15, 2011,
    http://www.guardian.co.uk/news/datablog/2011/jul/15/us-debt-how-big-who
    -owns.

24. Shruba Mukherjee, "Number of Engineers on Rise," *Deccan Herald* (New
    Delhi, India), January 10, 2010, http://www.deccanherald.com/content/46137/
    number-engineers-rise.html. "U.S. Risks Losing Global Leadership in Nanotech,"
    Lux Research, Inc., August 18, 2010, pdf available at http://www.foresight.org/
    nanodot/?p=4186.

25. "Diss Ingenuous," *The Daily Show with Jon Stewart*, August 15, 2006, http://www
    .thedailyshow.com/watch/tue-august-15-2006/diss-ingenuous.

26. Feagin, *Racist America: Roots, Current Realities, and Future Reparations*, 2nd ed., 221.

27. Tom Charlier, "Census Finds Hispanic Population Grows to 52,000 in Memphis
    Metro Area," *The Commercial Appeal* (Memphis, Tennessee), December 22, 1010,
    http://www.commercialappeal.com/news/2010/dec/22/hispanic-numbers-grow-in
    -bluff-city/?print=1. James C. Cobb and William Stueck, eds., *Globalization and the
    American South* (Athens: University of Georgia Press, 2005), 73–74.

28. William H. Frey, Alan Berube, Audrey Singer, and Jill H. Wilson, "Getting Current:
    Recent Demographic Trends in Metropolitan America," Brookings Institution, 21,
    pdf available from www.brookings.edu/~/ . . . /03_metro_demographic_trends.pdf.

"African American Profile," The Office of Minority Health, U.S. Department of Health and Human Services, November 2, 2011, http://minorityhealth.hhs.gov/templates/browse.aspx?lvl=2&lvlID=51.

4: Football: Louisiana State, ESPN, BCS, and the Gridiron Delusion of the SEC

I've elected not to provide source notes for the many team records, scores of games, and rankings mentioned in this chapter, as these are easily found on numerous Internet sites. For this type of information I relied mostly on websites from school athletic departments and ESPN.

1. Sally Jenkins, "It's Time for Congress to Sack the BCS," *Washington Post*, November 11, 2010, http://www.washingtonpost.com/wp-dyn/content/article/2010/11/10/AR2010111007161.html. Taylor Branch, "The Shame of College Sports," *The Atlantic*, October 2011, 81–110. Darren Everson, "Government Joins Bowl-Game Brawl," *Wall Street Journal*, May 5, 2011, http://online.wsj.com/article/SB10001424052748703849204576303483101861202.html. "House Panel Considers College Football Playoff," Associated Press, December 9, 2009, http://www.newsmax.com/Politics/us-bcs-congress/2009/12/09/id/338160.

2. Jeff Sentell, "Clay-Chalkville Loses on Appeal," *Birmingham* (Alabama) *News*, November 4, 2011, 1A.

3. Woodward, *The Burden of Southern History*, 190.

4. The number of college teams and conferences was calculated by counting conference and independent team standings from the National Collegiate Athletic Association, http://www.ncaafootball.com/#; and National Association of Intercollegiate Athletics, http://naia.cstv.com/sports/m-footbl/spec-rel/101911aab.html. It's possible that some obscure teams or conferences escaped my attention, but 721 teams and seventy-five conferences is the most verifiable number I could triple-count.

5. "BCS, Alliance & Coalition Games, Year by Year," Bowl Championship Series, updated 2012, http://www.bcsfootball.org/news/story?id=4809942.

6. The "white tailback" reference here is to former South Carolina Gamecocks tailback Ryan Brewer, http://www.gamecocksonline.com/sports/m-footbl/mtt/brewer_ryan00.html.

7. Rick Neuheisel's pre-firing salary from "Coaches Hot Seat Rankings," *Coaches Hot Seat*, August 30, 2011, http://www.coacheshotseat.com/RickNeuheisel.htm. Other coachs' salaries from "Salaries and Contracts," *Coaches Hot Seat*, December 17, 2011, http://www.coacheshotseat.com/SalariesContracts.htm.

8. Undisputed national titles since 1950 from "Consensus National Champions," 2011 NCAA Football Records," 2011, 71, pdf available at http://bit.ly/sns6wp.

9. Since the very first national college football championship was "split" between teams from the College of New Jersey (now Princeton) and Queen's College (now Rutgers) of 1869, choosing a titleholder has been a maddening process producing a number of dubious results. According to page 72 of the NCAA record book cited below, during the last 142 years more than thirty different bodies have been involved in selecting national champions. Often they have disagreed.

I used 1950 as the starting point for my national title calculations for three reasons. First, 1950 is the year the NCAA record book begins its listing of "Consensus National Champions," so there is that governing body's stamp of approval, debatable though it may be.

Second, 1950 is the year that the first Coaches Poll was published; originally the UPI poll, the Coaches Poll has more recently been passed between ESPN and *USA Today* and become an important part of the clumsy apparatus used to decide national champions.

Third, many of the older national championships, particularly those from the 1800s, were granted retroactively according to formulas that gained prominence in the 1920s and 1930s.

Even with the NCAA endorsement, figuring "consensus" champions is a challenge. For example, the NCAA's record book lists Tennessee as the 1951 consensus champion. What the record book fails to note, however, is that this title was granted before the number-one-ranked Volunteers' final game against number-three-ranked Maryland in the Sugar Bowl played on January 1, 1952. Maryland won that game, 28–13, to finish its season 10-0. That the Vols finished their 10-1 season with a loss to #3 Maryland yet somehow managed to retain their "consensus" championship is merely evidence that rigging titles in favor of the SEC is a long-standing tradition.

Alabama has also benefited from obvious fraudulence. In the 1973 season-ending Sugar Bowl, for just one example—I'll provide another shortly, simply because I can't resist pointing out all of this unadulterated rah-rah SEC bullshit—the undefeated and number-one-ranked Crimson Tide squared off against the undefeated and number-three-ranked Notre Dame Fighting Irish in a game that the entire country understood would decide the national championship. Well, almost the entire country. Rather than wait for the outcome of the game, the UPI went ahead and crowned Alabama national champions, even before the two teams met. (As well as having a tie blemish its 10-0-1 record, #2 Oklahoma was on probation for having ineligible players on its roster and not allowed to participate in bowl games.)

Notre Dame ended up beating Alabama, 24–23. The AP, Football Writers Association of America, National Football Foundation, and pretty much every fan in the country recognized the Irish as the 1973 champions. The UPI, however, did not change its decision, keeping Alabama as its champion. That "championship" is one of those alleged fourteen football titles hilariously mentioned by Alabama fans on T-shirts and websites such as Roll Bama Roll at http://www.rollbamaroll.com/2010/7/5/1549250/alabamas-13-national-champion.

I believe that 1973 Sugar Bowl, by the way, was the high point of my Notre Dame graduate father's sporting career. The game was also either the first or one of the first live sporting events ever televised in Juneau, Alaska, and the memory of Dad's smile in our living room after the game remains to me almost as satisfying as it was to him.

Incidentally, of the fourteen Alabama titles claimed on those ubiquitous (in Tuscaloosa) T-shirts and that Roll Bama Roll website, only four are recognized as "consensus" titles (1979, 1992, 2009, 2012) by any nonbiased organization or publication.

Much of that Bama titles list is padded with "national championships" "earned" by teams like the 1941 Crimson Tide. Alabama went 9-2 that year yet somehow managed to win a title endorsement from some outfit called the Houlgate Poll.

Meanwhile, ten other bodies, including the AP, Sagarin, and the National Championship Foundation, named the 8-0 and number-one-ranked Minnesota Golden Gophers as national champs. Alabama wasn't even the SEC champ in 1941. Mississippi State was. Anyone questioning my application of the C. Vann Woodward quote at the start of this chapter about southerners clinging to illusions, fantasies, and pretensions might do well to review the almost comical psychosis of fans who proclaim themselves champions in light of such obvious contradictory evidence.

There are, of course, a number of ways to play with numbers and statistics, but I believe my tabulations are fair to the SEC. I wrote that counting national titles from 1950 statistically favors the South and the SEC and indeed it does.

Were one to count all consensus national titles from the inception of college football in 1869 to the beginning of the BCS era in 1998, the championship winning percentage of southern teams would be just 9.375 percent, as opposed to the 20.83 percent I cited in the chapter. While starting the historical count from the very beginning of college football history seems logical, it also struck me as an unfair way of calculating the success of southern football programs, given that Alabama didn't even field a team until 1892 and the SEC wasn't officially created until 1932.

Point being, that while I acknowledge there are ways to cook most of these numbers—Should one count that 1973 Alabama UPI "title" as legit? I did not—I remained diligent and fair-minded while making my calculations. In this entire effort I received invaluable help and guidance from ace researcher Patrick Clark.

The primary source used for this section is "Consensus National Champions," 2011 NCAA Football Records, 2011, 71, pdf available at http://bit.ly/sns6wp. Other sources include: All college football national champions from 1869, "College Football National Champions," Hickok Sports, January 13, 2011, http://www .hickoksports.com/history/cfchamps.shtml. Results of the 1951 and 1973 Sugar Bowls from the official site of the Allstate Sugar Bowl at http://allstatesugarbowl .org/site.php. SEC history from the Southeastern Conference section of the *College Football Encyclopedia* at http://www.footballencyclopedia.com/sechome.htm.

10. Gene Wojciechowski, "At Last: Your Texas A&M/SEC Primer," ESPN, August 17, 2011, http://sports.espn.go.com/espn/columns/story?columnist=wojciechowski_ gene&page=wojciechowski-110816&sportCat=ncf.

11. Inter-conference records tabulated from Sports Reference at http://www.sports -reference.com/cfb/.

12. "Path to Primetime—Draft Tracker," NFL, 2011, http://www.nfl.com/draft/2011/ tracker#dt-tabs:dt-by-college/dt-by-round-input:1/dt-by-conference-input:acc. "Draft Finder," Pro-Football-Reference.com, 2011, http://www.pro-football-reference .com/play-index/draft-finder.cgi.

13. Gene Wojciechowski, "Ex-SEC Commish Discusses Expansion," ESPN, June 11, 2010, http://sports.espn.go.com/espn/columns/story?columnist=wojciechowski_ gene&id=5272309&sportCat=ncf.

14. Thirty-three of thirty-five 2011–12 bowl games broadcast by ESPN/ABC from "2011–2012 College Football Bowl Game Schedule," http://www.collegefootballpoll.com/bowl_games_bowl_schedule.html, December 2011. Ryan Hogan, "ESPN/ABC Has Monopoly over Bowl Games," *Bombastic Sports*, December 8, 2010, http://bombasticsports.com/?p=5208.

15. Mark Schlabach, "SEC Teams Dominate Early Look at 2011," ESPN, February 4, 2011, http://sports.espn.go.com/ncf/columns/story?columnist=schlabach_mark&id=6087284. "2011 NCAA Football Rankings—Preseason," ESPN, August 2011, http://espn.go.com/college-football/rankings/_/week/1.

16. More than a billion of SEC revenue from Taylor Branch, "The Shame of College Sports," *The Atlantic*, October 2011, 82. Cash, *The Mind of the South*, 326.

17. Ted Miller, "Les Miles Thinks the Huskies Stink," *Seattle Post-Intelligencer*, July 3, 2007, http://blog.seattlepi.com/sportsrant/2007/07/03/les-miles-thinks-the-huskies-stink/.

18. Fewer teams go undefeated in Colonial Athletic Association play than in SEC play from ESPN conference records site at http://espn.go.com/college-football/conferences/standings/_/id/48/caa-conference.

19. Brian Mazique, "BCS Rankings 2011: Boise State Doesn't Deserve a Shot at BCS Title," *Bleacher Report*, October 29, 2011, http://bleacherreport.com/articles/916040-bcs-rankings-2011-predicting-and-projecting-the-new-week-10-poll/entry/144803-bcs-rankings-2011-boise-state-doesnt-deserve-a-shot-at-bcs-title. Scroll down to find the Mountain West with the "Highest Winning Percentage by Conference" and "BCS all-time records by school," Bowl Championship Series, July 21, 2011, http://www.bcsfootball.org/news/story?id=4819309.

20. Clay Travis, "Kirk Herbstreit: The Face of College Football (Part Two)," *Outkick the Coverage*, November 11, 2011, http://outkickthecoverage.com/kirk-herbstreit-the-face-of-college-football-part-two.php.

21. Jim Kleinpeter, "LSU Tigers Coach Les Miles Says Matchup Against Alabama in BCS Title Game Was the Right Call," (New Orkans) *Times Picayune*, December 5, 2011, http://www.nola.com/lsu/index.ssf/2011/12/post_60.html.

22. Thomas Ray, Letters to the Editor, "UM's 'Heritage' Being Dissolved," *Clarion-Ledger* (Jackson, Mississippi), July 17, 2010, 9A.

23. Iron Bowl stabbings from Robert McClendon, "Fighter Sentenced in 'Roll Tide' Brawl," *Press-Register* (Mobile, Alabama), August 7, 2008, http://www.al.com/news/press-register/index.ssf?/base/news/121810052579450.xml&coll=3; and "SEC Football: There Will Be Blood," *Dawg Day Afternoon*, July 25, 2009, http://dawgdayafternoon.wordpress.com/2009/07/25/sec-football-there-will-be-blood/. Video game fight from "Stabbing Apparently over Football Video Game," *Gadsden* (Alabama) *Times*, October 4, 2006, http://www.gadsdentimes.com/article/20061004/NEWS/610040322. Alabama/LSU shooting from Connie Baggett, "Football Dispute Leaves 2 Dead," *Press-Register* (Mobile, Alabama), November 10, 2008, http://www.al.com/news/press-register/metro.ssf?/base/news/122631213873770

.xml&coll=3. North Carolina 2009 football murder from "Police: Man Shot over Football Argument," CBS News, March 3, 2010, http://www.cbsnews.com/stories/2009/12/08/national/main5932129.shtml.

24. Greg Garrison, "In New Book, Auburn's Gene Chizik Mixes Faith and Football," *Birmingham* (Alabama) *News*, July 2, 2011, http://blog.al.com/living-news/2011/07/in_new_book_auburns_gene_chizi.html.

25. "2010–2011 Bowl Performance by Conference," *SportsRatings: College Football*, January 2011, http://sportsratings.typepad.com/college_football/2011/01/2010-2011-bowl-performance-by-conference.html.

Chapter 5: Education: Arkansas, Mississippi, and the Three Rs of Southern Schools—Revenue, Resentment, Resegregation

1. Fifteen Little Rock superintendents in twenty-five years from "LRSD Superintendents," Little Rock School District, June 2011, http://www.lrsd.org/display.cfm?id=214. Pilloried Roy Brooks from Max Brantley, "LRSD Scandal," *Arkansas Times*, April 29, 2007, http://www.arktimes.com/ArkansasBlog/archives/2007/04/29/1035992-lrsd-scandal. Roy Brooks firing from "Racial Overtones Shroud Superintendent Firing," Associated Press, May 24, 2007, MSNBC, http://www.msnbc.msn.com/id/18853476/ns/us_news-education/t/racial-overtones-shroud-superintendent-firing/#.TueA50rmvM8. Dr. Linda Watson firing and "Not really" quote from Kelly Dudzik, "Little Rock School Board Ends Superintendent's Contract," FOX 16 (Little Rock, Arkansas), July 24, 2010, http://www.fox16.com/content/news/education/story/Little-Rock-School-Board-ends-superintendents/GhiWq1VQD0Cz-sCb399TcA.cspx.

2. National Park Service, Little Rock High School National Historic Site, "Little Rock Nine," *The Encyclopedia of Arkansas History & Culture*, September 9, 2010, http://encyclopediaofarkansas.net/encyclopedia/entry-detail.aspx?entryID=723.

3. "Stakeholder Input Report for Little Rock School District," submitted by McPherson & Jacobson (Omaha, Nebraska), L.L.C., March 2011, cited pages 1, 9, 13, 15, 21, 23, 24, 26, 31.

4. "Regional Murder Rates, 2001–2010" and "National Murder Rates 1970–2010," Death Penalty Information Center, September 2011, http://www.deathpenaltyinfo.org/murder-rates-nationally-and-state.

5. Cash, *The Mind of the South*, 92. Illiteracy and school attendance figures of 1860 from Cobb, *Away Down South: A History of Southern Identity*, 40, 51. H. L. Mencken, *A Mencken Chrestomathy* (New York: Alfred A. Knopf, 1949); Vintage, 1982), 186.

6. High school and college graduation rates from J. C. Grant, "State Education Rankings: Graduation Rates for High School, College, and Grad/Professional School," *Yahoo Voices*, July 21, 2010, http://voices.yahoo.com/state-education-rankings-graduation-rates-high-6357074.html?cat=4. Fewest adults holding high school diplomas from "Percent of People 25 Years and Over Who Have Completed High School (Includes Equivalency) 2009" (most recent

statistics available at time of publication), U.S. Census Bureau, http://factfinder.census
.gov/servlet/GRTTable?_bm=y&-geo_id=01000US&-_box_head_nbr=R1501&
-ds_name=ACS_2009_1YR_G00_&-redoLog=false&-mt_name=ACS_2005_EST_
G00_R1401_US30&-format=US-30. Composite SAT/ACT scores from "High
SAT and ACT Scores (80th Percentile and Above) per 1,000 High School Graduates," the National Center for Higher Education Management Systems, 2009,
http://www.higheredinfo.org/dbrowser/index.php?submeasure=35&year=2007&le
vel=nation&mode=graph&state=0.

7. Michael A. McDaniel, "Estimating State IQ: Measurement Challenges and
Preliminary Correlates," *Intelligence* 34, issue 6, November-December 2006,
607–19, also available at http://www.sciencedirect.com/science/article/pii/
S0160289606001061/.

8. "Library Visits per Capita (Most Recent) by State," StateMaster.com, 2011, http://
www.statemaster.com/graph/edu_pub_lib_lib_vis_per_cap-libraries-library-visits
-per-capita.

9. Diane D. Blair and Jay Barth, *Arkansas Politics and Government*, 2nd ed. (Lincoln
and London: University of Nebraska Press, 2005), 311.

10. Property tax figures from *2011 Facts & Figures: How Does Your State Compare?*
(Washington, D.C.: Tax Foundation, 2011), Table 27, "State and Local Property
Tax Collections per Capita, Fiscal Year 2008," 40. State education spending per
pupil from "Census Bureau Reports Public School Systems Spend $10,499 per Pupil
in 2009," U.S. Census Bureau, May 25, 2011, http://www.census.gov/newsroom/
releases/archives/governments/cb11-94.html. Louisiana accepts more in federal funding than almost any other state from "Federal Spending Received per Dollar of Taxes
Paid by State, 2005," Tax Foundation, October 9, 2007 (update and clarification of
data in interview with Tax Foundation economist Mark Robyn in Chapter 6 of this
book), http://www.taxfoundation.org/news/show/266.html.

11. "Quality Counts," *Education Week*, January 13, 2011, http://www.edweek.org/
ew/toc/2011/01/13/index.html. Summary of Arkansas performance in "Quality Counts" report from "Public Schools in Arkansas Garner Low B," *Arkansas
Democrat-Gazette*, January 11, 2011, http://www.apsrc.net/NewsLetter/Newsletter
Display.asp?p1=178&p2=Y&Sort=.

12. Arkansas school studies from 1921 and 1978 from Blair and Barth, *Arkansas Politics
and Government*, 309–10. Gould city statistics from "Gould, Arkansas," City-Data
.com, 2011, http://www.city-data.com/city/Gould-Arkansas.html.

13. Norman Merchant, "Little Rock Struggles with Desegregation Effort," Associated
Press, September 18, 2011, http://www.washingtontimes.com/news/2011/sep/18/
little-rock-district-struggles-with-desegregation-/.

14. Arne Duncan says 80 percent of schools failing from Larry Abramson, "Duncan
Develops 'Plan B' for Some Failing Schools," National Public Radio, June 14, 2011,
http://www.npr.org/2011/06/14/137182718/duncan-develops-plan-b-for-some
-failing-schools. Only 14 percent of Florida schools make AYP goals from Liz
Goodwin, "Report: More Schools Failing to Make Adequate Progress," *The Lookout*,
April 29, 2011, http://news.yahoo.com/blogs/lookout/report-more-schools-failing

-adequate-progress-151440489.html. Diane Ravitch, *The Death and Life of the Great American School System: How Testing and Choice Are Undermining Education* (New York: Basic Books, 2010), 104.

15. Little Rock School District student population is 68 percent black from Cynthia Howell, "Study: Student Losses No Harm," *Arkansas Democrat-Gazette*, May 31, 2010, http://www.speakuplittlerock.com/2010/06/study-student-losses-no-harm/.

16. Mark Carter, "Almost 20 Percent of Little Rock-Area Students Attend Private Schools," *Arkansas Business*, June 17, 2011, www.arkansasbusiness.com/article.aspx?aID=127082.

17. Jerry Cox's legislative efforts from "Our Staff," Family Council, 2010, http://familycouncil.org/?page_id=8. Arkansas Education Alliance information from the Education Alliance, 2007, http://www.arkansashomeschool.org/index.asp?PageID. Homeschool enrollment of 15,791 from "Home School Report 2009–2010," Arkansas Department of Education, 17, pdf available at arkansased.org/about/pdf/schools/hs_report_09-10_090110.pdf.

18. Transfers out of public school system, and Little Rock charter school statistics from Cynthia Howell, *Arkansas Democrat-Gazette*, http://www.speakuplittlerock.com/2010/06/study-student-losses-no-harm/.

19. Max Brantley, "Fun with Numbers: eStem charter v. LRSD," *Arkansas Times*, July 6. 2010, http://m.arktimes.com/ArkansasBlog/archives/2010/07/06/fun-with-numbers-estem-charter-v-lrsd. Walton Family Foundation support of charter schools from "Student Achievement Goals," the Walton Family Foundation, 2011, http://www.waltonfamilyfoundation.org/grantees/student-achievement-goals. Walter Hussman support of charter schools from "Hussman Honored with Distinguished Alumnus Award," UNC School of Journalism and Mass Communication, http://jomc.unc.edu/News-Items/Hussman-honored-with-Distinguished-Alumnus-Award. Leslie Newell Peacock, "Hussman, Walton Money Fuel e-Stem," *Arkansas Times*, September 4, 2008, http://www.arktimes.com/arkansas/hussman-walton-money-fuel-e-stem/Content?oid=964668.

20. Ravitch, *The Death and Life of the Great American School System: How Testing and Choice Are Undermining Education*, 129, 133, 138–40.

21. Andy Brack, "Brack: My, How Things Have Changed," Center for a Better South, May 29, 2011, http://www.bettersouth.org/2011/05/brack-my-how-things-have-changed/.

22. Brent Renaud (director), *Little Rock Central: 50 Years Later*, 2007, Minnijean Brown clip viewable at http://www.youtube.com/watch?v=d8Or8OBrMzg.

23. "Make a difference" and "Peace Corps" quotes from "About," Mississippi Teacher Corps, 2011, http://mtc.olemiss.edu/about. All MTC testimonials from "Mississippi Teacher Corps, Best of the Blogs, 2007–2010," Mississippi Teacher Corps, https://docs.google.com/document/pub?id=1p2_9t7b2PdUPkL3dTOP8xKjALUiw5mgGScHQykSFiiE#id.yephl1lz2h58.

24. Patrik Jonsson, "America's Biggest Teacher and Principal Cheating Scandal Unfolds in Atlanta," *The Christian Science Monitor*, July 5, 2011, http://www.csmonitor.com/USA/Education/2011/0705/America-s-biggest-teacher-and-principal-cheating

-scandal-unfolds-in-Atlanta. Patrik Jonsson, "Atlanta Cheating Scandal: Should Educators Face Jail Time for 'Robbing' Students?," *The Christian Science Monitor*, July 6, 2011, http://www.csmonitor.com/USA/Education/2011/0706/Atlanta-cheating -scandal-Should-educators-face-jail-for-robbing-kids. Language quoted from the Atlanta Public Schools website since removed.

25. Nichols Elementary School GreatSchools rating and general information from "Nichols Elementary School," GreatSchools, 2011, http://www.greatschools.org/ mississippi/biloxi/1433-Nichols-Elementary-School/. Nichols school closure from Stacey Patton, "Biloxi Schools Controversy; Punished for Achievement?," *The Defenders*, August 10, 2010, http://www.thedefendersonline.com/2010/08/10/ biloxi-schools-controversy-punished-for-achievement/. Robbie Brown, "A School Closing That Some See as Fiscal Responsibility, Others Racism," *New York Times*, July 10, 2010, http://www.nytimes.com/2010/07/11/us/11biloxi.html. Krystal Allan, "Racial Complaint Withdrawn Regarding Nichols Elementary," WLBT-TV (Jackson, Mississippi), February 17, 2011, http://www.wlbt.com/story/14048401/ racial-complaint-withdrawn-regarding-nichols-elementary?redirected=true.

26. Karoline Wightman, "New Superintendent Outlines District Goals," FOX 16 (Little Rock, Arkansas), May 18, 2011, http://www.fox16.com/news/local/story/ New-superintendent-outlines-district-goals/dnMDGDywP06Xa-vbNWkolg.cspx.

27. Max Brantley, "Judge Orders End to State Payment for Pulaski Desegregation," *Arkansas Times*, May 19, 2011, http://www.arktimes.com/ArkansasBlog/ archives/2011/05/19/judge-orders-end-to-state-payment-for-pulaski-desegregation. "No way for the LRSD to adjust its budget" quote from Rob Moritz, "Judge Won't Stay Desegregation Ruling," *The Times Record* (Arkansas), August 19, 2011, http://swtimes.com/site/bios//state_news/article_8cc30e18-9369-11e0-8cd6 -001cc4c03286.html. Judge Brian Miller as Bush nominee from "Brian Miller," http://judgepedia.org/index.php/Brian_Miller, November 4, 2011. Melanie Fox quote "eventual loss of the money" from Max Brantley, "Breaking: 8th Circuit Stays Little Rock School Money Cutoff," *Arkansas Times*, June 21, 2011, http://www .arktimes.com/ArkansasBlog/archives/2011/06/21/8th-circuit-stays-end-of -desegregation-funding.

28. "State Dissolves PCSSD Board, Removes Superintendent," FOX 16 (Little Rock, Arkansas), June 20, 2011, http://www.fox16.com/news/local/story/State-dissolves -PCSSD-board-removes-superintendent/cxkJoFW700yqrgBWIvaJBA.cspx. "Cafeterias are prepared, and floors are cleaned" quote from "New Superintendent Named for PCSSD," KTHV-TV (Little Rock, Arkansas), June 28, 2011, http:// littlerock.todaysthv.com/news/news/new-superintendent-named-pcssd/66804.

29. Little Rock Central High School information from "Frequently Asked Questions," National Park Service, February 9, 2009, http://www.nps.gov/chsc/faqs.htm.

30. David Fincher (director), *The Social Network*, 2010, http://www.imdb.com/title/ tt1285016/.

31. Katherine S. Newman and Rourke L. O'Brien, *Taxing the Poor: Doing Damage to the Truly Disadvantaged* (Berkeley, Los Angeles, and London: University of California Press, 2011), 50. Blair and Barth, Arkansas Politics and Government, 5.

Chapter 6: Economics: Florida, Texas, the U.S. Military, and the Fiscal Future of Secession

1. Governor Bob McDonnell bio material from "71st Governor of Virginia," Office of Governor Bob McDonnell, http://www.governor.virginia.gov/aboutthegovernor/ mcdonnell-bio.cfm. McDonnell "A" rating from National Rifle Association from "NRA Backs McDonnell," *Washington Times*, September 15, 2009, http:// www.washingtontimes.com/news/2009/sep/15/nra-backs-mcdonnell/?page=all. Anita Kumar and Rosalind S. Helderman, "McDonnell's Confederate History Month Proclamation Irks Civil Rights Leaders," *Washington Post*, April 7, 2010, http://www.washingtonpost.com/wp-dyn/content/article/2010/04/06/ AR2010040604416.html. Confederate History Month proclamation (with mention of slavery added retroactively) from "Confederate History Month," Office of Governor Bob McDonnell, http://www.governor.virginia.gov/OurCommonwealth/ Proclamations/2010/ConfederateHistoryMonth.cfm.

2. Population figures calculated from "Resident Population Data," U.S. Census Bureau, United States Census 2010, http://2010.census.gov/2010census/data/ appointment-pop-text.php. Landmass calculated with figures from "Table 17. Area Measurements: 2000; and Population and Housing Unit Density: 1980 to 2000," *United States Summary: 2000*, published by U.S. Census Bureau, 2004, 29.

3. Quotes from Governor Bob McDonnell's address at the October 5, 2010, Future of the South symposium held at the National Archives in Washington, D.C., come from two primary sources. The first is the governor's own notes for his speech ("Remarks of Governor Robert F. McDonnell, Oxford American Magazine 'The Future of the South' Symposium, Washington, D.C., October 5, 2010") provided to me by the governor's office. The second is my own notes. I was in attendance for the speech and able to fill in areas where the governor deviated from his own script. Third-party coverage of the governor's speech was also helpful in preparing this section of the chapter: Stephen Groves, "McDonnell Predicts a Modern Rise of the South," *Virginia Statehouse News*, October 7, 2010, http://virginia.statehousenewsonline. com/832/mcdonnell-predicts-a-modern-rise-of-the-south/.

4. "Population Estimates for the 100 Fastest Growing Metropolitan Statistical Areas: July 1, 2007 to July 1, 2008," U.S. Census Bureau, March 19, 2009, spreadsheet available at http://www.census.gov/newsroom/releases/archives/population/cb09-45.html.

5. List of key southern industries from Jeffrey S. Arpan, "Foreign Industry," *Encyclopedia of Southern Culture*, 741. GDP estimates and comparisons calculated from "Comparing US States with Countries: Stateside Substitutes," *The Economist*, January 13, 2011, http://www.economist.com/blogs/dailychart/2011/01/comparing _us_states_countries.

6. Jeffrey S. Arpan, "Foreign Industry," *Encyclopedia of Southern Culture*, 741.

7. "Death Toll Reaches 8 in Louisiana Blast," Associated Press, May 3, 1991, http://articles .latimes.com/1991-05-03/news/mn-1032_1_death-toll. "Process Safety Management of Highly Hazardous Chemicals," Occupational Safety and Health Administration,

U.S. Department of Labor, May 1996, http://www.osha.gov/doc/outreachtraining
/htmlfiles/psm.html. "Plant Explosion Leads to Nitro Shortage," *National Dragster*,
December 1, 1991, available at http://www.nhra.net/50th/news/index.html?story=457.

8. Howard Zinn, *The Southern Mystique* (New York: Alfred A. Knopf, 1964), 218.

9. Mary Quinn O'Connor, "Boeing Facility Opens in S.C., Despite NLRB Opposition," FOX News Network, June 10, 2011, http://www.foxbusiness.com/
markets/2011/06/10/boeing-facility-opens-in-south-carolina-despite-opposition
-from-nlrb/. Tim Devaney, "Boeing Opens $750 Million Plant in South Carolina,"
Washington Times, June 10, 2011, http://www.washingtontimes.com/news/2011/
jun/10/boeing-opens-750-million-plant-south-carolina/. Boeing chief executive
Jim Albaugh's "can't afford to have a labor stoppage" quote from Dominic Gates,
"Albaugh: Boeing's 'First Preference' Is to Build Planes in Puget Sound Region,"
Seattle Times, March 1, 2010, http://seattletimes.nwsource.com/html/business
technology/2011228282_albaugh02.html. "A stake in the ground" quote from Patrik
Jonsson, "Boeing's South Carolina Move: Illegal Union Bashing or Just Good Business?," *The Christian Science Monitor*, May 10, 2011, http://www.csmonitor.com/
USA/Politics/2011/0510/Boeing-s-South-Carolina-move-Illegal-union-bashing
-or-just-good-business. Nikki Haley's "We are fighting" quote from "Did Boeing
Move 1,000 Jobs to Get Back at Union?," CBS News, June 15, 2011, http://www
.cbsnews.com/stories/2011/06/15/earlyshow/main20071219.shtml. Map of right-
to-work states from National Right to Work, Legal Defense Foundation, Inc., 2010,
http://www.nrtw.org/rtws.htm. Economic Development Association of Alabama
quote from Michael Tomberlin, "Experts: Boeing Union Fight in South Carolina
Could Spill into Alabama," *Birmingham* (Alabama) *News*, August 9, 2011, http://
blog.al.com/businessnews/2011/08/experts_boeing_union_fight_in.html.

10. South Carolina repeals wage and hour restrictions from Cash, *The Mind of the
South*, 427.

11. Overview of Auto Alley available from "Interstate 65," Wikipedia, http://
en.wikipedia.org/wiki/I-65.

12. Dr. Hari Singh, "Right to Work and Economic Impact: What It Means for Michigan," academic paper, Seidman College of Business, Grand Valley State University,
2010, available at media.mlive.com/news_impact/other/RTWHari4word.pdf.

13. All statistics in this paragraph from Cobb and Stueck, eds., *Globalization and the
American South*, 1–2.

14. Quoted statements from Connie May Fowler and Diane Roberts were made at the
October 5, 2010, Future of the South symposium held at the National Archives
in Washington, D.C. Per my notes, Fowler and Roberts made their remarks while
co-moderating a panel discussion titled "The Future of Southern Culture and Identity."

15. Care2 information on plastic bags from "Ban Plastic Bags in New Zealand Su-
permarkets," Care2, 2011, http://www.thepetitionsite.com/31/ban-plastic-bags-in
-new-zealand-supermarkets/. Information on environmental impact of plastic bags
from "Plastic Bags and the Environment," Planet Ark, 2011, http://plasticbags
.planetark.org/about/environment.cfm. Achim Steiner quote from "Report Brings
to the Surface the Growing Global Problem of Marine Litter," United Nations

Environment Programme, June 8, 2009, http://www.unep.org/documents.multi lingual/default.asp?documentid=589&articleid=6214&1=en. Countries with plastic bag laws from "Plastic Bag Reduction Around the World," Planet Ark, 2009, http://plasticbags.planetark.org/about/othercountries.cfm. San Francisco plastic bag ban from "S.F. First City to Ban Plastic Shopping Bags," Charlie Goodyear, *San Francisco Chronicle*, March 28, 2007, http://articles.sfgate.com/2007-03-28/news/17235798_1_compostable-bags-plastic-bags-california-grocers-association. General information, attributed quotes, and specifics on plastic bag issues in Seattle, California, and Oregon from Kitt Doucette, "The Plastic Bag Wars," *Rolling Stone*, August 4, 2011, 37–39, available at http://www.rollingstone.com/politics/news/the-plastic-bag-wars-20110725. Californians use 120,000 tons of plastic bags each year from "Holes in the Bag Ban," *Los Angeles Times*, November 19, 2010, http://articles.latimes.com/2010/nov/19/opinion/la-ed-bags-20101119. Surfrider "goliath" quote from "Senate Fails to Pass Bag Ban—Local Govs Move F," Ban the Bag PDX blog, Portland Chapter of the Surfrider Foundation, June 10, 2011, http://www.banthe bagspdx.com/?p=174. Hilex Poly headquarters listing from Hilex Poly Company, LLC, http://www.hilexpoly.com/contact. Unistar headquarters listing from Unistar Plastics, LLC, http://www.unistarplastics.com/contactUs.cfm. Superbag headquarters listing from Superbag, http://www.superbag.com/contactus.html.

16. Average income figures from *2011 Facts & Figures: How Does Your State Compare?*, Table 31, "Income Per Capita by State, Fiscal Year 2009," 44. Corporate income tax figures from ibid., Table 13, "State Corporate Income Tax Collections Per Capita, Fiscal Year 2009," 24. Gallup-Healthways Well-Being Index from "State of Well-Being 2010," Gallup-Healthways Well-Being Index, 2010, 4, pdf available at http://www.well-beingindex.com/.

17. "Federal Spending Received per Dollar of Taxes Paid by State, 2005," Tax Foundation, October 9, 2007, http://www.taxfoundation.org/news/show/266.html.

18. Newman and O'Brien, *Taxing the Poor: Doing Damage to the Truly Disadvantaged*, 141.

19. Cobb and Stueck, eds., *Globalization and the American South*, 2.

20. Obesity costs and disability claims information from "The Economics of Overweight and Obesity—The High Cost of Overweight and Obesity," Net Industries, http://www.libraryindex.com/pages/1219/Economics-Overweight-Obesity-HIGH-COST-OVERWEIGHT-OBESITY.html. Obesity costs from Nanci Hellmich, "Obesity a Key Link to Soaring Health Tab as Costs Double," *USA Today*, July 28, 2009, http://www.usatoday.com/news/health/2009-07-27-costofobesity_N.htm. Disability claims information from Darius N. Lakdawalla, Jayanta Bhattacharya, and Dana P. Goldman, "Are the Young Becoming More Disabled?," *Health Affairs*, 2004, http://content.healthaffairs.org/content/23/1/168.full.

21. "U.S. Obesity Trends, Trends by State 1985–2010," Centers for Disease Control and Prevention, http://www.cdc.gov/obesity/data/trends.html.

22. GDP estimates calculated from "Comparing US States with Countries: Stateside Substitutes," *The Economist*, January 13, 2011, http://www.economist.com/blogs/dailychart/2011/01/comparing_us_states_countries.

23. Defense industry largest employer in Georgia, Louisiana, Mississippi, and Tennessee in 1970s from James C. Cobb, *The South and America Since World War II* (Oxford and New York: Oxford University Press, 2011), 173. Top three Georgia employers from "State Profile: Largest Employers," CareerOneStop, U.S. Department of Labor, Employment and Training Administration, 2011, http://www.careerinfonet.org/oview6.asp?soccode=&stfips=13&from=State&goto=/acinet/state1.asp%3Fstfips%3D22. Military bases and installations around the United States from "Installation Guide," Military.com, 2011, http://benefits.military.com/misc/installations/Browse_Location.jsp.

24. Florida with 181 and Virginia with 231 total military installations from "Department of Defense Base Structure Report Fiscal Year 2011 Baseline (A Summary of DoD's Real Property Inventory)," 2011, pp. 27, 34. Florida and Virginia as South's two largest economies (not counting Texas) from "Comparing US States with Countries: Stateside Substitutes," *The Economist*, January 13, 2011, http://www.economist.com/blogs/dailychart/2011/01/comparing_us_states_countries. Florida military installations and economic impact from "Rick Scott Says the Military Makes Up Nearly 10 Percent of Florida's Economy," PolitiFact Florida, December 6, 2010, http://www.politifact.com/florida/statements/2010/dec/07/rick-scott/rick-scott-says-military-makes-nearly-10-percent-f/. Virginia bases and installations from "Installation Guide," Military.com, 2011, http://benefits.military.com/misc/installations/Browse_Location.jsp.

Comparing total numbers of U.S. military installations is tricky. Is an unmanned antennae station in a remote location considered a military site? Technically, yes, according to Department of Defense accounting, but it hardly seems fair to compare the economic impact of such a facility with a major base or installation housing thousands of personnel.

When comparing military sites nationally, I confined myself to the DoD's classification of "large" and "medium" sites (defined as having a "plant replacement value" or PRV of more than $929 million) as provided in the aforementioned Base Structure Report for 2011. I used the total number of sites (including what the DoD classifies as "small" and "other") to emphasize the military's specific reach in Florida and Virginia.

Allowing for the fact that many of these numbers can be manipulated to some degree—from minuscule to mammoth, the DoD maintained 4,127 active and reserve sites in 2011—I believe mine is a fair accounting of the military's footprint in the South vis-à-vis the rest of the country.

25. Texas home to six of top fifty *Fortune 500* companies from "*Fortune 500*, State Ranking," CNN Money, 2011, http://money.cnn.com/magazines/fortune/fortune500/2011/states/TX.html. Texas GDP equivalent to Russia's, Texas second-largest state economy, and Florida fourth-largest state economy from "Comparing US states with Countries: Stateside Substitutes," *Economist*, January 13, 2011, http://www.economist.com/blogs/dailychart/2011/01/comparing_us_states_countries.

26. Wilson, *Patriotic Gore: Studies in the Literature of the American Civil War*, 232. Virginius Dabney 1942 editorial from Cobb, *Away Down South: A History of Southern*

Identity, 185. Virginius Dabney bio from Brendan Wolfe, ed., "Virginius Dabney (1901–1995)," *The Dictionary of Virginia Biography*, April 7, 2011, http://www .encyclopediavirginia.org/Dabney_Virginius_1901–1995. Newman and O'Brien, *Taxing the Poor: Doing Damage to the Truly Disadvantaged*, 31 and xli.

27. Electoral reapportionment from "In Reapportionment, Texas, Florida Gain Congressional Seats," *U.S. News & World Report*, January 3, 2011, http://www.usnews .com/opinion/articles/2011/01/03/in-reapportionment-texas-florida-gain -congressional-seats.

28. Nine of ten poorest states in the South from "America's Poorest States," *24/7 Wall St.*, September 14, 2011, http://247wallst.com/2011/09/14/americas-poorest-states/. Nearly 40 percent of impoverished Americans reside in South from Newman and O'Brien, *Taxing the Poor: Doing Damage to the Truly Disadvantaged*, xxx.

Epilogue: The South's Gonna Do It Again . . . and Again . . . and Again

1. Malcolm Gladwell, *Outliers: The Story of Success* (New York: Little, Brown, 2008), 170–73, quote from page 173.

2. "Francis Salvador," The Historical Marker Database, 2011, http://www.hmdb .org/marker.asp?marker=27489. "Solomon Blatt, 1895–1986," University of South Carolina School of Law, http://law.sc.edu/memory/1987/blatts.shtml.

3. "Top Largest Colleges and Universities," MatchCollege.com, 2009, http://www .matchcollege.com/top-colleges. With a southern top-twenty enrollment of 25,947 students, the University of Georgia placed #62 (fifteenth among southern schools, including Texas) on *U.S. News & World Report* 2011 rankings of colleges and universities in the United States, "University of Georgia," *U.S. News & World Report*, 2011, http://colleges.usnews.rankingsandreviews.com/best-colleges/university-of -georgia-1598.

4. "Flags of the Confederacy," Sons of Confederate Veterans, Texas Division, 2011, http://www.texas-scv.org/confedFlags.php. "Cotton Ed" Smith quote can also be found in Robert S. McElvaine, *The Great Depression: America, 1929–1941* (New York: Times Books, 1984; Three Rivers Press, 2009), 192–93.

5. Quote from former University of Texas president Kent Berdahl regarding unacceptable academic standards among SEC schools from Guerin Emig, "Apparently, We Have Texas A&M to Thank for the Big Twelve," *Tulsa World*, April 30, 2010, http:// www.tulsaworld.com/blogs/sportspost.aspx?/Apparently_we_have_AM_to_thank_ for_the_Big_12/12-8408.

6. In November 2011, The Citadel's History Department chair Keith N. Knapp sent an email to fellow history professors around the country soliciting input on academic-credibility ramifications surrounding a proposed course titled "Charleston and the War for Southern Independence." In a December 2011 email to me, Knapp wrote: "By a one-vote margin, the History Department approved of the new course entitled 'Charleston and the War for Southern Independence.' This, though, is just one stop along the way. The course proposal will now go before the college's curriculum committee. If it is approved there, it goes before our Academic Board, which consists of

the provost, deans, and department heads. In short, it is not yet approved. In the meantime, the course will continue to be taught under its provisional name, 'History 391: Special Topics—Charleston and the Civil War.'"

No matter what the final decision, it's compelling to consider the motives of a university professor at a leading southern military college proposing such a massively revisionist course offering.

7. Wilson, *Patriotic Gore: Studies in the Literature of the American Civil War*, first Lincoln quote from page 114, second Lincoln quote from page 111.

8. Sixty percent of University of Georgia students come from metro Atlanta from November 2011 interview with University of Georgia history professor John Inscoe.

Acknowledgments

1. Frederick Law Olmsted, *The Cotton Kingdom: A Traveller's Observations on Cotton and Slavery in the American Slave States, 1853–1861* (New York: Da Capo, 1996).

2. Chuck Thompson, "Sweet Home . . . Chattanooga?," *Outside*, October 2011, 28–30.

3. "The ARC Curved Shower Bar," Focus Bath group, http://www.arcsandangles.com/finditem.cfm?itemid=157. God bless you people.

INDEX

Abbeville Civil War Monument, South
    Carolina, 81–83
ABC (American Broadcasting Company),
    137
abolitionism, 51
abortion, 35, 36, 50, 171, 234, 255
abortion clinic bombings, 5
achievement gap, 158, 178
ACLU (American Civil Liberties
    Union), 34
Adley, Robert, 50
affirmative action, 251
Afghanistan, 66
African American History Monument,
    Columbia, South Carolina, 80
African Americans
    civil rights movement, 15, 16, 34,
        89, 238, 246, 256
    football and, 129
    hypothetical secession and, 245–249
    income of, 122–123
    Latinos and, 122
    obesity and, 220
    population in South, 101, 248
    religion and, 10–12, 34
    slavery and, xv, 2, 16, 54, 66, 67,
        79–82, 90, 100–103, 105, 121,
        251, 254, 256
    unemployment of, 123
    voters, 62, 63
aging population, 202–203
agriculture industry, 199
Alabama, xvii

automobile industry in, 119,
    208–209, 218
education in, 93, 117, 177, 218
English-only drivers license exams
    issue in, 118–119
football in, 126, 128
hate groups in, 94
library patronage in, 160
obesity in, 220
politicians from, 62, 64
politics in, 41–44, 49, 53
property taxes in, 93, 161
religion in, 3–5, 20–27, 39
test scores in, 162
2010 gubernatorial campaign in,
    118–120
Alabama Crimson Tide, 136, 138, 141,
    143–144, 147, 148
Alabama State University, 177
Alaska, xxi
    politics in, 44–45
Alaska Independence Party, xxi
Alaska Republican Party, 45
Albaugh, Jim, 206
Aliotti, Nick, 131, 147n
All the King's Men (Warren), 59
Allen, George, 120
Alston, James, 233
American Airlines, 227
American Community Survey (Census
    Bureau), 122
Anderson, Fulton, 48
anger, measurement of, 232–233

Angus Chemical Company, Sterlington, Louisiana, 204
Apex, North Carolina, 233
Apostles of Disunion: Southern Secession Commissioners and the Causes of the Civil War (Dew), 82
Appalachian Mountains, xi
Ard, Ken, 70
Arizona
    education in, 159
    reapportionment in, 228, 229
Arizona State University, 131
Arkansas, xvii
    defense industry in, 224
    education in, 153–157, 162–180, 183–185, 189–191
    happiness in, 214
    income in, 213
    politicians from, 62
    property taxes in, 161
    religion in, 3, 39
    test scores in, 162
Arkansas Democrat-Gazette, 176
Arkansas Department of Education, 187
Arkansas Education Alliance, 171
Arkansas National Guard, 155, 156
Arkansas Non-Public School Accrediting Association, 171
Arkansas Politics and Government (Blair and Barth), 160
Arkansas Razorbacks, 136, 140, 144
Arkansas School Boards Association, 179
Arkansas Times, 154, 170, 184, 186
Aryan Wear, 92
Asian Americans, 119, 120
    population growth and, 117
Atlanta, Georgia, 105
    African American population in, 101
Atlanta Journal-Constitution, 53
Atlanta Public Schools, 182
Atlantic magazine, 126

atomic bombs, 51
AT&T, 227
Atwater, Lee, 74, 75
Auburn Tigers, 128, 136, 145, 149
Austin Lounge Lizards, 4
automobile industry, xx, 56–57
    in South, 60, 119, 208–209, 218
    wages, 208
Awakening Young Voters (radio show), 36
Away Down South: A History of Southern Identity (Cobb), xx
AYP (Adequate Yearly Progress), 164–165

Bachus, Spencer, 64
Bahr, Dr., 103, 104, 115
Bailey, Phil, 70–72, 74–78, 80
Bangladesh, 210
baptists, 2, 4–14, 18, 20–25, 106
Barber, Rims, 18, 111–112, 233, 245, 247
Barbour, Haley, 85–86, 196, 198, 200
Barkun, Michael, 17
Barna Group, 3
Barrow, John, 248
Barth, Jay, 160, 186
Bauer, André, 70
Bechtel, 68
Beck, Glenn, 1
Beck, Woody, 239, 240, 244–247, 249, 253
Beirich, Heidi, 92–95
Bentley, Robert, 49
Bessinger, Maurice, 77–78
Bible, the, 5–6, 28–29, 33–36, 172
Bible Babel: Making Sense of the Most Talked About Book of All Time (Swenson), 28
"Biblestan," xi–xii
Bilbo, Theodore, 47–48
Biloxi, Mississippi, 20, 182–183
Birmingham, Alabama, 3
Birmingham News, 64

birth rates, 116
Black, Earl, 63
Black, Merle, 63
Black Republican Party, 66–67
Blair, Diane, 160
Blatt, Solomon, 234
Bleacher Report, 141
Blease, Coleman, 80
BMW, 208
Boehner, John, 63–64
Boeing, 206–208, 225, 250
Boise State, 141
Bombastic Sports, 137
Bond, Julian, 12
Bowden, Bobby, 132
Bowl Championship Series (BCS),
    128, 129, 132–137, 140, 142,
    144–145, 150
BP (British Petroleum), 209
    Gulf oil spill, 49–50
Bracey, Glenn, 85, 116
Brack, Andy, 176–178
Branch, Talmadge, 87–88
Brantley, Max, 154, 170, 173, 184
Breaux Bridge, Louisiana, 221
British spelling, xix
Brookes, Iveson Lewis, 4
Brookings Institution, 122
Brooklyn Dodgers, 88
Brooks, Roy, 153
Broun, Paul, xxi–xxii, 48
Brown, Charlotte, 164, 166–168
Brown, Minnijean, 180, 190
Brown v. Board of Education (1954), 62,
    175, 256
Broyles, Frank, 128
Bruno, Jason, 221
Bullock, Charles, 63, 239, 245–246,
    248, 250
Burden of Southern History, The (Wood-
    ward), 68, 127
Burns, Ken, 236
Bush, George H. W., 3, 165

Bush, George W., 5, 12, 24, 68, 69, 73,
    94, 104, 119, 128–129, 165, 186
Bush, Jeb, 196
Byrd, Robert, xiii

Cain, Herman, 41
Cal-Berkeley Golden Bears, 139
Calhoun, Andrew Pickens, 48
Calhoun, John C., xix–xx, 46
California
    hate groups in, 95
    plastic bag use in, 211–212
    religion in, 4
Calvert family, xv
Cantor, Eric, 64
Care2, 210
Carter, Jimmy, 62
Carville, James, 231
"Cascadia, Republic of," x–xi, xii
Cash, W. J., 34, 100, 139, 158, 179
Catholic Church, 7, 10
CBS (Columbia Broadcasting System),
    133, 139, 140, 190, 207
Center for a Better South, 176
Center for the Study of Southern Cul-
    ture, 2
Centers for Disease Control and Preven-
    tion, 48, 220
Chaison, Gary, 207
Charleston, South Carolina, 199
    as slave trading center, 101
Charlotte, North Carolina, 3, 199
charter schools, 170, 172–173, 187
cheerleaders, 126, 228
Chester's Cypress Inn, Donner, Louisi-
    ana, 220, 221
Chestnut, Mary, 68
Chicago Maroons, 139
child labor, 207, 208
China, 43, 52, 119, 191, 192, 202,
    206, 210
Chizik, Gene, 149
Christian academies, 171

Christian Broadcasting Network, 35
Christian Identity movement, 17
Christian Reconstructionism, 16
Christian rock, 5
Christian Science Monitor, The, 207
Civil Rights Act of 1964, xvii, 77, 251
civil rights legislation, 61
Civil Rights Memorial, Montgomery,
    Alabama, 90–91, 95
civil rights movement, 15, 16, 34, 89,
    238, 246, 256
Civil War, xiii, xiv, xix, xx, 24, 34, 39,
    42, 46, 51, 52, 54, 66, 69, 79,
    81, 82, 86, 197, 212–213, 251,
    256
Claghorn, Beauregard, 52
Claiborne County, Mississippi, 101
Clay-Chalkville Cougars, Alabama, 126
Clemson University, South Carolina, xx
Cleveland public schools, 33
Clinton, William Jefferson, 89, 194
CNBC, 199
CNN, 71
Cobb, James C., xx, 65, 159, 218,
    236–240, 243, 245–250, 253
Coca-Cola, 201
Cohen, Dov, 232
Colbert, Stephen, 70
Colby, Doug, 3
college football. *See* football
Colorado, xi
    obesity in, 220
Columbia, South Carolina, 77–81
Columbia Journalism Review, 173
Columbia University, 96
Concerned Women for America, 18
Confederate Army, xvi
Confederate flag, xvi, 42, 78, 80–81,
    195–196, 238, 245
Confederate History Month, 197
Confederate States of America, xiii, xiv
    fantasy presidential inauguration,
        196–201

First White House of Confederacy,
    89–90
    hypothetical secession and, xviii–xix,
        xxi, 26, 52, 120, 123, 127, 222–
        223, 225–227, 231, 233–257
Confederates in the Attic (Horwitz), 69
Congress of Racial Equality, 17
congressional committee chairmanships,
    63, 64
congressional election of 2010, 56, 63
Connecticut
    government assistance and entitle-
        ment programs in, 214
    property taxes in, 161
ConocoPhillips, 227
conservatives, 45–46, 103, 173–174
Continental Congress of 1776, xix
contraception, 52
cooking, southern, 220, 221
Cooper, Anderson, 190
Corddry, Rob, 120
corporate supplication, 47, 58–61
corporate tax rates, 214
cortisol levels, 232–233
Corwin Amendment, 67
Couch, Tim, 130
Council of Conservative Citizens, 18
Cowherd, Colin, 129–131, 137–138,
    147*n*
Cox, Jerry, 171
Creation Museum, Petersburg, Ken-
    tucky, 28–32, 38, 64, 149, 171,
    235
creationism, 33–34
Cresap, Thomas, xv
Cresap's War, xv
CT&T Ltd., 56
Curry, Jabez Lamar, 48, 49

Dabbs, James McBride, 46
Dabney, Virginius, 228
Daily Beast, The, 46, 60
Daily Show, The, 120

Daniel, 38
Danson, Edwin, xiv
Davis, Jefferson, 46, 89, 90, 241
Davis, Kenneth, 80
De La Beckwith, Byron, 17
Death and Life of the Great American School System, The: How Testing and Choice Are Undermining Education (Ravitch), 173
Declaration of Independence, xix
Deen, Paula, 222
Dees, Morris, 91, 95
Defending My Heritage: The Maurice Bessinger Story (Growing Up Southern) (Bessinger), 77, 78
Defense, U.S. Department of, 224, 225
defense industry, 223–225, 234, 247
Delaware, xiv
DeMint, Jim, 53, 70
Democratic National Convention (1936), 238
Democratic Party, xvii, 26, 49, 57, 61, 248 *See also* politics; presidential elections
    hold on South, 61–62
    in South Carolina, 70–72
DePass, Rusty, 70, 75–76
Descartes, René, 32–33
desegregation, 15, 93, 155–156, 169–171, 173, 185–186, 256
Detroit, Michigan, 208
Dew, Charles B., 82
Dhaliwal, Daljit, x
dinosaurs, 29–31
disability claims, 219
Diversity of Faith in Various U.S. Cities (Barna Group), 33
Dixiecrats, 62
Dixon, Jeremiah, xiv–xv
Dobson, James, 171
Donehue, Wesley, 70–78, 80
Doocy, Steve, 48

Doucette, Kitt, 211
Douglas, Stephen, 41
Douglass, Frederick, 86
Dr Pepper, 227
Drivers license exams, English only, 118–119
Duncan, Arne, 165
Duncan, South Carolina, 56

Earnhardt, Dale, 241
Eastern Kentucky Colonels, 140
economics, 195–230
    annual GDP of South, 202, 223
    automobile industry, 208–209
    defense industry, 223–225
    diversity of economy, 202
    energy, 226
    foreign investment, 213–214
    government assistance and entitlement programs, 214–218
    income, 213, 214
    international businesses, 203, 206
    labor force, 203–204, 206–208
    McDonnell on, 198–199
    rate of expansion, 201–202
    in Texas, 202, 227
Economist magazine, 227
education, 28, 59, 61, 116, 153–194, 198, 249, 255
    achievement gap, 158, 178
    in Alabama, 93, 117, 177, 218
    in Arizona, 159
    in Arkansas, 153–157, 162–180, 183–185, 189–191
    AYP (Adequate Yearly Progress), 164–165
    charter schools, 170, 172–173, 187
    cheating scandal, 182
    Christian academies, 171
    creationism/evolution issue, 33–34
    in Florida, 130, 165
    in Georgia, 182

education (*cont.*)
  high school graduation rates, 159
  homeschooling, 171–172
  illiteracy, 158–159
  IQ scores, 159
  library patronage, 160
  in Louisiana, 93–94, 161
  in Mississippi, 11, 159, 163,
    180–183, 218
  No Child Left Behind Act (NCLB)
    of 2002, 162, 165
  in North Carolina, 218
  private schools, 171
  SAT/ACT scores, 159
  segregation/desegregation, 15,
    87–88, 93, 106, 117, 155–156,
    169–171, 173, 175, 177, 180,
    185–186, 256
  in South Carolina, 74, 218
  state-by-state ranking, 11
  student apathy, 179–181
  student population, 117
  support for public, 160–161, 170
  in Tennessee, 34, 218
  test scores, 159, 162, 165
  in Texas, 11, 159, 165
  in Virginia, 159–161
Education Week magazine, 163
Eisenberg, Jesse, 191
Eisenhower, Dwight, 156, 190, 224
electoral reapportionment, 64, 228–229
electronic church, 15
Encyclopedia of Southern Culture, 2, 15,
    37, 38–39, 203
End Times psychosis, 38, 52
energy, xxi, 199–200, 223, 226
environmentalism, 210–211
  BP Gulf oil spill, 49–50
EPA (Environmental Protection
    Agency), 36
Erickson, Dennis, 131
ESPN, 96, 129–130, 133, 137–140,
    142, 144–146, 149

"ESPN/ABC Has Monopoly over Bowl
    Games" (Hogan), 137
eStem Public Charter Schools, 172
evangelicals, 4–6, 16, 18, 25–29,
    34–39, 51, 105
Evers, Medgar, 17
evolution, 34, 51, 172
Exodus, 35
ExxonMobil, 227

Fair Labor Standards Act of 1938,
    207
Falwell, Jerry, 17
Family Research Council, 18
Family Values Radio, 6
Faubus, Orval, 46, 48, 155, 156, 190
Faulkner, William, 158, 237
Feagin, Joe, 100–104, 118, 121
Federal Aviation Administration, 215
federal labor laws, 206–208
Federal Reserve System, 52, 64
Federalists, 68
Fields, Emma, 41–44, 57
Fields, Will, 42, 44, 57
Finebaum, Paul, 96, 97, 148
First White House of Confederacy,
    Montgomery, Alabama, 89–90
Fitzgerald, Zelda, 93
501(c)(3) organizations, 8–9
Florida, xiv, xvii, xviii
  defense industry in, 224, 225
  education in, 130, 165
  football in, 128
  hate groups in, 94, 95
  politicians from, 62, 64
  presidential election of 2008 and, 62
  racism in, 87–88
  reapportionment in, 228
  religion in, 3
Florida Atlantic University, 140
Florida Gators, 135, 142
Florida International Golden Panthers,
    141

Florida State University, 132, 133, 136
football, 96–97, 125–151
    Bowl Championship Series (BCS),
        128, 129, 132–137, 140, 142,
        144–145, 150
    championship disasters, 132–133
    cheerleaders, 126, 227
    ESPN, 96, 129–130, 133, 137–140,
        142, 144–146, 149
    inter-conference results, 134–135
    media and, 129, 132, 137, 138,
        140–142, 146
    NFL drafts, 135
    physique of players, 130
    poll fabrications, 138, 143
    preseason rankings, 136–137
    religion and, 149, 150
    salaries of coaches, 130–131
    Southeastern Conference (SEC),
        127–131, 133–146, 148–151
    status of, 126
    tradition and pageantry of, 128
    violence over, 148
Foote, Shelby, 236
Forbert, Steve, 115
Forbes magazine, 50, 199
Ford, Gerald, 62
Forest Heights Middle School, Arkan-
    sas, 164–170, 173, 204
Forrest, Nathan Bedford, 86, 241
Fort Benning, Georgia, 224
Fort Bragg, North Carolina, 224
Fort Knox, Kentucky, 224
Fort Pillow, Tennessee, 86
Fort Stewart, Georgia, 224
Fort Sumter, South Carolina, xix, 67
Fortune 500 companies, 227
Fortune magazine, 199
Fowler, Connie May, 209
Fox, Melanie, 186
FOX "News," 23, 48, 197
Frankfort, Kentucky, 229
free states, xv

Freedom Baptist Church, Hiddenite,
    North Carolina, 35
Friedman, Kinky, 222
"Future of the South" symposium,
    176–177, 179, 201

Gaines' Mill, Battle of, 67
Galileo, 33
Gallup-Healthways Well-Being Index,
    214
Game Change: Obama and the Clintons,
    McCain and Palin, and the Race
    of a Lifetime (Heilemann and
    Halperin), 73
Garcia, Alicia Williamson, 21–25, 27,
    28, 37
Garth, Fred, 88–89
Gator Bowl, 135
General Dynamics, 68
General Motors, 208
Genesis, 149
Georgia, xvii, 68, 73
    defense industry in, 223–224
    education in, 182
    hate groups in, 94, 95
    politicians from, 62, 64, 248
    reapportionment in, 228
    religion in, 6–12, 21
    state flag of, 53
Georgia Bulldogs, 136, 141
Ghetto Revolts (Feagin and Hahn), 100
Gibbs, Chad, 149
Gibbs, Charles, 20, 23, 26–27
Gingrich, Newt, 47–48, 72, 219
Gladwell, Malcolm, 232, 233
Glaser, James M., 64–65
global warming, 36
"Globalization, Latinization, and the
    Nuevo South" (Mohl), 122
Globalization and the American South
    (Cobb), 218
God and Football: Faith and Fanaticism
    in the SEC (Gibbs), 149

Gone With the Wind (movie), 192, 257

Gould, Arkansas, 163

government assistance and entitlement programs, 214–218

graduation rates, high school, 159

Graham, Lindsey, 53, 196, 231

Great Basin National Park, Nevada, 30

Great Santini, The (movie), 87

"Greater Soxany," xii

GreatSchools designation, Mississippi, 182

Greene, Alvin, 70

Greensboro, North Carolina, 246

Greensboro *News & Record*, 99

Grimes, Tonisha, 167

gubernatorial elections, 61
2010, 118–120

Guess, Jerry, 187

Gulf Coast, xviii

Gulnare Free Will Baptist Church, Pike County, Kentucky, 106

gun control, 252

Haas, Mark, 212

Hahn, Harlan, 100

Haile, Louisiana, 203

Hale, Stephen Fowler, 66–67

Haley, Nikki, 70, 71, 75, 207

Hall, Spencer, 115, 128–129, 147–148

Halliburton, 68

Halperin, Mark, 73

Ham, Ken, 28–29, 30–32, 35, 171

Hamby, Peter, 71

Hammond, James H., 68

Hampton, Wade, 79–80

Hampton Roads, Virginia, 199

Hand of the Past in Contemporary Southern Politics, The (Glaser), 64–65

Harding, Warren, 110

Harper's, 100

Harrington, Joey, 130

Hartford Convention (1814–15), 68

Harvard University, 139

hate crimes, 105–107

hate groups, 94–93

Hate Map (Southern Poverty Law Center), 94–95

Hatewatch blog, 92

Hayward, Tony, 50

Health Affairs, 219

"Heartlandia," xi, xii

Heilemann, John, 73

Herbert, Bob, 75

Herbstreit, Kirk, 144

Hickel, Wally, 45

Higgins, Mrs., 166–168

high school graduation rates, 159

Hilex Poly, 211, 212

Hill, Lance, 93–94, 102–103

Hill, Michael, 1, 37, 94, 233–234, 237

Hispanics. *See* Latinos, 121

Hitler, Adolf, 24

Hoffman, Roy, 27

Hogan, Ryan, 137

Holmes, Morris, 184, 185

homeschooling, 171–172

homosexuality, 12–15, 17, 18, 35, 121, 174, 255

Honda, 208, 209, 218

Hopson, Charles, 162–163, 175–176, 178, 187–188, 218

Horwitz, Tony, 69

"House Divided" speech (Lincoln), 254

Houston, Texas, 101

Howard, John, 19–20, 107–113, 255

Howard, Wildman, 108, 110–111

Hurricane Katrina, 102, 104

Hussman, Walter, 172, 173, 176, 178

hypothetical secession, xviii–xix, xxi, 26, 52, 120, 123, 127, 222–223, 225–227, 231, 233–257

Hyundai, 119, 208, 209, 218

Idaho, xi
hate groups in, 94

Illinois, 35–36
   reapportionment in, 229
   religion in, 3
illiteracy, 158–159
IMC Fertilizer, 204
immigration rates, 116, 234
income, 60, 122–123, 213, 214
Independence Day, 53
India, 206, 210
   graduating engineers in, 119
Indian Institute of Technology Bombay, 119
Industrial Revolution, 209
InDyne, 225
influence, disproportionate, 47, 61–65
Inscoe, John, 99, 239, 240, 247, 251, 253
Institutes of Biblical Law (Rushdoony), 16
Intelligence Report magazine, 92
International Association of Machinists & Aerospace Workers, 206
International Monetary Fund, 64
interracial marriage, 86, 99, 106
interstate highway system, 215
Iowa
   presidential primary in, 74
   religion in, 3
IQ scores, 159–160, 191
Iraq War, 68–69, 217
Ireland, 210
IRS (Internal Revenue Service), 8–9
Is God a Mathematician? (Livio), 33
Isaiah, 10
Islam, 23
Islamic fundamentalism, 50–51
Israel, 22–23, 36
Issues in Education, 36
Italy, 210

J.A. Fair High School, Little Rock, Arkansas, 154–157, 185
Jackson, Mississippi, 111
Jackson, Stonewall, 103

Jacobson, Tom, 154–157, 162, 163, 183–185, 188
James, Fob, 120, 218
James, Tim, 118–120
Jamestown colony, Virginia, 101
Japan, 119, 192–193
Jefferson, Thomas, 73
Jena Six, 107
Jim Beam whiskey, 229–230
Jim Crow, 16, 62, 101, 244–246, 256
Jindal, Bobby, 49, 65
job sites, dangers of, 203–204
Johnson, Lyndon B., xvii, 42, 245
Joshua, 172
Joyner, Charles, xv–xvi, 227, 235–236
Justice, U.S. Department of, 126

Kansas, xii
   hate groups in, 94
   religion in, 3
Kasper, Lynne Rossetto, 221
KBR, 68
Kellogg Foundation, 183
Kelly, Megyn, 48
Kennedy, John F., 43, 45, 73
Kent State University, 140
Kentucky, xiii, xv, xvii, 28–33, 38, 64, 68, 107
   automobile industry in, 208
   defense industry in, 224
   government assistance and entitlement programs in, 214
   happiness in, 214
   income in, 213
   Jim Beam whiskey factory in, 229–230
   obesity in, 220
   politicians from, 62, 63
   property taxes in, 161
   religion in, 39
   secession and, 238
Kentucky Wildcats, 140

Kerry, John, 24, 53
Keynes, John Maynard, 200
Kia, 119, 208
Kimbrell, Tom, 187
King, Coretta Scott, 12
King, Martin Luther, Jr., 89
Kinnaman, David, 3
Kloran: Knights of the Ku Klux Klan, 108–110
Knapp, James B., 209
Knotts, Jake, 70, 71, 75–76
Koran, 51
Korean War, 66
Kramer, Roy, 132, 137
Krugman, Paul, 46, 200, 231
Ku Klux Klan, 16–20, 86, 91, 107–113, 115–116, 255

Labor, U.S. Department of, CareerOne-Stop website, 223–224
labor force, 203–204, 206–208
labor unions, 60, 61, 173, 187, 206–207
Lamis, Alexander, 75
Lancaster, Eleanor, 6
land disputes, xiv–xv
Latinos
    African Americans and, 122
    growth of population of, 116–117, 121, 248
    in Memphis, Tennessee, 122
Laurens, South Carolina, 107–113, 255
League of the South, xix, 1, 94
Lee, Robert E., 82, 86, 241
Left Behind Rapture book series, 38
Levin, Joe, 91
Leviticus, 172
liberals, 45–46, 102, 103, 173
library patronage, 160
life expectancy, 221
Limbaugh, Rush, 38
Lincoln, Abraham, xiv, xv, 42, 48, 49, 51, 66–67, 73, 254

Lind, Michael, 46, 60, 232
literacy tests, 245
Little Louie's Bar-N-Grill, Laurens, South Carolina, 54–58, 122
Little Rock Central: 50 Years Later (documentary), 162, 180
Little Rock Central High School, Arkansas, 155–156, 180, 189–191
Little Rock Christian Academy, Arkansas, 171
Little Rock Nine, 155–156, 162, 180, 189–190
Little Rock School District, Arkansas, 153–155, 162, 164, 169, 170, 172–174, 178, 183–189, 193
Living Waters Program, 6
Livio, Mario, 33
Lockheed Martin, 225
Long, Eddie, 11–13, 21, 31, 177
Long, Huey P., 59
Longwood Plantation, Natchez, Mississippi, 90
Los Angeles, California, 3
Los Angeles Times, 212
Lost Cause mind-set, 38, 39, 52, 221
Louisiana, xvii, 107
    BP Gulf oil spill, 49–50
    defense industry in, 223
    education in, 93–94, 161
    football in, 128
    hate groups in, 94
    homicide rate in, 158n
    New Orleans. *See* New Orleans, Louisiana
    obesity in, 220
    plastic bag industry in, 212
    politics in, 53
    property taxes in, 161
    reapportionment in, 229
    test scores in, 162
Louisiana State Tigers, 128, 131, 136, 138–140, 143–148
Luke, 5

lunch counter sit-ins, Greensboro, North Carolina, 246
Lux Research, 119

Mabus, Ray, 194
Maddow, Rachel, xiv
Made in Texas: George W. Bush and the Southern Takeover of American Politics (Lind), 232
Maine, xii
religion in, 4
March to the Sea (1864), 197
Mark, 5
Marshall, Bob, 35, 52
Martin, Trayvon, 106
Maryland, xiv, xv
Maryland Legislative Black Caucus, 88
Mason, Charles, xiv, xv
Mason-Dixon line, xiv, xv
Massachusetts, reapportionment in, 229
Matthew, 36
Matthews, Chris, 197, 201*n*
Mazique, Brian, 141
McCain, Bridget, 73
McCain, John, 73, 74
McConnell, Glenn, 80
McConnell, Mitch, 63
McDaniel, Michael A., 159
McDonald's, 201
McDonnell, Jeanine, 197
McDonnell, Robert Francis, 35, 196–201, 213
McMath, Sidney, 194
McPherson & Jacobson, 154, 156, 157, 163, 183, 184
media, football and, 129, 132, 137, 138, 140–142, 146
Medicare/Medicaid, 203, 214, 217, 219
megachurches, 6–9
Memphis, Tennessee, 121–122
Mencken, H. L., 159, 160
Mercedes-Benz, 208, 209, 218
methodists, 2

Mexican War, 68
Mexico, 206
South compared to, 60
Miami Hurricanes, 131
Michigan
automobile industry in, xx, 60, 208
reapportionment in, 229
religion in, 3
Miles, Les, 131, 139, 140
military adventurism, 47, 65–67
military bases, 199, 201, 224
military-industrial complex, 223, 224
Miller, Brian, 186
Mind of the South, The (Cash), 34, 100, 158
Minnesota, government assistance and entitlement programs in, 214
Mississippi, xvii, 228, 247
African American population in, 101
defense industry in, 223
education in, 11, 159, 163, 180–183, 218
government assistance and entitlement programs in, 214
happiness in, 214
hate groups in, 94, 95
income in, 213
obesity in, 220
politicians from, 62
politics in, 53
religion in, 3
test scores in, 162
Mississippi Burning murders, 17, 75
Mississippi State University, 131, 140
Mississippi Teacher Corps (MTC), 180–181
Missouri, xii, xiv, xv
secession and, 238
Mitchell, Jerry, 17
Mobile, Alabama, 20–27
Mobile Press-Register, 27
Mohl, Raymond A., 122

Montana, xi
hate groups in, 94
religion in, 4
Montgomery, Alabama, 88–93, 95, 119
Montgomery Bus Boycott (1955), 89
Montgomery County, Georgia, 106
Moral Majority, 17, 34–35
"Mormonia," xi, xii
Mormons, 3
Mountain West Conference, 141
Mullen, Dan, 131
multinational corporations, 69, 203, 206
Murdoch, Rupert, 165
Murdock, Steve, 193, 202–203
Murphy, Terrell, 11–12
Muslims, 23, 27
"My, How Things Have Changed" (Brack), 176

N word, 111–112
NAACP (National Association for the Advancement of Colored People), 77
NAFTA (North American Free Trade Agreement), 226
Natchez, Mississippi, 90
national defense, 223
national health insurance coverage, 221, 222
National Japanese American Memorial to Patriotism During World War II, 83
National Labor Relations Board (NLRB), 206–207
National Parks Service, 189
National Rifle Association (NRA), 197
Native Americans, 121
Natural Bridge, Alabama, 41–44
natural gas, 200, 226
NCAA (National Collegiate Athletic Association), 133
Nebraska, hate groups in, 94

Nettleton Middle School, Mississippi, 106
Neuheisel, Rick, 131, 147
Nevada, xi, 159
government assistance and entitlement programs in, 214
New Birth Missionary Baptist Church, Lithonia, Georgia, 6–12, 21
New Black Panthers, 105
New Christian Right, 15
New Hampshire, xii
government assistance and entitlement programs in, 214
presidential primary in, 74
property taxes in, 161
religion in, 4
New Jersey
government assistance and entitlement programs in, 214
hate groups in, 95
property taxes in, 161
reapportionment in, 229
New Life Family Worship Center Pentecostal Church, Dallas, Texas, 38
New Mexico, 159
religion in, 3
New Orleans, Louisiana, 93, 199
Hurricane Katrina, 102, 104
as slave trading center, 101
New York, New York, 3
New York state
property taxes in, 161
reapportionment in, 229
religion in, 4
New York Times, 75, 96, 99–100
Newberry, South Carolina, 105
Newman, Katherine J., 194, 209, 215, 228
Newman, Randy, 83
Nichols Elementary School, East Biloxi, Mississippi, 182–183
Nisbett, Richard, 232
Nissan, 208
Nite Krawlers, 54, 55

Nixon, Richard, 45, 74
No Child Left Behind Act (NCLB) of
    2002, 162, 165
Noah, 36
Norfolk, Virginia, 225
North Carolina, xvii, 85–86
    defense industry in, 224
    education in, 218
    hate groups in, 94
    politicians from, 62
    presidential election of 2008 and, 62
    religion in, 35
North Charleston, South Carolina, 206
North Dakota, hate groups in, 94
North Texas Mean Green, 141
North-to-South migration, 99–100
Notre Dame Fighting Irish, 132, 140
nullification, doctrine of, xix

Obama, Barack, 23–24, 36, 41, 43, 44,
    50, 52, 56–58, 62–63, 70, 71,
    75, 79, 94, 106, 126, 177, 219,
    234, 256
Obama, Michelle, 24, 70, 75, 219
Obamacare, xxii
obesity, 158, 219–222
O'Brien, Rourke, 194, 215, 228
obstruction, willful, 47, 51–53
Occidental Dissent, 114
Occupy Wall Street movement, 64
Ohio, xvi, 33, 68
    hypothetical secession and, 236
    reapportionment in, 229
Ohio State Buckeyes, 129, 135, 140
oil, xxi, 73, 199–200, 226
Oklahoma, xiv
    religion in, 3
Oklahoma Sooners, 142
Oliver, Jamie, 220
Oregon
    government assistance and entitle-
        ment programs in, 215
    plastic bag use in, 211, 212

Oregon Ducks, 143
Oregon State Beavers, 142, 145
Orlando, Florida, 106
Orlando Sentinel, 96
Osteen, Joel, 31
Outback Bowls, 129
Outliers: The Story of Success (Gladwell),
    232
Oxford American magazine, 177

Palin, Sarah, xvii, 8, 25
Papal States, 10
Parks, Rosa, 89
Patriotic Gore: Studies in the Literature of
    the American Civil War (Wilson),
    xx, 52, 228
Penn family, xv
Pennsylvania, xiv, xv
    reapportionment in, 229
Pensacola, Florida, 225
pensions, 116
Perry, Florida, 87–88
Perry, Rick, xviii, 72
Perry Package Store & Lounge, Perry,
    Florida, 87–88
Petersburg, Kentucky, 28–32, 38, 64
Pew Forum "Importance of Religion"
    study, 3, 25
Pew Forum on Religion & Public Life,
    39
P&H Cafe, Memphis, Tennessee,
    121–122
Philadelphia, Mississippi, 75
Philadelphia, Pennsylvania, xv
Picayune, Mississippi, 103–104
Pike County, Kentucky, 106
Pine Bluff Arsenal, Arkansas, 224
Planned Parenthood, 35
plastic bags, 210–212
Politics
    in Mississippi, 53
politics, 41–83, 248–249, 255
    in Alabama, 41–44, 49, 53

politics (*cont.*)
  in Alaska, 44–45
  corporate supplication and, 47,
    58–61
  demagogic dishonesty and, 47–49
  disproportionate influence and, 47,
    61–65
  disregard for own self interest and,
    47, 53–57
  in Louisiana, 53
  military adventurism and, 47, 65–67
  race and, 74–76
  reapportionment and, 228–229
  religion and, 8–9, 47, 49–51
  Seven Deadly Sins of Southern,
    47–67
  in South Carolina, 56–58, 69–79
  willful obstruction, 47, 51–53
PolitiFact, 225
Pope, John, 194
population
  of African Americans in South, 101,
    248
  growth of minority, 116–117, 121,
    248
  growth of southern, 64
Portland, Oregon, 3, 175, 212
Potok, Mark, 4–5, 92–95, 161
poverty rate, 123
presidential elections
  1860, 48, 49
  1976, 62
  1980, 74–75
  1984, 45
  2000, 62, 73
  2004, 62
  2008, 53–54, 62, 73
  2012, 72
  primary process, 72–74
private schools, 171
Progressive Bag Affiliates (PBA),
  211–212
Prohibition, 57

property taxes, 93, 161
Proverbs, 33
Prudhoe Bay, oil in, xxi
Prudhomme, Paul, 222
Pub Politics (webcast), 71, 72
Pulaski County Special School District,
  Arkansas, 162–163, 174–176,
  187

Queer Duck (cartoon), 17

race and racism, 85–123, 255 *See also*
    African Americans
  costs to North, 88, 116, 123
  football and, 96–97
  hate crimes, 105–107
  hate groups, 94–93
  Ku Klux Klan, 16–20, 86, 91,
    107–113, 115–116, 255
  Mississippi license plate issue, 86
  politics and, 74–76
  slavery, xv, 2, 16, 54, 66, 67, 79–82,
    90, 100–103, 105, 121, 251,
    254, 256
  southern preoccupation with,
    114–116, 120
  systemic or institutionalized racism,
    87, 101
  white denial, 98–99, 101–105
Racist America, 118, 121
Ravenal, Thomas, 70
Ravitch, Diane, 165, 173
Ray, Thomas, 147
Reagan, Ronald, 45, 74–75
reapportionment, 64, 228–229
Reconstruction, 74, 79, 213, 233
Redneck Shop, Laurens, South Carolina, 107–110, 112
Regent University, 35
Reid, Harry, 92
religion, 1–39, 243–244, 255
  in Alabama, 3–5, 20–27, 39
  in Arkansas, 3, 39

baptists, 2, 4–14, 18, 20–25, 106
Bible, the, 28–29, 33–36
black churches, 10–12, 34
Catholic Church, 7, 10
evangelicals, 4–6, 16, 18, 25–29,
   34–39, 51, 105
football and, 149, 150
in Georgia, 6–12, 21
Ku Klux Klan and, 16–20
megachurches, 6–9
percentage of self-described Christians, 3
politics and, 8–9, 47, 49–51
science and, 29–30
segregation and, 15–17
Republican Party, xvii, xviii, 45–46, 48,
   49, 52, 53, 56, 58, 61, 248 *See*
   also politics; presidential elections
   "Christian" takeover of, 61
   gubernatorial election of 2010,
      118–120
   in Mississippi, 86
   Solid South and, 61–63
   in South Carolina, 70–76
Research Triangle Park, North Carolina,
   158
Reston, Virginia, 225
Revolutionary War, 66
Reynolds, Paul, 49
Rhee, Michelle, 173
Rice, Condoleezza, 73
Richmond, Virginia, 67, 89
Richmond Times-Dispatch, 228
Riley, Bob, 194
Rise of Southern Republicans, The (Black
   and Black), 63
Roberts, Diane, 210
Robertson, Pat, 35
Robins Air Force Base, Georgia, 224
Robinson, Jackie, 88
Robyn, Mark, 216–218
Rock, Chris, 164
Rodgers, Jimmie, 115

Roe v. Wade (1973), 244
Rolling Stone, 211, 212
Romans, 29
Romney, Mitt, 72
Roosevelt, Franklin D., 73, 201
Roosevelt, Theodore, 73
Roots (miniseries), 86
Ruffins, Wanda, 164, 166
Rushdoony, R. J., 16
Russia, 43, 51
Rutledge, Edward, xix
Rutledge, John, xix
Ryan, B. J., 10, 18–19

Saban, Nick, 131
sacrificial donations, 10–11
Salvador, Francis, 234
same-sex marriage, 12, 52
San Francisco, California, 3, 211
Sanford, Mark, 70
SAT/ACT scores, 159
Saturn, 208
Saunders, Dave "Mudcat," 63
Savannah, Georgia, 199
savings and loan scandal, 43
Schwarzenegger, Arnold, 211
science, religion and, 29–30
Scopes, John Thomas, 34
Scopes Monkey Trial, 34, 36, 256
Scott, Rick, 225
scripture, 5–6, 28–29, 33–36, 172
Sea Island, Georgia, 251
Seattle, Washington, 3, 211
secession, xiii–xv, 82
   hypothetical, xviii–xix, xxi, 26,
      52, 120, 123, 127, 222–223,
      225–227, 231, 233–257
segregation, 15–17, 77, 79, 87–88, 106,
   175, 177, 180
self-interest, disregard for own, 47,
   53–57
Selma, Alabama, 89, 118
Selma-to-Montgomery March (1965), 89

senatorial elections, 61
sexism, 17
Share Our Wealth Society, 59
Shared Traditions: Southern History and Folk Culture (Joyner), xvi
Shelby County, Tennessee, 122
Shimkus, John, 35–36
Shreveport, Louisiana, 3
Sidney Lanier High School, Montgomery, Alabama, 93
Simmons, William Joseph, 19
Simms, William Gilmore, 68
Singh, Hari, 208
slavery, xv, 2, 16, 54, 66, 67, 79–82, 90, 100–103, 105, 121, 251, 254, 256
Smith, Horace, 179–180
Smith, Tony, 103–105
Smith "Cotton Ed," 238
Smithfield Packing Company, 201
Social Contract, The (magazine), 95
Social Network, The (movie), 191–192
Social Security, 116, 203, 217
Solid South, 61–63
Sons of Confederate Veterans, 42, 80, 86
South Africa, 210
South Carolina, xix, xvii, xx, 98, 228
    Abbeville Civil War Monument in, 81–82
    automobile industry in, 208
    Boeing plant in, 206–207, 250
    corporate tax rates in, 214
    education in, 74, 218
    federal labor laws and, 206–208
    foreign investment in, 213–214
    government assistance and entitlement programs in, 214
    hate groups in, 94–95
    income in, 213, 214
    Jews in, 234
    Ku Klux Klan in, 107–113
    obesity in, 220

    plastic bag industry in, 212
    politicians from, 62, 64
    politics in, 56–58, 69–79
    presidential primary in, 72–74
    reapportionment in, 228
South Carolina Gamecocks, 129, 140
South Carolina State House, 78–81
South Dakota, hate groups in, 94
South Korea, 119
Southeastern Conference (SEC), 127–131, 133–146, 148–151, 249, 250
southern cooking, 220, 221
Southern Poverty Law Center (SPLC), 4, 91–96, 161
southern strategy, 74–75
Spartanburg, South Carolina, 56
speed limit, 57
Sports Illustrated, 96
SportsRatings, 150
Stallworth, Bill, 183
Stanford University, 139
Starr, Bart, 93
StateMaster.com, 160
Steiner, Achim, 210
Sterlington, Louisiana, 204
Stewart, Jon, 70
Stone Mountain, Georgia, 81, 263
Stonewall's BBQ restaurants, 103–105, 116
Stowe, Harriet Beecher, 2
Summerfield, Alabama, 117–118
Superbag, 211, 212
Surfrider Foundation, 212
Sutton, Ken, 169, 173–174, 179
Swenson, Kristin, 28
Swift, Taylor, 37

Tax Foundation, 213, 214, 216–217
taxes, 60, 61, 93, 161, 213, 214
Taxing the Poor: Doing Damage to the Truly Disadvantaged (Newman and O'Brien), 194, 209, 215, 228

Tea Party, xvii, xviii, 57
Tebow, Tim, 37
Tenille, Toni, 93
Tennessee, xvii, 68, 106
  automobile industry in, 208
  defense industry in, 223
  education in, 34, 218
  government assistance and entitlement programs in, 214
  hate groups in, 94
  politicians from, 62
  property taxes in, 161
  religion in, 39
Tennessee-Chattanooga Mocs, 141
Tennessee Valley Authority, 215
Tennessee Volunteers, 132
test scores, 159, 162, 165
testosterone levels, 232–233
Texas, xiv, xvii, 64
  defense industry in, 224
  economy in, 202, 227
  education in, 11, 159, 165
  hate groups in, 95
  hypothetical secession and, 236, 249
  income in, 213
  library patronage in, 160
  obesity in, 220
  plastic bag industry in, 212
  reapportionment in, 228, 229
  religion in, 4
  southern identity of, 226–227
Texas flag, 249
Texas Longhorns, 132, 142
textile industry, 207
Thomas Road Baptist Church, Lynchburg, Virginia, 17
Thompson, James L., 45
Thompson, Josh, 161
Thornwell, J. H., 47–48
Thumma, Scott, 9
Thurmond, Strom, 46, 79
Tillman, Ben, 78–81
"times we're living in" phrase, 37–38

tourism, xviii
Toyota, 208
Traditional Values Coalition, 18
Trinity Broadcast Network, 4
Tubman, Harriet, 86
Tucker, James, 203–204
2011 Facts & Figures: How Does Your State Compare? (Tax Foundation), 213

UCLA Bruins, 131, 139
Uganda, 210
Uncle Tom's Cabin (Stowe), 2
unemployment, black, 123
Unistar Plastics, 211, 212
U.S. Army 101st Airborne Division, 156
U.S. Census Bureau, 11, 101, 116, 122–123, 159, 160, 201
U.S. Coast Guard Air Station Elizabeth City, North Carolina, 224
University of Alabama, 131
University of Florida, 128
University of Georgia, 237–239, 247, 256
University of Kentucky, 130n
University of Michigan, 232
University of Mississippi (Ole Miss), 2, 140, 142, 147
University of North Carolina Press, 2
University of Oregon, 145–146
University of Texas, 249, 250
USC Trojans, 133, 139, 142
Usery, Stephen, 121–122
Utah, xi
  religion in, 3

Valley Grande, Alabama, 117–118
Van Zant, Charles, 210
Van Zant, Ronnie, 158
Vatican, 10
Vermont, xii
  religion in, 4

Vesey, Denmark, 80
Vicksburg, Mississippi, 53
Vietnam War, 16, 24, 68, 69
Villard, Oswald Garrison, 100
Virginia, xvii
    defense industry in, 224–225
    economy in, 52
    education in, 159–161
    government assistance and entitle-
        ment programs in, 214
    hate groups in, 94
    hypothetical secession and, 225
    income in, 213
    library patronage in, 160
    McDonnell as governor of, 35, 197
    politicians from, 62, 64
    presidential election of 2008 and, 62
    religion in, 3, 4
Virginia Commonwealth University, 159
Virginia Tech, 133
Volkswagen, 208
Voting Rights Act of 1965, 245–246

Waiting for "Superman" (documentary),
    173
Walker, Herschel, 131
Wallace, George, 41
Wallace, Hunter, 114
Wallace, Mike, 190
Walmart, 172, 201
Walt Disney Company, 137
Walton Family Foundation, 172, 173,
    178
War of 1812, 67–68
Warren, Rick, 4
Warren, Robert Penn, 59, 83
Washington, George, 73, 81
Washington Generals, 139

Washington Post, 35, 126
Washington state, plastic bag use in,
    211
Watergate, 16
Watie, Stand, xvi
Watson, Diane, 235
Watson, Linda, 153–154
West Mobile Baptist Church, Mobile,
    Alabama, 20–25, 27
West Virginia, xiii, xvii, 106–107
    government assistance and entitle-
        ment programs in, 214
    happiness in, 214
    income in, 213
    obesity in, 220
    property taxes in, 161
West Virginia Mountaineers, 132
White, H. Rock, 114
white supremacy, 17, 79
Who Speaks for the South? (Dabbs), 46
Williams, Christopher, 179
Wilson, Edmund, xx, 52, 228
Wilson, Joe, 70, 71, 75–76, 234–235
Winnfield, Louisiana, 59
Wisconsin, religion in, 4
Woodward, C. Vann, 68, 127
workplace safety, 208, 209
World Bank, 64
World War II, 51, 66, 83
Wyoming, xi
    hate groups in, 94
    property taxes in, 161

Zapato, Lyle, x–xi
Zimmerman, George, 106
Zinn, Howard, 205
Zook, Ron, 129
Zuckerberg, Mark, 191

Photograph © Corky Miller

ABOUT THE AUTHOR

Formerly the features editor for *Maxim* magazine and editor in chief of *Travelocity* magazine, and currently the supervising editor for CNN.com Travel, Chuck Thompson is the author of the comic travel memoirs *Smile When You're Lying* and *To Hellholes and Back*, as well as a two-volume World War II survey (*The 25 Best World War II Sites: Pacific Theater* and *The 25 Essential World War II Sites: European Theater*), regarded as the most comprehensive catalogue of World War II sites in existence. Raised in Juneau, Alaska, he graduated from the University of Oregon with degrees in history and journalism; he has lived in Japan, New York City, Dallas, and Portland, Oregon, and traveled on assignment in more than fifty countries. Thompson's writing and photography have appeared in numerous publications including *Outside*, *Men's Journal*, *The Atlantic*, *Esquire*, *Maxim*, *Cowboys & Indians*, and the *Los Angeles Times*.

Want more Chuck Thompson?
Check out his other books!

smile when you're lying
confessions of a rogue travel writer

CHUCK THOMPSON

TP: 9780805082098
EB: 9781429924870

to hellholes and back
bribes, lies, and
the art of extreme tourism

CHUCK THOMPSON

TP: 9780805087888
EB: 9871429954747

"Savagely funny."
—*The New York Times*

"Extremely irreverent."
—*Outside*

"Wickedly entertaining."
—*San Francisco Chronicle*

"Riveting, hilarious, and
wildly entertaining."
—*Booklist*

"If there's such a thing as
extreme tourism, Thompson
is surely its guru."
—*The Boston Globe*

AVAILABLE IN TRADE PAPERBACK AND EBOOK
WHEREVER BOOKS ARE SOLD.

www.chuckthompson.com

SIMON &
SCHUSTER
A CBS COMPANY

Mount Laurel Library
100 Walt Whitman Avenue
Mount Laurel, NJ 08054-9539
856-234-7319
www.mtlaurel.lib.nj.us